DATE DUE			
AUG 1 9 1986			
AUG 1 9 1986			
NOV 0 5 1987			

MUIRHEAD LIBRARY OF PHILOSOPHY

An admirable statement of the aims of the Library of Philosophy was provided by the first editor, the late Professor J. H. Muirhead, in his description of the original programme printed in Erdmann's *History of Philosophy* under the date 1890. This was slightly modified in subsequent volumes to take the form of the following statement:

'The Muirhead Library of Philosophy was designed as a contribution to the History of Modern Philosophy under the heads: first of Different Schools of Thought—Sensationalist, Realist, Idealist, Intuitivist; secondly of different Subjects—Psychology, Ethics, Aesthetics, Political Philosophy, Theology. While much had been done in England in tracing the course of evolution in nature, history, economics, morals and religion little had been done in tracing the development of thought on these subjects. Yet "the evolution of opinion is part of the whole evolution".

'By the co-operation of different writers in carrying out this plan it was hoped that a thoroughness and completeness of treatment, otherwise unattainable, might be secured. It was believed also that from writers mainly British and American fuller consideration of English Philosophy than it had hitherto received might be looked for. In the earlier series of books containing, among others, Bosanquet's *History of Aesthetic*, Pfleiderer's *Rational Theology since Kant*, Albee's *History of English Utilitarianism*, Bonar's *Philosophy and Political Economy*, Brett's *History of Psychology*, Ritchie's *Natural Rights*, these objects were to a large extent effected.

'In the meantime original work of a high order was being produced both in England and America by such writers as Bradley, Stout, Bertrand Russell, Baldwin, Urban, Montague, and others, and a new interest in foreign works, German, French and Italian, which had either become classical or were attracting public attention, had developed. The scope of the Library thus became extended into something more international, and it is entering on the fifth decade of its existence in the hope that it may contribute to that mutual understanding between countries which is so pressing a need of the present time.'

The need which Professor Muirhead stressed is no less pressing today, and few will deny that philosophy has much to do with enabling us to meet it, although no one, least of all Muirhead himself, would regard that as the sole, or even the main, object of philosophy. As Professor Muirhead continues to lend the distinction of his name to the Library of Philosophy it seemed not inappropriate to allow him to recall us to these aims in his own words. The emphasis on the history of thought also seemed to me very timely; and the number of important works promised for the Library in the very near future augur well for the continued fulfilment, in this and other ways, of the expectations of the original editor.

H. D. LEWIS

MUIRHEAD LIBRARY OF PHILOSOPHY

General Editor: H. D. Lewis

Professor of History and Philosophy of Religion at the University of London

The Absolute and the Atonement by DOM ILLTYD TRETHOWAN
Absolute Value by DOM ILLTYD TRETHOWAN
Action by SIR MALCOLM KNOX
The Analysis of Mind by BERTRAND RUSSELL
Ascent to the Absolute by J. N. FINDLAY
Belief by H. H. PRICE
Brett's History of Psychology edited by R. S. PETERS
Broad's Critical Essays in Moral Philosophy edited by DAVID R. CHENEY
Clarity is Not Enough by H. D. LEWIS
Coleridge as Philosopher by J. H. MUIRHEAD
The Commonplace Book of G. E. Moore edited by C. LEWY
Contemporary American Philosophy edited by G. P. ADAMS and
    W. P. MONTAGUE
Contemporary British Philosophy first and second series edited by J. H.
    MUIRHEAD
Contemporary British Philosophy third series edited by H. D. LEWIS
Contemporary Indian Philosophy edited by RADHAKRISHNAN and J. H.
    MUIRHEAD 2nd edition
Contemporary Philosophy in Australia edited by ROBERT BROWN and C. D.
    ROLLINS
The Discipline of the Cave by J. N. FINDLAY
Doctrine and Argument in Indian Philosophy by NINIAN SMART
The Elusive Mind by H. D. LEWIS
Essays in Analysis by ALICE AMBROSE
Ethics by NICOLAI HARTMANN translated by STANTON COIT 3 vols
Ethics and Christianity by KEITH WARD
The Foundation of Metaphysics in Science by ERROL E. HARRIS
Freedom and History by H. D. LEWIS
G. E. Moore: Essays in Retrospect edited by ALICE AMBROSE and MORRIS
    LAZEROWITZ
The Good Will: A Study in the Coherence Theory of Goodness by H. J. PATON
Hegel: A Re-examination by J. N. FINDLAY
Hegel's Science of Logic translated by W. H. JOHNSTON and L. G. STRUTHERS
    2 vols
A History of Aesthetic by B. BOSANQUET 2nd edition
A History of English Utilitarianism by E. ALBEE
Human Knowledge by BERTRAND RUSSELL

MUIRHEAD LIBRARY OF PHILOSOPHY

EDITED BY H. D. LEWIS

EXPERIENTIAL REALISM

EXPERIENTIAL REALISM

BY

A. H. JOHNSON

LONDON · GEORGE ALLEN & UNWIN LTD
NEW YORK · HUMANITIES PRESS INC.

ISBN 0 04 100036 6

USA ISBN 391-00243-0

Printed in Great Britain
in 11 on 12 point Fournier type
by Unwin Brothers Limited
Woking and London

To Sandra and Sheila

PREFACE

This book is an attempt to outline some aspects of a philosophical system. It is based on an examination of comprehensive human experience.

I find myself in agreement with some of the basic insights of A. N. Whitehead. However, there are marked differences in the ways in which some of those insights are developed. Further, matters are here discussed which were not covered in Whitehead's writings.

I am profoundly grateful to my teachers, colleagues, students and other members of the philosophic fraternity. Without their stimulus this project would not have been undertaken, nor would it have taken this form.

I wish also to express my deep gratitude to the Nuffield Foundation and the Canada Council for travel and subsistence grants which greatly facilitated my investigations and meditations, the Canada Council for providing secretarial assistance, the University of Western Ontario for reducing my formal academic responsibilities and thus making available time which I was able to devote to the writing of this book, Mrs Pauline Campbell of the Department of Philosophy for invaluable secretarial assistance, graduate students Mr Paul Ritsema, Mr David Rivett and Mr Foster Walker for help in preparing the manuscript, my wife Helen, a constant source of encouragement and assistance, Professor H. D. Lewis, editor of the Muirhead Library, and Mr Peter Evans of George Allen and Unwin for their interest in this book, Dean John G. Rowe, Faculty of Arts, University of Western Ontario, for his support, and the Faculty of Arts for a grant in aid of publication. Further, the book has been published with the help of a grant from the Humanities Research Aouncil of Canada, using funds provided by the Canada Council.

I dedicate *Experiential Realism* to my daughters Sandra (Mrs Albert H. Oosterhoff) and Sheila (Mrs Hugh M. Kindred). Through the years they have brought to my attention, and helped me to deal with, problems which may appropriately be termed philosophical.

Section Two of this book includes brief quotations from a considerable number of sources. I wish to express and record my gratitude to those who have made available to me material from books and articles—as indicated herewith (in each case I have listed author, title, and publisher and, when requested, copyright holder. In some instances, in order to obtain world rights, it has been necessary to secure permission from two publishers):

A. J. Ayer, *Language, Truth and Logic*, Victor Gollancz, London and Dover Publications, New York; Gilbert Ryle, *The Concept of Mind*, Hutchinson University Library, London, and Barnes and Noble, New York; Ludwig Wittgenstein *Philosophical Investigations*, Basil Blackwell, Oxford; Norman Malcolm, *Dreaming*, Humanities Press, New York, and Routledge and Kegan Paul, London; G. E. Moore, *Principia Ethica* and A. N. Whitehead, *The Concept of Nature*, both published by Cambridge University Press, London; W. Desan, *The Tragic Finale*, Harvard University Press, Cambridge, Mass.; H. D. Lewis (ed.), *Clarity is not Enough*, George Allen and Unwin, London and Humanities Press, New York; A. Flew (ed.), *Essays in Conceptual Analysis*, Macmillan, London and St Martin's Press, New York; G. Humphrey, *Thinking*, Methuen and Company, New York; M. Lazerowitz, *The Structure of Metaphysics*, Routledge and Kegan Paul, London and Humanities Press, New York; P. P. Wiener (ed.), *Leibniz Selections* (The Modern Student Library), Charles Scribner's Sons, New York; Jean-Paul Sartre, *Existentialism* (trans. Bernard Frechtman), Philosophical Library, New York; G. Berkeley, Vol. II of *The Works of George Berkeley* (ed. P. E. Jessop), Thomas Nelson and Sons, Sunbury-on-Thames.

In some cases, one house is the publisher of several of the books which I have quoted. Clarendon Press, Oxford: *The Republic of Plato* (trans. W. D. Ross from the *Oxford Translation of Aristotle*, ed. W. D. Ross, Vol. IX, 1925); J. L. Austin, *Sense and Sensibilia* (1962); F. H. Bradley, *Appearance and Reality* (1930). Books by A. N. Whitehead, published and copyrighted by the Macmillan Company of New York, and Cambridge University Press, London: *Science and the Modern World* (1925); *Religion in the Making* (1926); *The Aims of Education* (1929); *Process and Reality* (1929); *Adventures of Ideas* (1933); *Modes of Thought* (1938). The following books copyright by the Liberal Arts Press Division of Bobbs-Merrill, Indianapolis: Epitectus, *Enchiridion* (trans. T. W. Gigginson); Descartes, *Meditations* (trans. L. J. LaFleur); I. Kant, *Prolegomena to any Future Metaphysics* (trans. L. W. Beck); I. Kant, *Fundamental Principles of the Metaphysics of Morals* (trans. T. A. Abbott); J. S. Mill, Utilitarianism (ed. O. Piest).

English Philosophers from Bacon to Mill (ed. E. A. Burtt), Random House, New York: Francis Bacon *Novum Organum;* T. Hobbes, *Leviathan;* J. Locke, *An Essay Concerning Human Understanding.*

A. J. Ayer (ed.), *Logical Positivism,* copyright © 1959 by the Free Press Corporation, New York (permission granted by the Macmillan Company, New York and Allen and Unwin, London); D. Hume, *Enquiry Concerning Human Understanding,* Open Court Publishing Company, LaSalle, Illinois (Philosophical Classics Series); John W. Yolton, *Thinking and Perceiving,* Open Court Publishing Company, LaSalle, Illinois; *New Essays in Philosophical Theology* (ed, A. Flew and A. MacIntyre, S.C.M. Press, London, and the Macmillan Company, New York; 'from the book *Ethics,* and on the *Correction of the Understanding* by Benedictus de. Spinoza, Trans. by Andrew Boyle, Everyman's Library Edition. Published by E. P. Dutton and Company, Inc. and used with their permission.' Permission to use this book was granted by J. M. Dent and Sons, London; *The Function of Reason* by A. N. Whitehead, copyright © 1957 by Princeton University Press; E. W. Hall, *Philosophical Systems,* © 1960 by the University of Chicago Press, published 1960 Chicago, Ill., USA; Roderick M. Chisholm, *Theory of Knowledge,* © copyright 1966 by Prentice-Hall Inc., Englewood Cliffs, New Jersey, USA.

Philosophical Review: A. I. Melden, 'Action' (Vol. 65); G. Ryle, 'Ordinary Language' (Vol. 62); *Analysis:* J. J. C. Smart, 'Professor Ziff on Robots' (Vol. 19); *Philosophy*, G. N. A. Vesey, 'Volition' (Vol. 36); Harvard University Press, 'Report of a Symposium in Honor of the 70th Birthday of Alfred North Whitehead'; Max Black, *Philosophical Analysis;* Alexander R. Jones, *Essays in Radical Empiricism* by William James. *Mind:* B. Russell, 'Physics and Mind' (Vol. 31), A. M. Turing, 'Computing Machines and Intelligence' (Vol. 59), M. Scriven, 'The Mechanical Concept of Mind' (Vol. 62).

Proceedings of the Aristotelian Society (Vol. 56): J. L. Austin, 'A Plea for Excuses'; G. E. M. Anscombe, 'Intention'. *Aristotelian Society Supplementary Volumes:* A. N. Whitehead's contribution to a Symposium entitled 'Time, Space and Material', (Vol. 2); J. L. Austin, 'Other Minds (Vol. 20); G. A. Paul, 'Is There a Problem about Sense Data?' (Vol. 15); F. Waismann, 'Verifiability' (Vol. 19); G. E. Moore, 'Is Existence a Predicate?' (Vol. 15).

I have been unsuccessful in eliciting replies to my requests for permission to quote, from several publishers. Full acknowledgement of source is made in footnotes covering the material involved. It falls within the category of scholar's right to quote.

University of Western Ontario   A. H. JOHNSON
London, Canada
October 1971

CONTENTS

19

CONTENTS

CONTENTS

Philosophy is not a mere collection of noble sentiments. A deluge of such sentiments does more harm than good. Philosophy is at once general and concrete, critical and appreciative of direct intuition. It is not—or, at least, should not be—a ferocious debate between irritable professors. It is a survey of possibilities and their comparison with actualities. In philosophy, the fact, the theory, the alternatives, and the ideal are weighed together. Its gifts are insight and foresight, and a sense of the worth of life, in short, that sense of importance which nerves all civilised effort.

Mankind is now in one of its rare moods of shifting its outlook. The mere compulsion of tradition has lost its force. It is our business— philosopher, students, and practical men—to re-create and re-enact a vision of the world, including those elements of reverence and order without which society lapses into riot.

A. N. Whitehead, *Adventures of Ideas*, pp. 125–6, Cambridge, 1933.

SECTION ONE
EXPOSITION

INTRODUCTION

I

A general statement of the nature and function of philosophy

All adult human beings, so far examined, under appropriate conditions react to some physical objects, lower animals, and persons. Symbols are used to refer to these facts, express emotions or influence behaviour by giving orders or asking questions. Thus there is interaction among individual men and women.

Within the context of this situation, many disagreements arise and are discussed. People turn to reputed sources of assistance in dealing with these problems. One of them is philosophy. However, here also there is much diversity.

This book is an introduction to a philosophy which is offered as a candidate for acceptance. It is developed in the context of a specific view concerning the nature of philosophy.

Philosophy, as here envisaged, is a distinct sort of complex human activity and the results obtained thereby. More specifically, philosophy is an attempt to answer questions such as the following. What is the nature and destiny of human beings? What are the basic ingredients of the world? How is knowledge obtained? What is valuable? Is there a divine being? These questions are obviously very broad in scope. Philosophers also deal with more restricted though still complex problems such as meaning, truth, the laws of thought.

It is well to emphasise that, while philosophy answers general[1]

---

[1] The term 'general' is here used in the sense of 'universally present' or 'common to all members of a group', for instance, all moral issues have specific common characteristics, all syllogisms of a specific sort have the same structure.

It is to be noted that the term 'general' also has the sense 'not detailed', 'not definite or specific' or not dealing with particular differences among members of a group. The term is also employed in the sense of 'inclusive'. The various uses of the term will be noted in subsequent occurrences of 'general'.

questions, it is not restricted to such questions. Particular questions are also suitable for consideration and answers may appropriately be given to them. For example a philosopher may answer the question: what is the structure of any moral situation? and then go on to answer the question: Is this situation, this behaviour, morally good? Philosophy may state the structure of (all) categorical syllogisms and then answer the question as to whether or not a particular categorical syllogism is valid.

In any case philosophy is both (a) the activity of attempting to answer certain sorts of questions and (b) the answers thus obtained.

It is clear that answers to general questions obtained by philosophers can assist them in producing answers to particular questions. Thus by knowing the structure of all valid categorical syllogisms a person can ascertain that the structure of a particular syllogism is valid. In this sense, within the sphere of intellectual activity, philosophy has an 'applied' aspect.

It is important to note that the philosophical approach to any problem is an attempt to be as comprehensive as possible. It undertakes to examine with care all available data. Present in philosophy, thus delineated, there is a critical function. It endeavours to help to identify, call attention to, and correct errors of (a) commission and (b) omission, in the thought processes and some other activities of human beings.

The topics selected by philosophers for examination are those which, in their judgement, are not adequately dealt with elsewhere, otherwise. With the passage of time, responsibility for dealing with some problems has been transferred from the hands of philosophers to those of natural or social scientists or other specialists. They, within the limits of narrowly restricted problems, are like philosophers, comprehensive and critical in their approach.

So far philosophy has been portrayed as (a) an intellectual activity, an attempt to obtain answers to a number of questions, some general, some particular, and (b) the results of these activities, the answers obtained.

It does not follow that a philosopher, as such, should cut himself off from participation in the affairs of everyday life. Philosophy is characterised by a comprehensive approach to any relevant problem. This involves as much first-hand experience of as many facts as possible. Further, a philosopher as here envisaged not only seeks answers to questions for the sake of knowledge, but also, when possible, he uses the answers (information and skills)[1] in guiding activities of all sorts. Just as in science there is (*a*) activity in solving intellectual problems and (*b*) the application of this knowledge to human affairs, as in the practice of medicine, so it is in the case of philosophy. In other words, science is 'pure' and 'applied', likewise philosophy. Specifically, a philosopher may quite legitimately not only answer the question: What should be done in this situation? He, as a philosopher, may then proceed to implement his answer in some particular moral, political, educational, religious, aesthetic problem situations.

He may do so on his own, or by giving advice to others who follow it, or both. Thus philosophers may sit in Parliament or Congress, serve on school boards, form civic reform groups, etc., and so help by their action and thought to bring about changes in men and their environment. In this sense philosophic thought is translated into philosophic action. In other words philosophy is not just thought (intellectual activities and the results obtained) about certain sorts of problems. It is also action based on such thought.

It must be admitted, and stressed, that a professional philosopher cannot cover all phases of philosophy with equal competence. Indeed, most such men specialise in a few phases of thought or action, or both, in varying degrees.

It is nevertheless essential to retain the comprehensive and critical approach to the problems which fall within the scope of philosophy.

In so far as the non-professional can emulate the philosopher, he will be drawing on philosophy in solving his own problems of thought and action.

Some illustrations, and more detailed explanatory comments, are now in order concerning the statement of the intellectual phase of philosophy, as here envisaged.

Some more detailed, explanatory comments

In formulating a world view, that is finding and reporting the basic ingredients of the world, or attempting to deal with the nature and destiny of human persons a philosopher should try to consider, with

---

[1] Readers of this book may be perplexed by the number of parentheses. However, I feel that all of them are necessary in order to achieve accuracy and to prevent possible misunderstanding (A. H. J.).

critical care, all relevant data.[1] Specifically he should concern himself with the subject matter and techniques of the humanities and the natural and social sciences, also professional pursuits such as law, engineering, medicine and theology as reported by specialists in these fields. Full and serious attention must be paid to ordinary, non-technical experience as well. Further, it is essential to note that, a philosopher on his own account provides information and skills in addition to what is derived from fields mentioned above. There are at least some aspects of logic, ethics and aesthetics, indeed value in general, which are regarded as the special preserve of philosophy.

This remark about the special preserve of philosophy requires clarification. Men engaged in various special fields, such as physics, psychology, law, theology, etc., are of course concerned with the logic of their disciplines—definition, structure of argument, evidence and so on. However, philosophy in its logic aspect is concerned with the logic of all special disciplines, that is with a more comprehensive view. It notes common elements in all logics, for example the laws of thought. The distinctively philosophic aspect of logic introduces some special techniques and deals with some logical elements neglected by others. These are additional unique contributions.[2] Obviously ethics is not the exclusive territory of philosophy, neither is aesthetics. Religion, for example, has much to say concerning such matters, and the common man has also. However, here again philosophy tries to take into consideration approaches to moral and aesthetic issues in all fields. Further, it adds a great deal as its own distinctive contribution in the way of standards, delineation of issues and so on. Further, there is an interest in what is common in all value situations.

These philosophic data and methods must, of course, be involved in any adequate general[3] (world) view of man and his environment, as well as data from other sources. Some data contributed by philosophers will be relevant in dealing with some more restricted problems.[4]

[1] It is very important to notice that in some cases an attempt to consider all relevant data implies a consideration of additional facts. In other instances it implies an elimination of facts which might appear appropriate for consideration, but are not. Here obviously philosophy's critical function is at work.

[2] Further, as a matter of fact, on occasion philosophers spot errors of commission and omission perpetrated by specialists in various fields. In this fashion, philosophers also contribute data and hence aid in achieving comprehensiveness.

[3] In the sense of inclusive.

[4] The preceding comments on logic apply also to epistemology (theory of knowledge).

It should be realised that philosophy is not the only attempt to formulate a world view. Some scientists and most experts in religions undertake this assignment. However, it is contended that philosophy as here envisaged achieves a more comprehensive result.

Likewise it must be admitted that philosophers are not alone in dealing with other problems which are not restricted to one special area of human experience. Health involves physics, chemistry, biology, psychology. A medical doctor must be concerned with all these matters. In this case a philosopher should recognise the authority and responsibility of the doctor. In a sense a doctor deals with the nature and destiny of human beings, as does a theologian. But, to repeat, a philosopher attempts a more comprehensive approach to this problem.

In drawing information from the humanities, the natural and the social sciences and the learned professions, a philosopher as here envisaged is not obliged to duplicate the labours of specialists in these fields, nor should he presume to supersede these specialists. Rather, in many instances, a philosopher contents himself with understanding and accepting the methods and conclusions of the specialists. For example, a philosopher learns from an anthropologist that the Egyptians believed in a life after death. He does not feel obliged to duplicate the anthropologist's process of investigation, by devoting a lifetime to field work and reflection on that area of knowledge. Further, a philosopher frequently accepts conclusions reached by an expert, without concerning himself with all the technical concepts and procedures and complex, minute details involved in the process of reaching and stating those conclusions.[1] For example, a philosopher concerned with the many factors which influence human behaviour may learn from a research scientist the effects of the excessive consumption of alcohol on mental and physical activities. He need not have a detailed technical knowledge of the chemistry of alcohol, blood chemistry, anatomy, the nervous system and so on, such as possessed by specialists in these fields.

Thus, when wrestling with a complex problem involving data from many sources, a philosopher frequently finds it necessary, in order to achieve an adequate, comprehensive view, to leave concentration on minute technical details to the specialists in various fields. The

[1] In this sense the philosopher is satisfied with a general approach.

philosopher is satisfied with a report of results. Thus, to use another clarifying illustration: in dealing with the problem of memory, a philosopher may well content himself with the physiologist's claim that changes in the cortex are involved. The philosopher will not become immersed in a detailed study of the physiology of the brain.

The philosopher's function (in this case, of memory) is that of fitting together the separate pieces of information derived from various sources. He supplements the report of the physiologist by reference to the results of psychological investigation of the phenomena of memory on the conscious level. He then goes on to deal with questions which do not usually fall within the purview of physiology or psychology, for example personal identity, the status of the memory image, possible factors other than brain processes which are involved in memory.

When a philosopher turns from relatively restricted problems, of varying degrees of complexity, to the most broad one, that of formulating an adequate world view, the comments just made concerning specific problems are even more relevant. To the best of his ability, he must familiarise himself with the conclusions reached by specialists in various fields, including his own. This, of course, involves an awareness of basic concepts and methods employed. There is no substitute for first-hand knowledge of facts. However, a man cannot formulate an adequate world view and also be a full-time specialist in some one field, for example, mathematics, physics, or psychology or aesthetics. Therefore he must rely on some first-hand experience of 'manageable' typical cases and much second-hand information lacking in minute technical detail.

It must be admitted that there are dangers involved in accepting conclusions derived from the work of others. Also, it is difficult to draw the line beyond which, in grappling with a problem, a philosopher need not go in acquiring first-hand technical competence. However, this situation faces specialists in every field, including the natural and social sciences. As a matter of fact, the line is drawn in these fields. It can also be drawn in philosophy.

Ideally, however, a philosopher should be fully competent in the field of special knowledge, for example, physics, in which he is exercising his critical function on a distinctly technical level, for instance in discussing the theory of relativity.

Nevertheless, it is important to notice that some of the errors of omission and commission to which some specialists have fallen victim, in dealing with restricted technical topics, are spotted by philosophers, not on the basis of their knowledge of the technical details of the subject matter under consideration, but because of their awareness of data, non-technical or otherwise, which the specialists have overlooked. For example, a critic of Marxism may note phases of human behaviour that do not fall under the complex technical analysis of the Marxist system[1] which as a matter of fact the critic does understand. Further, consider the case of a critic of behaviouristic psychology who does not understand all the complexities of physiology, yet is aware of distinctive mental ingredients in his activity, as well as physical ones.[2]

The purpose of this book

In brief, it must be stressed that philosophy as here envisaged is (a) a complex type of intellectual activity and (b) the results achieved. In other words, philosophy consists of answers to certain sorts of questions and the various concepts and methods employed in formulating the answers. It also (c) involves action based on philosophic thought. Philosophy exists because of the recognition of specific types of human problems and the desire to achieve their solution.

Philosophy, in this sense, is a much more ambitious project than many men wish to undertake. Indeed, some deny that such an enterprise should be termed 'philosophy'. They prefer to concentrate on a few very restricted problems, for example, in the field of language, logic or ethics. Some of the results achieved and the methods employed in the philosophy outlined in this book are regarded as nonsense, or distasteful, by some professional philosophers and some laymen. However, the word 'philosophy' has been applied for centuries to the types of undertakings and results, both broad and restricted, both thought and action, referred to above. The topics discussed are meaningful and important to many reflective men.

In the context of the preceding interpretation of the nature of philosophy, this volume is an attempt to report and describe the main features of man and his environment. On the basis of this examination, an attempt is made to outline a general world view. Speaking technically, this is metaphysics in a broad sense. However, there is also a discussion of some more restricted problems. In brief this is an introduction to one type of philosophy. This volume focuses

---

[1] Error of commission, that is, misinterpretation.
[2] Error of omission.

attention on the following topics: *Minds, physical objects, concepts, words and meaning, knowledge, values*. It is not pretended that this study is an exhaustive treatment of the topics with which it is chiefly concerned. This book does not include a detailed discussion of logic, ethics, aesthetics, or the so-called 'philosophies' of science, history or religion.

In the context of this volume, advice is provided explicitly and implicitly concerning a number of human problems. Also an attempt is made to use relevant information and skills in dealing with the problems discussed.

Some philosophers in formulating their world views, or in dealing with some more restricted problem, place great emphasis on the creations of their imaginations. The philosophy here presented does not propose to explain the non-imaginary in the terms of the imaginary. Its main concern is with what is found in non-imaginary experience. No attempt will be made to discuss what is not present in human experience.

More specifically: the type of philosophy here presented is characterised by reliance on human experience which is as comprehensive as is possible at this stage of human development.

II

Some fundamental terms; 'experience', 'comprehensive'

In outlining this philosophical system, a number of terms are used to state its essential features. Brief reference will now be made to some of these.

In the second from last preceding paragraph the terms 'human', 'experience', and 'comprehensive' are employed. In order to avoid misunderstanding it is appropriate, at this point, to indicate what it is to which these terms refer.

The term 'human' has its obvious usage. Reference is being made to creatures regarded by biologists as human, as distinguished from lower animals, machines, or so-called higher, superhuman, types of creatures. The term 'experience', in its most general[1] sense, means being occupied in any participation in the affairs of life. More specifically it refers to: (*a*) observation of (*b*) facts or events. Thus a philosophy

---

[1] Inclusive.

based on human experience will take into consideration facts and events which are observed in the course of the many activities in which human beings engage.

In view of the complexities of meaning which the term 'observation' has acquired, it is proposed, in the context of this discussion, to employ the more neutral term 'awareness'. 'Awareness' and 'consciousness' are, roughly speaking, synonymous terms. However, 'consciousness' has acquired some unfortunate meanings (because of mistaken theories concerning human minds), which do not attach to 'awareness'.

Awareness, as here understood, provides an immediate, that is first-hand relation of a person to facts and events. In other words, an activity of awareness is immediate since it is direct, not roundabout. It is not the case that something stands for something else or decisively intervenes between the process of awareness and a fact or event. As will become obvious from subsequent discussion, the terms 'immediate' and 'direct' in this context do not imply a denial that in being aware of an external object a brief time elapses as energy travels along the nervous system, or that the nervous system, physically, is located between the external object and the brain which is involved in the occurrences of awareness. The point being made is that a fact, of which one is aware, is itself present to awareness, not a substitute which serves as a sign or symbol. The nervous system is a factor which enables this to occur. Apparent difficulties do not arise so obviously in the case of internal mental states, such as a memory image, or pain. There is no physical gap because of any intervening medium. Awareness is to be contrasted with assumption or postulation which are characterised by a lack of first-hand immediate presence.

It seems advisable to substitute 'entity' for 'fact' and 'event'. The term 'entity', as used in this discussion, is regarded as preferable to such terms as 'fact', 'event', or 'thing', because these are either ambiguous or restricted in obvious scope of application. For example, 'fact' is used to refer either to a proposition or to what a proposition reports. The term 'event' refers to a process of change. It is not applicable to that which endures. The term 'thing' most obviously applies to physical objects, though sometimes it has more extended application, as in 'anything'. Hence a more neutral term, unrestricted in range of application, is required in dealing with very general topics as well as differing particular ones. In the context of this book, the term 'entity' will be used to refer to whatever a person is aware of in the course of comprehensive experience. Thus for example 'entity' is used to refer to wood (a relatively enduring physical object), pleasure (a transitory mental content), awareness (a transitory mental activity), and the number five (a relatively enduring concept).

In this study the term 'experience' is frequently employed in a broad sense to refer to a complex situation which has two main ingredients, (*a*) awareness and (*b*) entities (present to awareness). However the term 'experience' is sometimes used in its verb form, (a limited sense) 'experience' or 'experiencing' or 'experienced' as synonyms for 'awareness'. It must be realised that 'experience', in its verb form, is sometimes used to refer not only to the activity of awareness but also to a vast range of other activities, some of which are necessary if awareness is to take place, for example, travel or manipulation of the environment. The term 'experience' is employed in another limited sense, namely in its noun form, to refer to the entities of which a person is aware. The various usages of the term are, in most cases, easily determined by reference to their context or spelling.

It is important to stress the complexity of meaning of the term 'comprehensive'[1] as employed in the context of this discussion. Most obviously, the philosophy based on comprehensive experience gives careful attention to all types of entities of which human beings are now aware, or have been aware, that is the results and methods of specialists in various areas as well as the ingredients of 'non-professional' ordinary human experience. This implies no mere passive spectator role. Wide as possible first-hand participation in human affairs, practical and theoretical, is necessary. Of course, no one person can be aware of all available entities. But under carefully controlled conditions, second-hand reports can be used.

There are a number of aspects of comprehensive experience which may be overlooked. For example, when a person takes a comprehensive approach to a situation, he may find the presence of prejudice, special interest, and mistaken interpretations in his own reactions and those of others. He will be aware of the importance of avoiding these if other entities are to be placed in their proper perspective.

Further, in comprehensive experience the imaginary is distinguished

---

[1] The use of the term 'comprehensive' here outlined may be open to objection. However the term is essentially a convenient shorthand label sanctioned by ordinary use to refer to specific characteristics of experience, in the broad sense.

from the non-imaginary; artificial distinctions are identified. The relevant is distinguished from the irrelevant.[1]

A world view based on comprehensive experience takes into consideration the vast range of differing entities. But this does not imply an indiscriminate piling together. Among the entities are value distinctions. There are many different relations among entities: different orders are found. In some cases no order is as yet discoverable.

A possible misunderstanding may arise concerning reliance on comprehensive experience in dealing with some restricted, limited, entity, simple or complex. It may be claimed that if comprehensive experience involves consideration of all entities present to human awareness, how can one stop short of considering everything when attempting to deal with a particular entity, that is with part of the whole content of experience? The reply is: On the basis of awareness of a range of entities, distinctions are noted. Once these are brought into focus, for example in noting that a chair is distinct from a table and other things in the world, then a comprehensive approach to a particular problem such as finding the dimensions of a particular chair as measured by a yardstick, can be undertaken without referring to everything else in the world of which persons are aware. Comprehensive experience of the dimensions of the chair merely requires an awareness of all the dimensional entities in this particular situation (involving the chair, yardstick and its use). Thus it must be borne in mind that 'comprehensive experience' is a relative term. Obviously what constitutes comprehensive experience in the case of the dimensions of a chair is much more limited in scope and content than comprehensive experience of a universe of entities. To repeat, comprehensive experience is experience of all entities, but it is comprehensive experience of a specified situation, restricted or broad, simple or complex.[2]

A person who relies on comprehensive experience takes into consideration whatever human beings are or have been aware of in a specific situation.[3] However, there is no claim that there is a grasp of

[1] Such activities, of course, are the bases of philosophy's critical function.

[2] It may appear that some phases of the discussion in this book are lacking in comprehensiveness. It should be realised, however, that what is here presented is intended to be an introduction. For this purpose, the 'comprehensive' requirement may well be met.

[3] As has been noted, a person can make use of the results of the awareness of others, that is take into consideration entities of which he himself is not aware.

all entities. It seems obvious that there are entities beyond the range of any human awareness at the present time or in the past. It is obvious in the sense that we are now aware of areas of ignorance, and that with the lapse of time new entities are discovered. In other words, the range and content of comprehensive experience is enlarging with the passage of time. What it may be in the future cannot be accurately predicted.

It is of course the case that a person who is not aware of all entities of which a person is aware in comprehensive experience, may be aware of some of them. In other words, lacking comprehensive experience, a person is not reduced to complete incompetence—rather his range of competence is limited.

III

Method of presentation of Experiential Realism

It will be noted that, as this study proceeds, technical jargon is kept to a minimum. Thus an attempt has been made to emulate the example set by Plato (in some of his dialogues, for example the *Republic*, the *Phaedo*), Locke, Berkeley, Hume, James, Whitehead in *Modes of Thought*, Austin in *Sense and Sensibilia*, Wittgenstein in *The Blue Book*, Ryle in *The Concept of Mind*. It is here suggested that much of the technical verbiage of professional philosophers arises because, for their purposes, they invent imaginary entities, or introduce distorted interpretations, and are hence forced to invent names for them outside the range of familiar terms applicable to the non-imaginary world.[1]

However, some technical terminology is required to bring into focus entities in the non-imaginary world, and the imaginary as well, which are overlooked by most men, and hence have not been linked with familiar terms. Also, as noted earlier, some familiar terms are so ambiguous, or misleading, that accurate statement of experience requires the invention of new technical terms, or apparently cumbersome qualifying terms. Nevertheless, wherever possible, non-technical terms will be employed.[2]

Some philosophers, in presenting their views, state them in simple straightforward fashion, merely saying what their views are and why

---

[1] See Chap. 10, pp. 255–60 and Chap. 19, pp. 416–17, 418–19
[2] See Glossary in Appendix.

they hold them. There is little or no reference to other philosophers in order to (*a*) list possible alternatives, (*b*) show their deficiencies, (*c*) claim their support. In brief, the philosophers who use the simple method invite the reader to judge for himself.

Other philosophers proceed in a more tortuous, cumbersome, fashion. These present their views in the context of a step-by-step, detailed comparison with those of other philosophers, (*a*) listing possible alternative views, (*b*) criticising other views, (*c*) claiming support from great men in the field. These complicated procedures have the advantage of placing the views being offered for acceptance in a broad context. However, all this tends to interfere with the understanding of a person's views. One has to endure a great deal of background discussion, much of which may seem, and in many instances is, rather irrelevant, in order to find out what a man's position actually is.

In this study there are two sections. Section One is chiefly an attempt to simply report the major entities found in comprehensive experience. Some uses of this information are indicated. In Section Two the views of other philosophers are evaluated in terms of comprehensive experience. In this fashion the philosophic position termed 'Experiential Realism', outlined in Section One, receives further clarification.

It is deemed advisable to provide as complete a report as possible of the major entities found in comprehensive experience (in Section One) before using comprehensive experience to comment (in Section Two) on other philosophies in general or concerning particular problems. Further, in Section Two it will be shown that Experiential Realism is neither unique nor queer, since it is supported at crucial points by many respectable philosophers.

The two-section arrangement is an attempt to retain the best features of the two methods of presenting philosophic views, and also to avoid defects present in either method when used exclusively.

In Section Two of this volume, views opposed to Experiential Realism are brought into clear focus by means of quotations from representative exponents and by summaries of their points of view. The replies of Experiential Realism to the criticisms involved in these alternative views, and its general reaction to these views, is developed in some detail. Some supporting quotations from the work of philosophers who are in agreement with Experiential Realism are also included in the text of Section Two.

IV

A final introductory comment

At this point, a few defensive[1] remarks are in order. Some phases of Experiential Realism's sketch of the general structure and content of the world, and the justification of this view, which will be outlined in subsequent chapters, may seem so obvious that it appears hardly necessary to mention them. However, it is advisable to bring into clear focus what is common and familiar because it is sometimes neglected by philosophers when considering a situation. There is such a disease as professional myopia. Nevertheless, despite the preceding comments, there are admittedly persons who will reject at least some of what has here been termed 'comprehensive experience'. They agree that such experience recognises prejudice, special interests, mistaken interpretations, a superficial approach to entities, and artificial distinctions. On the basis of this, they contend that at least some of the entities referred to in this study are the result of restricted, or indeed distorted experience. For example, it is contended by some critics that words deceive us into believing that there are mental entities and concepts, whereas there are only physical entities in the non-imaginary world. Even in cases where there is no fundamental disagreement with much of the general discussion so far outlined, many philosophers will anticipate disagreement ahead. The point is this: even if there is general agreement with Experiential Realism that there are physical objects, mental entities and concepts,[2] profound philosophical disagreements arise when one begins to examine them. In short, the philosophy to be presented in the remainder of this volume is likely to arouse opposition in some circles.[3] Indeed, much of what will be presented will be denied the title 'philosophy' in some (ivory) towers or traditions, because it does not use the technique and reach the conclusions of the critic. One can only hope for tolerant suppression of suspicion or rejection, until the discussion has proceeded to its conclusion.

In the course of this study, statements will be (indeed, have been) made, particularly in the early stages, which may seem to a critic to be

---

[1] Indeed, they may be regarded as 'offensive' in at least one sense!

[2] See pages 39–40

[3] Certainly among those who look with favour on the Vienna Circle (or who, scoffing at details of its doctrine, still feel its influence).

unjustified or at least to require further support and clarification. In particular, objection may be taken to reports to the effect that one is aware of a particular or general situation. The critic may legitimately ask how these statements are justified. Those questions will be faced as the discussion proceeds.

In any case, it is here suggested that the final appeal which any man makes is to his own experience that is to the entities of which he is aware. It is, of course, the case that some men admit entities which are not accepted by others. It is sometimes possible to work from a shared group of entities to an expansion of range in the experience of one person, due to the initiative of another, thus bringing into focus an entity previously overlooked. Ultimately, all that can be done, in the face of disagreement, is for each person to look again carefully at the entities he finds in his own experiencing, and decide what he is prepared to accept as reliable reports by others, and continue an open-minded search for new entities.

What follows, then, is a report by one person concerning the major ingredients of men and their environment. In other words, it is a report of the entities present to his awareness, supplemented by reports from others who are considered, as the result of his experience, to be reliable. Some uses of this information and relevant skills are indicated.

Since it is contended that entities are found, not generated by mental acts of awareness, this point of view is, speaking technically, a form of Realism. Since it is based on experience (awareness of entities), the philosophic position may appropriately be termed 'Experiential Realism'. In the spirit of one of the founders of modern philosophy, Descartes, and one of the leaders of contemporary philosophy, Ludwig Wittgenstein, these mediations and investigations are presented in the hope that they may be of assistance to others, and that other persons will see fit to discuss what they consider to be errors in the reports here presented.

Readers of this book will note that I have made very extensive use of material in parentheses. It may appear that this procedure involves unnecessary complexity and is stylistically unfortunate. However, I judge, after due consideration, that the presentation of supplementary material in this fashion is necessary in view of: (i) the notorious ambiguity of many key terms, (ii) the need to indicate as exactly as possible the nature of an entity or a situation, (iii) the need to deal immediately with crucial questions which may occur to a perceptive reader—without repetition of points at issue. In some instances, some persons may not require this 'assistance'. They can, then of course, disregard the material in parentheses.

1

ENTITIES OF COMPREHENSIVE EXPERIENCE

I

It is appropriate at this point to provide a brief preliminary examination of a representative sample of entities, that is whatever people find in the course of comprehensive experiencing of men and their environment.

An example

Consider the following situation: I walk into a room and see a desk a chair and a table. Each is brown. I am informed that the table is made of oak wood, the desk of pine, and the chair of maple wood. I feel pleasure when I contemplate these useful objects. Among the entities noted are: wood, brown, pleasure.

Obviously there are several occurrences[1] of each. It must be realised that each occurrence (piece) of wood involves some differences. While the composition of the cells is not very diverse, the patterns of their arrangement vary considerably in the cases of maple wood, pine wood and oak wood. However, each is wood. Similarly, it is found that the brown of the maple wood differs in shade from that of the pine and both differ in shade from the brown of the oak wood. Nevertheless, in each case brown occurs. Likewise in all probability the several occurrences of pleasure involve differences of intensity, but pleasure is there in all cases. This situation, that is differences in occurrences, is typical of many entities. However, in some cases occurrences of an entity do not involve such differences. For example, if a person dips a paintbrush into a tin of well-mixed brown paint and

---

[1] The term does not have a predominant verb sense. 'Case' or 'instance' might have been used, but while similar in meaning they are more open to misunderstanding.

makes three strokes of paint at different places on a wall, these occurrences of brown will probably not involve differences in shade.

Language and entities

The English language sometimes presents difficulties when a person attempts to discuss many-occurrence entities. There is no problem in cases such as wood, brown, pleasure. It is conventional usage to speak of many occurrences (that is pieces, patches, pulses) of wood, brown, pleasure. Singular words are available to refer to[1] these three different entities, each of which has many occurrences. However, the situation is different with other entities. A person does not usually refer to[2] many occurrences of chair, table, desk, since singular 'entity words' sound odd. A person refers to chairs, tables, desks, that is he uses plural words. Yet as a matter of fact, chair, table and desk are entities, that is distinct 'somethings' which a person finds, each of which has many occurrences in like fashion as wood, brown, pleasure. There are many chairs, just as there are many occurrences of pleasure. In the course of discussion in this book conventional locutions will be used, except when the somewhat odd-sounding version is required to bring into focus a point which is being made, for example that all chairs are occurrences of one 'something,' that is chair.

In referring to particular occurrences of a many-occurrence entity, the term 'a' is prefixed, in conventional English, to a singular form of the term used. Thus one speaks of a chair, a table. But in other cases it is necessary to add a more complicated phrase, for example a piece of wood, a pulse of pleasure. Once again, in some instances, it is advisable to use a more technical locution and speak of a particular occasion of one entity, for instance wood, table, chair, pleasure.

It is to be noted that the term 'entity' is sometimes employed in an

[1] Frequently in this book the term 'refer' ('refer to') is (a) employed as a synonym for 'talk about' or 'comment on'. Sometimes (b) what is at issue is chiefly a way of talking or writing. However (c) in discussing the meaning situation (see Chapter 5, pp. 111–13) the term is used in several technical senses. Of course a person cannot use the term 'refer' in talking or writing without understanding its meaning situation.

The 'refer to' to which this note is attached is a case of sense (a), that is singular words are available to talk about.

[2] This use of 'refer to' is a case of sense (b) as outlined in the preceding footnote; 'many occurrences of chair, table, desk' is a way of writing or talking in which a person does not usually engage.

apparently redundant fashion. However, this is ordinarily done in order to emphasise the point that what one is talking about is present to awareness. It is found and hence is a legitimate topic for discussion.

It is important to understand that the term 'entity' is used to refer, for example, (*a*) to wood, brown, pleasure as such, (*b*) to each particular piece of wood, patch of brown, pulse of pleasure.

Many-occurrence, particular-occurrence and simple-occurrence entities

It must be realised, for example, that wood, brown, pleasure are not found apart from their occurrences. In other words wood is present, brown is present in the situation described. The three items of wooden furniture are there with their brown surfaces, and the person is there experiencing occurrences of pleasure.

In the interests of clarification it may be pointed out that 'many-occurrence entity' refers to the nature of what is present. A particular occurrence is the fashion in which the many-occurrence entity is present. Thus, for example, the many-occurrence entity wood is present in the fashion of (i) a desk (a particular occurrence), (ii) a chair (another particular occurrence), (iii) a table (another particular occurrence).

The phrase 'occurrences of an entity' is possibly a source of misunderstanding. It is very easy to be misled by language. It may sound paradoxical to state that each occurrence of an entity is that entity. However, turning from words to what is the case, it is the case that a piece of wood (one occurrence of the entity wood) is wood.

Thus in talking about, for example, the occurrences of wood there is no implication that wood, a many-occurrence entity, is a mysterious something which appears in the guise of its so-called occurrences. The term 'entity' is not here used to refer to an assumed reality which appears in various particular instances and is reputed to be other, in nature and status, than they. An entity is a distinct 'what is present' to comprehensive experiencing. In many cases what is found occurs more than once.

Because some entities have many occurrences this does not constitute a problem. This is a situation which is found in comprehensive experiencing. It is not difficult in many instances to determine that there are many occurrences of an entity.

In addition to many-occurrence entities it seems obvious that there are single-occurrence entities, for example Socrates and Napoleon. Westminster Abbey and the Empire State Building. The question as to whether in a sense a particular piece of wood, a particular patch of brown, a particular pulse of pleasure are single-occurrence entities will be left for later discussion when more background has been provided. (See treatment of individuality, Chapter 7 pp. 191–201.)

Further examples of many-occurrence entities

Thus far we have concentrated on the following entities: wood, brown, pleasure, chair, table, desk. However, reference has also been made to other entities, for example maple, pine, oak, room, person, experience, occurrence, particular, difference, and there are others.

Having attempted to clear up some possible misunderstandings, let us now proceed to examine further representative samples of many-occurrence entities. Each occurrence of wood[1] has the characteristic[2] 'physical', that is 'physical'[3] is an entity (something found), a distinct feature, which has the relation of being a characteristic of wood. Thus 'physical' and 'characteristic' are entities which occur more than once.

It should be obvious from the preceding discussion that among the entities found in the course of comprehensive experiencing are: many-occurrence, and particular-occurrence. For example wood, brown, pleasure are characterised by many-occurrence. Each piece of wood, patch of brown, pulse of pleasure is characterised by particular-occurrence.

It is to be noted that many-occurrence and particular-occurrence are, as such, many-occurrence entities. This apparent paradox should

---

[1] Strictly speaking this is an over-simplification. While in a general sense it is the case that wood is a many-occurrence entity, the issue is this: pine wood, maple wood, oak wood, in one sense, are many-occurrence entities. In another sense they are occurrences of the same (one) entity, wood. The same comments apply to intense pleasure, mild pleasure and so on.

[2] The term 'characteristic' (more exactly 'characteristic of') is employed in order to avoid the use of terms which may seem more obvious such as 'quality', 'relation', or 'property'. This is done because of the unfortunate theoretical implications of these terms, based on restricted views of man and his environment (see later discussion).

Here and elsewhere, quotation marks are used to draw attention to an entity. Subsequently these marks are omitted. Quotation marks are also used to indicate that a word (term) is being discussed. Differences in use are indentifiable by reference to context.

not give rise to confusion. It is the case that many entities are, that is have the characteristic many-occurrence and each particular occurrence is one of many particular occurrences. In other words many-occurrence and particular-occurrence are characteristics of many entities, and hence as such are many-occurrence entities.

In referring to the characteristics which all occurrences of pleasure have in common, it is convenient to speak of the characteristics of pleasure. In referring to the characteristics which all chairs have in common it is conventional to talk about the characteristics of chairs. The same topic is under discussion despite the fact that the term 'pleasure' is singular in form and 'chairs' is plural. In some instances, in the interests of clarity, it is advisable to use the more clumsy locution 'the common characteristics of all occurrences of pleasure', that is in cases where one might mistakenly assume that reference was being made to one particular occurrence of pleasure.

These references to pleasure and chairs are of course only illustrations of procedures to be followed in using the English language to refer also to other entities in like fashion, that is to be either conventional or more technically accurate, in accordance with the requirements of the situation.

It should be noted that, in discussing a many-occurrence entity, attention will be focused usually on what is the case in any occurrence of the entity under consideration.

As has been indicated above, a person relying on comprehensive experiencing finds that some entities are characteristic of others. For example, 'physical' is a characteristic of wood. When an entity has another entity as its characteristic, it (the former) is frequently referred to as 'being' its characteristic. Thus wood is said to be physical. However, it is obvious that the sense of the verb 'to be' is not that of identity or existence but rather of possession.

It is very important to realise that some entities have the characteristic 'basic,' that is they have other entities as their characteristics and they are not characteristics of other entities, and further they do not have the characteristic 'presently dependent resultant'. Pleasure is a presently dependent resultant. It continues only as long as a mind continues to function in generating it. Despite the fact that pleasure has characteristics (for example intensity), it is not basic, because of its presently dependent status. On the other hand a piece of wood, which is the result of process of growth by a tree, is no longer dependent on it. While it exists, it has the characteristic 'basic', that is it has other entities as characteristics, for instance rectangular, brown. This is so even though earlier, as part of the tree, it was a presently dependent resultant. The term 'basic' may be misleading. It is not used to refer to ultimate, unchanging, indestructible building blocks of which the universe is constructed.

It is obvious that the world is very complex. Entities which are characteristics of other entities, in turn have entities which are characteristic of them. For example brown, which is a characteristic of wood, itself has the characteristic intensity, and the characteristic colour. A more complex and very important illustration is the following. Some characteristics (entities which are characteristics of others), have the characteristic 'key'. For example wood has the characteristic physical and it also has as characteristics shape and size, as well as numerical and relational ones. Speaking technically, physical is the key characteristic of wood, and the other characteristics of wood are invariant associates (in other words, what is physical is also characterised by shape, size, etc.). It is to be noted that physical is an inherent characteristic of wood, and colour is an inherent characteristic of brown.

Not all associated characteristics are invariant. For example, while physical entities always are characterised by shape and size (invariant characteristics), some physical entities are characterised by green and others by brown. (Green and brown, while associates when present, are not invariant.)

The distinction between inherent and associate characteristics is difficult to express in words. The examples given should serve to indicate what is involved. In the case of wood, the associated characteristics as it were cluster around or in a sense are superimposed on it. Its inherent characteristic is what characterises it as such.

Some entities are (have the characteristic) simple—for example physical, brown. Others are complex: for example wood is composed of many cells, the human body has many parts.

The immediately preceding discussion has added a number of items to the earlier list of many-occurrence entities, for example: characteristic, physical, basic, resultant, shape, size, key, relation, mind, invariant, associate, inherent, simple, complex, cell, human, body.

A group of occurrences of an entity may conveniently be termed a class, for example all occurrences of wood. The members of a class may be further distinguished in terms of sorts, for instance maple, pine. However, all occurrences of maple wood constitute a class.

When a group of entities are together, not because it is a case of many occurrences of one entity as in the case of a class, but rather because they share an inherent characteristic, this group is termed a type. The members of this group are termed types. For example wood, iron and stone are types of physical. In other words they have the inherent characteristic physical in common.

In the context of comprehensive experiencing a person finds, in addition to the entities already mentioned, the following: mental, concept, value. In other words there are entities which are (are characterised by) mental and value. There are occurrences of the entity 'concept' that is concepts. These and some other entities, which fall within the scope of philosophy, as here delineated, will be discussed in an introductory fashion in this volume.

II

Illustrations of the contrast between comprehensive and restricted experience

It is useful to bring comprehensive experience into focus by contrasting it with its opposite, human experience which is severely restricted. For a new-born child the world is a 'blooming, buzzing confusion'. He is not aware of many entities. A savage has difficulty in distinguishing mental from physical, for example a dream image from physical objects. A person who is seriously mentally ill will deny that he has a mind, that there is a physical world or that he is aware of concepts. All such people are unaware of many occurrences of value. However, a person whose experience is comprehensive does distinguish physical, mental and value entities and also concepts.

The process of development from savage to civilised or from childhood to adulthood is a long and difficult one. Also difficult is the avoidance of at least some abnormality. However, to repeat, these achievements do take place and a more extensive type of experience is attained by some human beings. The way in which all this comes about, and the details of any case of the functioning of any such human beings are primarily the subject matter of the natural and social sciences. We receive (or should receive) from such sources general and, when relevant, specific information concerning these matters. Philosophers, of course, should use this information for their purposes, namely a comprehensive view of a topic. But they should avoid getting bogged down in minute details.

Even if, as is the case, scientists and philosophers cannot, at present, understand all phases of this development, and these complex functionings, there is no justification for denying that these developments have taken place or that these experiences occur. This is known to be the case. These mental, value and other entities are found and are recognised in comprehensive experience.

Basic entities

It was noted in a previous very brief reference to various entities that some of these are (have the characteristic) basic. In other words some entities have other entities as characteristics and are not characteristics of other entities. Further, they (basic entities) are not presently dependent resultants. In the context of comprehensive experiencing it is found that the entities which have the characteristic basic are either mind or concept or entities which also have the characteristic physical.

It was pointed out earlier that if an entity which is basic, has the inherent characteristic physical, it will have a number of entities which are invariant associates. Mind has mental as inherent characteristic. Here too there is a cluster of invariant associates.[1] In the case of concept there is no inherent characteristic 'conceptual' (see later discussion). However the entity 'concept' does have characteristics which are invariant associates. (See relevant chapters).

Incidentally, as a convenient locution, instead of referring, for example, to 'a basic entity which has the inherent characteristic physical' the phrase 'basic physical entity' will be used. Likewise in general[2] the phrase 'basic entity' will be used instead of 'entity which is basic'.

It is very important to realise that no basic entity occurs without any other characteristics.

In referring to the characteristics of basic physical entities, it must be remembered that when, for example, it is stated that shape is a characteristic, this is so because the entities in question have as characteristics 'square', or 'rectangle', or 'circle', etc. Thus in dealing in simplified fashion with members of the type physical, a person refers

---

[1] Either actual or potential. See Chapter 2, pp. 60–3.
[2] That is, usually.

in cases such as these to characteristics (such as shape) of characteristics (square, rectangle, circle). It should be clear that a shape is an invariant characteristic of basic entities which are physical, on the other hand 'square' is not. The same simplified presentation is used with reference to the other basic entities.

III

This book is, in part, an attempt to discuss the characteristics of basic entities. In order to clarify and support the preceding introductory statements, further comments and illustrations are in order.

Explanatory comments on physical objects

It will have been obvious that, so far, the phrase 'physical object' has not been used very frequently. This is because, in its ordinary employment, it is ambiguous. In one of its uses (*a*) it is a synonym for 'basic physical entity'. However, more commonly and usually it is employed (*b*) to refer for example to, chairs, tables, turnips and coins. These occurrences of the entities—chair, table, turnip, coin,—of course involve the presence of the characteristic physical. Difficulty arises when a person speaks of the characteristics of physical objects in sense (*b*), for example the colour, shape, size of chairs, tables, turnips, coins. Strictly (technically) speaking, chairs (for example) do not have characteristics such as colour, shape, etc. It is the basic physical entity, namely wood, which has the characteristics colour, shape, size. However, it is a convenient locution to speak of the 'characteristics of physical objects' (chairs, tables, etc.) in place of the more cumbersome locution 'characteristics of basic entities which have the characteristic physical and out of which entities such as chairs and tables are made.'

It is important to note that in accordance with the first use (*a*) of the term 'physical object', that is referring to basic entities having the inherent characteristic physical—physical objects differ on the basis of being wood, copper, stone, etc. However, in accordance with the other (*b*) more common use of the term, physical objects may have the same basic physical entity but be different physical objects because of differences in associated characteristics such as shape, size, etc.

Pennies and plaques may well be of the same basic physical entity (copper), but differ in shape and size. They are different physical objects (in the second sense). Likewise chairs and tables are composed of the same basic physical entity, wood, but differ in shape and in many cases in size. In this sense shape and size are constitutive characteristics as far as chairs and tables are concerned.

Explanatory comments on 'mind' and 'concept'

So far attention has been focused chiefly on the associated characteristics of basic entities which have the characteristic physical. Some comments concerning characteristics of mind and concept are now in order.

In the context of comprehensive experience[1] a person is aware of an entity which has the inherent characteristic mental and has as associate characteristics a number of activities which are also mental. Among these activities is the generation of a number of entities (content) which are presently dependent resultants, for example memory images. They are also mental. The entity which, as basic, engages in these activities is ordinarily termed 'mind'. Strictly speaking, a person is aware of only one occurrence of the entity mind, namely the occurrence which is his own. There is, however, evidence to indicate that there is, and has been, a vast number of other occurrences of mind, manifesting an impressive range of individual differences (see later discussion).

There is also a vast range of differing occurrences of the entity 'concept'. Each occurrence has a linkage with some other many-occurrence entity (simple or complex). It is a customary and convenient locution to refer to each occurrence of the entity concept as 'a' concept. Thus there is a concept linked with pleasure and a concept (another one) linked with wood. However, the entity concept has characteristics in addition to that of linkage with other entities. Consider for example: useful (value), numerical, individuality.

It is important to note that, with the exception of linkage as just discussed, the characteristics of concept as mentioned are not its

---

[1] In presenting a discussion of entities reference is frequently made to the fact that a person is aware of them. This is done to emphasise the fact that in the philosophy here being presented it is proper to deal only with what people are aware of in comprehensive experiencing.

exclusive possession.[1] Numerical and value characteristics are also possessed by basic physical entities. The mental entity which is basic (mind) also has them and so do its mental activities and content (its characteristics). For example, wood is characterised by one (is one entity) and hence by a number. Further, wood as such may be characterised by 'useful', and a memory image (a mental characteristic) as well. A person's mind is one and useful. The same general comments apply to the resultants of basic physical entities.[2]

Entities and their characteristics

It is essential to realise that while entities have characteristics, and hence it is appropriate to refer to them in terms of their characteristics, for example wood as physical, nevertheless an entity is what it is. It is pointless to attempt to account for or define an entity in terms of its characteristics alone. Wood is wood, brown is brown. Wood has shape and size characteristics and is characterised by physical. Brown may have beauty and is one entity. These are characteristics of wood and brown, but they do not constitute wood or brown as such. It is no help to say that wood is characterised by 'woodness' or brown by 'brownness' or concepts by 'conceptual'. This is false. Further, the concept 'wood' applies, the concept 'brown' applies, but the concepts are not constitutive characteristics of wood or brown as such. To remark that a piece of wood is composed of cells does not refute the contention which has here been made. The cells are components of the wood, but not constitutive characteristics. The basic point is: a characteristic is another entity. It is different from the entity of which it is the characteristic. It is different in this sense: an entity has a characteristic but it is not identical with it (or with the sum of its characteristics) even though in customary locution, for example, wood is said to be physical.

In the case of chair and horse for example, the preceding comments may seem not to apply. It may be argued: an entity is a chair if its component wood has a distinctive shape and size, and other sorts of characteristics which are decisive in distinguishing chairs from tables. A living organism is a horse if it has as characteristics

[1] See subsequent discussion of resultants of basic physical entities. (Chapter 3, pp. 79-83).

[2] See subsequent discussion of physically based resultants. (Chapter 3, pp 79-86).

distinctive shape and size and performs specific characteristic activities. It thus seems as though chairs and horses are accounted for and defined in terms of their characteristics. However, as has been noted earlier, strictly and technically speaking, chairs and horses as such do not have characteristics. The characteristics in question belong to the component wood and living organism. It is only a sometimes convenient (but actually misleading) locution to refer to the characteristics of chair or horse. In any case there is more to a chair or a horse than shape, size, etc. There is more than characteristics alone. There is also in each case a basic physical entity.

The state of affairs is this: there is an occurrence of the entity chair when there is present wood (or metal, etc.) with specified characteristics. There is an occurrence of the entity horse where there is present a living organism with specific characteristics. In other words, given a specific complex situation, one is confronted by the entity chair or the entity horse. In this sense one can account for or define (in one meaning of the term 'define') chair or horse. But, to repeat, it is not an instance of accounting for these entities in terms of their characteristics only. Rather it is a case of noting (*a*) basic entities (which are components) and (*b*) characteristics of basic entities which are components of entities such as chair and horse.

It will be obvious from subsequent discussion that from the point of view here being developed, not only physical objects but also minds and concepts are not merely a collection of characteristics. There is an addition, in each case a basic entity to which these characteristics belong.

IV

At the end of this very brief outline of comprehensive experience it is well to reiterate a point made earlier. Some human beings have comprehensive experience, that is they perform many activities and hence are aware of as wide a range of entities, involved in some situations, as are open to human awareness at this stage of man's development. On the other hand, it is the case that a person who has not achieved comprehensive experience may still be aware of some of the entities open to comprehensive experiencing. It is merely a case of restricted range of awareness of entities.

The status of language

In outlining a world view, and in dealing with some specific problems, in the context of comprehensive experience, a person is forced to rely on available language to a very considerable extent. It is one of the chief means of recording information and of communication. This is not a perfect instrument, but careful and patient use of dictionary and grammar and other such aids can provide a basis for a relatively effective discussion of many, but not all, instances of comprehensive experience.

Language also performs another useful function. It is a source of information concerning experience in the sense that its content and structure provide significant clues concerning entities.

However, it is here contended that statements about men and their environment, and a study of the vocabulary and grammar of language, are at best a second-hand source of information. Sometimes they are dangerously misleading media. Therefore one should place primary emphasis on what is present in comprehensive experience. In using indirect sources of information, as indeed one must, their reliability should be certified on the basis of present awareness, of the reliability of these sources of information. In any case, there is more to life than language.

2

MIND

As noted previously, mind is a basic entity. In the context of comphrehensive awareness there is only one occurrence of this entity of which a person is aware, namely his own. The question as to the existence of other minds (other occurrences of the entity mind) will be dealt with subsequently.[1]

Mind and its characteristics

It was noted in the preceding outline of Experiential Realism, the basic mental entity engages in a number of activities which are also mental. These activities are characteristics of the basic mental entity. One of these activities is the generation of entities which may be appropriately termed 'mental content'. These also are characteristics of the basic mental entity. 'Mental' is an inherent characteristic of the entities here under consideration. The activities and contents are associated characteristics of the basic mental entity. Further, they are presently dependent resultants, entities which depend on the basic mental entity for their continuing present existence, and go out of existence when the engaging in and generating cease.

Mind, its activities and its contents constitute a realm different from that which is composed of physical entities. However, while the realm of the mental is private and that of the physical world public, the mind's activity of awareness is not restricted to the realm of the mental.

Consider the following situation: A person is aware of an imagination image of a cup of coffee[2] and feels pleasure at the prospect of drinking it. He desires and hopes to do so. If the person in question

[1] See Chapter 6, pp. 157–8.
[2] He can of course be aware of a cup of coffee (physical object): however the concern at this point is with mental activities and content.

relies on comprehensive experience he will note (be aware) that there is a basic mental entity engaged in the activity of awareness (in a number of acts of awareness) and also in the activities of desiring and generating imagination images as well as hoping. In this case his mind also generates pleasure. It will be obvious that a basic entity, the activities mentioned, and the imagination image and pleasure (the mental content) all have the characteristics: mental, my own, private. They also have numerical and relational characteristics. The pleasure has the inherent characteristic: feeling.

Comprehensive experience, which is not restricted to the situation described above, indicates that the basic mental entity, in addition to engaging in the activity of awareness,[1] on occasion not only engages in the activities mentioned but also performs other activities such as willing and choosing. When it is not engaged in these activities it has the ability to perform them. In this sense these potential activities are associates of the basic mental entity.

Mental activities

A statement of major mental activities and mental content of the basic mental entity is now in order.

The mental activities in question can be arranged in three groups. These are group A—being aware, being interested, being disinterested, liking,[2] disliking directing toward, believing, disbelieving, linking entities, desiring, hoping, willing, choosing, intending, expecting: group B—generating (i) images (memory, imagination, dream), feelings and emotions and (ii) all other mental activities: group C—meaning, imagining, dreaming, remembering and reasoning.[3] These are more complex mental activities in the sense that they involve some of the mental activities listed above, and others.

It is to be noted that apart from being aware, each of these activities on occasion occurs without any of the others. There are of course many cases where more than two mental activities occur at the same time (that is not just awareness and one other).

[1] See discussion of lapse into unconsciousness, Chapter 7, pp. 198–9.

[2] In broad sense to include approving.

[3] All activities listed are, as such, mental and only mental, except directing toward, linking, generating. These, on occasion, are activities of physical entities. See Chapter 7, p. 173 for comments on generating. It is important to note that when generating is an activity of a physical entity it does not thereby become physical (pp. 179–80).

The term 'thinking' is here broadly used to refer to the following mental activities, choosing, intending, expecting, linking entities, meaning, imagining, remembering, reasoning. In other words, thinking is an inherent characteristic of these activities.

Mental content

Among the sorts of mental content[1] are memory, dream and imagination images, and images which a mind generates when stimulated by extreme external physical processes (for example after-images due to a bright light or stars seen following a blow on the head), excessive use of alcohol or drugs, images resulting from mental illness and extreme physical illness. Speaking technically these are various occurrences of the entity 'image'. Among mental content there are also emotions (for example fear, anger) and feelings (for example pleasure, pain, itch).

It is important to note that on occasion feelings and emotions, when generated by a mind, are directed toward, focused on (a mental activity), some person or thing. Thus for example anger, fear, love, hate, reverence are sometimes directed towards a person or a thing. However, there are occurrences of fear, anger and so on which are not focused on any particular entity. Likewise pleasure and pain are sometimes focused on an entity, sometimes not. Some emotions, such as joy and sorrow, are experienced in a specific context, but while directed towards a particular person or thing are more pervasive of experience than some feelings and emotions.

It follows that, for example, strictly speaking there is no distinctive particular activity which is appropriately termed 'loving', or 'hating', or 'revering' analogous to such activities as believing, willing, choosing. In the situation under consideration these are emotions (love, hate, reverence) together with the activity of 'directing toward' (focusing on).

The various sorts of images mentioned above (that is their mental entities)[2] have some associated characteristics in common with physical objects (those whose basic entity is physical), for example shape, size, colour. (Consider an imagination image of a cup of coffee.) It is

[1] The term 'content' is here being used in a somewhat special, restricted, sense. The term might also be applied to mental activities, since they are also characteristics of mind and are mental, and are as internal as, for example, images, feelings and emotions.

[2] See discussion, this Chapter, p. 64.

essential to realise that these shared[1] characteristics as such are neither physical nor mental, nor are any occurrences of these physical or mental. In this sense they are neutral characteristics. The brown (colour) of a piece of wood is not physical, though of course the wood is. The same brown colour of an imagined cup of coffee (i.e. image) is not mental though the imagination image is mental. The same general point must be made concerning many other shared characteristics, as will be brought out in later discussion.

It is the case that the particular occurrence of colour, shape and size characteristics of an imagined cup of coffee are mind-generated—but, to repeat, as such the colour, size and shape are not mental. They are characteristics of mental entities. Characteristics which are mind-generated are characteristics of entities which in many cases are both mind-generated and mental. For example, the imagination image is mind-generated and mental. On the other hand, imagination images are characteristics of a mind. The images are mind-generated, the mind is mental—whether or not it is mind-generated cannot now be settled. (See later discussion.)[2]

Mental contents differ from physical objects which they superficially resemble, (a) in having a different inherent characteristic. They differ also (b) in some of their other characteristics (associate ones). Under the most favourable conditions for awareness, memory and imagination images are more dim than physical objects of which they are memory and imagination images. This is also the case with some dream images but not all. Further, dream images are experienced as restricted in scope and lack background environment (in comparison with physical objects). This is also the case with memory and imagination images. Generally speaking, after-images and images produced by a blow on the head or resulting from mental or physical illness, as well as those produced by drugs, have a distinctive brightness of surface which is not found in physical objects, at least under normal conditions of observation. In any case, such images do not fit in with physical objects in accordance with physical laws. For example an imaginary pink elephant does not move physical blocks of wood in accordance with the laws of physics. In other words, if all the laws which apply to one type of entity do not apply to entities under consideration, these entities are not the type to which the laws apply.

[1] That is, not restricted to any one type of entity.
[2] See Chapter 17, pp. 384–5.

Some further clarificatory comments are in order concerning memory, imagination and dream images.

Such images, of the visual sort, are present when a mind generates shaped colours of a specific size. These entities occur within a mental medium.[1] The situation is analogous, in some important respects, to the occurrence of clouds in the medium of the atmosphere. Specific memory images, for example, are distinguished from one another on the basis of colour, shape, size, intensity, and so on. However, the mental-medium factor is what distinguishes a memory image from a physical object or a physically based resultant with the same colour, shape and size.

Just as one refers, in a convenient locution, to the characteristics of a table, meaning more accurately the characteristics of the wood of which the table is composed, so analogously one may refer to the characteristics of a memory image, meaning the colour, shape and size which occur in the mental medium involved in the specific memory image. Just as a table is termed physical because of the nature of the entity out of which it is made, so a memory image is termed mental because of the mental medium which is fundamental in the occurrence of a memory image.

In the case, for example, of memory images involving sounds, tastes, odours, thermal 'qualities', here again these entities occur in a mental medium. The same general comments apply to these as to memory images of the visual sort.

What has been reported concerning memory images applies in general to imagination and dream images as well as to the other types of images discussed above.

In the case of mental contents which are feelings and emotions (which have the inherent characteristic feeling or emotion), shape, size and colour are not associated characteristics. Consider, for example pleasure or anger. Further, feeling and emotion do not have the specific spatial aspect (location) which characterises physical objects.

In like fashion mental activities do not resemble physical activities in their obvious associated characteristics. In any case their inherent characteristics differ; they are mental, not physical.

However, physical objects, mental activities and mental content have some characteristics in common: for example numerical and relational ones.

---

[1] Which is mind-generated.

More detailed examination of mental activities and of mental contents is now in order. Since the philosophy here being developed is a report and description of the entities of which persons are aware in comprehensive experience, a careful examination of awareness is essential.

Awareness

In the course of comprehensive human experience, there is awareness of a great variety of different entities, including the occurrences of mental and physical activities.

Different names are applied to acts of awareness. External 'sensation' (for instance visual sensing) is awareness of physical objects (basic physical entities or entities such as tables and chairs). A person also sees (by internal sensing) dream images when asleep and other sorts of images when awake. The activity termed 'feeling' (in its verbal sense) is awareness of pleasures and pains ('feeling' in its noun sense) and emotions. In being aware of concepts one is engaged in 'rational' or 'intellectual' apprehension. Awareness of mental activities, content, and of the mind itself, is called 'introspection'. Awareness of value characteristics, aesthetic or moral, is sometimes termed aesthetic or moral 'sensation' (sensing). In any case, awareness is always awareness of something. The point being made is this: for the purposes of this discussion it is to be noted that the different names apply to one mental activity which is most conveniently and appropriately termed 'awareness'. It is to be noted that no pure act of awareness exists by itself.

It is very important to realise that awareness, by a person who takes a comprehensive approach, frequently is a very complex process. It is not merely a case of being aware of one entity at a time. Rather there is awareness of many entities. There are distinguishable single acts of awareness which constitute a complex process of awareness. Consider a[1] person who sees a chair, is aware of the concept chair as applicable to it, feels anger because it is uncomfortable, is aware of the concept anger as applicable to his emotion.

The complex process of awareness, just described, is a case of recognising. Speaking technically, recognising occurs when a person

---

[1] Here and elsewhere in this book, in discussing many-occurrence entities, reference will sometimes be made to particular occurrences of an entity, in the interests of bringing the discussion into clear focus.

is aware of an entity and aware that a familiar concept applies to, is linked with, it. The nature of this linkage will be discussed later.[1]

In some instances many adults recognise entities immediately. In other situations there is much mental effort and a lapse of time as a person tries to find the appropriate concept which is applicable to the entity of which he is aware. However, in all such cases recognising (recognition) is not a distinct type of simple mental activity. It is a complex of activities of awareness. Strictly speaking, a so-called error in recognition is not a case of recognising at all. It is misinterpreting an entity, applying the wrong concept ot it.

As ordinarily used, the term 'perceiving' (perception) is a synonym for 'recognising'.

The term 'recognising' has another usage which must be very carefully considered. It is to be noted that it sometimes is a synonym for 'awareness' of a familiar entity. In this case concepts can be recognised if they are entities with which one is familiar.

It must, of course, be realised that the ability to be aware of a simple or complex entity, or to carry out a complex activity of awareness is a skill, a competence, which in many cases is acquired after much experience. It involves a number of complex mechanisms and conditions which are not yet fully understood by psychologists. However, the fact remains, this type of activity does take place.

The temporal duration of a complex activity of awareness is wider than a 'knife edge' present. It is possible to consider in conjunction not only entities which are in 'centre focus', but also peripheral entities, for example, those which are in process of fading into the status of 'past'. Thus comparison is possible over a fairly extensive range of entities.

At the moment when the mind is engaged in activities of various sorts, for example hoping, believing, choosing, it is aware of all these activities.

It is to be emphasised that a mind, in being aware of all other entities, is also aware of itself engaged in awareness of entities. In other words, a basic mental entity can be aware of its own acts of awareness. For example, the person (in the preceding illustration) who is angry at the hardness of a chair is not only aware that he is angry but also is aware that he is aware of the chair, the anger and relevant concepts.

---

[1] See Chapter 4, pp. 95–6.

It is obvious that some of the entities of which a person is aware are in the foreground of experience, others are in the background. Of course, there may be a shift of entities from background to foreground and vice versa. Consider the case of a person smoking a pipe. He is aware of smoke and pipe (foreground), his own mind and the awareness of smoke (background). However it is possible to have mind and awareness of smoke in the foreground as well as smoke—and pipe in the background.

This awareness of awareness may seem to involve an infinite regress. Consider for example the situation referred to above: the mind is aware (A) of smoke and also aware (B) of the awareness of smoke. Does it not follow that there is an awareness (C) of (B) and then an awareness (D) of (C) and so on *ad infinitum?*

A careful comprehensive examination of the awareness situation indicates that this difficulty does not arise. A mind is aware (X) of the many activities of awareness (and other activity) in which it engages. One of these many activities of awareness (Y) is awareness of (X). In other words (X) is awareness of (Y) (and other entities); (Y) is awareness of (X). Hence there is no infinite regress involved in awareness of awareness.

It is essential to stress the point that awareness of any entity does not occur unless conditions are suitable. Specifically permissive conditions must be present and preventive conditions must be absent.[1] Depending on the entity, suitable conditions vary. Among permissive conditions are the following: In general[2] a person's brain and other parts of his body are functioning on at least a minimum level of efficiency in reaction to stimuli. There must also be at least a minimum of mental competence. In many specific cases, considerable past experience of the types of entities of which one is trying to be aware, is necessary. Of course external conditions are important. If one is to see an object, there must be sufficient light.

Turning now to preventive factors, a person who is in a state of extreme anger or dizziness produced by a high fever, or suffering from some specific physiological defect, for instance of the eye, or mental disability such as prejudice, may not see a physical object

[1] As will be obvious from the following illustrations: frequently, specific entities when present are permissive conditions and when absent are preventive conditions, and vice versa, that is, absence of an entity is a permissive condition.

[2] That is, in all cases.

which is before him under external conditions permissive of awareness; or he may neglect some of the characteristics of the physical object. Likewise, a person in these internal states may neglect, that is not be aware of some of his own mental activites of content or some concepts. Also, external factors may make impossible the awareness of physical objects, mental entities and concepts, for instance darkness in the case of physical objects, excessive noise in the case of physical objects, mental entities and concepts, even if internal factors are permissive.

However, and this point is crucial, in a situation containing an entity, if interfering preventive factors, internal and external, are absent, and favourable permissive conditions are present, so that conditions are fully suitable for the awareness of a specific entity, then one is aware of that entity.

Another very important fact is to be noted. Awareness of an entity cannot be erroneous in the sense of misleading one concerning the entity of which one is aware. However, a complex process of awareness may be deficient with reference to a complex situation if it does not involve awareness of all entities in the situation, in other words if it is deficient in scope. Error arises when, for example (a) it is assumed that all entities are present to awareness and this is not the case, or (b) some mistaken interpretation is placed on entities which are present to awareness. In some cases b occurs in a context which involves a. Consider the case of a person who is aware of the vegetable nature of a toadstool, but is not aware it is poisonous, and assumes he is aware of all its important characteristics. He interprets the toadstool as being good to eat.

Similarly, consider a savage who is not aware of the distinction between a dream image and a physical object. Error arises if he assumes he is adequately aware of the situation before him. A further error occurs if he interprets the dream image as being a physical object.

It is important to realise that what constitutes a sufficiently wide range of awareness, that is awareness of all relevant entities in a complex situation, depends on the situation in question. If it is a matter of determining whether or not to eat something, such as a toadstool, it is not enough to be aware of the vegetable nature of the entity. One must also be aware of its poisonous potentialities. This is enough information for ordinary purposes. If, however, the question is that of the chemical components of entities which have a bearing on edibility, then a person must be aware of these data if the range of awareness is to be adequate. It is here reported that in some cases an observer can settle the question of what constitutes an adequate range of awareness and whether or not this has been achieved. People eat mushrooms and avoid toadstools. The details of the process of reaching sound conclusions ordinarily are left to specialists in the fields.

It is possible in some instances for a man who is trying to become aware of an entity, to be aware of the presence or absence of preventive factors and of permissive ones which have a bearing on whether or not one is able (is going) to be aware of an entity. When one is aware that conditions are suitable, he is satisfied that no problem arises concerning awareness of the entities of which he is trying to be aware. Consider, for example, a particular instance when I am justified in claiming that I am looking at (aware of) a pen which I am holding in my hand. I am aware that suitable conditions are present for the awareness of this object. Specifically, I am aware that my body and mind are in healthy condition and that no external distortion is being introduced by light or sound. Also, I am at an appropriate distance for seeing the object.

On the other hand, I am able to be aware of interfering conditions such as lack of light or a high fever when they are present. On the basis of this awareness of unsuitable conditions, I can refrain from attempting to be aware of the pencil or the claim that I am aware of the object.

If a person is aware of a piece of vegetable matter growing in the grass, but is also aware that he has had little experience in distinguishing toadstools from mushrooms, he is aware that his range of awareness in this situation is defective, and hence is unable to have an awareness of all essential characteristics of the vegetable before him, as far as the question of eating it is concerned.

In brief, the ability to function in this complex fashion with reference to[1] some entities, to be aware of the preventive and permissive factors which have a bearing on awareness, as well as what constitutes an adequate range of awareness in a complex situation, and the ability to profit from this information and avoid the error of misinterpretation, involves a great deal of experience. But this competence characteristic is one ingredient of comprehensive human experience.

In order to clear up a possible misunderstanding, it is necessary to

---

[1] That is 'in relation to'. This is not the verb form 'refer' discussed in Chapter 5, p. 112.

point out that the presence of an internal disturbing factor does not inevitably eliminate all activities of awareness of all entities. The important point is that, in many cases, while the distracting factor, for example anger, renders impossible the awareness of a physical object some mental entities or concepts—the awareness of anger is not likewise prevented. Further there is awareness of the relation of prevention between anger and the awareness of the other entities under consideration. That is to say, these activities of awareness concerning the preventive function of anger occur because suitable conditions are present. Of course, if anger reaches the stage where every other entity is blotted out, and one is reduced to an awareness of an emotional tornado, there is no possibility of a person's being aware of the preventive effect of a paralysing emotional storm. This, however, can sometimes be noted by an external observer. For example, it is possible to determine that another person is paralysed and blinded by rage.

It is, unfortunately, the case that one may lose permanently the ability to be aware of whether or not conditions are suitable, or whether or not the range of awareness is adequate for the awareness of entities in the situation before one. Extreme senility reduces a once competent adult to the level of a young child. It is of course obvious that a young child in many instances does not have the competence under discussion.[1]

In the preceding discussion of awareness the term 'sensation' has been mentioned only in passing. 'Sensation' has a complicated use. It is employed to refer (a) to an act of awareness, (b) to the entity of which one is aware, (c) as a comprehensive term to refer to both a and b. Confusion as to reference arises because it is frequently employed without qualification as to whether, act of sensation is meant; or content of act of sensation or complex of both act and content. Qualification is necessary if clarity is to be obtained. Further, sometimes pleasure and pain are termed 'sensations'; at other times 'feelings' or 'emotions'. In presenting Experiential Realism it has seemed preferable to employ the term 'awareness' to refer to the activity and to specify the type or sort of entity of which one is aware. However, on occasion it is convenient to indicate the type of object of which one is aware by using the term object of 'sensory awareness'.

[1] The preceding discussion of awareness introduces the vast problem of knowledge. (See Chapter 6.)

II

The ability to perform many mental activities

One phase of the preceding discussion of awareness brings into focus a very important point. In general, a person relying on comprehensive experience is able, in some cases, to determine whether or not conditions are suitable for the occurrence of many mental activities—not just that of awareness.

Let us now consider illustrations. If a person prepares to engage in an activity of reasoning concerning some complex human problem, on being aware of anger or extreme fatigue, he will be aware that conditions are not suitable, and hence that at least an impartial reasoning process cannot occur. It is, of course, the case in some instances that, as the result of a controlled state of anger, one may develop a very effective rational plan for revenge or remember some relevant facts pertaining to the achievement of revenge.

This general comment applies not only to activities which a person is now engaged in or attempting. An elderly person is aware of his inability now or in the future, to remember promptly the name of a friend or how to take appropriate steps in dealing with a problem in symbolic logic.

III

Imagination

Imagining is a mental activity which is of very great importance in understanding the behaviour of all men, in particular of some philosophers.

In general, imagining is one of a group of creative activities which produces entities simple and complex which would not otherwise be present to awareness.

It is well to examine some of the main sorts of imagining and their results. Imaginative activity involves (a) in many cases the generation of mental entities namely, images which in varying degrees resemble but frequently do not accurately represent other entities, or (b) the production by mental activity of complex entities which frequently do not resemble entities otherwise produced or present in awareness.

These complex results of imagining may be composed of more than one type of entity. For example, a person having seen a human face (physical object) imaginatively generates an ideal human face image. Speaking technically, it is a mental entity which has as associated characteristics a specific shape, a specific size and a specific colour which are not the same as those of the face (that is the basic physical entity of the face does not have these ideal characteristics). Similarly, having experienced excessive anger, one can in imagination create ideal righteous indignation. Consider also a case of an imagination image which does not resemble a physical object. Having seen a fish and a woman, a person can imaginatively generate a mermaid image. Similarly, a person can imaginatively link the concept fish and the concept woman to form the complex concept mermaid. Further, concepts may be linked in imagination to physical objects and to mental entities in a fashion which is not justified by reference to the non-imaginary world. For example, one can think (using concepts) of a seen stone as gold, an occurrence of blind rage as righteous in- dignation. An imaginative linking of a physical object and a mental entity is also possible, for instance a sky blue elephant sitting in one's favourite chair.

So far attention has been focused on 'imagination-produced' entities which do not accurately report or resemble other entities. It is important to realise that, in some cases, a mind can generate an imagination image which is, for all practical purposes, an accurate resemblance of some physical or mental entity. For example, one can accurately imagine how a well-known friend will react to a specific joke. Incidentally, in some cases an imagination image is very similar in appearance and perhaps in origin (but not in direction of reference) to a memory image. Consider for example the imagining of a cup of coffee. In any case it is possible, imaginatively, to produce complex entities which are accurate representations of other complex entities. For example, one can imagine what a new building will look like at a certain place on the campus. Further, a person can imaginatively combine concepts which fit the facts even though the facts at the time are unknown to the imaginer.

Some imagined entities are regarded by some men, including some philosophers, as ultimate (real), and hence take precedence over en- tities in the non-imaginary realm. Consider, for example, the notion of the Aryan race or the theory that the universe is the experience of an all-inclusive Mind (which cannot be present non-imaginatively to human awareness). These imaginary creations are used to justify the destruction of specific groups of human beings (the Aryan race theory) or to deny the ultimate importance of individual human minds (the all-inclusive, Absolute Mind theory). These may be termed in a broad sense 'fantastic' imagining (fantastic entities produced by imagining).

Other imaginary entities are (state) possiblities which later may be actualised. A student can imagine himself as being the recipient of an academic degree. In due course he receives it. This sort of imagination entity may be termed 'realisable'.

Some imagined entities may be useful intellectual instruments employed in dealing with problems in the natural and social sciences, for instance the atomic theory in modern form. Some such experience as coming up with a solution after being asleep, may be explained in terms of the unconscious. But in both cases these theories are only assumptions of imaginary entities. They are not found as present in experience, apart from imagining, and should be understood as such. They are at best a useful imaginary construction. This sort of imagination entity may be termed 'instrumental'.

One sort of imagined entity has an important place in human experience because it provides symbolism involved in one phase of artistic creation.

A play or a painting is presented for the sake of aesthetic enjoyment. Its author does not present it as a possibility or an instrumentality. It is not a case of running away from or negating the world of non-imaginative awareness. It has value as an aesthetic object.

Another sort of result of imagining is found in some tentative speculative constructions, philosophical or otherwise. Vague insights are suggested (by imaginary entities) concerning intriguing questions which seem at present to lie beyond the range of human experience. While not now realisable, in the sense of being translatable from possible to actual, and neither supported by the entities of non imaginary experience nor claimed to be an accurate blueprint of ulti-mate reality—these imaginary entities have a function which goes beyond the merely instrumental or artistic, as defined above. For example, such imagination entities, at the very least, satisfy the desire of some minds to engage in tentative speculation concerning the vast mysteries which lie beyond present experience, or to express aspira-tions concerning human behaviour. Consider, for example, some cases of science fiction or the dreams of social reforms concerning the new Jerusalem.

But in all cases the distinction between imaginary and non-imaginary must be retained and, linked with this, a refusal to assign exalted status to the imaginary—if comprehensive experience is one's frame of reference. Yet there is no room for dogmatism here. With the passing of time, there have been cases where what seemed to be merely imaginary entities, instrumental or speculative, turned out to be in accordance with the world of non-imaginary entities—at least, in some general characteristics, if not in particular details. Compare, for example, Bacon's *New Atlantis* and present scientific achievements.

The generative activities, by which a mind produces imagination, memory and dream images, as such do not differ in kind. Imagining of this sort, remembering and dreaming[1] (as far as images are involved) are distinguished in terms of their results and the context in which they occur. Imagining, including what is termed 'day-dreaming', and remembering take place when a person is awake. Dreaming (in distinction from day-dreaming) occurs when a person is asleep. There is no awareness of effort during dreaming when asleep, no sense of effort in order to produce a dream image. On the other hand, in day-dreaming, imagining, remembering, sometimes there is such effort, sometimes not. Dreams have as content entities which have a reference to past, present or future. Imagination content is likewise. Remembering is concerned with past entities. As noted previously, the image content involved in imagining and remembering is more dim than in dreaming when asleep. It is also obvious that the content of remembering activities (in distinction from trying to remember and failing) must produce an accurate report of other entities. This may happen in dreaming but is not the case in most instances of imagining. Imagining is not confined to image content, neither is dreaming or remembering. A person in remembering may use a concept or physical object. The activities of imagining or dreaming sometimes involve a mixture of imaginary with non-imaginary entities, including concepts as well as mental entities. However, only in the case of imagining can the non-imaginary physical world be actually present to awareness as part of its content.

Some people, on occasion, seem to have difficulty in differentiating what they imagine or dream from what is seen in the physical world.

[1] Dreaming is a creative activity of the same general sort as imagining (see pp. 71–2).

It is the case that, to take dreaming as an example, as dream content and activities occur, they are not recognised as dream entities. Some dream experiences have as clear and vivid content as orderly a sequence, and are as common, as in the case of waking awareness of some parts of the physical world. However, the dream content does not have the same inherent characteristic as non-dream material (of the physical world). The emotional background of dream experience also is different from that of non-dream experience. Perhaps the most noticeable difference is that perspective and environmental context are limited as far as the visual aspect of dream content is concerned.[1] It is, of course, the case that many dreams are vague and chaotic in comparison with waking experience. Further, on waking, the fact that dream experience cannot be verified, that is, fitted in with most other experiences (entities), in particular those shared with others, as many non-dream experiences can be, is quickly determined. In brief, on waking, there may be momentary uncertainty as to whether an experience (awareness and content) is dream or non-dream, but with the passage of time this uncertainty is cleared up by using the criteria mentioned above, and remembering the sort of activity which occurred. The same uncertainty as to the status of entities may also occur in non-dream experience, and yet be cleared up. It is significant to notice that, while in waking experience one may wonder whether one is dreaming, the reverse does not occur!

Remembering

Remembering, as such, is not primarily a creative activity. It is essentially a case of reporting past facts by a process of recall and referring back. In some instances this does involve the generation of memory images. As such they are more or less accurate representations of the entities to which they refer.[2] Thus memory images may serve as a vehicle for the remembering process. In other cases the vehicle is a proposition which is a true report concerning past entities. The machinery which makes possible the provision of these vehicles (brain storage, etc.) need not concern us here.

In a sense, the performing of a once-learned skill which has not been exercised for a time, and is now being expressed, may be termed 'remembering'. Indeed its mere retention without use may be so termed.

[1] See pp. 62–3.
[2] See discussion of meaning, Chapter 5, pp. 111–13.

Some general comments on mental activities

It is important to note that the mental activities composing group A mentioned at the beginning of this chapter differ from the items in group C so far considered (namely remembering, dreaming, and imagining) in very important respects. The members of group A are all cases of reaction to entities which they do not create (as distinct from the case of imagining and dreaming). They are not as such reporting entities, as in remembering. Further, members of group A do not use other entities as raw material or as vehicles in their functions (as in remembering). It is true that as a consequence of these activities in group A entities sometimes may be produced. But to repeat, the activities as such are not cases of creation of other entities not otherwise present. Hence obviously the members of group A differ from those of group B.

The use of words is sometimes a source of confusion concerning mental activities and contents. For example, as a matter of fact there is no distinctive mental content (emotional tone) which is the 'object' of the activity of desiring, in a fashion similar to the memory image in some cases of remembering. The same is true of willing. What one desires or wills is not desire or will but mental entities, physical objects, concepts or physically based resultants. On the other hand, emotions such as fear and anger are not generated by a specific mental activity which can appropriately be termed 'fearing' or being 'angry'. When confronted by a loud noise, for example, a mind generates fear or anger and is aware of it (feels it), and in some cases directs it toward some entity.

The term 'attitude' applies to the activities in group A, apart from linking together and directing toward, either present or potential.

The remaining mental activities, reasoning, choosing, believing, willing, desiring, being interested, and so on, can be most effectively dealt with in detail later, after more extensive discussion, and in a wider context. Likewise, other mental content will be examined in subsequent chapters, also other questions concerning mind.

3

SOME PROBLEMS CONCERNING PHYSICAL OBJECTS

I

Invariant associated characteristics

In discussing basic physical entities mention was made of their associated characteristics. It is now advisable to deal with this topic more fully. In the context of comprehensive experiencing, it is found that basic entities that are physical have the following invariant[1] associated characteristics: length, width, thickness, hence shape and size, also colour. Resistance to pressure and bounded by a surface (either smooth or rough) are also such characteristics. In addition all basic physical entities have weight, thermal, numerical, relational and value characteristics. Individuality is an invariant characteristic. Some basic physical entities also are characterised by odour and taste. These are not invariant associates.

More specifically, it is found that each particular occurrence of a basic physical entity, for example each piece of wood, has a definite specific shape, size, colour and so on. For example, my desk top is rectangular in shape, five feet by three in size and brown in colour.

'Apparent' difficulties: shape, size, colour

In considering this report concerning basic physical entities, it is advisable to examine several particular cases. Concentrating for the time being, on a few of these characteristics, namely shape, size and colour, let us consider a stick,[2] a mountain and a penny. While strictly speaking colour, shape and size, are characteristic of their component basic physical entities, it is convenient, and a common locution, to

---

[1] That is, All basic physical entities have these characteristics.

[2] A more convenient wooden object than my desk, for the purposes of discussion.

refer to the characteristics of such physical objects[1] as a stick, a mountain and a penny. This is much simpler and more effective than referring to the associate characteristics of basic entities which are physical, such as a piece of wood, a stone, and a piece of metal.

Some human experiences (awareness of entities) seem to cast serious doubt on the claim that physical objects have definite specific characteristics. For example, depending on varying conditions under which one is aware of a physical object, many different shapes, sizes and colours, are experienced. In looking at a mountain from a distance, a person sees a purple colour and a small shape uniform in height. When he moves closer, he sees a larger shape, jagged in outline, and a green colour. Shape problems arise when a penny is viewed from different perspectives, or when a stick is seen partly in and partly out of water. How can these variations occur if a person is experiencing one and the same physical object (a basic physical entity and its associated characteristics)? In brief, it seems to follow that a mind which relies on its activity of awareness is in serious, if not insuperable, difficulties when it proposes to discuss the associated characteristics of particular occurrences of basic physical entities.

However, it should be noted that a person relying on comprehensive experience is not ordinarily confused concerning the characteristics of physical objects, for example the shape of a stick, because he sees a bent shape when part of the stick is in the water. Nor does he have doubts about the characteristics of a penny, its shape, and size, because he sees different shapes and sizes under varying conditions of distance and perspective. If he is technically inclined, he makes use of the science of physics, physiology and psychology which are relevant here. In any case, as a result of past experience and accurate observational techniques, any apparent difficulties with the so-called bent stick and different results of observing the penny and mountain are overcome.

The stick, which in the water is seen as bent, is found to be straight when a finger is run along its length. A person sees different shapes and sizes when looking at a penny. But this entity is found to have one shape and one size when proper conditions of observations, as specified by an oculist, are in effect and use is made of appropriate measuring devices. Likewise the shape and size characteristics of the mountain can be determined without too much difficulty.

[1] See Chapter I, pp. 55–6 for a discussion of the dual use of the term 'physical object'.

In general, as far as a person relying on comprehensive experiencing is concerned, the colour characteristics of a physical object can be ascertained despite seen differences in colour. A distant mountain 'looks' purple (that is a person sees purple). Near at hand, it 'looks' green. What is the colour of the mountain (what is its colour characteristic)? In the context of comprehensive experience, it (the leaves of trees growing on it) is found to be green. To repeat, there are recognised appropriate normal conditions under which observation should take place.

II

Physically based resultants

There are, however, a number of important issues which must be considered. When I look at (am aware of) a penny from an angle, I see metal (basic physical entity) with an elliptical-shaped top. When I see a distant mountain, I see a complex of matter with a purple colour. When I look at a stick partly immersed in water, I see wood with a bent shape. In all these cases, though I am aware of basic physical entities, I am not aware of the shape and colour characteristics of these entities (except, in some instances, one is aware of the colour of the penny). The bent part of the stick is seen with a colour shade which is not a characteristic. As a matter of fact, the metal (penny) is round, the mountain (that is, the trees covering it) is green and the wood (stick) is straight.

Therefore a fundamental question remains. What is the nature and status of these colours and shapes[1] which are present in awareness with basic physical entities, yet are not actually (as a matter of fact) characteristics of physical objects? Are they physical, or mental, or concepts of something else? What is their nature?

As background it is important to realise that, in the context of comprehensive experience, it is found that all colours and shapes, as such, are neither mental nor physical nor concepts, nor is a colour or a shape ever physical or mental or a concept.[2] If this is not obvious, it may help to note the following: though concepts apply to them,

---

[1] In the interests of simplification of discussion, references to size will be omitted.

[2] They are neutral. See Chapter 2, p. 62.

79

colours and shapes are apprehended by sense, while concepts are not apprehended by sense. They are different types of entities. Colours and shapes are in some cases characteristics of basic physical entities, in some cases characteristics of mental entities (for example, imagination images). Obviously, they are not restricted to, or as such belong to, the physical or the mental realm. They do not have either physical or mental as inherent characteristics. In general, as will become obvious in subsequent discussion, there are many entities which are as such (that is, in nature) neither physical or mental, nor are they concepts.

In the case of the elliptical shape, the bend shape and the purple colour, here under consideration, shape and colour are not characteristics of any mental or physical entity. (Here status is being considered.)

Let us consider in detail this fundamental contention. They are not characteristics of the penny or the stick or the mountain, as has been shown. They are not the characteristics of physical entities other than the mountain, the stick or the penny. The evidence is that, in comprehensive experience, there is no awareness of any basic physical entity other than the components of the mountain, stick, and the penny available to have, as characteristics, these shapes and this colour. The elliptical shape, bent shape and purple colour are not the characteristics of some mental entity, for example an imagination image. This conclusion is reached because in comprehensive experience of the situation involving the mountain, the stick or the penny, there is no awareness of any mental entity of which the shapes and colour under consideration are characteristics, that is, none is found, therefore it is pointless to contend that there are such mental entities. Supporting evidence for this latter contention is provided by the fact that the characteristics of mental entities are private and cannot be reproduced photographically. On the other hand the elliptical and bent shapes and the purple colour can be recorded photographically.

How then can one account for the presence of the elliptical shape, the bent shape, purple colour, if they are neither physical, mental nor concepts and are not the characteristics of basic physical entities or of mental entities (basic or characteristic) or of concepts? It has not been previously pointed out, but it is the case, that they are not characteristics of characteristics of basic physical entities or of concepts. The reply is that they are resultants; more specifically, physically based resultants. They are there present to awareness because of the interaction of a number of physical entities none of which possesses them as characteristics. There are, for example, the state of the atmosphere, the angle of the eye to the physical object, the factor of distance and so on. To repeat, they are physically based resultants. No mental activity or concept is efficacious in producing or changing them. Specifically, while the colours and shapes of mental entities (for example memory and imagination images) can in some cases be changed by mental effort, and in all cases are found to be generated by a mind, this is not the case with reference to the shapes and colour here under consideration. Further there is no awareness in comprehensive experience of, for example, the concept green generating a patch of green.

It is important to note that physically based resultants, such as those under discussion, do not have the status present in the universe even though no process of awareness occurs. Thus they differ from characteristics of physical objects. The straightness of the stick is there, even though no one is looking at it—likewise the roundness of the penny. On the other hand, the bent shape and the elliptical shape are present only in a situation where a mind is aware of a physical object under certain physical conditions. However, it is not the case that these physically based resultants are dependent for the presence, either in whole or in part, on the causal initiative of a mind or its activities—specifically the activity of awareness. Rather it is the case that 'mind engaging in the activity of awareness', in the situations under discussion, is a necessary condition for the presence of physically based resultants. The causal initiative lies with physical entities, not with mental ones (see discussion in Chapter 7).

It has been noted that the physically based resultants, here under discussion, can be reproduced photographically. Here again it is not a case of the bent or elliptical shape being present in the same fashion as the straightness or circular shape. The bentness and elliptical shape are present only on a developed film print, after a camera has been in roughly the same position as the man who is aware of the bent or elliptical shape. The print is present in the universe even though no one is aware of it.

In some instances it is possible to be aware of the shape characteristic but not of the size characteristic of a physical object, under the same conditions. For example, when a person is looking at a distant object which has a square surface, what he is aware of—the square shape—is a characteristic of the physical object. However, he is not aware of the size characteristic of that shaped surface. The size entity of which he is aware is a physically based resultant. It is of course the case that in some instances distance does make impossible the awareness of shape characteristics. For example, a person looks at a cube and sees only one surface, that directly facing him.

It is important to realise that there are many sorts of physically based resultants found in comprehensive experience. Consider, for example, shadows and mirror images. These are shaped colours[1] which are (a) neither physical, mental or concepts and (b) are not the characteristics of any physical or mental entity (on a concept); rather they result from the interaction of physical entities. Like the other physically based entities mentioned above—the elliptical and bent shapes and the purple colour—shadows and mirror images can be reproduced photographically.

This, however, is not the case with all physically based resultants. For example some mirages of water in the desert and of water on the pavement, also the so-called 'floating finger' illusion, cannot be photographically reproduced. Incidentally, some mirages in the desert may be the result of mental initiative or combination of mental and physical factors in interaction.

It is significant to note that shaped colours which are here termed 'physically based resultants' lack characteristics which are found in mental entities such as memory, imagination and dream images. Specifically they do not have either the dimness of memory and imagination images or the peculiar brightness of some dream images. They do not have the restricted environmental context of images of the sorts just mentioned. Rather, physically based resultants are experienced as fused with a physical environment (as with the elliptical shape of a penny), or superimposed on it (as with a mirror image on a mirror). This is not the case with imagination, memory or dream images. Memory and imagination images stand out in distinction from a physical environment which may be seen at the same time.

---

[1] Strictly speaking it is the colour which (as component) is characterised by shape (size and other experienced characteristics). This, however, does not turn the colour into a basic entity. It (the colour) is, in these cases, a presently dependent resultant. Colours may have the status of (a) neutral characteristics of mental or physical entities, or (b) in this case, a physically based resultant, the colour being neutral.

On the basis of the foregoing discussion, one can conclude that images produced by a violent blow are mental. On the other hand, seeing parts of a straight line as crooked, as the result of some eye defect, or of seeing parallel rails converging, because of perspective, are cases of being aware of a physically based resultant.

In the context of this discussion some comments are relevant concerning a familiar phenomenon. In looking at the following diagram

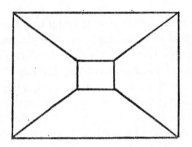

a person sees, alternately, a corridor or a stand—one for a brief period then the other, then the first again and so on. It should be obvious that the seen corridor and the seen stand are physically based resultants occurring because of the nature of the physical diagram and the physiological functions of the human body, specifically the eye. It is the case that if a person is told, for example, he is confronted by a corridor, he will see a corridor, but very quickly it is 'replaced' by a stand. Thus the mental suggestion is not ultimately decisive in the situation. Fundamentally one sees both a corridor and a stand, in sequence, without benefit of mental conditioning (by a suggestion).

It should be obvious that, like other entities, physically based resultants have numerical, relational and value characteristics. However, these characteristics are not physical or mental or concepts, neither are they physically based resultants as such.

Physically based resultants and scientific aids to observation

So far the discussion, for the most part, has concentrated on the level of human experience unassisted by scientific aids to observation. The use of a microscope reveals to awareness entities not otherwise seen. It also raises questions concerning some entities of which one is aware when using unaided sense organs. For example, with reference to the colour of blood: what looks completely red without benefit of microscope is found not to be so when viewed under a microscope—it is red and yellow. In viewing a leaf with the naked eye, and then under a microscope, one sees different entities in the two cases, a mass of distinct cells in the latter but not in the former. Some of the cells are found to be green, others not. When a microscope is used, it is found that as a matter of fact the surface of a tabletop is rough, not smooth as it appears to the unaided eye.

In general,[1] a person wishing for as comprehensive an awareness as possible of physical objects, must for example supplement the eye with the microscope. Only in this fashion will some entities which are components or characteristics of physical objects, both living and non-living, be accurately ascertained. In short, a human being relying on comprehensive experience will turn, when appropriate, for accurate and detailed knowledge of basic physical entities and their characteristics, to the persons who are best fitted to observe at least some aspects of these physical objects, namely natural scientists.

However, some so-called components and characteristics of physical objects are not literally observed in any fashion. Scientists and non-scientists must take care not to overlook the distinction between non-imaginary entities, found in the course of careful observation, and entities imaginatively assumed to be present in order to provide either an 'instrumental' or 'fantastic'[2] explanation or interpretation. Scientists can see cells, they cannot see electrons. They see or feel what they interpret in terms of electrons. In this, as in all cases, use should be made of the most effective instruments of observation.

Nevertheless, care must be taken to ensure that the use of some sophisticated instrument does not produce distortion or destruction of the characteristics of the object, or introduce new entities. For example, in trying to locate an electrical particle one may change its velocity. In observing a cell under a very high power microscope it is necessary to kill the cell. Hence, some of its characteristics are lost, such as colour in the case of some cells. Likewise, one must realise that some scientists, in the interests of simplicity in theorising, deny the presence or importance of some experienced characteristics of physical objects. For example, it is claimed that no physical object is really coloured.

[1] In all cases.
[2] See Chapter 2, pp. 72-3.

As in the case of the experienced bent shape of a straight stick immersed in water, the experienced elliptical shape of the penny which is actually round, and the experienced purple in the case of the mountain which is actually green—problems arise concerning the status of the experienced smoothness in the case of a table which is found, when viewed with a microscope, to be uneven, the experienced all-redness of blood, or all-greenness of leaves, which are found under the microscope to be somewhat different, and the experienced 'all of one piece-ness', say, in the case of a leaf or a slab of wood which, when examined under the microscope, is found to be comprised of separate cells.

The experienced smoothness, 'all of one colour-ness' and 'all of one piece-ness' have the same status as the experienced bentness, elliptical shape and purple colour referred to above. They are the result of the interaction of physical factors: they are physically based resultants. It follows that some of the data of our awareness, when we are confronted by physical objects, have the status of physically based resultants, though with care one can be aware of characteristics.

A further complication arises. It may be argued for example that if one relies on a microscope, a penny will be found to be not round, but somewhat uneven, in outline of shape. Similarly the stick is not straight.

It must be admitted that no physical object, so far found, completely measures up to an ideal circularity or straightness. But, in the context of this world, and the meaning of 'circular' and 'straight', it is possible to find an undamaged penny which is appropriately recognised as circular and some sticks which are, in this sense, straight. In the case of roughness, the apparent difficulty does not arise. It is not a matter of a merely high degree of approximation to ideal roughness, as in the case of ideal circularity and straightness. Roughness is found in many physical surfaces. However, to repeat, the roughness of the edge of a penny or side of a stick does not rule out approximation to circularity or straightness. The situation is different with reference to smoothness. The penny is found to be circular either with the naked eye or under a microscope, the straight stick likewise. But the wood which looks smooth to the naked eye is found to be rough.

The report, based on the use of the unaided eye, that blood is red and some leaves are green, is not completely refuted when a person makes use of a microscope. It is found that as a matter of fact many of the component cells of some leaves are green, while others are not;

likewise blood cells are red, while plasma is yellow. Speaking technically, as noted above, the 'all-redness' or 'all-greenness' are physically based resultants. But to repeat, many of the components of some leaves are green and many of the components of blood are red. In this sense, it is correct to report that green is a characteristic of some leaves and that red is a characteristic of blood.

Incidentally, referring back to the brown table, desk, and chair mentioned in Chapter 1, p. 47, it should be realised that under a microscope it is found that the component surface cells of a piece of wood take a colour stain with varying degrees of intensity. Specifically, an individual cell will have a more intense degree of brown at its boundaries than at its centre. Thus the 'all one shade of brown' which one sees with the unaided eye is a physically based resultant. This however, does not deny the fact that brown is a characteristic of the surface of the wood composing the chair, desk or table.

In reporting that the naked eye under proper conditions of observation sees wood, one is correct, despite the fact that one is not aware of the component cells. A person sees one blob of matter, not its many component parts, for instance a pile but not the individual distinctions of the components of the pile.

III

Sound, heat, taste and other characteristics

So far there has been no discussion of sound. Is this a characteristic of basic physical entities? In the context of comprehensive experience it is found that some sounds are physically based resultants; some are characteristics of memory, imagination, or dream images. No sound is characteristic of a basic physical entity. In cases where a sound seems to be such, it is actually a case of interaction between physical entities, for example the tongue of a bell hits the side of the bell, and the sound produced is a physically based resultant. Otherwise, when a sound is experienced it is found to be characteristic of mental content (that is present in a mental medium). In any case the nature of sound as such is neither physical nor mental nor is it a concept (though of course there is a concept linked with the entity 'sound').

In the context of comprehensive experience basic physical entities are found to have thermal characteristics and some to have odour and taste characteristics. It is to be noted (*a*) that not all experienced thermal entities, odours and tastes are characteristics of basic physical entities. (*b*) The experienced variety of such entities does not constitute an insuperable problem. As in the case of shapes and colours, it is quite possible to distinguish characteristics of physical objects from physically based resultants and from thermal, taste and odour entities which are characteristics of mental content.

A thermometer enables a person to determine the thermal characteristics of a basic physical entity. If a thermal entity is experienced and it is found neither to be a characteristic of mental content (that is occurring in a mental medium) nor to be experienced as being mentally generated, it is possible to locate physical causes of which this is a physically based resultant. Consider abnormal environmental or internal physical conditions. For example, if a person has deliberately heated his hand, water which is actually mildly warm will seem very cold.

A professional tea-taster can identify taste characteristics of a relevant fluid. A wine expert likewise can identify the bouquet of another type of fluid. Here again it is possible to distinguish entities which are characteristics of physical objects from those which are physically based resultants or characteristics of mental content. For example a person can distinguish a taste of an imaginary apple from one into which he physically bites. He can identify the bitter taste of the apple as a physically based resultant if he notes that he has eaten something very sweet beforehand. Actually the apple is characterised by a mild sweetness.

A more detailed treatment of these issues would involve the needless repetition of matters already discussed at some length in dealing with problems concerning colours and shapes. In general, such topics are more appropriately left, for very extended examination, to experts in the fields of psychology and physiology.

The weight of a stick or a penny can be easily determined by placing it in a balance. The weighing of a mountain obviously presents difficulties, but at least in theory not insuperable ones. Of course some experienced weights are physically based resultants, as when a person with tired muscles lifts a light object which seems heavy. Likewise mental expectation may determine one's experience of weight.

Resistance to pressure is found to be a characteristic of a stick, a penny, a mountain, or a mass of air or water. A discussion of individuality will be postponed until later. (See Chapter 7, pp. 191–201.)

In addition to the characteristics just discussed, some physical objects have physical, chemical and biological characteristics which are revealed by our experience. For example, the ability to explode of some compounds is experienced when it happens.

Physical objects obviously have numerical characteristics. A penny is one object. It has two sides. The value and relational characteristics, including spatial and temporal, of physical objects[1] will be dealt with in subsequent chapters.

IV

Supplementary comments

A crucial point concerning the characteristics of particular occurrences of basic physical entities remains for consideration. It is obvious that the definite specific characteristics of such an entity vary, depending on changing internal and external conditions. For example, in the spring a maple leaf is green, in the autumn it is yellow or red, or both. A piece of metal and a piece of wood expand or contract, that is their size and shape change, depending on the heat or cold, and in the case of wood, the humidity. A person's body, in growing from childhood to adulthood, changes in shape and size, including length. An object which on earth has a specific weight loses it at some points in space and has less weight on the surface of the moon. The temperature of an entity varies depending on changes in internal or external factors, or both.

Obviously in stating what the characteristics of a particular occurrence of a basic physical entity are, one must take into consideration the environment in which the entity is located and also relevant internal conditions, for instance the temperature of a human body changes depending on health or illness. However, this does not result in hopeless relativity. Given suitable conditions for observation, it is possible to determine (ascertain) what the characteristics of an entity are in a specified situation—at least in some cases.

It is obvious that the foregoing discussion of the characteristics of particular occurrences of basic physical entities has been concerned

---

[1] The difference between the reports on the characteristics of physical objects offered in this Chapter and those found in relativity theory (for instance, changes of length with rapid motions) will be discussed later (see Chapter 14, p. 320, fn. 1).

with the situation which is present on the planet earth, under normal conditions, and whatever areas beyond which are open to human awareness. When exceptional or abnormal conditions are present this has been mentioned.

The preceding discussion has been concerned with some of the problems which arise when a person reports that he is aware of the characteristics of basic physical entities. It was pointed out at the beginning that attention is here focused on particular occurrences of several basic physical entities (one of each). It was shown that each of these had for example shape, colour, and other characteristics as listed in the first paragraph of this chapter.[1] It will have been noted that while each of the entities discussed had colour as a characteristic (the penny brown, the leaf green, the blood red), they did not have the same colour. More specifically and technically, they had the characteristic colour in the sense that they were brown, green or red and all these entities have, in common, the characteristic colour. In like fashion the shape of the stick and the penny varied—one was oblong, the other round. They had the characteristic shape in the sense that they had the characteristic oblong or round and these entities have the characteristic shape. The same situation does not arise with reference to length, width, thickness, resistance to pressure, bounded by a surface, individuality, rough, smooth. They are not characteristics of characteristics of the basic physical entities under consideration. On the other hand, size, thermal, numerical, relation, value, taste, odour, do have this status.

It should be obvious that no attempt has been made to consider all the particular occurrences of any one basic physical entity, for instance all pieces of wood or all pieces of metal, nor has an attempt been made to consider all the different basic physical entities. The justification for the general statement in the first paragraph of the chapter that all basic physical entities have the characteristics as listed, will be discussed later (Chapter 6, pp. 160–3). As was noted in Chapter 1, pp. 47–8, a many-occurrence entity is frequently present in varying fashions, for example in the case of the desk and chair, one entity brown was present with variations in its shade.

---

[1] More accurately, some characteristics of physical objects were discussed by referring to objects other than sticks, pennies, mountains.

So far this chapter has been concerned with a discussion of the associated characteristics of basic physical entities. In the interests of convenience, attention has been focused on particular familiar entities which are commonly termed physical objects, namely a stick, a mountain, a penny and the like. These of course are composed of basic physical entities: wood, stone, metal.

It is appropriate at this point to stress, at the risk of undue repetition, a matter referred to in Chapter 1: the term 'physical object' has a dual use. One (*a*) is to refer to basic physical entities. Its second use (*b*) is to refer to more specific entities which involve basic physical entities and also their characteristics. For *a* we have for example wood and metal. For *b* we have for example a stick and a penny. A stick is wood characterised by a specific shape and size. A penny is metal with a specific shape, size and colour. If the wood has different shape and size characteristics it is a cheese board. If the metal has different shape and size, and perhaps colour, characteristics, it is a plaque. In this sense, the distinctive shapes and sizes of the stick and penny are constitutive of them.

It is very important to note that all characteristics of a basic entity, out of which a physical object in the second *b* sense is made, are not constitutive of that physical object. For example. the wood of a stick may have the characteristic 'nearness to another object'. However, nearness is not constitutive of the stick. It is that same stick even if it is moved some distance away from the other objects in question.

Many physical objects, in both senses of the term, are complex. Indeed in some cases these complex physical objects are composed of other physical objects of the same class. For example, a wooden TABLE (a physical object in the second *b* sense) has a top and legs, which are pieces of wood (sticks). Here the relation to each other of the component entities, which make up the table, are spatial. Wood (a physical object in the first *a* sense) when viewed under a microscope, is found to be composed of a complex structure of vegetable cells (physical objects in the second *b* sense). In other words, in this case also, a physical object is a complex organisation of smaller, component, physical objects. A biological organism is likewise composed of entities which are biological organisms, but the components differ more markedly than in the case of wood. In addition to spatial relations, there are organic interactions involving physical and chemical changes.

The identification and detailed technical discussion of simple physical objects (those which do not have component physical objects) also many complex ones, should be left to science, to physics, chemistry and biology.

It is obvious that sorts of complex physical objects have various distinctive characteristics. For example, animate physical objects of the vegetable species have as distinctive characteristics growth, nourishment, reproduction, preservation and repair functions. Animals are characterised in addition by movement, and rely on vegetables to make available some necessary food minerals.[1] More highly developed animals are a very complex type of entity composed of physical and mental basic entities, accompanied, of course, by their characteristics. Inanimate physical objects lack the distinctive characteristics of vegetables and animals.

The characteristics of a complex physical object of the second *b* sort, particularly an animate one, are not merely the sum of characteristics of its component physical objects in either the first *a* or the second *b* sense. For example the human body is capable of walking. This particular characteristic is not a characteristic of the particular component parts of the body, let alone the component cells of these parts.

What characteristics physical objects may have which are beyond the range of awareness, simply cannot be determined, and no claim to knowledge should be made concerning them. However, every effort should be made to extend the range of what is now comprehensive experience.

---

[1] There are some cases of borderline entities with both some vegetable and some animal characteristics.

4

CONCEPTS

In the context of comprehensive experience a person is aware of many concepts.[1] There is a concept for every class of entities. A concept refers to each member of the class of which it is the concept. For example the concept green[2] refers to all occurrences of green, the concept wood to all occurrences of wood, and so on.

Characteristics of concepts

Concepts are basic entities since they are neither presently dependent resultants nor characteristics of other entities. They have other entities as characteristics. Among the characteristics of the entity 'concept' are individuality, and also numerical, relational and value characteristics.

It is obvious from the preceding discussion of basic physical entities, basic mental entities, and resultants (and their characteristics) that individuality, value, relational and numerical characteristics are not confined to concepts.[3]

Awareness of concepts

It must be admitted that concepts are not as obvious as, readily open

---

[1] Speaking technically each is an occurrence of the entity 'concept'.

[2] A concept is given the same name, that is, verbal label, as the entity with which it is linked.

[3] It has already been noted that such characteristics are neutral; that is, as such they are neither physical nor mental, nor concepts, nor physically based resultants, nor is any occasion of these either mental or physical, etc.—with one exception. In some cases of the relation of causation (for example generation and stimulation) there are relations which as such are neither physical nor mental, etc., but on occasion are characterised by 'mental'.

to awareness, as most of the entities so far discussed. The following comments may be relevant to this situation.

When a person sees a physical object and recognises it to be a table, this recognition experience involves, in at least some instances, the awareness of an entity which is not seen. There is a concept in addition to what is seen. As one is listening to a person speaking, or is reading in a newspaper about absent entities such as the war in Vietnam, the understanding[1] of what is being stated occurs because there is, in addition to and linked with seeing and hearing present entities, an awareness of another type of entity, that is of concepts. This is particularly obvious, by contrast, when a person is dealing with an unfamiliar foreign language. Merely seeing or hearing the words[2] is not enough.

Most people most of the time experience concepts in association with some sensed entities either physical or mental. For example, in thinking of the concept 'home' (the concept referred to by the English word 'home') one may also be seeing a physical object, house, or a memory or imagination image which is a more or less pictorial representation of a particular house. However, in the more complex situations referred to above, namely the listening to and understanding of one's native tongue, the process of understanding does not involve the presence of a series of specific pictorial representations (or any other set of specific sensory entities) which parallel, or are, that to which the words immediately refer. Rather the words (the sounds and inscriptions) are understood because one is aware of their related concepts. There may, of course, be a vague background of some sort of sensory accompaniment. The point being made here, in the terms of an illustration, is that, at least in comprehensive human experience, a person is aware of the distinction between a sensed entity (internal or external), mental or physical, and a concept. In some cases, such as rapid calculation by a proficient mathematician deep in concentration, sensory experience fades to a minimum or is absent. In the latter instance, one is aware of concepts, without sensory accompaniment.

It is therefore obvious that words (written or spoken to oneself or out loud), or other symbols, cannot be equated with concepts. If there were no difference between symbols and concepts, it would be impossible to translate from one language to another presumably

---

[1] See discussion of meaning, Chapter 5.
[2] More accurately: sounds or inscriptions, see Chapter 5, pp. 132–3.

expressing the same meaning. Despite some difficulty, translation in many cases is achieved. Further evidence is provided by the fact that one may be aware of concepts which cannot be expressed adequately in words, of other symbols. For example, a person may have an idea about a social situation or a person which he cannot state in available language.

II

Simple concepts and groups of concepts

There are simple concepts, for example, table,[1] leg, square, brown, top, mind, awareness (that is the entities referred to by the English words 'table', 'leg', 'square', etc.). There are various sorts of groups of simple concepts which constitute complex conceptual entities: (*a*) there is a minimum case where for example, as in free association, two concepts such as table and leg are together; (*b*) consider also the group of concepts which is conveniently termed complex concept, for example, square, brown, table, top. This is a complex entity composed of single concepts in a specific arrangement.

It is essential to realise that the concept table does not include the concept leg (as a part) just because a table has a leg. In other words, a simple concept such as table, is an individual entity without component parts.[2] However, among the meanings of the concept table is the concept leg.

There is a further (*c*) sort of group of concepts which constitutes a complex conceptual entity. The sentence 'The table has four legs' states a proposition. The concepts 'the table,' 'four', 'legs' and 'has' are together as a proposition. They are not here parts of a complex

---

[1] It is important to realise that a simple concept may be naturally linked with a complex entity. The concept table is a simple concept, the physical object table is a complex entity composed of a top and four legs. Similarly the concept person refers to a complex of body and mind.

[2] When one deals with the concept of table, one is referring to all concepts which together refer to the entities composing or linked with the physical objects to which the concept table refers. For example, the concept of table is all the concepts which refer to the parts of the table (leg, top), emotions involved, memory images which occur, intentions to use tables for specific purposes and so on. Thus, 'concept of' is a synonym for 'the conceptual ingredients in the meaning of a concept'. (See Chapter 5, pp. 122–3.)

concept. Nor is it a mere case of the minimum group like that of the concept 'table' and the concept 'leg'. Among the concepts is a verb— relations are stated.

It should be obvious that there are concepts which refer to (are linked with) physical objects, physically based resultants, minds and to other concepts (and the characteristics of all these entities).

The mention of the concept 'the' focuses attention on the contention by Experiential Realism that there are concepts which are referred to by the English words 'of', 'and', 'or', 'it', 'the', 'not', 'if', 'slowly', connectives, prepositions, adverbs, as well as by the sorts of words already mentioned, nouns, verbs, adjectives. The same is the case with names of persons. In this instance it is a very complex concept. Numbers are, as such, concepts. Some such as 1, 2, are simple; others such as $\sqrt{2}$ are complex.

A basic physical entity, such as wood, or the basic mental entity mind has many occurrences. There are many different pieces of wood and many different minds. Each particular occurrence of wood has one specific location in space and time. A piece of wood can occupy only one space at one time. Each particular occurrence of mind can have only one (continuing) association with a body. On the other hand one and the same concept (numerically) is applicable to, (linked with) a large number of other entities. For example, the concept brown is applicable to a brown chair, a brown desk, a brown table. Further, while physical objects and minds may be said to 'exist', concepts 'subsist'.

The 'natural linkage' characteristic of concepts

One sort of relational characteristic of concepts is particularly important to note—natural linkage.[1] As pointed out earlier, each concept is linked with each member of the class of entities of which it is the concept. This linkage is natural in the sense that it is found, not artificially created by human initiative.[2]

[1] It is important to realise the difference between the linkage of a concept to entities to which it applies and the grouping of concepts to form a complex unit.

[2] There are of course other sorts of natural linkage, such as causal ones. Many human activities are natural in the sense that this is the way human beings behave. Indeed, in this sense the application of some concepts to some entities for instance in imagination, may be termed a natural human activity. However, to repeat, the phrase 'natural linkage' here refers to a specific sort of linkage, namely that of concept to relevant entity (i.e. relevant concept to entity) which is found, not created by human initiative.

It may seem that the natural linkage of a concept with some other entity, of which it is the concept, indicates that the concept is a characteristic of the entity. This, however, is not the case. An occurrence of green has a natural linkage with the concept green. The natural linkage is a characteristic, though the concept green is not. The concept green has as a characteristic its natural linkage with an occurrence of green and any other occurrence of green. But a particular occurrence of green is not a characteristic of the concept green. In any case, the concept is not composed of its characteristics. It is what has the characteristics.

It is important to note that, for example, in a situation involving a green physical object, the green is there present on the surface of a physical object. On the other hand, the concept green can be present to awareness when no occurrence of green is present. However, as a matter of fact, a person initially becomes aware of a simple concept after having had one or a number of particular experiences of an entity to which the concept is found to be naturally linked. But this does not prove that simple concepts are human inventions. Simple concepts cannot be created by mental initiative as are imagination images. They are not mere imaginary assumptions 'dreamed up' to account for the recognition of entities or the understanding of language. A person is not aware of a process by which he creates simple concepts.

In brief, the position of Experiential Realism is that simple concepts, like physical objects are not generated by mental activity. They are found. They, in their own right, are part of the world in which we live. Not only are they found, but some simple concepts are found to be linked with other entities. This linkage is not due to human initiative. There are of course some cases where linkage is the result of imaginative activity. For example, the concept gold may be applied to a mountain which as a matter of fact has no gold in it.

In the interests of comprehensiveness it must be noted that it is possible for a person to think imaginatively a concept and an entity—in accordance with natural linkage—but not be aware of this. In this case the linkage, though resulting from imagination, is a correct linkage.

III

Groups of concepts: complex concepts and propositions
Let us turn now to a consideration of groups of concepts. Complex concepts (such as square brown table top) or propositions ('There is

a square brown table top') are naturally linked to groups of entities on the basis of the natural linkage of the individual ingredients of the complex concepts or propositions to their relevant entities. It is possible that the complex concept and the proposition mentioned might be imaginatively linked to relevant entities in accordance with natural linkage, even though the person doing the linking was not aware of that fact. On the other hand, the linkage of 'gold on the surface' to a mountain or 'there is gold on' used to talk about a mountain are uses of imaginary linkage of groups of concepts with complex entities, the linkage being incorrect, that is not in accordance with natural linkage.

Some concepts, both simple and complex, are naturally linked to imaginary entities as well as to non-imaginary ones. For example, the complex concept 'square brown table top' is naturally linked to a specific table with these characteristics and to an imagined table (imagination image) with these characteristics. The concept green is naturally linked to the green of a leaf and to the green of an imagination mirage of a leaf. The complex concept woman-fish (mermaid) has natural linkage only with the imagined entity mermaid.

IV

The status of groups of concepts where physical and mental entities are involved

One very important problem concerning concepts is that of the status of the 'togetherness' of concepts with concepts so as to form groups of the sorts noted above: (*a*) complex concepts, (*b*) propositions.[1] Attention will be focused first on concepts which have a reference to physical objects and minds (and their characteristics). Specifically, the question is this: are complex concepts and propositions objective facts found in the world—the togetherness of their component single concepts being a state of affairs which is independent of any other entity?

As far as comprehensive experience is concerned, there is no evidence to support the thesis that in any case, togetherness of concepts with concepts (to form complex concepts and propositions) is an ultimate independent factor in the world. When a person is aware of a number

[1] In the interests of simplification so-called 'minimum' grouping is not discussed.

of simple concepts, he cannot merely, by being aware of them (without reference to other entities) be aware of such conceptual groupings as for example, 'square brown table top'; or 'The table has a square brown top'. After the experience (his own or someone else's) of the entities table, top, brown, has, etc. (in the cases just mentioned), in relationship together, and the relevant simple concepts, naturally linked with each specific entity—then various groups of concepts with concepts are present in awareness. Likewise, when a new drug is discovered and its concept noted, any togetherness of this concept with other concepts relevant to the nature and function of the drug is open to awareness not merely by examining a single concept, but only after observing the chemical components of the drug and what happens when it is used. The same holds true of concepts which refer to mental entities. The mental state produced by the first ever use of LSD, is naturally linked with a concept. The togetherness of the concepts LSD with this one is found by observation of the drug and its resultant mental state.

These comments may be misleading. The main concern here is not with how one becomes aware of the groups of simple concepts. Rather the point is this: a person is not aware of groups of concepts, as such, in isolation from other entities.

Thus in the context of comprehensive experience the situation is as follows: there are groups of concepts of the complex concept, and proposition sorts. These groups occur, in some cases (when not imaginatively grouped) because other entities are together and the concepts which are grouped are naturally linked with these entities. Thus, for example, there is a complex concept 'square brown table top' because there is present somewhere in the environment a physical object 'table top' which is brown and square.

In like fashion one can account for the proposition 'there is a table with a square brown top'.

It must be noted, however, that the complex concepts and propositions mentioned above can be accounted for by (result from) an imaginative activity whereby concepts are put together to obtain the same results, as in 'square brown table top'. The fact that the complex concepts and propositions fit facts does not rule out the possibility of an imaginative grouping. The history of mathematics and science records that speculative spinning together of concepts, with no attempt to find out factual relations, may result in complex concepts and propositions which later are found to fit the facts.

Further, obviously some groups of concepts are exclusively involved in the realm of imaginative activity. It may be (*a*) a purely imaginary grouping of concepts (that is they do not refer to any non-imaginary entity). On the other hand it might be (*b*) a case of the imaginative generation of a group of images, to each of which a concept is naturally linked. Because of the grouping of the images the relevant concepts would be in a group. Either situation would account for 'creature half woman and half fish' or 'There is a creature in the sea half woman and half fish.'

It is essential to realise that both ways of accounting for the presence of groups of concepts indicate that it is not the case that groups of concepts are ultimate in the sense of being independent of any other entity. In one situation simple concepts are together because of their natural linkage with entities which are together. In the other, concepts are put together by imaginative activity. The grouping (being together in a group) is not a characteristic of the concepts as such. It is a derivative characteristic resulting from relations of concepts to other entities.

Once someone has become aware, for example, of the togetherness of the concepts brown, square, table, top to form a complex concept, and remembers it, or receives reports of this combination of concepts from others—this concept is available for use and one can be aware of it without the presence of a physical object. Indeed all such physical objects may go out of existence.

It may be the case that concepts are naturally linked together, that is they are together regardless of their actual linkage to other entities or apart from imagination. Indeed it may seem that this thesis should be accepted in order to explain some of our experience. The comment of Experiential Realism is simply this: no theory (in this case natural linkage of such[1] concepts with concepts to form groups) will be accepted unless it is supported by relevant entities present to awareness. If it is offered as an interesting suggestion imaginatively generated, so be it. It should not be regarded as a statement of solid fact used to explain what is present in awareness with non-imaginary status.

v

The status of groups of concepts where other entities are involved

So far, discussion has focused first on the natural linkage of simple

[1] Those which refer to physical or mental entities or their characteristics.

concepts with mental and physical entities and their characteristics, and the relation of complex concepts and propositions to relevant entities. Further, it has been reported that groups of concepts which refer to various relevant entities of these types (physical and mental) are not found to be naturally linked together as such. The togetherness of concepts, if it is not the product of imagining, is the result of the togetherness of the physical and mental entities with which they are naturally linked. What is the situation concerning concepts which refer, not to mental and physical entities and their characteristics, but to other concepts?

Are there cases of a natural linkage of concepts with the concepts to which they refer, such that there are groups of concepts independently of the natural linkage of concepts with entities other than concepts and independent of human imaginative activity? The situation is as follows: the simple concept 'concept' is naturally linked to any concept. However, this group of concepts does not form a complex concept or a proposition. Rather it is a case of a simple concept, naturally linked to an entity which is a concept. This is the only case of a natural linkage of concept with concept. The concept 'one' for example applies to a concept only in the sense that it is naturally linked to the 'oneness' characteristic of the concept. Strictly speaking, it does not refer to, is not naturally linked with, the concept as such—any more than the concept square is naturally linked to the wood of the table as such. The concept square is naturally linked with the square characteristic of the wood. Thus a concept and the concept 'one' do not constitute a group on the basis of natural linkage. The concept 'proposition' applies to 'This is a square brown table top'. But the concept proposition and the other concepts do not form a group on their own. The concept proposition is not naturally linked with the concepts as such. The decisive factor is its natural linkage with a characteristic of their concepts—their togetherness in a specific pattern.

The complex concept 'complex concept' applies to 'square brown table top' because concept is naturally linked with (the concepts) square, brown, table, top. But the decisive factor is the fact that the concept 'complex' is naturally linked with the relational characteristics of the component concepts, which are parts of the group. The concept complex is not naturally linked with the concepts brown, square, etc., as such. The same situation is in effect in the case of a proposition (a) referring to proposition (b). Consider for example 'This is a square brown table top' (proposition *b*), and 'This is a group of concepts forming a proposition' (*a*). The concept 'concept' referred to in *a* is naturally linked with the component concepts of *b*. The other component concepts of proposition *a* are naturally linked not with the component concepts of *b*, but with some of their characteristics.

Summarising the preceding discussion one concludes, on the basis of comprehensive experience, that apart from the natural linkage of the concept 'concept' with other concepts, any group of concepts does not constitute a group on its own. Concepts are not naturally linked so as to form groups of concepts of the complex or proposition sort independently of other entities. They are together in groups because (i) of their natural linkage with entities other than concepts which are together (though the linkage may be with characteristics of concepts), or (ii) they may be together in groups because of human imaginative activity.

As noted previously, the imaginative grouping of concepts may or may not be in accordance with the togetherness of their relevant entities.[1]

VI

Further comments on the status of propositions

The report that there are no propositions which stand on their own feet independently of other entities, merits further consideration. This is so because it may appear that there are at least some self-evident autonomous principles which 'dictate to' rather than depend on other entities, also that some less august propositions state relations independently of external entities. Let us examine some typical

---

[1] It is to be emphasised that the togetherness of concepts, which results from the togetherness of the entities with which the individual concepts are naturally linked—is objective facts independent of human initiative. When found and remembered, these groups of concepts can be used even though their relevant entities are absent. An imaginative grouping of concepts (that is, produced by the activity of imagining), whether or not it is in accordance with the grouping of the entities to which the concepts refer, does not have the same objective status as the grouping just mentioned. Nevertheless, though as imaginative and hence a human product, such a group of concepts can be available for recurrent and common use on the basis of memory or some other recording device.

propositions which are not imaginary, that is not created by the putting together of concepts by a process of imagining.

The proposition (principle) 'A whole is composed of parts' depends on the fact that, for example, a table has a top and legs.

Turning to more particular propositions, the same general comment is in order. A proposition such as 'All men are mortal' is dependent on physical objects and their characteristics in the sense that without them, the concepts 'men' and 'mortal' are not together.[1] The proposition 'Black is black' is not a togetherness of different concepts, and hence an exception to the claim that no proposition joining different concepts is independent of some other entity. Even here, the relation (a sort of togetherness) expressed by it (Black is black), that is identity, is an entity which justifies the use of the concept 'is'.

Propositions in which the predicate states what is included in the subject or merely repeats the subject concept, are termed 'analytic'.[2] Hence the proposition expressed in English words thus, 'All bachelors are unmarried', simply states, on the basis of the situation in question, that the concept which constitutes the subject of the proposition and the concept which constitutes its products is the same concept (in the sense that it is repeated). The one concept is symbolised by using two words which, as a matter of fact, are known as the result of past experience to be used as synonyms. In the most glaringly simple case of an analytic proposition such as 'Black is black', obviously the predicate does not add anything not already in the subject. 'Black cats are black' is an instance of the predicate being included in the subject.

Propositions expressed in English thus, 'All wooden objects have extension' or 'All men are mortal' are statements of the characteristics of a basic entity. In these two cases, the subject concept as such does not include the predicate concept, as in the case of 'Black cats are black'. For example, the concept man does not include the concept mortal[3] though of course the entity man has the characteristic mortal. Therefore, such propositions are not analytic.

Propositions are termed 'synthetic' if the predicate concept (concepts) is not included in the subject concept nor is a mere repetition

---

[1] See also subsequent comments.

[2] Other uses of the term 'analytic' involve a reference to the truth of propositions.

[3] It is the case that the meaning of the concept man includes the concept mortal (see Chapter 5, pp. 122–3).

of it. The proposition 'Some men are slant-eyed' is clearly synthetic. It may appear that 'All men have eyes' is analytic but as in the case of 'All men are mortal' and 'All wooden objects have extension', the predicate is not included in the subject as such. The subject is simple not complex, nor is the predicate a mere repetition of the subject.

Groups of propositions

At this point some further comments are in order. They have to do with groups of propositions in cases where the propositions are not due to imaginative activity nor is the fact that they are in groups.

Consider a situation in which several propositions are together in such a fashion that one (or more) serves as a premise and another proposition is a conclusion of an argument or proof. We are here concerned not with the activity of arguing or proving, making use of propositions, but rather of the relations of propositions in the premise-conclusion situation.

On the basis of comprehensive experience it is found that premises as such do not give rise to a conclusion as such. Rather, it is ultimately a case of premise propositions reporting a factual state of affairs and the conclusion proposition reporting a state of affairs related to what is reported by the premises. In brief, propositions as such do not produce as progeny other propositions. What links propositions together in argument or proof, leading from premises to conclusion,—is not a so-called logical generation or determination of a proposition by others. Rather, the grouping of propositions is due to the grouping of the entities with which the concepts of the propositions are naturally linked. It is of course the case that when a person is engaged in the activity of arguing or proving he may use propositions in varying relations. Specifically he may present several propositions—and his hearer or reader will accept another proposition as a conclusion. But, to repeat, this is not a case of propositions generating other propositions. Propositions are related on the basis of relations of other entities with which they are naturally linked. Propositions may cause a person to remember another proposition which is termed a conclusion. On the other hand, the so-called conclusion proposition may be present to a person not as the result of remembering, but rather because he has remembered or been informed about (by propositions, the so-called premises)—a group of facts from which he then derives a conclusion proposition.

Returning now to the main point which is being made, namely

that the non-imaginary groups of non-imaginary propositions in the premise-conclusion relation are due ultimately to the relations of the entities to which the component concepts of the propositions are naturally linked—let us consider some examples;

(1) The familiar syllogism

> All animals are mortal
> All dogs are animals
> ∴ All dogs are mortal

is a group of propositions, each of which reports a group of facts. The conclusion is based on the togetherness of the facts reported in the premises, that is facts of class membership and characteristics of classes.

(2) The 'argument' that (a) the apple is red, therefore (b) the apple is coloured, reports (a) the apple is characterised by red and that (b) since colour is an inherent characteristic of red, in this sense the apple is coloured. Hence the transition from premise a to conclusion b is based on factual relations. A proposition containing the concept red cannot generate or lead to a proposition containing the concept colour. As noted earlier, there is no natural linkage between concepts except that of concept with 'a' concept. All other non-imaginary togetherness of concepts is based on the togetherness of entities to which the concepts are naturally linked. (Hence in case (1) there is no natural linkage of dog or animal or mortal.)

(3) The 'argument' (a) Men are rational animals therefore (b) men are animals—may appear to be a case of the conclusion being generated by (derived from) the premise, since the content of the conclusion is part of the content of the premise. It is the case that, given the premise, the conclusion (that is part of the premise) is there. However, in the last analysis, the content of the so-called conclusion is part of what originally went to make up the so-called premise. In any case the 'content concepts' of the conclusion are grouped as they are because of their natural linkage with the entity man and its characteristics (which are of course together). This is also the case with the premise 'concept contents' in their entirely.

One very important consequence of the point of view here being developed is that propositions which state the structure of propositions, or syllogisms and other patterns of concepts, including the so-called laws of thought, are not ultimately independent in status but are based on and derived from relations found among the entities to which the (component) concepts of propositions are naturally linked. For example, the 'A' type of proposition which states, 'All S are P', is based on the fact that a number of propositions (stated in English sentences), such as 'All men are mortal', 'All dogs are animals' have this structure. Further, and this is a fundamental point, propositions of type A occur in this form because of the fact that entities of the class man have the characteristic mortality (belong to the class of mortal beings), and likewise, with other similar cases.

Similarly, the syllogism of the sort

M P
S M
S P

as illustrated in:

All animals are mortal:
All dogs are animals:
All dogs are mortal:

is based on and derived from the facts of class membership which are reported in such propositions and the syllogisms which they compose.

Let us turn to the 'laws of thought'. The 'law of identity', 'A is A' for example is also due to the fact that, in thinking about an entity, one thinks of it, using concepts, as identical[1] with itself because, as a matter of fact, it is. In other words, change is not absolute nor is the entity something else.

Thus, in general, the so-called laws or principles of logic so far discussed state ways of putting concepts together—the ultimate determination being provided by the world of entities to which the concepts refer in natural linkage. It is to be remembered that, so far, we have been concentrating on non-imaginary situations.[2]

Once a logical structure has been identified and is remembered, (a) one can play intellectual games, in the context of an imaginary world, or (b) use meaningless words (sounds and inscriptions), and

[1] See discussion of identity, Chapter 7, pp. 196–201.
[2] That is, the natural linkage of concepts and relevant entities and groups of concepts which are not together because of imaginative activity.

concern oneself with only logical validity, where, given specific premises and an appropriate structure, a specific conclusion follows.

But such a game must be recognised for what it is—something ultimately dependent for its patterns or structure on the relation of non-imaginary entities.

Thus (*a*) one argues with logical validity that

M	P

All round objects are made of green cheese:

S	M

The moon is a round object:

S	P

∴ The moon is made of green cheese:

or (*b*)

M	P

All boojuns are snorks:

S	M

All wigwogs are boojuns:

S	P

∴ All wigwogs are snorks.

These conclusions follow because the logical structure is sound. However, to repeat, the structure is sound because it is based on a general structure in the non-imaginary world.

It is to be further noted that some patterns, that is principles or rules and definitions used by some logicians are not based on general factual situations (in the non-imaginary world of entities). Rather, some logics employ some rules (patterns stated as rules) which are imaginary creations—specifically conventions arbitrarily set up. For example, it is claimed that if two propositions which are false are linked in the 'if-then' relations; the compound formed by them is true, for instance ,'If giraffes have short necks then water is always solid'. Here 'true' is used in a special sense, and a logical rule is employed which is not based on the experience of the non-imaginary world.

VII

Some problems involved in the use of concepts

In comprehensive experience one is aware of various simple concepts, and complex entities composed of groups of concepts—and their linkage (natural or otherwise) with other entities, including other concepts. Many errors arise: (*a*) natural linkages are overlooked, (*b*) concepts are incorrectly applied, (*c*) the natural linkage situation as such presents difficulties. In comprehensive experience (so far achieved) this is recognised and these mistakes are corrected in some cases. However, this competence is difficult to attain in many instances. For example, the question arises as to whether or not one has had enough experience—repetition and a range of awareness, to justify the claim of linkage of a concept to an entity.

Further, as a human being develops from childhood to maturity, concepts which were once relevant no longer are, but in most cases the moment of transition is hard to locate. Consider the case of a young person learning to drive a car. It is difficult to determine the moment at which the concept 'competent driver' can be accurately applied (is naturally linked). However, there is little difficulty in the case of concepts such as: chair, man, one. The linkage of the concept chair to what I am now sitting on does not constitute a genuine problem.

Even if a person is not sure of all the characteristics of a living organism, such as his own body, he has no difficulty in accepting the experienced linkage of it and the concept 'living organism' now, and without further checking or hesitation because of lack of complete knowledge. But, even in comprehensive awareness, at this stage of human experience, there is frequently uncertainty as to the appropriateness of the applicability of a concept, particularly when the situation is complex. For example, a fungus is usually regarded as a vegetable but, in some aspects, it is like an animal. On the other hand a parasite may seem to be chiefly animal but to have some vegetable characteristics. However, at least some of these difficulties are not insuperable.

It may well be the case that apparently mutually exclusive concepts are both relevant in some cases. For example, as just noted, some living organisms have both distinctive animal and vegetable characteristics, and hence both concepts apply. At the present stage in the development in the physics of light, both wave and particle seem to be relevant concepts.

There is at least one other difficult problem. Consider the applicability (natural linkage) of the concepts God, science, philosophy, to their relevant entities. A general prerequisite in such cases is a careful examination of the entities in question. In some cases, it is found that the concept applies to many entities, despite striking differences in characteristics. This is because there is one fundamental characteristic in common (or more). It is frequently very difficult to discover what this fundamental characteristic or group of characteristics is. But the fact remains, it is found (the machinery can be discussed by psychologists), and the concept is relevant. For example, the concept God applies to a specific stone, a curious[1] old gentleman with a white beard peeking out from behind a bush in the Garden of Eden, the unmoved mover, the spirit of love. All those entities, despite their differences, have the common fundamental characteristic 'great in influence and importance'. Related concepts bring out the differences, for example primitive God, metaphysical God and so on.

In the case of philosophy, the common core characteristics are concern, positive or negative, for specified problems, such as of method (logic), value, knowledge (epistemological), reality (metaphysical), or world view, There is a great variety of positive or negative approaches, in thought and action, to these problems. Here again, related concepts clarify distinctions, for example, between idealistic philosophy, realistic philosophy, ordinary language philosophy.

The concept 'science' refers to a common concern for important factors in specific types of situation under examination.[2] Here again, there is a great diversity as to methods and ingredients as indicated by related concepts, ancient deductive, modern inductive, atomic science, biological science, and so on.

It is only proper to realise that some concepts are relative in the sense that the linkage of a concept with other entities depends on the context. For example, the concepts 'large' and 'small' are linked to 'seven-foot man' and 'five-foot man'. But the concept large is not linked with a 7 by 7 foot building. As noted in an earlier discussion, some concepts, for example, shape concepts, have a fairly wide range of appropriate application (natural linkage). The concept round applies to the smooth circumference of a coin seen with the naked

---

[1] He wants to find out what Adam and Eve are up to!

[2] It is relevant here to refer the reader to the work of men termed scientists.

eye from above, and also to the somewhat uneven circumference of the coin seen under a microscope. As previously noted, it is possible to find borderline cases where it would be difficult to decide, for instance, whether a free-hand attempt at circularity might be termed either round or elliptical, or irregular.

It is, of course, the case that in some instances hesitation and, indeed, suspension of claimed linkage is in order. For example, when confronted by a so-called cure for cancer now, one should refrain from applying the concept with any high degree of confidence, though it may be relevant as an ingredient in a scientific hypothesis. However, there may come a day, as in the case of immunisation against polio-myelitis, when a concept which was once used with hesitation is now accepted with confidence. Legitimate difficulties have been cleared up.

There are, of course other sorts of propositions and complex concepts apart from the (a) referential (describing or reporting) and, hence characterised by 'true' or 'false'. There are in addition[1] (b) poetic propositions and (c) ceremonial ones, as well as those (d) expressing (giving vent to) emotions and (e) ordering or suggesting or (f) asking questions. In sorts b–f factual description or reference is not primary, though it is involved in varying degrees. Nor is the question of truth and falsehood, in the usual senses of the terms, relevant. For example, the poetic proposition expressed by the English words, 'I wandered lonely as a cloud That floats on high' is not primarily a description of facts. Likewise, 'Thank you for a most pleasant evening', while ceremoniously appropriate, may unfortunately not be an accurate report of facts at all, or intended to involve truth or falsehood. 'You write illegibly' states a proposition which might be used to give vent to emotions or to make a suggestion, as well as state a fact.

The determination of the sort of proposition may on occasion present difficulties. For example, it is sometimes hard to distinguish a statement of fact from a purely ceremonial or poetic proposition. However, an examination of the context in which the proposition is used often clears up any crucial initial difficulty. The arrangement of concepts comprising propositions is also sometimes significant. The

---

[1] Some philosophers decline to apply the term 'proposition' to the following groups of concepts. In this discussion it is done because they are groups of concepts which include a verb content. These propositions will not, in this volume, receive detailed examination.

structure of poetic and ceremonial propositions is frequently different from descriptive ones, for example 'I wandered lonely as a cloud That floats on high'. Incidentally poetic and ceremonial propositions sometimes use concepts which are not ordinarily used in descriptive propositions, for instance 'lonely' in this context.

In the case of questions and orders also the same comments are relevant. Questions are frequently identified by a key concept, such as 'why'. The arrangement of concepts may distinguish an order from a description, as with 'Shut the door' contrasted with 'The door shut'. 'I want you to be quiet' is an order or a description depending on the context, for example tone of voice and the situation in which it is used.

5

MEANING AND WORDS

I

The meaning situation

The meaning situation (the various entities to which the ambiguous term 'meaning' is applied) is very complex. In its most general and simple form it is a situation in which an instance of entity A is in the relation of 'pointing to' an instance of entity B. When instances of this relation of entity A to entity B are available, a person uses an instance of entity A in the activity of pointing to an instance of entity B.

The relation of 'pointing to' takes three major forms. In the context of this discussion these are termed 'signifying', 'referring', 'expression-based'.[1] Clarification concerning these terms is obviously in order.

When an instance of entity A points to an instance of entity B on the basis of a causal relation—this is termed a case of 'signifying'.

When an instance of entity A points to an instance of entity B and the relation as such is not based on a causal sequence—this is termed 'referring', if the meaning relation is established by human decision (decree or stipulation), or is based on a natural linkage of a concept with its relevant entity.

When an instance of entity A points to an instance of entity B on the basis of (i) a 'whole-part' relationship or (ii) 'a part to a part of a whole' relationship—this is termed a case of 'signifying', unless the relations in question are established by human decision or are based on a case of natural linkage of concept with entity meant (which would be a case of 'referring').

When an instance of A is in the referring relation, it is a substitute for an instance of B: this is not the case in a signifying relation.

When an instance of entity A points to an instance of entity B be-

---

[1] These are here termed 'primary meaning relations'. There are also derivative 'associated meaning relations'. See pp. 119–20.

cause (that is on the basis of the fact that) an entity A gives vent to or expresses an emotion, feeling or attitude this (meaning relation) is termed 'expression-based'.[1] It is not a case of referring.

An instance of entity A is termed a 'symbol' if its 'pointing to' relation to an instance of entity B is established by human decision (decree or stipulation). When an instance of entity A is in a pointing relation to an instance of entity B, and a human decision is not involved either directly or as a condition, it is termed a 'sign'.

Entities of sort A are said to 'have meaning'. Entities of sort B are termed 'entities meant'.

When a person has available (or can make available) instances of A in a meaning ('pointing to') relation with instances of B, he can use A to point to B, that is engage in the activity of meaning. When he makes use of a symbol or a sign which is in the referring relation, it is appropriate to term the activity of meaning 'referring'. Likewise when a symbol or a sign is in the signifying relation, it is appropriate to term the meaning activity in which it is used 'signifying'.[2] However, when a symbol or sign has a meaning relation which is based on an entity giving vent to (expressing) emotions, feelings and attitudes, the use of the symbol or sign in a meaning activity may most appropriately be termed 'pointing to emotions, feelings and attitudes'. An alternate location sometimes more convenient is 'pointing to, which is neither referring or signifying'.

Thus, in brief, in the context of comprehensive experience, a person finds in the meaning situation instances of (i) entity A, (ii) entity B, (iii) 'pointing to' relations of the following sorts: signifying, referring, expression-based, and (iv) the complex human activity whereby a person (on the basis of available relations) uses instances of

[1] The somewhat barbarous phrase 'expression-based' is applied because there does not seem to be available a suitable term corresponding to 'signifying' or 'referring'. The term 'expressing' is too broad in scope, since it covers relations other than 'pointing to' and is not based on other relations or activities, as is the case with signifying and referring.

[2] The dual application of the terms 'signifying' and 'referring' to (i) a meaning relation and (ii) a meaning activity, which makes use of a specific sort of meaning relation, need not present difficulties. The context will indicate whether one is concerned with a relation or an activity (which uses the relation). The terms (in question) have this dual application because it is important to indicate the sort of meaning relation which is being used in a meaning activity. The nature of the activity is determined by the nature of the meaning relation it uses. See further pp. 123–4.

A to refer to or signify[1] instances of B or point to emotions, feelings attitudes (instances of B).

More specifically, signs and symbols, because of their place and function in the total meaning situation, are cases of an entity having meaning. The linkages termed 'referring', 'signifying' and 'expression-based', whether found or established by human decision, are the relational aspect of meaning. The entity meant is any entity of sort B, namely whatever is referred to or signified or expressed by a sign or symbol.

It is essential to stress that human activity in so far as it has a bearing on the meaning situation is of several sorts:

(a) In (i) a person decides for the first time in human history to use a symbol to refer to or express an entity. In this fashion he establishes a linkage between A and B. There is also (ii) the activity of noting meaning relations of signs and entities meant in cases where the relations are not based on human decision, but rather on other factors (such as causal, whole-part and other relations). The activities so far mentioned are not cases of meaning activity.

(b) Meaning activity occurs when, after meaning relations of symbols and signs with entities meant have been established or noted, the symbols and signs (in cases where signs can be introduced directly by human initiative) are used in the activity of pointing to entities meant.

It should be obvious that for the most part, a person relies on (uses) the meaning relations established or noted by others. The fruits of the labours of others, of these sorts, are retained in the memory or recorded in dictionaries and grammars.

Examples

Let us consider some examples which will serve to clarify the preceding very condensed outline of the meaning situation.[2] The inscription (a series of marks on a surface) 'table' (symbol) has meaning because

---

[1] Some instances of signs in the relation of signifying cannot be used in the signifying activity of meaning.

[2] Technically speaking, the examples considered are usually particular occurrences of a many-occurrence entity. However, in dealing with such particular occurrences, reference will ordinarily be made to what they have in common with other members of their class, that is all the particular occurrences of that (many-occurrence) entity.

it is involved in a relation of meaning, that is referring to a physical object, which is its entity meant. This inscription is termed a symbol because it and its linkage are human inventions (the linkage is established by human decision). The spoken sound 'table' would of course serve equally well in this situation. An unlearned gesture, such as a shudder (sign) is in both the signifying and expression-based relation of meaning with the emotion fear (entity meant). A learned gesture, such as crossing oneself, is a symbol pointing to (expression-based relation) reverence. Sounds and inscriptions (symbols) such as 'ouch' have a relation of pointing to a feeling (entity meant). A thunder clap (sign) signifies (meaning relation) rain (entity meant). A concept (sign) refers to (has the relation 'referring') a physical object, a concept or a mind (and characteristics).[1] A pain (sign) signifies the presence of a decayed tooth (entity meant). A cell (on the basis of being part of a whole) is a sign which signifies the organism (entity meant) of which it is a part. A table leg is a sign which signifies a table top (entity meant) since leg and top are both parts of a whole (the table). Likewise since the concept leg and the concept top are naturally linked to relevant entities and these entities are together as part of a whole, therefore the concepts have the same status—one (a sign) can signify the other (entity meant).[2] It is important to realise that in the context of this discussion the 'part to part of a whole' relation is exemplified in the relation of an entity and its characteristics, that is, the entity is a part of a whole: 'entity with characteristics'. This wood (a basic entity) signifies its characteristic: shape, size and so on.

When a person has available the meaning relation of the symbol 'table' to the physical object table, he can use the inscription to refer to the physical object (activity of meaning). Likewise when the relation between crossing oneself and reverence has been established a person can use the learned gesture as a symbol in the activity of pointing to the feeling of reverence (activity of meaning). It should be

---

[1] If it is a case of a meaning relation based on natural linkage. (See discussion, Chapter 4, pp. 95–6).

[3] It may appear that since a table leg and its related table top are together because of human initiative, that therefore the leg is a symbol and the meaning relation between leg and top is that of referring, not of signifying. However, this is not a situation similar to 'table' (an inscription) and table (a physical object). It is the case that a man nails or glues a top and a leg together, but the relation of part to part of a whole is not established by a human decision any more than the nature of the relation of a cell to the organism of which it is a part.

realised also, since the shudder gesture (a sign) has the relation of pointing to fear (when this is known), it can be employed by a person in the activity of pointing to fear. A table leg can be used in the meaning activity of signifying a table top. When a person is aware of the referring linkage of a concept (a sign) with some other entity, this relation can be used in the activity of employing the concept to refer to the entity meant. Some of the signs mentioned, such as the thunder clap and the pain (of a decaying tooth), cannot be introduced directly by human initiative and hence cannot be used in the activity of meaning. It may be objected that one can directly produce an imaginary pain and use it in a meaning activity. However, this comment is here[1] irrelevant. We are dealing with non-imaginary pains. While one can introduce a thunder-clap imitation, it cannot be done directly. A machine is needed. In any case it is an imitation, not the real thing.

In discussing the use of symbols or signs in the meaning activity, on the basis of their available meaning relation with entities meant, it should not be forgotten that instances of entity A and instances of entity B are used, in the sense of being ingredients, in the composition of that complex entity 'an instance of entity A in meaning relation to an instance of entity B.[2]

In subsequent discussion it will be convenient to make the following ing distinctions:

(a) The meaning situation which is constituted by (i) instances of entity A, (ii) instances of entity B, (iii) meaning relations termed 'referring', signifying 'expression based' and (iv) the activity of meaning which uses an instance of entity A to point to an instance of entity B in the context of available meaning relations.

(b) What is termed 'the meaning-relation situation' is the complex situation where an instance of entity A is in the meaning relation to an instance of entity B. The issue of the activity of meaning does not arise.

(c) When the term 'relation' (or 'meaning relation') is used alone, the concern is chiefly with the relation as such: that there is a relation, what sort it is, what its status is, how it becomes available, etc. Of course, a relation is always a relation of some entity to another, so instances of entity A and instances of entity B do become involved in any discussion of a relation. However, a detailed consideration of

---

[1] But see later discussion of a more complex meaning situation where a different state of affairs occurs.

[2] Thus the term 'use' has at least two entities meant.

symbols and signs, on the one hand, and entities meant on the other, occurs in what has been termed the 'meaning-relations situation'.

II

The preceding outline of the meaning situation requires further clarification and more consideration of details. Attention will initially be focused on the first three aspects of the meaning situation.[1] The phrase 'activity of meaning' will be dealt with in detail later.

Further comments on the status of meaning-relation

At this point it is advisable to comment further on the status of meaning relations in order to avoid possible misunderstanding. It was stated at the beginning that meaning relations are based on other relations or activities. This point can now be clarified against the background of the illustrative material previously presented.

The status of a referring relation, as far as a symbol is concerned (for example 'table' refers to a table) is simply that of an agreed procedure (based on a human decision, an activity). Specifically, the symbol is to be regarded as pointing to (referring relation) the entity meant. The signifying or referring or expression-based relation of a sign to an entity meant is not (established by) human decision (decree or stipulation). In the case of these relations, a sign points to its entity meant because (on the basis that) the sign and entity meant are related in some other fashion, such as causal, natural linkage of concept and relevant entity. Specifically, they will not be in the meaning relation unless they were in at least one of these other relations. In that sense the meaning relation is derivative from other relations. Further—and this is crucial—although the meaning relation is based on some other relation (in the case of signs and entities meant), the meaning relation cannot be identified with the other relations: there is a genuine distinction.

Let us consider previously introduced illustrations. On the basis of the fact that frost causes leaves to become yellow, frost (sign) signifies yellow leaves (entity meant). It should be obvious that the causal relation which results from the causal activity, though it is the basis of the 'pointing to' (signifying) relation, is not identical with it.

---

[1] That is, the meaning–relative situation.

Causation is one entity, 'pointing to' is another. The status of the 'pointing to' relation (signifying) in this sort of case is that of a fact of nature, independent of human decision.

Consider next the referring relation of a sign to an entity meant. The concept table refers to the physical object table. This referring relation is based on the fact that the concept and the physical object are naturally linked.[1] Without this relation, the pointing relation would not be in effect; it is derivative. However, the two relations, (i) natural linkage, (ii) 'pointing to' are not identical. In general this is the situation concerning the referring relation in so far as signs are involved. As in the case of the signifying relation (involving signs) the status of the relation is a fact of nature independent of human decision.

A complication arises concerning the relations of some signs to entities meant. Specifically, the 'pointing to' relation in some cases has two bases. Consider a shudder which points to fear. In so far as the relation is based on the causal sequence 'fear, shudder', the derived meaning relation is that of signifying. In so far as shudder points to fear on the basis of the fact that shudder expresses fear, the meaning relation is a case of 'expression-based'. Of course the causal and expressive relations are distinguishable aspects of one process. As in the case of signifying and referring, so the expression-based relation, while derived from another relation (generation by the expressive activity), is not to be identified with the expressive relation. Here again is a meaning relation which is a fact of nature, independent of human decision (decree or stipulation).

A complexity of another sort arises in cases where an expression-based relation involves a symbol. For example 'ouch' is in the expression-based meaning relation to pain because (*a*) a human decision has provided it as an agreed instrument for giving vent to this feeling. This having been done, (*b*) the symbol is used for that purpose. Obviously the pointing relation is not to be identified with the activity of setting up the symbol as a venting instrument, or the activity of using it in giving vent to feelings. The expression-based meaning relation, that is the pointing of 'ouch' to pain, is a fact derived from the set of circumstances as listed, namely *a* and *b*. Technically speaking, the mere decision to use 'ouch' to express pain, the setting up of the expressive relation without its being used, would not provide an expression-based meaning ('pointing-to') relation.

[1] See discussion, Chapter 4, pp. 95–6.

Simple and complex forms of the meaning-relation situation

The following comments concerning the meaning-relation situation are now in order. The relation of symbol or sign and entity meant is symmetrical (works both ways). For example, an emotion, fear, has as meaning (entity meant) a shudder—or vice versa. Either frost or yellow leaves may be sign or entity meant. More specifically, in examining the signifying linkages of any two entities, it must be realised that entities meant or signs may be either causes or effects. For example the 'entity meant' of rain may be the cloud disturbance (cause). On the other hand, a cloud may have rain (effect) as its entity meant. Likewise, either a part or the whole may be the entity meant. The physical object table may function as a symbol in relation to the inscription 'table' which could be its entity meant.

It is important to note that the meaning-relation situation, in its simplest form,[1] involves linkages (relations) of various sorts between two entities. Specifically, there are relations between physical entities, between mental entities, between concepts (and the characteristics of these entities) and, further, between any pair of different types of ingredients in experience. For example, there may be a meaning relation between frost (cold air) and yellow leaves, or pain and anger. The concept wine may be linked with the concept grape. Also, there may be a linkage of the physical object table and the concept table, a fire and the emotion of fear, fear and the relevant concept.

In brief, emotions and attitudes can be pointed to (they can be in the 'pointing to' relation of the expression-based type) by mental and physical entities, concepts and their characteristics. Concepts, physical and mental entities and their characteristics can be referred to (be in the relation of referring) by other concepts, physical and mental entities and their characteristics. The situation is the same as far as the relation of signifying is concerned.

Usually the meaning-relation situation is far more complex than that of some type of simple or single linkage involving only two entities. For example, the inscription (symbol) 'table' refers to (a) a physical object, and (b) to the concept table.[2] Consider another example:

[1] But see later discussion of a more complex meaning situation where a different state of affairs occurs.

[2] This is simply a matter of using the same sound or inscription for an entity and the concept which is naturally linked with it as relevant.

a (physical) table (sign) signifies the use made of the table, emotions[1] connected with the table as a physical object, also all the memory and imagination images linked with the table. The entity table also signifies its characteristics, including its causal efficacy in producing emotions, images, etc.

It is important to realise that the inscription (or sound) 'table', because of its relation with the table (physical object), acquires additional entities meant. For example, because the physical object (table) signifies its characteristics, also emotions, memory images, etc., these also become associated with the symbol 'table'. The concepts which are naturally linked with associated entities such as emotions, memory images, parts of the table, etc. (likewise the sounds and inscriptions which have an established linkage with these entities), are also associated entities meant of 'table'.

Primary and associated meaning of symbols

It is essential to note the distinction between primary meaning and associated meaning of symbols. The meaning-relation situation wherein 'table' is linked with the physical object (and its naturally relevant concept[2]) is primary in the sense that 'table' is applied as a label to a specific sort of physical object, not for example to an emotion. It is applied to an image only if the image is a more or less accurate reproduction of a specific sort of physical object. Further, without the symbol's linkage to the physical object table, it would not be linked with the emotions, images, etc., and their relevant concepts, also sounds and inscriptions—which are associated with the physical table. The symbol's linkage with these latter entities constitutes the associated meaning-relation situation. In this sense the associated meaning-relation situation is derivative from the primary situation.

It should be obvious that the three sorts of meaning relations so far discussed, referring, signifying, or expression-based, are primary meaning relations. In general, associated entities meant of a word

---

[1] The table stimulates a mind to generate the mental states mentioned herewith. Also the table when used to hold books signifies them in the 'part to part of a whole' relation.

[2] Because of the natural linkage of a concept to its relevant entity, when an inscription or sound is linked by human decision to an entity meant which is a primary entity meant—for example 'table' with the physical object table—the inscription 'table' has the concept 'table' as acquired primary entity meant.

(an inscription or sound) are linked to the primary entities meant by the signifying relation, supplemented in most cases by the referring relation and in some cases by the expression-based relation. It will become evident that attention is being focused on the primary and associated meaning-relation situations of symbols. This is complex enough. For the purposes of this introductory presentation, the even more complex situations involving signs are not here discussed in any detail.

Further complexities in the meaning–relation situation

The gradually expanding examination of the meaning–relation situation brings other factors into focus. One must consider the general context, and in particular the activities which occur in establishing or finding the meaning relations involved. Further, in cases of using sounds or inscriptions in the context of an available meaning-relation situation, in order to engage in the activity of meaning, this (the activity of meaning)[1] is part of the range of entities meant. This is also the case concerning the purpose or other causes which give rise to the establishment of the meaning relation or to the meaning activity. Specifically among the entities meant of the inscription or sound 'table' (in addition to those already listed[2]) are: the activity of selecting the sound or inscription, the activity of establishing their relation of referring to the physical object table, the activity of using this instance of entity A to refer to entity B (in the context of the meaning relation), the cause for establishing meaning relations, engaging in this meaning activity, and all the consequences of the use of the inscription or sound such as to facilitate communication, arouse interest and so on. All these are associated entities meant in the case of 'table'.

The causes, activities and results are particularly important when one comes to examine the entities meant by such inscriptions and sounds as 'stop', 'thanks', 'why' in at least some of their meaning-relation situations.

In some instances 'stop' only has as entity meant, the cessation of an activity (to which it refers). In some contexts it also has as entity meant (signifies),[3] an intention to force a person to cease an activity

---

[1] For an examination of other uses of sounds and inscriptions, that is, further extension of the range of entities meant, see following comments.

[2] See pp. 118–19.

[3] Based on a causal relation; see also pp. 116–17, 123–4.

(plus a strong emotional factor). In any case, impressive authority is part of the expanse of entities meant. More specifically, in the case of 'stop' the cessation of activity and relevant concept are not the entire range of primary entities meant. Equally primary are the causes which gave rise to the utterance of 'stop', such as the intention to force a person to cease activity, and the method of presentation. Examples of associated entities meant would be a 'flash' of anger on the part of a person obeying this so-called order term, or a physical act of retaliation.

In like fashion 'thanks' may point to only a feeling of appreciation (entity meant). But it may also signify a desire to say what is socially appropriate (entity meant), or a wish to arouse a pleasant reaction in the hearer (entity meant). Be that as it may, when these entities meant and their relevant concepts are involved in the meaning-relation situation with 'thanks', they all constitute part of its primary range or primary entities meant. Examples of associated entities meant would be admiration of one's apparent good manners produced in other guests on the occurrence of such a performance, or one's own feeling of satisfaction in doing what was socially acceptable.

In the case of 'why', the term may have as its entity meant some purpose or physical cause to which it refers. On the other hand 'why' may point to an attitude of enquiry or a desire to know (entity meant). It also signifies an answer, (an entity meant). Hence there is no referring relation to a purpose or physical cause. The inquiring attitude or the cause (or purpose) are primary entities meant. Examples of associated entities meant would be a feeling of satisfaction when a question is answered or desired physical activities occur resulting from a purpose or a physical cause.

It is, of course, the case that the inscription 'table' refers to the physical object table because of a desire on the part of human beings to carry out this activity; but the situation is not the same as in the case of 'stop', 'thanks', 'why'. The desire to refer is not a primary entity meant of the inscription 'table', while for example the intention to force a person to cease an activity is a primary entity meant of 'stop' (in some instances). The primary entity meant is what is primarily referred to or what are primarily involved as entities meant in a signifying relation or an expression-based relation.

One very important type of meaning-relation situation is that in which there is a linkage (for example) of inscriptions with other inscriptions to form groups of inscriptions. It is to be noted that inclusion in such groups of inscriptions may make a difference in the meaning (entity meant) of an individual inscription. For example, the emotions (associated entities meant) referred to by the inscription 'street' when used in isolation from others is different from the emotions linked with (and indeed expressed by): 'This is the street where J. F. Kennedy was killed.'

The same general comments made concerning the inscription 'table' apply to the concept table. In the primary meaning situation this concept has meaning because it is naturally linked with, and hence refers to, the physical object table (entity meant). In so far as the physical object is associated with emotions, images, etc., and concepts relevant to these entities, the concept table, because of its primary linkage with the physical object table, is involved in an associated relational meaning situation. Thus it has additional associated meanings, additional associated entities meant.[1]

The same state of affairs is found in the signifying type of meaning situation. Consider the case: 'yellow maple leaves signify frost'; this is a primary meaning relation situation. The feeling of exultation some people experience in autumn, the expectation of winter sports, and so on, which are linked with the fact of frost, may be associated with the yellow leaves. This would be a case of associated meaning-relation situation as far as the leaves are concerned.

It is important to realise that by a process of association, in particular, contiguity in space or time (in cases which do not involve a whole-part or part-to-part-of-whole relation), almost any entity can be associated (linked) with a specific entity. Thus the range of associated meanings, in particular entities meant, can be almost unlimited. What happens in such a case must be carefully noted. When, for example, two physical objects are merely present together in space, this does not as such constitute a meaning relation. This occurs in this situation only if a person has experienced this togetherness and then, where confronted by one, remembers the other. For example, having seen a fly on a table, when next he sees the table he thinks of the fly. Thus the table means (meaning relation) the fly. Here the table is a

---

[1] The analysis of a simple concept is usually a discussion of the meaning (three aspects) of the concept. It is the case, of course, that a complex concept, as such, can be analysed, that is, it can be pointed out that it is composed of a number of simple concepts. However, a simple concept as such does not have any parts.

sign which signifies fly (the idea of fly), which the presence of the table stimulates (causes) the mind to generate.[1]

The preceding discussion of complex meaning-relation situations has indicated that associated entities meant must be added to primary entities meant. At this point possible misunderstandings concerning meaning relations in such complex situations should be cleared up. There is the closely related problem of a possible change in status of an instance of entity A in a complex meaning-relation situation. This latter problem will be considered first. In the interests of simplification and convenience, attention will be focused almost exclusively on one case—that of the inscription 'table' and the physical object table.

In the primary meaning-relation situation, 'table' is a symbol in the referring relation to the physical object table. The relation is established by human decision (decree or stipulation). However, going beyond the primary meaning-relation situation, 'table' has acquired associated entities meant, namely[2] emotions and memory images. These, it will be recalled, are signified by the physical object table, it being a sign in this situation. The question arises: Does this change the status and meaning relation of 'table'? After all, while human decision linked 'table' with the physical object table, a human decision (decree or stipulation) did not link the physical object or the inscription with the emotions and images, and these emotions and images are among the entities meant of the inscription 'table'.

The following comments are in order. The status of the inscription is determined by its relation to its primary entity meant. Without the relation to this it would not be related to its associated entities meant. Hence the inscription 'table' is still a symbol even though some of its entities meant are not linked to it by a human decision. Likewise its meaning relation is still that of referring. In effect, associated entities meant are contributed by primary entities meant on the basis of their relations.

In summary: in cases such as the one being considered, the status and meaning relations of an inscription are settled in terms of the primary meaning-relation situation.

There is a further complication which arises because of the occurrence of another sort of complex meaning-relation situation. Because

---

[1] Resemblance is another basis for association (as well as cause effect already discussed.)

[2] Full coverage of associated entities meant will not be attempted.

of the entities meant (primary and associated) possessed by the inscription 'table', it is able to (and on occasion does) stimulate a mind to become aware of the concept table or to generate emotions or images. More specifically the situation is this: in this sort of case an inscription, because it is a symbol (and hence in a referring relation), can also function in a causal fashion, and thus be involved in a signifying meaning relation. This, however, does not turn the inscription symbol into a sign. Ultimately its signifying relation depends on a human decision, that is the original linkage of the inscription and the physical object. The physical object was the original source of stimulation which caused the mind to generate emotions and images and become aware of a relevant concept. Because the inscription is linked with this physical object it (the inscription) acquired its causal efficacy. Incidently, the decision to establish an inscription as a symbol sets up a signifying meaning relation. The symbol signifies the decision and the activities involved in implementing it.

In view of the preceding discussion of the place of symbols in a causal sequence, further comments at this point seem unnecessary. Nevertheless, one should not neglect the fact that when a person uses a symbol, in the context of a meaning situation, to refer to an entity meant, the symbol signifies on the basis of a part-whole relation (a) the meaning-relation situation[1] and (b) the meaning situation, that is, the symbol is part of the established relation of symbol and entity meant (a). When it is used in the meaning activity it is part of a more complex situation (b).

It should be obvious that in some instances of the referential, signifying or expression-based relation, the entity meant does not vary from person to person. As far as the primary meaning situation is concerned the concept table is naturally linked with the physical object table. When the linkage of the sound or inscription 'table' has been firmly established, in most instances there is no room for variation.[2] Also, yellow leaves signify frost and a groan signifies pain, whether a specific person likes it or not.

However, when we turn to the details of the associated meaning situation there is great variation from person to person. 'The Royal Crown of England' has one associated emotional meaning (entity meant) for one person. A different meaning is attached to it by

---

[1] It, of course, signifies the relation aspect as such.

[2] One can, of course, admit that there are a few difficult cases. For example, an object might be a table for a small child and a footstool for an adult.

another. The same is the case with reference to the concept crown. The same general comments apply to yellow leaves and frost.

It should be clear that there is no simple common answer to the question: What is the meaning of X? It is necessary to specify whether the meaning situation is primary or associated. Further, in the case of the associated meaning situation, frequently it is necessary to identify a specific person in a specific situation.

Returning to the analysis at the beginning of this chapter, it is obvious that the inscription 'meaning' refers to (i) a symbol or a sign, (as having meaning) (ii) entity meant, (iii) the linkages termed 'referring', 'signifying', 'expression-based' and (iv) the activity whereby a person uses available signs or symbols to point to other entities.

The meaning of complex terms

So far attention has been focused on meaning-relation situations in which single inscriptions or sounds are involved. It is obvious that groups of inscriptions and sounds also have meaning.

The meaning of compound terms, those composed of two or more single terms, is sometimes merely the meaning of the togetherness of these single terms.[1] For example, 'brown table' as entity A is the two terms together. The meaning relation is that of referring. The entity meant is composed of brown and table together (and their relevant naturally linked concepts). These comments of course deal only with the primary meaning-relation situation. Obviously there may be many other, that is associated meaning relations and a vast ring of entities meant, as in the case of single terms. These are contributed by the single terms which go to make up the complex terms.[2]

Incidently, it is possible, for example, to write meaningfully inscriptions (have entities meant) such as the following: 'round squares', 'The present King of France', 'Santa Claus', or 'knowledge of all facts'. This merely involves taking familiar concepts: round and square, present, King of France; old gentleman with white beard and red suit; knowledge of all facts, and combining them to form referents (entities meant), and then use inscriptions to refer to them. Such combinations of concepts, the product of imagination, need not be

[1] 'Term' is here used as a synonym for 'inscription' or 'sound' in a meaning-relation situation.

[2] However for the most part, in the interests of simplified presentation, associated entities meant will only be mentioned occasionally.

supported by an existing entity (that is, existing as a physical object or a mind, or their characteristics) in order that the groups of inscriptions should be meaningful. However, with the exception of 'round square', reference can be made to imagination images.

Sometimes a group of symbols or signs have an entity meant which does not involve mere togetherness and a simple one-to-one linkage of simple symbol or sign with entity meant. For example, a blizzard and a burning house (signs) together have an entity meant which is not just the sum of individual reactions to heavy snow or a blazing house.

The phrase 'the meaning of life' has, as its entities meant, the basic principles in terms of which one understands what happens and/or the value ideals or purposes which it is claimed should be decisive in guiding human life.

What has been said concerning compound terms whose relations are referential applies in like fashion to those which are involved in expression-based relations. 'Begorra, dammit' points to a combination of surprise ('Begorra') and disgust ('dammit'), and their relevant concepts. This is the primary meaning-relation situation. What arouses these reactions and the consequences of the utterance of these sounds would constitute at least part of the associated entities meant.

In dealing with sentences, a more complex group of inscriptions or sounds, many difficulties arise. A sentence such as: 'A dog sits by my chair' (a statement of fact) has referential meaning relation to the various entities to which the component inscriptions of the sentence refer. They, in their togetherness, constitute the entities meant. The pattern of togetherness of inscriptions parallels the pattern of togetherness of entities meant.

In addition, depending on individual conditions, many associated entities meant may be involved as well. For example the inscription 'dog' may signify the pleasure which it causes my mind to generate.

Consider next the meaning-relation situation in the case of: 'Stop talking' (an order). Here the inscriptions (and sounds) have a referring relation. Together they point to the togetherness of the entities individually referred to by the individual inscriptions (and sounds). However, 'Stop talking' not only refers to the cessation of talking, the sentence also signifies other entities meant, namely the intention to force the cessation of talking. Also present as an entity meant is the emotional factor which is present when an order is uttered. Thus the sentence has an expression-based meaning relation to such emotions.

All these entities pointed to are part of the range of entities meant by the sentence.

It is to be noted that no primary meaning relation other than referring, signifying or expression-based,[1] is involved in a meaning-relation situation which involves an order.

In view of the fairly detailed discussion of the meaning-relation situation of 'stop' and terms like 'talking',[2] it is unnecessary to go into further detail concerning the sentence: 'Stop talking'.

The same general comments apply to sentences like: 'Why did he stop talking?'. All the individual symbols have referential relation to specific entities meant except 'why', which points to an attitude of enquiry (or a desire to know) or refers to a purpose. It is unnecessary to repeat the preceding discussion of the various entities meant (primary and associated) by 'why' or a more detailed discussion of the meaning relations.

In brief: here again the entity meant (by the sentence) is the togetherness of the entities meant by the togetherness of the ingredients of the sentence.

Concerning 'Thank you for a pleasant evening' the same sorts of remarks apply as to the sentences containing 'why', except that here the key term points to a different mental state and the details of the exposition of causes are different. However, the same general pattern of discussion applies.

One additional comment is in order. It should be noted that the way in which inscriptions and sounds are arranged is sometimes an important matter. Specifically the entity meant may vary depending on this factor. For example, in the case of 'Shut my door' each component has a referential relation to a specific entity, but in addition this grouping of the symbols signifies an intention to influence the behaviour of others giving an order. On the other hand 'My door shut' has the same referential relation and entity meant as in the other sentence, but differs in that it signifies an intention to convey information.

III

Some reflections on the establishment of the meaning-relation situation

The magnitude of the achievement and the difficulties involved in the

---

[1] An associated meaning-relation situation is derivative from these three primary ones.

[2] Which is (can be) treated in the same fashion as 'table'.

establishment of meaning relations between inscriptions or sounds and other entities must be clearly recognised. However, the difficulties must not be allowed to obscure the fact that in some areas of experience, at least, (a) inscriptions and sounds are linked with other entities, and (b) this situation is shared with many other persons. These meaning relations are used effectively in the meaning activity. For example, 'stick', 'stone', 'water', 'vegetable', 'amimal'. 'jump', 'ouch', have a firm referential or expression-based meaning relations which are well known, widely shared, and not open to disagreement or variations in use under normal and specific conditions. However, other inscriptions and sounds have a complexity and a variety of meaning relations and hence are ambiguous. Consider, for example, 'God', 'religion', 'value', 'meaning', 'mind', 'real', 'good'.

Nevertheless, in cases such as these the situation is not hopeless. Difficulties can be overcome if their nature and origin are carefully noted. Concentrating for the moment on 'God':[1] there are different referential linkages of one sound or inscription. For example, 'God is applied to a stone and to a spirit. But there is a common characteristic of importance and influence. Qualifying terms point out differences, for example, 'primitive' view of God, 'Christian' view of God. With care, the similarities and differences may be fairly adequately indicated.

It is further important to note that one of the major difficulties involved in the referential relation of inscriptions or sounds is that one such entity may refer to several different entities which do not have a common characteristic. For example, 'chair' refers to a physical object and to the concept which is applicable to this physical object. Also 'chair' refers to the chairman of a meeting and the relevant concepts. Further, some have an even more complicated usage (linkage). 'Bore' refers to (a) a person who talks too much (and the relevant concept), (b) part of a gun (and the relevant concept), (c) a wall of water moving up a river (and the relevant concept). Possible confusion can, of course, be avoided by reference to context, or the use of qualifying inscriptions or sounds, which indicate whether 'bore' refers to a person, a gun or a wall of water.

The matter is further complicated by the fact that different inscriptions or sounds are used to refer to the same[2] entity. In some

[1] The others are discussed later.
[2] That is, an entity.

instances, it is merely a case of different referential usage in different communities. For example, what is called 'gas(oline)' in the USA is termed 'petrol' in England. Further, some entities which have the same referential function have different emotional overtones. For example, consider *filet mignon* and 'cooked dead cow'. The emotional factor obviously has an important bearing on the practical efficacy of inscriptions and sounds in influencing human behaviour. However, these complexities are not hidden from a person relying on comprehensive experience. Any initial difficulty can be overcome in such cases.

Some inscriptions and sounds are, in a sense, abbreviations. They refer to a very complex situation. Trouble arises because one person uses the term to refer to one part of a complex situation and someone else refers to another part. Thus, some people may use 'anger' to refer to publicly observable behaviour, while others restrict it to internal states of which the owner alone can be aware. Actually, the internal and external states are experienced as being frequently interrelated. Thus, 'anger' can be used to refer to both the internal and external factors.

The neglect of (*a*) the complexity in referential linkage of some inscriptions and sounds with entities meant, and (*b*) methods of avoiding misunderstanding, frequently leads to mistaken conclusions concerning important issues. For example, when one entity (sound or inscription) is linked with situations where there is one common factor and many differences, the important differences may be overlooked. Consider the following: the term 'religious' (meaning, that is referring to the entity meant, 'having an object of supreme devotion), may be applied to all men. This may appear to justify the conviction that all men believe in a personal God. As a matter of fact, while some religions involve this belief (Christianity), others do not (Confucianism). Likewise, the 'one referent, (entity meant) many inscriptions or sounds' situation may lead to unfortunate results. An occurrence in which a man is the victim of external forces may be interpretatively termed a case of either mechanism or divine providence. For all practical purposes, the situation is the same despite the use of two apparently drastically different terms which have led people to divide into warring factions under the banners of atheism and religion.

This brief sketch of some of the issues involved in dealing with the linkages (meaning relations) of sounds and inscriptions[1] with other

---

[1] The discussion has been simplified by omitting a consideration of gestures and other symbols and signs.

entities, indicates the complexity of problems in one area of the meaning situation. Yet enough has been said to indicate that in some cases the linkage of sounds and inscriptions with other entities has been established.

Specialists in psychology and language offer descriptions and explanations of how this has come about. Dictionaries, grammars, and literature record the fact that these linkages have occurred. Thus the appropriate use and usages can be recognised and also digressions from established usage[1] can be identified. We have also ample reminders of the difficulties involved in the meaning situation.

IV

The status of rules in the meaning situation

These sources of information concerning (*a*) the appropriate linkage (in meaning relations) of inscriptions and sounds with other entities in effect provide rules which apply to meaning relations. These rules serve to guide human activities in the activity of meaning. There are also rules (*b*) which have to do with groups of inscriptions or sounds which together form sentences or complex terms. These rules of course provide guidance for the use of these compounds in the meaning activity.

The help provided by rules in these matters may give rise to a misunderstanding concerning their status in the meaning situation. It is therefore (*a*) important to realise that, as a matter of fact, the meaning relation (the relation of symbol or sign to entity meant) in many instances is not established by rules. The rules merely reflect and report what gradually develop to be (become), as the result of various causes and conditions (other than the use of rules), the appropriate linkages. Further (*b*) the decisive influence in determining whether or not the linkage of inscriptions with other inscriptions has meaning, in many cases is not the application of a rule. Rather, it is the facts to which the inscriptions point (the entities meant).

More detailed comments on points (*a*) and (*b*) above are now in order.

(*a*) A study of the learning process of a child (which presumably is analogous to the childhood of the race) shows that in many cases an

---

[1] See Chapter 11, pp. 266–7.

inscription is first used very broadly, and is progressively restricted in scope as the result of gradually becoming aware of crucial differences. Thus a child applies the term 'dog' to every animal or 'dada' to every man. Many sounds are apparently generated by trial and error and used as part of a process of activity development. The linkage in the experience of a group of persons of available sounds to experienced entities is initially frequently a case of 'accidental' association in a situation, rather than in accordance with a deliberately established rule. In the case of 'dada' being linked to a child's father, this is probably an instance of using the first sound a child utters to refer to the premier member of the family! (at least in the opinion of one member of the family). When people come to feel towards a social group, such as a nation, what they feel towards their father, the nation is regarded as their father, hence patriotism (from *pater*, the Latin for father).

The decisive influence of factors other than rules in setting up the linkage of inscriptions or sounds with other entities is also illustrated in the following case. The phrase 'British nobility' in the mid-nineteenth century in England had one set of entities meant (of an emotional sort) because of social conditions in that country. On the other hand, the same phrase at the same time had a different emotional content in parts of the United States where a violent anti-British feeling was generated by disgruntled Irishmen.

On the other hand, it is also essential to note that in some meaning situations rules do have a central position. For example, when some new entity, for instance, a physical one, is discovered, it is necessary to set up a meaning-relation situation, that is, establish a new 'inscription–new entity meant' referring linkage so that, using the new inscription, the new entity may be referred to. When what is now called insulin was discovered, the inscription was established by rule to be the appropriate name for that new entity. Also, the meaning-relation situation whereby a red light means 'stop', obviously is established by a rule.

What has been pointed out concerning the relevance of rules to a meaning-relation situation involving single words (inscriptions or sounds) applies in general to groups of words, such as phrases or sentences.

(*b*) A dictionary states (provides a guiding rule) that inscriptions can be linked to form a meaningful (having meaning) compound. For example 'patriotism' can be linked with 'willing to die for one's country'. Thus: 'A patriot is willing to die for his country.' The linkage of these 'word' entities in so far as it is meaningful is ultimately dependent on the fact that the entity 'patriotism' (love of country) is characterised by willingness to die for one's country. In this case, as in many others, the dictionary rule is a report of a linkage situation. It does not create the linkage (meaning relation) of entities whereby one or more are meanings (entities meant) for others.

In some cases compounds of symbols are meaningful because of rules. For example, so-called combination pass words in secret societies, either a few, or a group in the form of a sentence, may be set up and give a referring or expression-based relation to entities meant in accordance with a pre-determined rule. It is of course possible to group inscriptions or sounds in accordance with some arbitrary rule and claim that such groups are meaningful, that is in accordance with that rule.

v

'Inscription' or 'sound'—'word'

It will have been noted that so far, in discussing (reporting) the meaning-relation situation, the terms 'inscription' or 'sound' have been employed rather than the term 'word'. This has been done because the term 'word' is ambiguous. (*a*) It is widely used as a synonym for 'inscription' or 'sound'. In this sense a discussion of the meaning of a word is a discussion of the meaning situation involving a sound or inscription. However, it is essential to realise (*b*) that one customary usage of the term 'word' reflects the fact that an inscription or sound, which functions as a symbol in a meaning-relation situation, has an established relation of signifying, or referring or expression-based to some other entity. Specifically, in such meaning-relation situations the inscription or sound acquires a distinctive status and function. This is what is referred to by the term 'word'.

The state of affairs is analogous to that in which a piece of metal is termed a 'coin' if it has status as (characteristics of) a medium of exchange. When using the term 'word' in the second, *b* sense, to be strictly technically accurate, one should not talk about the meaning of a word. It is rather a case of a physical or mental entity (a sound or an inscription), a word in the first, *a* sense, being in a meaning relation, and hence is a case of function as a word.

A further point requires clarification. The inscription 'table' and the sound 'table' are, in English, said to be the same word, either written or spoken. To be strictly accurate, it is an instance of two different entities having the same denotative function, and the same entity meant. Thus two entities have the same specific word function. In this sense they are the same word.

The term 'sentence' is also ambiguous in the same fashion as the term 'word'. 'Sentence' may refer to a grouping of inscriptions or sounds (words in sense *a*), or to a grouping of inscriptions and sounds, each of which has a place in a meaning-relations situation, and hence functions as a word in sense *b*.

VI

The activity of meaning and other activities

At this point it is appropriate to discuss some very important issues which arise concerning the phase of the meaning situation which in this study has been termed 'the activity of meaning'.

As has been noted, when a person has available signs and symbols in a meaning relation to entities meant, (words in sense *b*) he is equipped with an instrument he can use in the activity of meaning. For example, he can use the inscription 'table' to refer to the physical object table. It is to be realised that a person can engage in the activity of meaning (referring) even though the entity meant is not present to awareness, though of course in many instances it is present before one. In like fashion a person can use the symbol 'ouch' or the sign shudder to point to an occurrence of pain (ouch) or fear (shudder). This is the case even though pain or fear are not actually present, though in most cases of the use of such symbols and signs the mental states are present.[1]

A difficulty arises in connection with the use of such symbols and signs as 'ouch' and 'shudder'. The point is this. Both the sound and the gesture are used also to express feelings and emotions. The following questions arises. In cases when, for example, pain and fear are present in a person's experience and he says 'ouch' and shudders—is he expressing them or pointing to them (activity of meaning) or both?

[1] In the interests of simplicity of presentation, attention has been focused on the primary meaning situation.

Can he engage in one activity without performing the other? The answers to these related questions are as follows. A person can point to a feeling or emotion without expressing them. For example he can say 'ouch' merely to point to the fact that he is experiencing pain, and he can shudder merely to point to the fact that he is experiencing fear. There are people who keep their emotions and feelings under control, and do not give expression to them, but are prepared to indicate that they have them. In cases of violent pain or fear, the use of 'ouch' and shudder is primarily expressive. A person is not (or at best is only slightly) concerned to point to (engage in) a meaning activity. In some cases both the meaning activity and the expressive activity may be of equal status. It is to be noted that in the case of the meaning activity, in distinction from an expressive activity, a person uses a symbol or a sign to point to an entity meant because of some purpose. This purpose may be in clear focus in some cases. In other instances it is not. Expressive activities are predominantly immediate reactions to stimulation, though in some instances there may be an element of deliberation or even purpose involved in determining whether or not there will be an activity of expression and, if so, what form it will take. In any case there is a fundamental difference between these two sorts of activities: 'pointing to' is different from 'giving vent to' or expression.

It is more than obvious that there is more involved in either the activity of meaning or the activity of expressing than the mere presence of symbols or signs. Both of these activities are very complex indeed. In this discussion the main concern is with the use of symbols and signs. Only the necessary minimum of attention is paid to the other ingredients in these activities in order to make obvious distinctions.[1]

This discussion of the activity of meaning and its distinction from another activity, that of expressing feelings, emotions (and attitudes), brings into focus the fact that it is necessary to deal with further complications of this type.

The situation is this: Symbols and signs are used not only in the activities of meaning and expressing, but in many other activities as

[1] Although many persons share a meaning-relation situation and engage in roughly the same activity of meaning a person can of course engage in a meaning activity when completely alone.

well. A number of additional important issues will now be dealt with, in terms of the preceding discussion. In the interests of simplified and convenient treatment, attention will be focused on one sort of symbol, namely words (in sense *b*). Signs will be considered only by implication. In many cases what is pointed out about words applies also to signs.

These additional uses of words occur most obviously and commonly in a social context, though they are not restricted to such a situation. Specifically, when a group of persons share a sufficiently large number of words singly or in groups (in the second, *b* sense of the term), they have at their disposal instruments which can be used in the following activities: providing information[1] (reporting, describing), giving orders, offering suggestions, asking questions, making ceremonial utterances. In many instances these activities influence the behaviour of other people, in the sense not only of arousing new overt actions but also bringing about changes in feelings, emotions, attitudes and ideas. The achievement of such results is of course the main reason for (purpose of) providing information, giving orders, and so on (through the other items on the list just given). It is to be noted that in some cases words are used in an attempt to arouse feelings, emotions, attitudes and actions directly, not through the medium of providing information, giving orders and so on.[2]

As pointed out above, a person when alone can use words in the same fashion as they are used in social interaction. Here also the same results can be produced. For example a man may give orders to himself and they are carried out, he may question himself and be stimulated to produce answers. He may even make ceremonial utterances about himself and his behaviour changes as a result, and so on.

It is important to realise that the practical efficacy of language in

---

[1] The term 'referring' may be and is frequently used in this discussion, as a synonym for 'providing information'. Specifically, when a person is using words to talk about an entity, he is referring to it. In talking about it, he is (or at least may be) reporting or describing, providing information. It may be objected that the term 'expressing' should be as a synonym for informing (reporting, describing). After all, is it not an accepted locution to claim that a person 'expresses his views concerning' something? However, the term 'express' is here used in an admittedly restricted sense, concerning the venting of feelings, emotions and attitudes, in order to avoid confusing this activity with that of reporting, etc.

[2] For example, calling a person a pig. (In some cases this is a ceremonial utterance.)

influencing human behaviour does not depend on the accuracy of its report of fact. To label a man a Communist, even if he actually is not, will have important practical positive or negative effects in almost any community. In like fashion ceremonial utterances as such are not required to be statements of fact. The 'Thank you for a pleasant evening' utterance is socially appropriate and may produce desirable results, but in neither case need it be true.

It should be obvious from previous discussion that a word or a sentence may have several uses. Further, the obvious use may not be the actual intended use. Consider the following examples. A person may correctly be said to be a Communist, but the main purpose may be to express dislike or arouse a strong emotional reaction. The use of individual words or groups of words to express emotions is worthy of careful note in these regards. 'Damnation!' or 'I am going to blow up' do not necessarily have a factual reference (informative use), though of course they may. When one says, 'I hate you', there may be both informative use and an expression of emotion. Indeed, it may be ceremonial and also influence behaviour by producing a strong reaction.

VII

Comments on reputed difficulties involved in activities of using words (discussed above)

It was noted in the case of sounds and inscriptions that apparent difficulties in (*a*) the matter of linkage with other entities and (*b*) sharing such a situation with other people, were not insuperable in many instances. In like fashion, it is obvious to comprehensive experience that overwhelming difficulties do not arise, in all instances, in the use of words to convey information, give orders, etc., influence behaviour, or to express emotions, feelings and attitudes. Thus under normal conditions, when I ask for (order) five apples in a store, a clerk gives them to me. When I warn a friend about an approaching car, he jumps out of the way. When I tell some people 'I am in pain', or snarl 'You are a dirty rat', they understand me and react accordingly. In more complex situations, such as trying to advise a young person concerning his future, and in so doing referring to ideals, or in working in the border lands of theoretical science, words are not similarly effective, unless in exceptional cases.

In the actual activity of providing information, giving orders, offering suggestions, asking questions, making ceremonial utterances—when using words—the entities most commonly present in the experience of the persons involved in these forms of social interaction (or within the experience of a person when alone) are concepts or groups of concepts such as propositions. This is so because the physical or mental entities to which the words refer, or which they signify, frequently are not present. Yet the words function in the context of these activities because they are able to provide, almost immediately, the presence of a crucial segment of the range of entities meant. In brief, informing, ordering, etc., do not occur unless the words employed are understood. Otherwise one is dealing with mere unrelated sounds and inscriptions.

It may be claimed that a person can provide information, give orders etc. and no one understands the words but himself, that is no one (else) receives information or an order. However, even in this situation, in the experience of the person who is informing or ordering, it is not the case that he is merely using inscriptions or sounds in complete isolation from meaning relations to entities meant. Here the most relevant common concepts will be present. In most instances there will be mental entities and perhaps some physical entities meant. In some exceptional cases (the vivid presence of some mental and physical entities) the function of concepts may be negligible or not present.

As in the case of the activities of meaning and expressing, there is much more to the activities of informing, ordering, etc. than the mere utterance (or writing) of words. These are very complex processes.'[1]

At this point these additional factors are not at issue, the concern is with the place of words in the activities under consideration. Further, it is not proposed here, or elsewhere in this book, to attempt to discuss the psychology of how the giving of information, orders, etc. produces change in the ideas, feelings, emotions, attitudes and overt behaviour of people. This is a topic best left to experts in this field.

[1] There may be, for example, such factors as gesture, tone, of voice and a wide range of other physical, mental and conceptual factors.

VIII

Some confusions concerning meaning and use

It is advisable to clear up possible misunderstandings concerning meaning and use.

(*a*) When a person uses sounds or inscriptions in the activity of providing information, giving orders, offering suggestions, asking questions, making ceremonial utterances, he is of course also involved in the activity of meaning.

As has just been emphasised, in the course of these activities, he is pointing to (activity of meaning) a number of entities meant (on the basis of available meaning-relation situations). However—and this is crucial—although the meaning activity is involved in the activities of informing, ordering, etc., the activity of meaning cannot be identified with these other activities. When a person simply (merely) uses a symbol to refer (point) to an entity meant, this is not equivalent to giving orders, asking questions, etc. It is the case that a meaning activity may be a source of information, but not necessarily so. In any case, the activity of providing information by using words involves the element of purpose. A person can engage in the activity of meaning without proposing to provide information.[1] In brief, the activity of meaning is involved in the activities of informing, ordering, etc., in the sense that one engages in the activity of meaning in the course of doing more than that, that is, ultimately doing something else.

(*b*) The next phase of the discussion of the 'meaning-use' topic has to do with the meaning situation itself. It will be recalled that there are four distinguishable aspects of this situation: (i) signs and symbols (which have meaning), (ii) entities meant, (iii) the 'pointing to' relations termed 'referring', 'signifying', 'expression-based', (iv) the human activity of using symbols or signs in the context of the meaning relations to point to entities meant. It has been noted that there are several senses of the term 'use'. (i) An entity is used when it is an ingredient (part of a situation), (ii) activity of using, (iii) It has a use, that is purpose to be fulfilled or goal to be reached.

Concentrating on what in this book has been termed the 'meaning-relation situation' (the first three aspects of the meaning situation)—it is clear that symbols (which have meaning), meaning relations and

---

[1] Another person can derive information by observing a man who does not propose to provide information.

entities meant are all used, hence are ingredients in, a meaning-relation situation. That is to say, such a situation can be analysed in terms of the ingredients which compose it.

The question then arises: Do the entities which have the status (i) sign or symbol, (ii) meaning relation, (iii) entity meant, have that status because of their use, that is, their place as ingredients in a meaning-relation situation? The answer, in all cases, is yes. In this sense and in these cases, meaning is based on use. For example 'table' has meaning because this inscription or sound is an ingredient in a meaning-relation situation. Likewise the entity which is the relation referring is a meaning relation because it is part of a meaning-relation situation. Similarly the physical object table is an entity meant because of its use, its place as an ingredient in a meaning-relation situation.

However, it must be emphasised, as above, that meaning is based on use in a meaning-relation situation. It is not just a case of use alone, i.e. being an ingredient in simply any situation.

It should be obvious that meaning, in the first three senses of the term, cannot be identified with the activity of using. Any one of these (i) a sign or symbol, (ii) a meaning relation, (iii) an entity meant, does not have its meaning status because it is an activity—let alone an activity of using.

Let us turn now to the activity-of-meaning phase of the meaning situation. It is essential to realise that a person can use (activity of using) sounds and inscriptions in the activity of meaning only if these sounds and inscriptions already have meaning, that is are linked in a meaning relation with entities meant. Hence the activity of using, as such, does not constitute the meaning of a sound or inscription (make it have meaning). The same comment applies to the use of a relation. Entities meant are not 'used' in the sense of the term here considered.

The next question to face is this. Granted that in the activity of meaning[1] one uses, for example, sounds and inscriptions which are

---

[1] As already noted, in most general terms the activity of meaning is an activity of pointing to. In most general terms the meaning relation is that of pointing to. Some possible confusion may arise, because of the use of the term 'pointing'. This situation is thus: The activity of meaning is an activity of 'pointing to' in which a person uses an entity in the course of pointing to (a complex activity which is mental and may also be physical) another entity. On the other hand, the relation 'pointing to', as such, is not an activity, though it may have resulted from one (human or otherwise). Yellow leaves point to frost. 'Table' points to a table in the sense that there is an agreed linkage as a fact available for use among members of a specific social group.

in meaning relations to entities meant—is the activity of using these signs and symbols identical with the activity of meaning? The answer is yes. The activity of using (in these cases) is identical with the activity of meaning. A person takes, for example, an available symbol, 'table', and uses it to refer to a physical object table. It is to be stressed that the activity of meaning is not to be identified simply with any kind of using of sounds or inscriptions. It is a using of them in the context of an already available meaning-relation situation. Thus using, as such, is not to be identified with meaning.

In short, when a person engages in the activity of using a sign or symbol, he is thereby engaging in the activity of meaning.

At this point a brief comment on the third sense of 'use' (namely, purpose to be fulfilled or goal to be reached), is in order. When a person uses an entity which is a sign or symbol, he in most instances proposes to point to an entity meant.

The preceding discussion has, as noted, been based on the report that the term 'meaning' has four major senses, that it applies to (i) entities which have meaning because they are (ii) pointing to (are in meaning relation with), (iii) entities meant and (iv) the human activity of using symbols or signs (since they have meaning) to point to entities meant. If a person wishes to restrict the application of the term 'meaning', contrary to customary use, he will of course neglect some of the entities discussed here. But in the last analysis, the fundamental topic is not a matter of how terms such as 'meaning' are applied, but what is involved in a situation where one entity points to another, and use is made of this fact by human beings.

IX

The status of words and their function

An adult who has only restricted experience, or a child, or a savage, or a person who is mentally ill, proceeds on occasion as though merely by using words (in either the first *a* or the second *b* sense), one can change a situation in accordance with his wishes. Specifically, by employing words a person assumes he can (i) bring something into existence or (ii) transform something into something else or (iii) remove something from existence. Illustrations of these manoeuvres (word magic) are not hard to find. A politician may delude himself, or others, into believing that he is wise or good merely by repeating the claim that this is so, even if the facts are otherwise. Likewise what, as a matter of fact, is narrow selfishness may be labelled and regarded by the speaker as firm devotion to lofty moral principles. Consider the case of a man who says, in all instances, 'Everyone should look after himself; I refuse to pamper the incompetent unemployed.' Also, a man may deny that a specific woman is a good driver because of his reaffirmation of the statement, 'No woman is a good driver.'

Such persons tend on occasion to concentrate so much attention on the manipulation of words that they are distracted from a serious consideration of other entities, in particular (*a*) the entities to which the words presumably refer, or (*b*) pressing practical problems. Words assume for them the status of an almost autonomous realm governed by rules which are beyond question. For example, a person may strive so hard to achieve literary or grammatical excellence, or some approved method of expression, that what he says has little factual reference, emotional expressiveness or practical efficacy (as the case may be). Consider the purely verbal elegance of many public orators when evaluated by persons who rely on comprehensive experience. A politician or a theologian may become so immersed in the language of his trade and the accepted phraseology of his party or church that he is indifferent to relevant facts. For instance, a person may assert, 'All men are free and equal' or 'Evil is an illusion' and neglect (in all senses of the term) important facts of comprehensive experience. Having let words blind him to facts, a person is in no mood to engage in activities designed to remove human misery or provide opportunities for those who are under-privileged. In brief, it is sometimes assumed, by devotees of words, that talk about talking is an activity of supreme importance.

A different result of word worship is the assumption that what one says about other entities, in some approved fashion, is an accurate report of what these entities are. Thus a man intoxicated by his own verbosity may indeed claim that 'What I say is so because (according to the rules I accept) I have expressed myself properly.' The fanatical addiction to the accepted formulae of any discipline, be it science, politics, education, or religion, as final authority in every field of experience, is an obvious fact in the case of many men. Consider, for example, a person devoted to a 'language' which tolerates as respectable only reference to what is public and verifiable in terms of distinct sense experience (what is clearly seen, heard, touched, etc.). He is quite satisfied that such language provides a completely adequate statement of all facts, even though comprehensive experience reports otherwise. Similarly, many politicians and educators see no reason to doubt the accuracy of the basic statements of their systems because these statements are so obviously appropriate.

Experiential Realism agrees that it is, of course, the case that words, when used with discretion, are a valuable record of what exists (and subsists) or what has taken place. The statements, 'The Romans built a coliseum in their capital city', and 'Rome is located in Italy', are examples of the use of words which are not open to the preceding objections. Equally accurate statements can be made by a person, who relies on comprehensive experience, about some of his own internal states and some aspects of the behaviour of others, for example, 'I feel pain', or 'Mr X is behaving like a fool'.[1] Statements about concepts and their relations may, in some cases, also be free of objection. For instance: 'The concept table is linked with the concept furniture in the experience of twentieth-century North Americans.'

However, many entities cannot now be reported or described adequately in words. Also, in some instances, words are inadequate in influencing human actions or expressing emotions. The experience of a beautiful sunset, the ugliness of a slum area, the consequences of the invention of the atomic bomb, all elude satisfactory complete verbal statement. Even the most efficient politician or wizard of Madison Avenue may fall short in influencing human behaviour despite his impressive vocabulary and verbal skill.

Nevertheless, we must use these admittedly sometimes imperfect instruments to the best of our ability and to the limits which they permit. A partial supplement is provided by the fact that words can be used to suggest what cannot be clearly stated.

It is extremely important to realise that words and forms of statement or argument may set up thought habits which issue in erroneous views of various types of entities and their characteristics. In general, it is frequently (fallaciously) assumed that, whenever a person uses a word meaningfully, it must refer to a non-imaginary existing entity (or one which has existed or will exist). Thus it is assumed there must be bad luck, since we use the phrase. Strengthening this assumption is the fact that the sentence, 'Bad luck should be avoided'

---

[1] See later discussion, Chapter 12, pp. 284-7.

has the same grammatical structure as 'Flu should be avoided'. The careful noting of the distinction between imaginary and non-imaginary is of great value in this situation. Equally important is the point already noted that one can think about, or with, concepts without having to refer also to physical or mental entities. For example, one can be aware of a round square or of bad luck (as a complex concept) without trying to see, in the imaginary or non-imaginary world, any 'concrete' particular entity. In addition, as has been pointed out, many words are used on occasion not to describe or report but to influence behaviour (by giving orders, etc.) or express emotions. Thus, in the case of 'go to blazes', the word 'blazes' need not be regarded as referring to any imaginary or non-imaginary actual conflagration.

It is important to realise that mathematical and logical symbols are open to the same general sorts of comments which have been made concerning words. The addition to statistical forms of expression is a case in point. The number of adherents claimed by a church, the number of days a student attends school, may, in some cases, be somewhat misleading concerning the health of the church or the status of the student. Specifically, such statements are not the whole story, nor are these the only respectable form of report. On the other hand, when properly interpreted, statistical forms of expression convey very useful information, for example, the incidence of polio in cases of the use of the Salk vaccine and its absence.

It is appropriate to recognise that the word 'average', in referring to a group of persons, is not, mistakenly, designed to refer to an existing particular person, who in some cases of a specified average cannot be found. Rather, it is a way of presenting a convenient general idea about a group. For example, the average mark for a set of results of an examination may not be obtained by any student. However, the phrase 'average mark' refers to a concept which provides a general picture of the situation.

The techniques of symbolic logic are a valuable tool in laying bare (describing) the structure of an argument, or proposition, and indicating whether or not it is logically sound. However, the excessive emphasis on the techniques of symbolic logic in some cases unnecessarily complicates life. A long complex proof or solution is indulged in, so as to reach a conclusion concerning a situation which may be simply obtained as the result of experience (awareness of the entities to which the statement refers). To use a very simple example, one can accept the truth of 'Socrates is mortal', without dealing with the machinery of the structure and rules of validity of the relevant categorical syllogism, 'All men are mortal', 'Socrates is a man', therefore 'Socrates is mortal'. The same general comment applies to some other logical techniques.

Further, some devotees of symbolic logic, especially those who set up arbitrary definitions and rules, indulge in intellectual games which take them far from practical problems and facts. Even when the definitions and rules are based on the facts of comprehensive experience, addiction to abstract symbols and their manipulation leads frequently to an excessively one-sided view of the world, in extreme cases a form of other-worldliness.[1]

[1] This is not to be interpreted as a criticism of creative imagination. See Chapter 2, pp. 73–4.

6

KNOWING AND KNOWLEDGE

I

The use of the terms 'Knowing' and 'Knowledge', and qualifying terms
The term (inscription or sound) 'knowledge' is ordinarily used to refer to various types of complex situations in which a person is acquainted with, has personal experience of, is aware of, understands, perceives, cognises, or is versed in or skilled in things, states or processes. Thus 'knowledge', in this broad usage, refers to a situation involving (*a*) an activity, knowing, and (*b*) something which is known. Both aspects of knowledge involve freedom from error or deception. In a narrow sense 'knowledge' is frequently used to refer to what is known, a range of information, a body of known facts or skills.

Let us then study this complex situation, examining the activities termed 'knowing' and its 'objects', what is known. In the interests of clarity, in subsequent discussion, the term 'knowledge' will be used in the narrow sense, namely 'what is known'.

It is to be emphasised that the subsequent discussion is not primarily concerned with the terms 'knowing' or 'knowledge'. Rather it is deemed important to examine the entities to which these terms customarily refer, as indicated. In short, these terms are employed in the course of an attempt to obtain an accurate grasp of one phase of human experience.

Four sorts of Knowing and Knowledge
It is necessary to introduce qualifying terms for 'knowing' and 'knowledge'. These classifications are employed so that factual distinctions may be brought into focus.

Immediate knowledge and knowing
The phrase 'immediate knowing' ('knows immediately') reports the fact that some of what is known is immediately present in awareness.

When a person is aware of an entity, this occurrence will be termed a case of 'immediate minimum knowing'. The entity of which one is aware will then be designated 'immediate minimum knowledge'. There is also a more complex situation. Here a person is not only aware of an entity but is also aware of a linked[1] concept and is aware of the appropriateness[2] of its linkage with the entity in question. This will be termed 'immediate identifying knowing'. It is a complex of acts of awareness which is a recognising of the entity, that is of finding out what it is. The linkage of the entity with its appropriate concept in such a situation will be termed a case of 'immediate identified knowledge'. The mere fact of an entity being linked with an appropriate concept is not a case of immediate identified knowledge. This only becomes such when there is awareness of this complex situation and also awareness of the appropriateness of the linkage. The awareness only of the linkage is not immediate identifying knowing. A person being aware of the linkage and not of its appropriateness would be aware of a linkage which may or may not be appropriate.

The term 'immediate' is applied to these types of knowing and knowledge because the awareness occurs and as such is direct. The entities involved are hence present. They are not assumed or postulated. Some examples and further comments are now in order.

One is aware[3] of, that is knows immediately in a minimum fashion, all three types of basic entities, physical, mental, and concepts, also resultants—and their characteristics. On occasion a person is aware of these entities without being also aware of any identifying concepts—the process of recognising does not occur. This type of experience is frequent among animals and very young human children. In adult experience there usually is at least some degree of recognition. For example an unknown entity is recognised as an entity and strange.

It may seem peculiar to term an entity, such as a physical object, of which one is aware, a case of knowledge. But after all, this is what is present to awareness. This is what one is knowing.

[1] The terms 'linked' and 'linkage' as used in this discussion do not have a present tense verb sense. They refer to a relation which has been found or has been established (by human activity) between a concept and an entity.

[2] The experienced linkage of a concept and an entity is termed 'appropriate' if the linkage (relation) is in accordance with its natural or agreed linkage and hence not the result of unsupported (unjustified) imaginative activity. The term 'accurate' could be here used as a synonym for 'appropriate'.

[3] See the previous discussion of awareness and in particular the contention that awareness as such is not erroneous. Chapter 2, pp. 65–70.

A person is able to recognise, on occasion, many entities, basic, resultants and their characteristics, of which he is aware. That is, he is able to be aware of concepts and that they are appropriately (correctly) linked to the entity in question. It is, of course, the case that many different concepts are appropriately linked with an entity. As long as one of these, and also the appropriateness, is present in awareness, knowing of the immediate identifying type has occurred, and the entity and its appropriately linked concept constitute a case of knowledge of the immediate identified sort. The larger the number of appropriate concepts present, the wider is the range of knowledge. For example,[1] a person who is aware of a piece of wood and is also aware of the appropriateness of linkage of the concept wood with the physical object, has immediate identified knowledge of restricted range. If in addition he is aware of the appropriateness of the linkages of concepts such as large, expensive, mahogany, his range of knowledge is extended.

It is important to realise that both types[2] of immediate knowledge, minimum and identified, can be recorded in propositions, in some instances. The accuracy of a proposition can be checked against the knowledge it purports to report. One can be aware of whether or not it is an accurate report. One can have immediate identified or minimum knowledge of the accuracy characteristic of some propositions. In other words, one may be merely aware of the accuracy of the report (hence, immediate minimum knowledge), or in addition be aware of the appropriateness of the linkage of the concept accuracy with the characteristic accuracy (immediate identified knowledge).

In considering immediate knowledge (of either type) it is to be noted that most of the involved physical, mental and concept entities, and their characteristics, present in[3] awareness are experienced as familiar. The terms 'know' and 'knowledge' are sometimes used to apply to this situation. However, on occasion, new (unfamiliar) physical entities are present in awareness and new mental entities as well. The same is the case with concepts and their linkage. Some of these are recognised at once.

It is essential to realise that the distinction just reported, between the two types of immediate knowing and knowledge, may appear unjustified or at least confusing. Nevertheless there need not be, and

---

[1] To use a compressed form of exposition.
[2] The term is used non-technically.
[3] That is, a person is aware of.

in many cases there is not, awareness of the linkage of appropriate concepts with entities of which one is aware. Incidentally, while one is aware of one's own awareness, this does not necessarily include awareness of a linkage with identifying concepts. We can perform many activities and be aware of entities without being aware of appropriate identifying concepts. Yet, as a matter of fact, most entities are experienced as linked with varying amounts of conceptual environment. In any case, if the need arises for identifying these entities, one can become aware of the concepts with which the entities are appropriately (naturally) linked, and be aware of that fact. When one formulates propositions about these entities, concepts linked with them are, of course, present in awareness.

In the interests of simplified presentation, references to immediate knowing and immediate knowledge will not always be couched in terms of the distinction between 'minimum' and 'identifying' (or 'identified'). In some cases it is appropriate to note this distinction.

Knowledge about

When one is aware of an accurate report proposition as the result of remembering[1] and knows (is knowing immediately) by remembering the accuracy of its report concerning other entities, which as such are not present, this is a case of knowing about these other entities. Since the entities to which the accurate proposition refers are not actually present now in awareness, therefore one is not knowing them in the sense of immediate knowing. One is only immediately knowing (being aware of) the proposition and its accuracy. But in so far as the proposition is an accurate report, it provides accurate information about the absent entities. Thus, one has 'knowledge about' them.

Strictly speaking, the term 'knowledge about' refers to a proposition, now present to awareness, which is an accurate report concerning entities which are not now present to awareness for the person who is aware of the proposition in question, and aware of its accuracy.

Propositions are not the only entities involved in cases of 'knowledge about'. A memory image, for example, which accurately conveys information about absent entities can be an item of 'knowledge about'. However, the image as such, when dealt with as merely present in awareness, is an item of immediate knowledge.

In passing, it is to be noted that there are alternate synonyms for 'immediate knowing and knowledge' on the one hand, and for

[1] See subsequent discussion, in particular the reliability of memory.

'knowing and knowledge about' on the other. The terms 'by acquaintance' and 'by description' are employed. Likewise, one can refer to immediate 'knowing and knowledge' in contrast to 'knowing that and knowledge that'. However, from the point of view of Experiential Realism, the terms it employs are in most cases less ambiguous than the alternatives mentioned. For example, 'acquaintance' in its ordinary usage can apply both to direct awareness or to indirect report.

Propositions which are cases of 'knowledge about' are derived not only from one's own experience, and made available through the medium of remembering, but also are obtained from other persons by a process of communication.

In this context, the question arises: Why should Mr A accept as 'knowledge about' (that is, information, propositions regarded as accurate reports), what Mr B offers, in cases where Mr A has not been aware of these entities? For example, why should Mr A, who has never left North America, include in his 'knowledge about', the proposition: 'There is a Great Wall in China', because Mr B reports having seen and touched it? The reply is this. Information (knowledge about) is accepted by A from B, if A is convinced of the reliability of B as a source of accurate reports. Whether or not B is trustworthy in reporting can be checked by A, in cases where they are both experiencing the same entity and can compare reports.

It should be obvious that the entities so far discussed, which have the characteristic 'knowledge', have this characteristic only in so far as they are present to awareness, that is knowing. These entities as such in isolation are not cases of knowledge.

Knowledge of how

The terms 'knowing' and 'knowledge' refer not only to the situations discussed above, but also are used with reference to the fact that a person is performing, or is capable of performing, mental and physical skills other than that of being aware. Thus one speaks of 'knowing how' or 'knowledge of how' to perform a skill. A skill in this sense is an activity which a person has learned to perform. In this context the terms 'knowing how' and 'knowledge of how' are used as synonyms. It is not a case of one ('knowing how') referring to an activity and the other ('knowledge of how') referring to an entity on which, or towards which, the activity is focused. In this situation the term (phrase) 'knows how' is most conveniently used. Thus, to repeat, a person knows how when he (*a*) is performing an activity which he has learned or (*b*) is able to perform it but is not at the moment doing so. These two situations are, of course, very different.

The first type of 'knows how' situation, the case when a person is now performing an activity which he has learned, involves awareness of (immediate knowing) entities (immediate knowledge) which are being dealt with in the course of the activity in question. For example, in driving a car one is aware of the road, the traffic, and some of the mechanical components of the car. At an early stage in driving, one is also aware of various guiding propositions (knowledge about) which tell one what to do. Later, these lapse into unconscious habits. However, these items of knowledge and the activities of knowing (immediate and knowing about) are not identified with the skill 'driving'. They are only entities involved, in various ways, in the occurrence of this skill—driving a car. Merely to be aware of the rules of driving does not constitute the processes of the activity of driving.

Knowledge 'in storage'

In the case of the other *b* 'knows how' situation, namely, when one is able to perform a learned activity (skill) but is actually not doing so, there is no awareness of entities of any sort. It is a case of 'knowledge in storage'.[1] The physiological or other basis of either type of 'knows how', that is the actual performance of a skill or the ability to perform it, need not be discussed here. This is a subject appropriately left to physiologists and psychologists.

It is important to note that type *b* of 'skill knowledge', is not the only case of 'knowledge in storage'.

If a person is capable of restoring to present awareness, cases, or similarities, of past immediate knowledge, or past knowledge about, he can be seen still to have knowledge, knowledge 'in storage' of those entities and the activities involved. The somewhat barbarous phrase 'knowledge in storage' records the fact that, in some cases, when one claims that he knows or has knowledge, the entities thus referred to as a matter of fact are not present in awareness, nor are they occurring. But such knowledge in storage can be restored to presence in awareness or actual functioning. Written and other records constitute another type of knowledge in storage—providing what is recorded can be brought to present awareness.

[1] This is a less barbarous phrase than 'know how or knows how in storage'.

Supplementary comments

Within the context of the preceding discussion it is well to distinguish particular from general knowledge. Particular knowledge is concerned with an individual (particular) entity ('I have a brown desk in my office'). General information concerns all members of a class ('All men are moral'). In most cases, general information is chiefly 'knowledge about' based on (derived from) awareness of only some members of a group. The other members of the group (class) in many instances are not present to a particular person's awareness or to a group of persons. Yet as members of the group (though not present to awareness) they have the same characteristics. If they do not, they are not members. In so far as particulars are unique,[1] there are cases where no transition from particular to general knowledge is possible, for instance, the distinctive traits of the man Plato or the skill of the best diamond cutter in the world in 1970.

In cases where 'knowledge of how' (knows how) is involved, here again, the distinction between particular and general can be noted and the same comments made. A person has knowledge of how to drive one car. He can with care proceed to a knowledge of how to drive all cars of that class, for example with automatic transmission. The crucial problem concerning general knowledge is to be sure that we are dealing with members of a genuine class; or that the diversities within the class are not such as to make impossible the transition from some particulars to all, in the case of some characteristics. For example, if the class is transportation vehicles, knowledge of how to drive a car will not help with reference to a plane.

Obviously, any one type of knowing and knowledge cannot be reduced to or replaced by another, despite the fact that they are not completely mutually exclusive (for instance the 'immediate' types are involved as the basis of the 'about' types and some cases of the 'know how' types).

It is important to note that immediate knowing and knowledge, also knowing about and knowledge about, frequently constitute useful tools for solving problems. However, they do not necessarily involve present or future practical use, that is doing something. Some types of immediate knowledge and knowledge about, are acquired in order to satisfy a desire to know. Consider, for example, an interest in the religious ceremonies of the Aztecs. This information (knowledge

---

[1] See Chapter 7, pp. 191–96.

about) may serve to help one avoid their type of worship. On the other hand, it may have no specific practical use, as far as one can determine. In other words, one does not proceed to apply this knowledge by sacrificing human beings. Or, to take a more plausible example, the 'knowledge about' that a middle-aged man has of the present standing in the football league (or the final standing for a specific year) is a case of satisfying interest, not a guide to future specific action or even a providing 'grist for the conversation mill'.

There is no evidence to justify the claim that a person has complete immediate knowledge or knowledge about all the data concerning a particular entity, even with the assistance of memory and drawing on information provided by all available sources, such as other persons and books. For example, one cannot know all about the heredity and environment of an individual human being or trace a particular table back along a line of causal factors and their environment to the primeval nebuli and beyond. Some of the characteristics, such as relational ones, of even a relatively simple entity such as the concept blue likewise elude us.

II

The context of immediate knowing and knowledge

The activity of awareness (immediate knowing) of physical objects, involves the use of sense organs, the nervous system, the brain and other parts of a person's body.[1] In addition, external instruments and the experimental manipulation of the environment are necessary for the awareness of some entities and their characteristics. The awareness of one's mind and of concepts (and of the characteristics of concepts) does not require specific sense organs. In a few cases, such as kinaesthetic sensations, and pain, sense organs are involved in the production of mental entities. There is no awareness of organs of inner sense for mental activities, concepts, or for so-called aesthetic, religious or moral entities. However, one is aware of one's own mind, concepts, mental activities, images, emotions and also of value characteristics of all three types of entities, under appropriate conditions.

[1] It is here contended that, though in a sense the nervous system is between the brain and an external physical object, nevertheless under normal conditions it facilitates the presence to awareness of the physical object and hence does not render such awareness impossible.

Scientific procedures used in obtaining knowledge of all types are limited (introspective psychology is a possible exception if it is admitted to be a science) to specific entities open to public awareness by the so-called external senses after controlled experiments and employing theoretical constructions based on these data. An attempt is made to state the results in exact mathematical terms. Thus interpreted, science cannot deal with some entities, namely, those which are private, not open to the awareness of more than one person and/or entities not apprehended by sense awareness, or implied by it, or appropriately subject to mathematical notation. For example, moral, aesthetic and religious entities are 'outsiders'. However, the scientific attitude of tentative and cooperative search is applicable in our approach to all entities; also the scientific devotion to the value truth.

There are, of course, less rigorous approaches than that of natural science. For example: it may be admitted that one person may undertake verification and pay attention to (his own) private data. However, it is assumed that in all cases verification by many persons is superior to verification by one person, or that public data take precedence over private data in the knowing situation.

The following comment is relevant: in either instance it is basically a case of awareness of entities. Some entities a person shares with others, some he does not. The much vaunted check-up by others is not decisive in all instances. A man can, with due care, legitimately do his own checking on some public and all private data. The basic requirement is the widest possible range of awareness. Many restricted 'heads' are not as good as one comprehensive, accurate, 'head'. It is easier to check on one's own data of awareness than that of other men. Indeed, to repeat, as far as an observer is concerned, the reports by other men and, in general their activities, have the same status as his own. At best they are taken seriously, only if (a) they are found in the course of his (the observer's) activities of awareness and (b) these activities and results are accepted by him as providing an accurate presentation of the situation under consideration.

III

Public, private and common entities
More detailed comments concerning public (and, hence in this sense

common) and private entities are now in order. A mind itself and the mental activities and content which that mind has generated are for that mind private entities. Public entities are not mind-generated. It is possible to identify public entities by observing that many persons react to them by the same physical behaviour, that is gross bodily movement or language reports made by one and accepted by others. For example, all persons involved in a ball game react in the same way to the ball and would give roughly the same general verbal description of plays in the game. In the case of private entities of one person, he alone reacts to them and talks about them. For instance, others do not shudder at my fear feelings or report them (if I do not shudder). It is important to note that ultimately the distinction between public and private is found by each person on the basis of his own awareness of entities. This process of awareness is private!

So far in discussing public and private entites attention has been focused on those which are either physical or mental. The question arises as to whether physically based resultants are public or private. It has been noted earlier that these entities are not mind-generated, also that some of them are such that they can be photographically reproduced by a camera. No mental entity can be dealt with in this fashion. Specifically, the purple I see when I look at a distant mountain, the elliptical shape I see when I look at a penny from an angle, can be reproduced by a camera on a film and a picture provided. This is not so in the case of an imagination image or a feeling.

It might seem that the purple and elliptical shape under consideration are public entities in view of the fact that many people report them and react in other fashions such as drawing a picture (or photographically reproducing a picture) of the shape or selecting a purple colour from a series of colours on being requested to match the colour seen. However, the purple colour and elliptical shape are not public in the sense that the ball and the human bodies (mentioned above) are.

The physical objects seen are not dependent for their nature or existence on the position or condition of a receptive organ of a human body or the medium intervening, such as atmosphere in the case of the distant mountain or elliptical shapes seen when looking at a penny from an angle. The mountain and the penny, also body or ball, do not come and go depending on atmosphere and position of body. On the other hand, the purple colour and elliptical shape entities which are physically based resultants do so. The situation then is this. A physically based resultant is presently dependent on a particular human body or a medium or other particular physical factors, or a combination of them. When these entities are present a purple colour or an elliptical shape is present—as a physically based resultant. But each occurrence of purple and each occurrence of elliptical shape is different from others of the same class because different processes of generation are involved; specifically different bodies are involved. The purple I see is numerically distinct from the purple you see, similarly the elliptical shape. This is so because your body is numerically different from mine. On the other hand, it is the numerically identical mountain and the numerically identical penny which we both see. Thus the physical entities which are involved in the generating of a physically based resultant are public. But a particular physically based resultant is not something open to the awareness of many minds as a numerically identical entity. Rather it is a case of many occurrences of the entity 'purple' or the entity 'elliptical'. A person is aware of a particular physically based resultant only if his body is in a specific position. If he changes position he is aware of another different physically based resultant. Only one body can occupy one position at one time, therefore only one person can be aware of a particular physically based resultant. A particular physically based resultant is private because it is not available to anyone else. But its privacy does not depend on its being mind generated, because it is not.

Of course, to repeat, under similar conditions another human body could be involved in the generation of a numerically different physically based resultant which is a member of the same class, namely that is 'purple' or 'elliptical shape'. It is thus possible for those persons to react to purple when seeing a distant mountain from the same distance and elliptical when seeing a penny from the same angle but not the same position, and to have the reports confirmed. The situation is in some respects similar to one earthquake causing two numerically distinct shudders in the bodies of two persons within range, except the generating conditions are not as specialised as in the case of the shape and the colour.

The preceding discussion of physically based resultants has concentrated on a few examples, namely colour seen when looking at a distant mountain, shape seen when looking at a penny. The same comments are relevant in general in dealing with other physically based resultants, except some are not subject to pictorial representation. Mirror images, shadows, some odours, tastes, etc., are also presently dependent on a number of physical factors and in particular the presence or condition of individual human bodies. In some cases the condition of the body is decisive, for example physical illness affects taste and thermal entities. Each particular physically based resultant is necessarily distinct from other members of its class because each is the result of a numerically distinct generative process involving numerically distinct human bodies (specifically position and condition of the body) and other physical factors, some of which are numerically different for each generative process. Thus as in the case of particular purple colours and particular elliptical shapes, other physically based resultants are private because they are available only to the mind which is associated with the particular body involved in the generation of the particular physically based resultant under consideration.

In comprehensive experience a person is aware of the fact that concepts are found. They are not, like mental activities and mental content, 'owned' by a mind. As has been noted, a person can be aware that he shares with others a public world of physical objects. The question arises as to whether a person can also be aware of the same status for concepts. Of course, one cannot literally see others using the same concepts in the fashion in which one can see others 'playing with' the same (numerically identical) ball. However, there is knowledge about a shared world of concepts. When confronted by a shared public, physical object, many people use the same sound or inscription (there are many occurrences of a sound or an inscription) to indicate a reference to this object. On other occasions, the symbol is used when the physical object is not present nor any sensory imagery, and yet the symbol is understood. As argued earlier, this involves the public presence of a concept. For example, A wishes to have a dozen apples brought from a store and expresses a proposition to this effect in symbols. B, having heard the sounds, obviously has grasped, that is, shared the proposition with A. B goes and gets the apples. More specifically, the concepts and their linkage with symbols, and both with the entity apple, are a shared situation. Consider likewise the case of an adult giving a problem in simple calculation (say 8×9) to someone who answers 72 and the questioner agrees. In the case of adults there is no setting up of an imaginary blackboard or counting of fingers and toes or any such sensory manoeuvres of an exclusively individual (private) nature.

IV

Other minds

As just pointed out a person is not, strictly speaking, aware of other minds. A person who relies on comprehensive experience is aware of (some of) the activities, including talking, of human bodies, which are not his own. These activities are like his own bodily activities when influenced by his own mind, mental activity and content. This lends support to the claim that there are human minds other than his own, if there is no completely physical explanation of the behaviour of the other bodies.

This claim about other human minds has far more substantial support than the theory that scientific entities such as atoms exist as non-imaginary. No one is aware of atoms. A person is aware of a body linked with a mind (his own) and can, so far, successfully challenge a machine to do what a human body can do, in some phases of its behaviour, when linked with its mind.

In the case of the theory of a divine mind, as traditionally envisaged, such support for another mind is not present. For example, the physical universe is not, in any genuine sense, similar to a human body. However, returning to the question of other human minds, it is obvious that there is not experience of other minds in the sense of presence in awareness and hence, there is no immediate knowledge of them.

Nevertheless, it is legitimate to claim that, on occasion, a person (A) has knowledge about another person's (B's) mind. As in the case of knowledge about physical objects which A has not experienced, he accepts from B a proposition, regarded as an accurate report of B's mental life, on the basis of a check of B's general reliability in providing accurate reports.

It must be admitted that in the specific case of mental entities no direct check is possible. While A can check B's reliability by checking it in the context of physical objects which are experienced in common, and as public, no specific mental entity is present as public in the awareness of both A and B. Hence, to repeat, A can only rely on the general reliability of B as determined by reference to a non-mental shared public world.

Also, quite apart from the question of knowledge about B's mind derived from his statements about it, the accuracy of specific[1] claims

---

[1] Definite, detailed.

concerning the content and activites of other minds based on the model of one's own mind-body relations is open to question. The bodily activities are interpreted as indications of his mental content and activities. However, going back to the model, a person observing his own internal and external behaviour is aware of the fact that sometimes his own external behaviour is not an accurate indication of his internal state. A person may go through the motions of being angry when he feels no such (internal) emotion. On the other hand, a person may be aware of the fact that he feels anger as an internal state, but he does not show it, even when highly complex observational instruments are used to facilitate observation of overt behaviour, including internal bodily changes. The lie detector test is open to suspicion in many cases. In some cases a person is not aware of the real nature of his own mental activities and content.

Nevertheless, in some instances, a person by careful observation over a period of time develops a relatively reliable skill in spotting self-deception or misinterpretation, and deception by others. In other words, such cases can be identified. Let us consider a specific instance: Mr A, in the context of a combat situation, punches Mr B. When punched, Mr B may not show an external sign of anger, but, if subsequently he spreads destructive gossip, this is an indication that he did feel anger at the time.

V

Knowledge concerning future and past

Immediate knowledge (knowing) of the future is not possible because the future is not, or has not been, present as an entity in awareness. It is, of course, the case that one can plan and predict concerning some entities (particular occurrences of an entity) in the future on the basis of present and past experience. To this extent there are references to the future and the future has a bearing on the present. In thinking about the future, what is present to awareness are concepts or imaginative images, or both, with a characteristic 'reference to the future'. It is further to be noted that if a person has immediate knowledge of some members of a class, future members of the class will be the same. However, there is no knowledge as to whether or not there will be any members of that class in the future.

As noted previously, knowing about (knowledge about) the past is made possible by memory.[1] A past entity, physical or mental, is not now present as such to an immediate knowing process, and hence cannot be an item of immediate knowledge. Rather, a particular mental image or a concept or proposition may be present which refers to the past in an authentic fashion, which is known to be such. In the case of a proposition referring accurately to the past, a linked concept indicates this, or it is remembered as being accurate. It is to be noted that since concepts endure for long periods of time, a concept of which one was aware in the past may be grasped again in present awareness. In this sense there is immediate knowledge (knowing) of the past. An entity which was in the past—is now present (again).

More specifically, concerning memory images, the referring of the image to the past is something of which one is aware. The accuracy of the report provided by the memory image is open to awareness in the sense, as noted earlier, (a) that one can be aware that a specific activity, in this case remembering, is functioning, that conditions are suitable. Also (b) the memory image has the characteristic of familiarity (and no source of deception is present).

That a proposition is being referred to the past is open to awareness. The proposition as remembered is linked with the concept or has the characteristic: accurate. One accepts all this on the same basis as the memory image, that is (a) an awareness of functioning of the process of remembering, in other words one is aware of the fact that conditions are suitable, (b) an awareness of the properties as 'back again'.

A check on the accuracy of this sort of experience can be found in some instances. For example, in the case of the proposition 'Caesar crossed the Rubicon', there are historical documents. In the case of others, more direct evidence is still available, for instance concerning the number of rooms in one's birthplace. One's memory image can be directly verified, if the house still stands and has not been remodelled.

VI

Reasoning (in general)

The process of obtaining immediate knowledge or 'knowledge about' is sometimes very complicated. It is claimed that in many instances,

---

[1] Or written or other such records.

reasoning is operative. In general, what has been termed 'reasoning' involves proceeding in awareness from one entity to another to a conclusion. The content of awareness in this process may include, in addition to concepts, imagination or memory images and physical objects. The passage from one entity to another in reasoning may be based on imagination, memory, analogy, and/or in accordance with the logic of induction or (and) deduction. When functioning properly, the process of reasoning is reputed to be accurate and hence free from emotional bias. For example, in thinking about the requirements for a picnic, a person may call to mind a conceptual list of appropriate food, remember vividly past picnics, give scope to imagination, propose a menu analogous to that of a banquet recently attended, focus attention on kitchen equipment before one.

Analogy

Reasoning by analogy functions satisfactorily in cases when both entities involved are present in immediate knowing or presented by 'knowledge about', and crucial similarities are grasped. For example, there are enough similarities between a banquet and a picnic to lead to the suggestion that one might well include after-dinner mints in the picnic menu. But one cannot argue from the experienced, wise and benevolent contractor who makes a subdivision—to a wise and benevolent creator of the Universe. Here a crucial element is missing, namely, the awareness of a creator (of the Universe). Likewise, the similarities of a world and a subdivision are not sufficiently central to justify the conclusion that God made the world.

Induction

In one sort of induction,[1] one proceeds from an examination of a few items to a general conclusion about all members of the group, present, past or future. The formulation of these general propositions presents difficulties. Immediate knowledge and one sort of 'knowledge about' are based ultimately on someone's awareness of present entities. Further, even if the cases investigated have been accurately observed, the problem still remains as to whether crucial cases have been neglected. For example, all swans observed up to a certain time in specific places were white. Later, black swans were found. In any case, all instances of an entity present, past and future cannot be

---

[1] More restricted sorts need not be considered here.

examined. This sort of situation has led many to conclude that induction (of the sort under consideration) can provide only probability, not completely accurate general information, because all cases have not been checked. That is to say, such general propositions are not technically speaking knowledge.

However, an accurate (true) general proposition can be obtained concerning some characteristics possessed by all members of a group (hence, a case of knowledge). This occurs if care is taken to ensure that no distracting factors are present. Further, one must observe in all areas of the environment. If cases are found in the future or present or past which do not have the characteristic (or characteristics) thus carefully noted, such entities are not members of that class of entities. Consider, for example, the proposition 'All men are mortal', or 'All sticks of wood burn'. If, in the future, a creature is found that seems to be a man but, nevertheless, does not die, this creature is not a man.[1] Let us return now to a problem which was raised earlier. Even if some members of a class are not now present to awareness (immediate knowledge), or a proposition referring to them is not supported by the reports of others based on what is now or was present in awareness, nevertheless, the fact of class membership enables one to claim knowledge about such entities including future ones. That is to say, we have immediate knowledge of some members of the class. An unexperienced member of a class would have the class characteristics;[2] otherwise an entity is not a member of that class. In this sense, one can have knowledge about some unexperienced entities which are in the past, present or future.

It is important to stress that while there is knowledge about the characteristics of future members of a class, if they exist in the future, there can be no knowledge (accurate information) as to whether or not members of the class will exist in the future.

This problem of the accuracy of general propositions obtained by induction is related to the question of the possibility of general environmental or other conditions undergoing sufficient change in the future so as to modify the essential characteristics of entities under investigation, and hence give rise to a different class of creatures. There is, of course, no guarantee that this will not happen. In this respect, because of lack of full information, there is no knowledge of any specific sort

---

[1] Speculations about the possibility of extending life expectancy indefinitely are still indefinite.

[2] And of course basic entity where relevant.

concerning the future (apart from that mentioned above). But to repeat, one can know that if no significant changes take place, entities observed in the past and present will continue in the future. This is based on immediate knowledge and knowledge about members of a class of entities which have the same characteristics despite the passage of time.

It is very important to realise that any physical or mental entity exists only if environmental conditions are suitable. If changes are sufficiently drastic so that no member of a class continues to exist, the generalisation applying to these entities is not, therefore, completely undermined. It is now true only of entities which once existed and no longer do so.

Many changes in environment have known causes and can be predicted with a high degree of accuracy. But, for example, while an atomic war would produce drastic environmental changes, it is impossible to predict when, if ever, such a war is going to occur.

Particular present conditions may also be other than normal (suitable), so that a generality which applies under specified conditions no longer does so. For example, at high altitudes water does not boil at the usual temperature. Thus, many generalisations which constitute knowledge presuppose normal conditions. This remark is relevant to the 'All sticks burn' generalisation.

Of course, many inductive generalisations are at best probable and do not provide accurate information (knowledge) about all members of a complex group, many of which have not been experienced. To take an extreme case, the claim that Old Doc's nostrum will cure all diseases may have some support in a few cases, but diseases do not have common characteristics similar to the mortality of men. More plausibly the proposition 'There will always be wars because of the nature of humanity' lacks evidence to fully support the generalisation.

It has been contended in the preceding discussion that, with due care, one can be confident about some inductive generalisations. Nevertheless, nagging doubts remain. For example, how can one be sure that a sufficient number of cases has been examined in a sufficient number of places, or that items have been examined with sufficient care? These difficulties must not be disregarded. However, they must not be permitted to paralyse thought. It is difficult to say exactly how many human beings should be examined and in exactly how many places before one is justified in accepting as knowledge (accurate report) the proposition: 'All men are mortal', or 'The chemical formula of water is H_2O'. The fact remains, the point is reached where a person relying on comprehensive experience is prepared to accept these propositions as cases of knowledge. In some instances one observation is sufficient. Consider the famous experiment (one) by which Pasteur disproved the theory of spontaneous generation and so concluded that in all cases under consideration, life comes from life. It is here suggested that specialists in a field will determine when the obvious objections have been met (as noted above) and knowledge has been obtained.

Deduction

In deduction one proceeds from premises to a conclusion. Here no new entities are involved. In other words, there is nothing in the conclusion which was not in the premises. However, new immediate knowledge or 'knowledge about' may be obtained, in the sense that the conclusion is making obvious what was not previously obvious. Ultimately, in deduction the premises are reports of entities imaginary or non-imaginary which are present in experience of some person at some time, or they are arbitrary formulations. As noted earlier,[1] the laws of thought (principles) and patterns of deduction are likewise reports, or imaginary creations. There are no complex concepts or so-called self-evident principles (propositions) present to a mind apart from remembering of patterns of relations of other entities, or present experience of them or imaginary creations now present or remembered (or arbitrarily formulated).

Use of the term 'reason'

The preceding discussion of reasoning is based on a very broad use of the term 'reasoning'. Some prefer to employ the term in a far more restricted scope, applying it only to the manipulation of concepts in accordance with a group of carefully specified laws of thought or logic. Thus in many cases, a discussion of reasoning will omit any reference to content in the reasoning process such as memory or imaginative images or methods of reasoning such as analogy or imagining.

Here as elsewhere the basic question is not as to the legitimacy of a wide or narrow use of a term such as 'reasoning', but with an area of human experience which is referred to by the term 'reasoning' in one of its usages (a broad one).

---

[1] See Chapter 4, pp. 104–5.

Accuracy-truth-criteria

As has been noted, immediate knowledge and 'knowledge about' have accuracy as one of their essential characteristics and, in the case of propositional items, what is termed 'truth'. The question of (*a*) how the accuracy characteristic of knowing and knowledge can be achieved and (*b*) how it can be ascertained that it has been achieved, will be dealt with very briefly and in general fashion in the context of the following discussion. In the case of immediate knowing and knowledge of the minimum type, awareness of an entity occurs if the conditions are suitable for that entity. When one is aware of an entity, there is no question of the presence of that entity. With reference to many entities, a person can be aware of what constitutes suitable conditions for awareness and also be aware of whether or not they are present.[1]

In the case of immediate knowing and knowledge of the identifying-identified sort, there are several related processes of awareness, in particular the awareness of the linkage of a concept to an entity. Error, of course, may arise in the matter of the linkage of concepts to entity. One may be aware of the linkage but not aware of its erroneous nature, as the result of prejudice or hate. But here again there are suitable conditions for awareness and these can be determined and one can be aware of them and so ascertain whether or not the linkage is accurate.

In a well-established knowledge situation criteria are available to guide people in deciding on the appropriateness of the linkage of concepts with entities. In the case of a complex entity such as a table, one can specify with sufficient care the essential parts and fundamental (constitutive) characteristics of a table in such a fashion that a person can correctly apply, or accept the application of, the concept table to this entity. Likewise in dealing with a physical object which is distinguished from other physical objects chiefly by distinctive characteristics, one can by stating these characteristics with care provide criteria to guide others in appropriate concept use. For example, a horse and a man are both biological organisms. But they differ in shape and size and the functions they perform. In the case of a great

[1] See Chapter 2, pp. 67–70.

ape and a man the differences are fewer but can still be specified as criteria.

However, in the case of simple entities, which of course have characteristics, one cannot provide criteria in the sense discussed above. One cannot distinguish red from green in terms of parts (there are none) or characteristics (there are no distintive ones). In other words, one cannot provide criteria for identifying red or green in terms of parts or characteristics. This same comment applies to many entities, such as value, one, morally good, beautiful, colour.

It is the case that one can assist others in identifying a simple entity by describing, with great care, the conditions under which it normally occurs. Further, one can attempt to arrange the environment in such a fashion that the entity in question will stand out in clear focus for a normal human being.

Strictly speaking, these aiding devices are not criteria in the usual sense of the term.

Knowing and 'knowledge about' involves propositions used to refer to entities not now present in awarenes. However, the propositions are reports of immediate identified knowledge as the result of immediate identifying knowing. Given suitable conditions, the process of proposition-finding and checking will proceed without difficulty, and there will be awareness that the results are accurate, that is there will be accurate knowing and knowledge. As noted before, the characteristics of suitable conditions are open to awareness (in some cases). Hence, one can determine whether or not accuracy has been achieved and is aware how it is achieved.

Concerning 'knowing how' (knowledge how, skills), some of the same general comments apply. One develops skills, has skills, if the conditions are suitable. That being so, the activity is characterised by accuracy. What constitutes suitable conditions in the case of some such entities is open to awareness. Given suitable conditions for awareness of skill, one can be aware of the presence of skill. Hence the occurrence of accurate activity can be determined.

It is to be noted that skills are possessed in varying degrees. Among those who have the skill of car driving some are more effective (accurate) than others. Indeed the term 'skill' is somewhat ambiguous. It means (*a*) the performance of a complex learned activity[1] (such as playing ball) or (*b*) excellence in performing the activity (for example

[1] Which as complex involves some efficiency (accuracy) in integrating component activities and in achieving specific results.

a skilful ball player). It will have been noted that the term 'skill' has been used in the first sense throughout this discussion.

One can determine whether or not a person has knowledge in storage by observing his activities, depending on the sort of knowledge in storage involved. A person who claims to know Latin, even when not (now) using the language, can validate his claim by (later) translating from English to Latin. Conditions suitable for accurate storage can be specified.

The claim that in many instances in the knowledge situation (broad sense) accuracy is achieved implies there is not remaining ground for doubt (uncertainty). This seems to fly in the face of evidence to the effect that human experience is incapable of escaping from uncertainty. It is, of course, the case that some human beings claim to doubt or be uncertain (a psychological state) about every entity found in experience. This is based on a fundamental pessimism concerning human powers of apprehension. In the context of comprehensive experience, as has been noted, it is reported that human beings are able to, indeed do, in some instances, pass beyond doubt and uncertainty (as mental states) because there is sufficient evidence to provide sound, certain grounds (a state of affairs, not a mental state) for acceptance of some entities as knowledge. The question of whether or not one is practising self-deception in those instances must be faced. Some instances of self-deception, some cases of justified uncertainty, can be noted and either admitted or, on the basis of wider experience, overcome. As a matter of fact, every man is convinced, certain (mental state) that some experiences are beyond doubt. In the case of the extreme sceptics, in referring to the inadequacies of all human apprehension, they claim there is sound evidence (adequate factual, in this sense certain, support) for their point of view and are certain (mental state) of it. That this involves a contradiction does not seem to bother them.

In any case, a person who relies on comprehensive experience distinguishes sound evidence from what is not. Such a person reaches the point where further verification is no longer necessary as far as he can determine. He then claims certainty, in two senses: (a) a mental state (b) sound evidence. This is as far as a human being can go. When such a person is aware that all relevant internal and external conditions are satisfactory, then what he is aware of is accepted as an item of knowledge. No further evidence is possible or necessary. A demand for anything further is the wish to be other than a human being. It involves a departure from the context in which words and related concepts are used, in the milieu of comprehensive human experience.

VIII

No one simple answer to the question: How is knowledge obtained?

It should be obvious from the preceding discussion that there is no simple answer to the question: how is knowledge obtained? There are four main sorts of knowledge. The answer varies from sort to sort and within sorts. Immediate knowledge results from awareness of and, in some cases in addition, identified awareness of accuracy of linkage of a concept and the entity, for example recognition of an entity. In other words, what is known is what one is aware of in the activity of knowing. The awareness of external physical objects and some of their characteristics involves the use of the so-called external senses. In some cases supplementary instruments and experimental manipulation and complex thought processes are required. Of course, all instruments, natural (sense organs, nervous system, brain, etc.) and supplemental (such as a microscope) must be functioning properly. In some instances a person can 'go it alone'. In other cases he requires help from others. In obtaining immediate knowledge of some of his internal physical components a person, in some cases, treats his body as an external physical object. In other instances he uses the so-called internal senses. Here again, supplementary instruments, complex thought processes and experimental procedures may be required.

In being aware of his own basic mental entity, its characteristics and recognising them, no sense organs are available (though some of these entities are said by some philosophers to be apprehended by internal sense). In some cases the processes of awareness are as complicated as the cases mentioned above (except no direct help from others is involved), that is, supplementary entities such as theories or explanatory hypotheses are required in order that the process of awareness may be effective. The awareness of concepts and their characteristics is conditioned by the awareness of other entities, mental and physical, and here again, a very complex process may be involved for reasons indicated above.

167

It is to be noted that the awareness of value characteristics found in physically based resultants, physical objects, minds, concepts, and their characteristics frequently requires considerable exposure to these entities before these value characteristics become present to awareness. Here again, the process may be very complex, requiring experimental manipulation and the use of instruments, including complex thought processes. In brief, each case of immediate knowledge must be discussed in terms of its own nature and situation.

'Knowledge about' is based on cases of immediate knowledge, either one's own as present or remembered knowledge, or someone else's as reported.

'Knowledge how is obtained by developing skills through practice. Here again, there is great variation, depending in some cases on supplementary instruments of all sorts and involving the two other types of knowledge at least initially in varying degrees.

Knowledge in storage is obtained by remembering cases of the three sorts just mentioned.

In general: all sorts of knowledge are obtained only if internal and external conditions are suitable, that is permissive factors are present, preventive factors absent. Here again, there is great variation. Obviously, an item of knowledge is obtained only if the process by which it is obtained occurs.

To repeat, knowledge of each entity must be considered as an individual case. There is no one simple answer to the question: how is knowledge obtained? However, with care and patience an adequate answer can be provided in some instances, at least in outline. One additional comment is in order. A person cannot obtain knowledge of any sort which is independent of human experience.

As noted on several occasions previously, propositions concerning physical and mental entities, physically based resultants, concepts and their characteristics, are cases of 'knowledge about' only if a person is aware of their 'accuracy of report' characteristics. This inescapably involves previous immediate awareness. Specifically technically speaking, there is no a priori knowledge (that is prior to experience) of the entities mentioned above. The proposition 'All men are mortal' is a case of knowledge, because the entity 'man' has been found in experience to be characterised by the entity 'mortal'. Hence the concepts forming the proposition are known to be an accurate report. The proposition is true (accurate) even if no one is aware of it. But it is not a case of knowledge unless someone is aware of (it and) its truth. The only way to be aware of its truth is to experience its accuracy of report characteristic.[1] The proposition 'black is black' is a case of 'knowledge about' only if a person is aware that the entity 'black' retains its identity; and hence the conceptual report provided by the proposition is accurate.

[1] See Chapter 4, p. 105.

7

MAN AND HIS ENVIRONMENT

An adequate discussion of man and his environment must be set in the context of a careful examination of cause-effect relations.

I

Cause—general comments

The term 'cause' is used in two major ways when applied to basic physical entities, basic mental entities, physically based resultants and their characteristics. In one case the term refers to (*a*) the presence of an entity. In the other instance (*b*) reference is made to the absence of an entity.

Let us examine (*a*) the 'presence' sense of 'cause' first. An entity is a cause (has the characteristic 'cause') when[1] it functions in such a fashion as to produce[2] another entity (its effect). There are several sorts of causal functions, such as impact (hits against, pressure), stimulation (providing a stimulus), or generation. Effects may be (i) a new characteristic or characteristics of an already present entity or (ii) a new entity which is not a characteristic of a present entity, or (iii) the elimination of an entity either basic or characteristic.[3] In general, a causal function is a change in a specific complex situation. The effect of that cause is another change in that situation. In the

---

[1] The discussion will focus on occurrences of the entity 'cause'. That is, causal function is present. It is to be noted that the same entities are termed 'causes' even though they do not have the characteristic. It is a case of potentiality, of being a cause if a situation which does not now exist does exist later.

[2] The term 'cause' is used as a noun, an adjective and also as a verb. The noun and verb forms frequently are identical in appearance (when written or spoken). In order to avoid misunderstanding, in the following discussion (at least initially) the verb form of the term will be replaced by terms which are synonyms but indicate more specifically what is under consideration.

[3] Or physically based resultant.

case of an impact or the stimulation type of causal function, this change obviously is prior in time to the change in the situation which is the effect. When the causal function is generative, the effect is not as clearly distinguished from the causal process. However, the effect does not exist prior to the causal process.

In the interests of clarity it may be well to emphasise the point that, in the context of this discussion, what is termed a 'causal function' is a function (an activity or characteristic) of an entity whereby that entity produces or eliminates another entity, which is its effect. Thus the first entity acquires the characteristic 'cause'. In this sense, it is a cause. In this context a causal function is not *a* cause, it is the means by which a cause functions.

It is essential to realise that a function (impact or stimulation or generation) of an entity—which when present has a bearing on the entity being a cause (it is not a cause unless it produces effects)—is present only if the entity in question has specific characteristics. The entities in the environment are also relevant. A function when present is a causal function of the entity only if the entities in the situation are such that by this function the entity produces effects. These requirements as listed above are termed 'suitable conditions'. Such factors are here termed 'conditions'[1] not 'causes' because they may be present and yet there is no effect. When they are present, the decisive factor (what produces the effect) is the entity (the cause) which functions in such a fashion as to produce the effect.

It is important to note that in discussing causes and effects a person is usually dealing with a limited situation, not with the entire universe. Some limited situations are very restricted, other broader.

In the second *b* sense, the term 'cause' is used to refer to the absence of an entity which is termed a 'condition' in the situation discussed above. More specifically, if a condition is absent, then a present entity cannot exercise its usual causal function. In this sense the absence of the condition is the cause of the absence of the entity which would otherwise be present as an effect. A more obvious[2] case of the absence sense of 'cause' is that in which an entity is absent because the entity which would have produced it if it were present (and conditions were present) is, as a matter of fact, absent. Here the concern is obviously not with conditions alone.

---

[1] An abbreviation for 'suitable conditions'.
[2] So obvious that it is mentioned only in the interests of comprehensiveness.

In the context of comprehensive experience a person finds various sorts of cause-effect relations in both the presence and absence sense of 'cause'.[1] Let us consider typical examples.

Cause physical, effect physical

(a) Cause in the 'presence' sense of the term

There are physical entities which are causes of other physical entities. For example a billiard cue is the cause of the motion of a billiard ball when the cue moves and strikes the ball (impact, causal function), and the ball moves. The effect is a change in the characteristics (was static, now moves) of an entity (ball) already present in the situation. It is subsequent to preceding change, to the movement and impact of a cue (previously static and distant).

The question of how the cue acquired its causal function requires a reference to a broader situation than that now under consideration. It has been noted that a causal function is termed by some investigators a 'cause', for example, the impact. But it seems advisable to distinguish the cue as cause from the impact as causal function. After all, it is impact of the cue which produces the motion of the ball.

In order that the cue may function (by impact) as a cause in this situation, it must have suitable characteristics. It must be solid and movable. The ball must also have appropriate characteristics. It must be round and light. The environment must be suitable—the ball must be on a smooth table and not wedged[2] in a corner. The entities just mentioned are conditions, not causes.

So far, attention has been focused on one sort of cause-effect relation, namely a physical cause producing change in the characteristics of another present physical object. However, a physical object may produce a new entity which is not a new characteristic but rather a new physical object. For example, a blow torch may be used to ignite a dry tree branch and hence transform it from wood to carbon.[3] Here again, of course, conditions must be suitable.

---

[1] As in the case of comments on the use of other key terms, the concern in this study is primarily with the entities to which the words refer.

[2] Under these conditions of course the ball would not move even though there were impact by the cue. Hence the impact is a causal function only if an effect is produced by the impact of the cue.

[3] This and the immediately following are cases of the causal function as stimulator: the cause stimulates chemical changes.

A physical entity on occasion functions as a cause (i) by eliminating a basic physical entity or (ii) by removing a characteristic of a basic physical entity. Consider the latter case first. Fire will turn a green leaf yellow (remove the characteristic green). In the former case, fire will vaporise a cube of ice—in this sense eliminate a basic physical entity. (Strictly speaking it is a case of changing it into something else. The causal function is stimulation.)

So far, illustrations have dealt with situations involving one basic entity as cause and another basic entity or its characteristics as effect. It must be realised that one living physical entity by its own (generative) causal function can produce as effects new characteristics which belong to the entity. For example, a fruit tree (the component wood cells) produces blossoms and fruit. Here again, of course, conditions must be suitable.[1]

Further, a living organism (physical entity) can function causally to eliminate some of its own characteristics. For example, a fruit tree having produced blossoms can get rid of them, replacing them by fruit.

Cause in the 'absence' sense of the term

If a billiard ball is firmly wedged in a corner, the absence of suitable conditions for movement, even if the cue does strike the ball, is the cause of the absence of motion. Turning to another sort of situation to which the 'absence' use of 'cause' refers: the absence of water is the cause of the absence of flower and fruit, in the case of a fruit tree, in instances where water is a condition for healthy vegetation. Likewise the absence of air is the cause for the absence of breathing in the case of a human organism, thus the cause of death. In these cases it is a matter of one entity being unable to carry out its usual causal activities,

[1] It is to be noted that when conditions are suitable for generation (generative activity) and an entity engages in this activity, an entity (an effect) is produced. On the other hand, as in the case of impact as noted above, when conditions are suitable for stimulation and providing a stimulus occurs, the function is not causal. No effects are produced unless other conditions in the environment and conditions in the entity affected are suitable. For example, the wood will not be turned into carbon by the stimulus of the blow torch if the wood is wet or the atmosphere is very damp. Technically speaking, blossoms or fruit as long as they are attached to a living tree are characteristics. When they are removed they have the status of basic entity with characteristics. In this sense a living organism can produce another basic entity. In the case of a mother giving birth to a child, it is a living organism producing another living organism.

produce effects belonging to itself, because of the lack of suitable conditions. It is not a case of one entity being unable to produce effects in another entity because conditions are not suitable. However, it is to be noted that in the fruit tree illustration the absence of water is a condition for the causal function of the sun (in the stimulation sense) in producing withered vegetation as an effect, where initially there was water and the tree was healthy.

The more obvious sort of 'absence' sense of 'cause' is illustrated by a situation where a billiard ball does not move because there is no cue to be used, or where there is no fruit because there is no tree (even though conditions are suitable).[1]

Cause mental—effect mental

(a) Cause in the 'presence' sense of the term

A mind is a cause when it generates (causal function) various mental activities. As has been noted, these include awareness and desiring. The mind also is a cause when it generates images[2] (imagination, memory, dream), emotions and feelings (its content). Strictly speaking, it is not the generative processes as such which are causes of the activities, images, and so on. Generative processes are how a mind goes about directly producing (by its causal function) other mental activities and all mental content. However, some activities, once they are produced by a mind, do on occasion have a causal function, that is they are causes. For example when a person is desiring food, the desire[3] may cause his mind (its causal function is stimulation) to generate imagination images.[4] Mental content may also on occasion

---

[1] The 'absence of' locution can of course be replaced by a positive form of statement ('the ball is static'). 'Withered vegetation' is a 'presence' locution.

[2] The generation of mental activities and content is a mental activity. Other cases of generation are not mental.

[3] Willing in a limited situation is an internally initiated effort to produce some result, namely, what one has chosen. An exertion of will is also required to bring into existence what one is interested in, intends, believes, desires, in the way of mental entities and bodily activities within one's power, in cases when merely being interested, believing, intending, desiring, are not as such sufficiently strong to function as causes. In some cases these activities are capable of producing effects (without the assistance of willing) if, of course, conditions are suitable.

[4] More specifically the stimulus produces a reaction in the mind. Thus mind, in this state of affairs, then proceeds to generate images.

function as cause. For instance, an imagination image (its causal function is stimulation) may cause a person's mind to generate the emotion fear.

It has been noted that all mental activities and mental content of a mind are characteristics of that mind and are its effects. It may seem to follow that as a matter of fact no activities and content, as such, can appropriately be considered causes—only the mind that generated them can have that status. However, to repeat, such is not the case. Possibly some of the difficulty arises because some persons tend to think almost exlusively in terms of a specific physical model. It is the case that no characteristics of some basic physical entities can ever stimulate their own basic entity and cause it to produce effects on or in it.[1] However, a living organism can generate a chemical characteristic which stimulates the organism to produce a new effect.

Only some mental activities and content may have causal function. It must be emphasised that the activity 'awareness' does not have causal function either in the sense of generating or impact or stimulation.

Further, a mind or its characteristics, cannot exercise direct causal efficacy on another mind or its characteristics. Mr X cannot produce imagination images in Mr Y's mind in the same fashion as he can in his own. A mind can eliminate its own and only its own mental entities, either activities or content, by ceasing to generate them. There is no evidence to support the claim that a mind can eliminate itself by direct causal functions—or any other mind.

In order that a mind or any of its characteristics may exercise causal functions, conditions must be suitable. For example, a mind must be in a relatively calm state, otherwise it will be unable to settle down and generate memory images. Likewise the external environment must be quiet, otherwise a desire may be unable to stimulate a mind to generate an imagination image, for example, of a piece of apple pie.

(b) Cause in the 'absence' sense of the term

Examples are not difficult to find. If conditions suitable for the mind's generation of activities or content (or the causal function of such entities) are absent, then the effects, which usually occur under normal conditions, are absent, because the generative activity did not

---

[1] Consider a billiard cue.

occur. Thus the absence of the required conditions is the case of the absence of the normal causal functions and effects. For example, the absence of a calm state of mind or quiet external environment causes the absence of the generative activity whereby mental activities and content would otherwise have been produced. Turning to an example of the more obvious 'absence' sense of 'cause' (of basic entities), there will be no desires and no memory images if there are no minds, even if conditions are suitable.

In referring to the other main sorts of causal situations, attention will be concentrated on the 'presence' sense of 'cause'. The 'absence' sense of 'cause' has now been illustrated with reference to situations involving only physical objects or only mental entities. Further comments on the 'absence' sense of 'cause' in mixed situations (cause mental, effect physical or vice versa) would be unnecessarily repetitious.

In general, from now on attention will be focused on sense *a*, the 'presence' sense of 'cause' since it is here that the main problems arise. Once such issues are solved, the 'absence' sense of 'cause' is implicitly covered. In other words, once one becomes aware of causes and their effects and requisite conditions, one has noted what entities when absent are the causes, in sense *b*, of the absence of entities which are effects when suitable conditions are present; or, to take the obvious case, when a causal entity is present.

Cause mental—effect physical

For example, desiring to raise one's arm produces, as an effect, the raising of the arm. An emotion of anger produces clenching of the fist or churning of the stomach. In these cases the causal function is stimulation.[1]

As in the other cases of causal function, conditions must be suitable, the mental entity (cause) must have sufficient intensity, the physical entity must be such that some of its characteristics can be added to or removed by a mental cause. The environment must be suitable also.

It is very important to realise that a mind as such does not have direct causal function with reference to any physical object. In influencing its own body a mind first generates mental entities. These then exercise pressure on or stimulate that body. No mental entity can exercise direct causal function on any physical object other than its own body. Its only causal function is to change characteristics

[1] For a more detailed discussion, see pp. 179–80.

of an existing body. A mind can never generate a new basic physical entity or eliminate a basic physical entity.

Some clarificatory comments and illustrations are now in order. Mr X's desire to have his fingers snap (if conditions are suitable) produces that complex movement which admittedly involves a series of complicated internal bodily processes by direct causal function. Here characteristics of the person's own body are changed. This is replacement of one characteristic (rest) by another (motion), that is elimination of rest. But Mr X cannot by desiring that Mr Y's fingers snap, directly[1] cause them to move. He can of course achieve this result indirectly. Mr X's desire is conveyed to Mr Y by language and Mr Y carries out the suggestion. No matter how hard a mind tries, no matter how strongly it desires, say, the elimination of a venerable family car and the presence of a Rolls-Royce, these results are not produced directly by mental activity as such. The desires (desirings) in question can of course directly influence a person's body and so set in motion a long chain of physical processes, and a set of related mental processes, which finally can lead to these results (if conditions are suitable)! In this sense there may be indirect mental causal function with reference to physical objects other than one's own body.

It must be stressed that in cases where mental activities and mental contents have causal functions with reference to (1) other mental entities and likewise also (2) physical entities their status as characteristics of a mind cannot be neglected. As noted earlier, these mental entities (activities and content) are causes in the context of a limited situation. However, in a more extensive situation they are effects of (caused by) a mind. In this sense, in a broad context, the mind is the cause of the effects, mental and physical, produced by its characteristics. As just pointed out, in some instances it is a case of mediated causal function.

Cause physical—effect mental

The causal function is stimulus of the mind, thus arousing it to generate mental activities and content. There is no reliable evidence that a physical object (human body or a machine) can generate a mind (see subsequent discussion).[2] However, turning to cases where there is physical causation of a mental entity, consider a book falling on

---

[1] In the sense illustrated above, that there is a series of events but it is within the same person. There is no external mediation.

[2] Chapter 17, pp. 385–86.

one's foot. As a result of this, the mind is stimulated to generate anger and also probably to a desire to kick at the offending book. However, if some very attractive item of food or drink is taken into the person's body, this physical object will arouse his mind to stop generating anger, hence eliminate it and replace the anger by pleasure.

In view of the preceding comments, it seems unnecessary to repeat remarks and provide illustrations concerning the point that conditions must be suitable in order that an entity may have a causal function.

Physically based resultant

In an earlier discussion it was pointed out that, given a complex of physical entities, in some cases, a type of entity is found (is present to awareness) which has been termed 'physically based resultant'. The purple colour seen when looking at a mountain that has the characteristic green; the elliptical shape seen when looking at a penny which is round; the mirror image of one's face—all are the results of a combination of physical entities: the observer's body, condition of the atmosphere, angle of vision, distance, reflection of light waves, and so on, including of course the presence of a mountain, a penny, and a face. The causal function of such a complex of physical factors is not a case of stimulating a mind, causing it to generate mental content. The entities under consideration can be duplicated in a photograph by a camera, while mental content cannot be so treated. Further, and more significantly, the entities in question are different in nature from mental content as far as comprehensive experience is concerned. The causal function here is perhaps most appropriately termed 'physical generation' (generation by physical entities). However, it is to be emphasised that the entities generated are neither basic physical entities nor are they characteristics of basic physical entities (see discussion Chapter 3, pages 79–83).

There is generation[1] by physical entities of entities other than physically based resultants. For example, two parental cells, when brought together, generate a human body; a plastic (an entirely new basic physical entity and its characteristics) is produced as the result of the combination of appropriate chemicals; water results from the appropriate mixture of hydrogen and oxygen. In these latter two cases the

---

[1] Stimulation may also be involved, see pp. 172–3.

basic physical entities which are effects are of different sorts from the entities out of which they were produced. Some of their characteristics also differ from those of the entities which had the causal function.

II

Comments on causal functions

A further somewhat technical comment concerning impact, stimulation, generation (causal functions) is required. These three sorts of activity on occasion are mental (have the characteristic mental). For example, the activity of generating memory, imagination and dream images has the characteristic mental. When a desiring (mental activity) or an imagination image (mental content) stimulates or pressures (impact) a mind or body and produces results, the activities of stimulating or pressuring are 'mental'. On other occasions pressuring, stimulating and generating, are activities of physical entities. For example, the impact of the cue pressures the ball; the blow torch stimulates the wood to chemical change; the tree generates blossoms. These activities, generation excepted, are not physical activities—they are not characterised by physical, as wood and metal are. These activities are activities of physical entities. If, as a convenient locution, one calls such activities physical, meaning that they are activities of physical entities, this situation should be understood.

It will be recalled that some activities, such as awareness, desiring, willing, are as such mental (they have the characteristic mental). They are, strictly speaking, not mental just because they are activities performed by a mind. Some entities have been termed 'neutral' (see Chapter 4, p. 92) in the sense that as such they are neither physical, mental, concepts, nor physically based resultants, nor are they on any occasion characterised by mental, physical, or concept, or physically based resultant. Consider for example: shape, size, colour, individuality, value.

It should be obvious that the activities: impact (pressuring), stimulating, generating are as such neither physical, mental, nor physically based resultants. However, as noted, on occasion, they may all be mental (characterised by mental). In any case, they are never characterised by physical, concept, or physically based resultant, physical generation being an exception.

179

Incidentally, it is well to note that the comments made concerning pressuring, stimulating and generating apply also to some of the other mental activities listed in Chapter 2, p. 61, for example directing toward, pointing to (in meaning situations), arranging, proceeding from item to item.

In many instances the causal function in the typical cases so far discussed is of brief duration and so is the effect; and it is obvious in most instances that the causal function is prior in time to the effect. In other cases the cause continues to operate and the effect continues to occur, for a considerable period of time. This leads some to conclude mistakenly that some causes and effects are co-temporal rather than prior and subsequent. Consider for example poverty[1] and crime, fire and heat. However, when crime and heat are effects of the causes stated, at least initially the poverty and fire came first at some point in the history of the phenomena under discussion.

Complexities in cause-effect relations

One event (entity) may be the result of any one of several different particular causes. For example, cooked meat may be the effect of either a camp fire or an electric or a gas stove. For this reason it is not correct to claim that a cause is the factor (entity) necessary to produce a specific effect. The gas stove which in one situation is the cause of cooked meat is not the only, the necessary cause required to produce this result. It has already been noted that a cause cannot correctly be regarded as sufficient (that is, functioning by itself) to produce a specific result because it is operating under conditions which must be suitable. For example, meat exposed to a source of heat must be capable of being cooked (for instance not a stone) and environmental conditions must be favourable. The fact that in some cases a specific entity is not necessary for the production of a specific effect (though when present it does), and in any case no entity is sufficient by itself to produce an effect, indicates the inadequacy of the attempt to define cause as the sufficient and necessary condition.[2]

---

[1] To state that poverty is the cause of crime is an over-simplified locution. More exactly: a person desires something which requires the expenditure of money, which he lacks. He knows that by committing the crime of robbery he can obtain the required money. He proceeds to perpetrate the crime.

[2] The distinction between a cause and a condition must again be emphasized. See pp. 171–2.

Cause-force

Further complexities in some causal situations must be noted. In some situations, no one entity is a cause. To consider a further example the presence of a cluster of causes, all of which are required to produce the effect, is illustrated by the competent decision of a committee which depends on (results from) the cooperative efficient functioning of all members of the committee, under satisfactory conditions.

Also, one cause may have a number of different effects. For example, a horn emitting a loud noise may produce a flash of anger or a feeling of curiosity, depending on conditions.

It is important to realise in addition that, in some situations, two entities are present which are in a mutual cause and effect relation. For example, Mr X and Miss Y are in love; Mr X causes affection in Miss Y and Miss Y causes affection in Mr X.

In some cases at least, when mental entities are at work, there is an awareness of the exertion of force (pressure), as when for example a person forces himself to concentrate on a difficult idea, or forces himself to keep his eyes open. On the other hand, a person is not aware of force being exerted by a cue on a billiard ball. However, even when the cause is not mental, one can be aware of force, as in the case of the impact of the physical environment on one's body. For example, a person is aware that a bright light is forcing him to blink. A person also on occasion experiences a physical cause exerting force in producing a mental effect, as with a bright light causing an experience of pain.

It is essential to realise that the 'is aware of' locution is a way of referring to facts and reminding the reader that facts as here reported are found in the cause of comprehensive experience.

In cases where the existence of force is not experienced, and hence one is not justified in reporting its presence, one can still be aware of a cause producing an effect (the causal function: impact, stimulation or generation). Causation is not merely a case of continuity of entities termed 'cause' and 'effect'.

Complexity of some cause-effect sequences

It is obvious that some of the preceding illustrations of cause-effect relations have been over-simplified. For example, in the case of a person desiring to raise his arm and the arm is raised, a series of causes (C) and effects (E) is involved in a series of limited causal situations. A mind (C) generates a desire (E). The desire (C) touches off a nerve (E). This, in turn, is a cause which produces a muscular contraction as effect. This then functions as a cause which produces an effect, namely the rising of the arm. Thus it should be clear that the terms 'cause' and 'effect' are relative in their application to any specific entity. Their appropriate use depends on the situation involved. The desire to move (C)—nerve impulse (E) is one situation; the nerve impulse (C)—muscle movement (E) is another situation. Indeed, there are limited situations within a broad one which as such is less limited[1] than the situations which compose it.

It is also to be noted that the term 'condition' is relative in its application, once again depending on the situation involved. In the cases just considered the state (nature) of the nervous system is a condition which makes possible the transmission of nerve impulses. But in the context of another situation, a wider one in the sense of time, space and complexity, the state of the nervous system and the muscle is the effect of causes going all the way back to the origin of the human organism and its environment.

The complexity (extensiveness) of some causal sequences does not introduce serious difficulties into a discussion of cause-effect relations. A person can, in some situations, legitimately identify the cause of some entity (effect) which involves a long sequence of events before the entity (effect) occurs. For example, to change the illustration, if a man is shot and dies, it is correct to claim that the bullet (fired by the gun) is the cause of his death. This implies that a distinction be made between basic[2] and subsequent causes in a specified limited situation. True, the bullet causes the heart to stop beating (E_1) which in turn causes the cessation of the flow of blood (E_2), and so on. But none of these events would have occurred without the firing of the bullet. The bullet is the basic physical cause in this specific, limited situation, the others are subsequent. The bullet in this situation may appropriately be termed the cause.

Going further back, step by step, and hence extending the range of the situation, there is of course the cause of the firing of the bullet. Anger may well be the basic psychological cause. This may involve environmental physical and social causes if one extends the situation

---

[1] However, it is still a limited situation because it is not the totality of entities.
[2] Ultimate.

further. Each of these will be a basic cause, depending on the scope of the situation considered.

Of course, there are causes for the environment and for the person affected by it. But within a specified context, that is the given situation, in other words a limited segment of the entire universe, the question of the basic cause (*the* cause) of the death of a person is a manageable one. It may well be the case that, if one deals with a very complex extensive situation, there will be a cooperating group (plurality) of basic causes. In brief, identification of cause-effect relations occurs in the context of some limited situation which must be carefully specified.

III

Final causes

The preceding discussion of physical entities and minds, physically based resultants and their characteristics, which are cases of efficient causation, should not lead to the neglect of another sort of causation, namely the causal function of envisaged goals, so-called final[1] causes. A goal may be presented in the form of an imagination image, an actually present superior person, or in the form of a concept or a proposition which states an ideal goal. If conditions are suitable, a concept for example may have a 'lure' function, arousing a reaction (conduct approximating the ideal) in a receptive and able mind, one possessing the proper capacities and interests.

Some clarification of the preceding very general remarks about final causes is in order. Unless a person is interested in obtaining guidance (a condition), a great leader or an idea will not have a lure (causal function) and hence will not be a final cause. To take a mundane example: if Mr X desires money (a specific interest), a rich man, money or the idea of great wealth are causes in so far as they have a lure function producing money-making activities. Thus in such a situation money is a final cause. As a matter of fact, it is artificial to attempt to limit the situation to a case of final causation. Both efficient and final causes are at work. For instance, a person engaged in money-making activites because he desires (efficient cause) money and money has a luring function: it is a final cause.

[1] The term 'final cause' is also sometimes used to refer to a person's purpose to achieve the implementation of a goal.

As noted earlier, some final causes, such as an ideal social organisation, are 'creatures' of human imagination. In other cases a non-imaginary man or ideal (concept or proposition) is a final cause.

Concerning the causal function of concepts, it may appear that difficulties arise since causation so far considered obviously involves the factor of temporal priority and change in the total situation. It has been reported that, in the context of comprehensive experience, concepts do not have temporal characteristics, nor are they characterised by generative, stimulative or impact function (that is change). Thus they are different from the moving cue, the generating mind, desires to raise an arm, and so on. However, a concept is first found, then has a luring or stimulating cause function. In this sense it is prior to the effect, that is, it is temporally prior in the cause-effect sequence. When a concept acquires a lure function it has a new characteristic (that is change occurs). Nevertheless, there is one sort of causation where a temporal factor is entirely lacking. In the case of a deductive argument the conclusion is an effect which follows (in this sense a change occurs) from or is produced logically by the premises which are thus causes. More specifically, while a mental process of reasoning from premise to conclusion takes time, the priority of premises over conclusion is not temporal but logical. Time makes no difference in the realm of logical relations.

It is of course obvious that in many situations a number of entities are present which compete for the status of cause, that which produces whatever entity (effect) occurs. In the context of his experience, a person may be aware of the lure of an ideal, and the impact (stimulus) of a desire which is opposed to the ideal. If he turns in the direction of the ideal, this effect indicates that the ideal, in the situation, is the cause—the opposing desire is denied that status.

IV

Cause, laws of nature, prediction

In some instances, the activities of specific causes in producing effects are found to be recurrent and without known exceptions, under normal conditions. That is, all members of a group produce standard effects. For example, inanimate physical objects fall when support is removed; all cases of fire burn paper; in all cases when a human being is wounded he feels pain—under normal conditions. Thus, reference is made to laws of nature. Hence, there is a basis for predictions which are verified with the passage of time. For example, one confidently predicts that when a book is pushed off a table, it will fall to the floor. This has been verified innumerable times.

However, there are cases of an entity which functions as a cause only once. For instance, Leonardo produced 'The Last Supper' only once, not many times. It is of course the case that he produced many pictures. Even if an entity termed a 'cause' on many occasions is followed by a standard effect (the same effect on many occasions), mere repetition does not constitute the causal function. Likewise neither does prediction. The first time X-rays caused burns did not involve prediction. No formulated law was available for verification. It is obvious, in the context of comprehensive experience, that the causal function of an entity should not be confused with a repetition of a sequence, or knowledge of it expressed in a law, or accurate prediction based on this knowledge, or verification of a prediction.

In brief, in discussions of cause-effect relations, reliance should be placed on the results of comprehensive experiencing. It is not considered necessary in this book to attempt to report in detail how a cause produces an effect. How causal sequences are identified, making use of the methods of agreement, difference, concomitant variations and all other such investigational and verificational techniques, is primarily the business of specialists in relevant fields. A philosopher may legitimately, if need arises, warn an observer of possible pitfalls in reaching conclusions. For example, it may be pointed out that in using the methods of agreement and difference, an essential factor may be overlooked or an unessential factor stressed. In the case of the method of concomitant variations, one may initially be in doubt as to which is cause and which is effect. However, to repeat, it is essential that the philosopher rely on the competence of specialists in various fields of investigation. For example, one comes to accept the conclusion that the spoiling of food is due to the presence of bacteria which once were neglected. Causal explanations in this field were once made in terms of the activities of evil spirits. Of course, the acceptance of the work of an expert, by a philosopher or anyone else, is based ultimately on the support found for it in one's own experience. In the last analysis, a person with the assistance of an expert and instruments can observe bacteria and also observe the effect they have on one type of food such as milk. Also no souring occurs when bacteria are absent. This experiment on the part of the non-exper leads him to accept a general competence on the part of the expert.

The cases of causation so far examined have been considered in relative isolation from the total situation, as far as it is 'open' to comprehensive human experience. The causes mentioned have been identified as operating in a specified limited situation. Obviously, the question arises as to whether everything which is or happens has a cause.

v

Determinism-indeterminism

The position of Experiential Realism concerning the questions of determinism (all entities have causes) and indeterminism (there are some uncaused entities) is as follows: there are not adequate grounds in comprehensive experience for concluding that all entities,[1] physical, mental, concepts and their characteristics, are the result of causes. In other words, a human being does not experience or have knowledge about causes for all experienced entities, let alone entities which are assumed to be but are beyond the present range of experience. For example, event A may be experienced as producing event B; but a person may not be aware of causes producing A, though they may be assumed. For instance, cancer produces death but, as yet, the cause of cancer is not open to awareness. A 'comprehensive' person will be modest (and honest) and so admit the limitations of his experiencing. No person or committee of persons has, or can, observe all entities past, present and future, including interrelations of basic entities and their characteristics. New entities are continually being discovered.

The fact that a person does not find causal sequence 'everywhere' does not deny the fact that some particular causal sequences do occur. They are found in limited situations. Under normal conditions on the planet Earth one does find that, for example, the impact of cues moves billiard balls, minds form imagination images.[2] On the other hand,

---

[1] Speaking technically, reference is here being made to particular occurrences of a many-occurrence entity as well as to many-occurrence entities as such.

[2] This is the case even though a person is not aware of the cause of all the conditions involved in a limited situation, or a complete causal network stretching back into the far distant past.

one cannot claim that, since some entities cannot now be traced to causes, therefore they do not have them. Further, concerning indeterminism, it is important to note that some entities which once did not seem to have causes, later have been found to have causal relationships to other entities. For example, the cause of immunisation against poliomyelitis has recently been found. Yet it must be emphasised that at the present time there is no conclusive evidence to show there are no entities without causal relations. In short, a person cannot now finally settle the question of determinism versus indeterminism. He can only report: I have found that in a limited situation some entities result from causes; I have not found causes for some entities. Since some particular pieces of wood, stone and metal (are found to) have causes, also persons, etc., it may be assumed that any member of these classes (any occurrences of the entities) will have causes. However, this is not justified. We were not aware of the first (ever) occurrence of persons or the first occurrence of trees or the material out of which stones and metal are made. We do not know whether or not causes were operative.

So far, discussion has proceeded for the most part on a general level referring to many-occurrence entities as such. We turn now to examine particular occurrences of entities.

The point of view here being developed receives further clarification from an examination of a situation where a particular person[1] chooses between two possibilities, for example whether or not he will have parsnips for dinner. The selection he makes can be explained causally by known recently occurring events, both internal and external. For example, in the past he has eaten the vegetable and does not like the taste. Also, his friends object to the odour. Therefore, he chooses not to have parsnips for dinner. The decision, however, operates within a very limited situation. Ultimately, since we do not now have a complete causal explanation of any man's behaviour—all causes presumed to operate all the way back to the origin of the universe and beyond—there is no evidence to justify the belief that he is the victim of a definite, predetermined divine blue-print or of heredity or pre-existing environment.

To say concerning a man's behaviour, 'He is not responsible', 'He didn't do it' because the initiative (cause) comes from outside, is

---

[1] The author

correct, if it is a case, for example, of a violent gust of wind blowing him through a window. Yet, in a sense, everything is outside (in space and time) a person and his experience, if you go back before his conception.

But in the context of a limited situation, there is, on occasion, decisive causal efficacy exerted by a person on his own activities (discovered in comprehensive experience), despite external factors. Thus a person is responsible (in the sense of 'he did it') for at least some of his actions on the basis of the experienced causal initative localised in the person. For example, a person decides to offer a friend a drive and then proceeds to do so. There are no obvious immediately present external causal factors such as a police order or a gun pointed at him.

The term 'freedom' has been used to refer to many different states of affairs. It is frequently employed as a synonym for complete lack of causation. However, freedom, in one sense, consistent with the preceding discussion, is not escape from all causes. Rather it consists in the fact that a person does carry out his intentions without prevention by the external environment or some factor present in himself, or both. For example, I intend to go to the dining-room of my home. This intention is caused by hunger. I get up and walk to the table. In this situation I am free. Lack of freedom also involves causes. For example, I plan to go to the dining-room, but I am locked in the study, or I faint because of a severe headache; I plan to think about comprehensive experience, but my anger aroused by dogs barking prevents me.

There is no firm evidence to support the belief that the individual is ultimately immune from some causal influence by heredity and environment. In any case, one's awareness of causal factors supports the contention that an individual exists and possesses some of his characteristics, such as a tendency to decide to help friends, because of the causal influence of his environment (the customs of his group). This does not constitute a denial, in the case of a limited situation, of an immediate internal initiative on the part of the individual. It is merely a recognition, by reference to a wider inclusive situation, of the causal factors which are found to be relevant in producing an individual who exercises internal initiative of specific types.

The question arises as to whether or not a person could have done otherwise than he did, or more specifically could have done some other particular thing. The thing done here under discussion is frequently (*a*) the choice of some activity or (*b*) desire concerning an activity, or (*c*) the occurrence or performance of an activity.[1] The phrase 'could have' is ambiguous. It may refer either to conditions or to causes.

It must be noted at the outset that, if an entity occurs (something is done), conditions must be suitable. This is the case whether one accepts determinism, indeterminism or the view of Experiential Realism. Thus for example, if a man has walked a few paces, the question as to whether he could have flown by flapping his arms is quickly settled by pointing out that in this situation he could not have flown because he is incapable of flying in this fashion—conditions are not suitable. However, given normal conditions of heredity and environment, a person is physically capable (another condition) of either walking or running to his destination. Likewise, given as conditions a knowledge of English and normal physical and mental health, light and so on, one is mentally capable (a condition) of reading either Plato or *Playboy*. Thus in some cases the question as to whether or not some specific activity could be performed can be answered with reference to a specific definite identified capacity (condition). However, in a case where an individual as a matter of fact walked and did not run, or read Plato rather than *Playboy*, the question (a causal one) of whether he could have done otherwise than he did becomes much more complex.

If a person takes an indeterminist position, it might be argued that the activity which occurred, since it had no cause, might equally well have been replaced by the one which did not occur (conditions being equally suitable for either). That is to say, if there are no causes for an activity, one could occur equally as well as another. Nevertheless, it is essential to note that this type (causal or lack of cause) of 'could have done' (could have occurred) is very different from the (condition) 'walk-run' or 'read Plato–read *Playboy* situation. In this latter case, it is a matter of capacities which are definite, identified and specific. In the other case, it is one of the capacities (potentialities) implemented (actualised) and a specific activity occurs—according to the indeterminist position, without a cause. The claim in the context of indeterminism that anything can happen, that is the implementation of any capacity[2] which a person possesses, is to refer to a type of 'could

---

[1] In all cases the cessation of a present activity might be an option.
[2] Some indeterminists do not have even this qualification.

happen' which is completely vague, unspecified and indefinite. Indeed, it is so vague that it hardly counts as a positive answer at all. One might just as well answer 'no' as 'yes' in the situation where the question is: could he have done otherwise than he did? (that is in cases where, even admitting the presence of capacity and other normal conditions or activity, the activity occurred without a cause).

The preceding comments about walking, flying, reading, etc., are equally relevant to questions as to whether or not choice or desire might have been otherwise, in the context of an indeterminist approach.

In the context of a causal explanation, of course if causal factors and conditions had been different the results would have been different. However, there is no practical point in talking about 'if causes and conditions were otherwise something different would have resulted'. As a matter of fact they were not different, as far as comprehensive experience is concerned. In any case we do not know that every event has a cause, only that some have.

At the risk of some repetition, the immediately preceding comments will be briefly clarified.

In some cases where a man chooses to do good, that is due to the causal influence of some saintly person. But there is no complete answer to the question: why does one man respond to such an ideal's 'lure' and another not? Hence the questioner seems to be getting out of his depth. To repeat, we are aware of only a relatively few causes and these within a relatively restricted temporal sequence. They do not provide a complete explanation when we are dealing with a very complex entity such as a human person. We have no conclusive evidence that there are no uncaused events.

Thus, to repeat, in a specific case, whether a specific man in a specific situation could have overcome the lure of evil where he did not, or could have bowed in dedication to evil where he chose good—that is, whether the choice could have been otherwise than it was—these questions cannot be settled. We do not have sufficient evidence. One can only report what actually happened.

As far as comprehensive experience is concerned, a past event was what it was. We can only note what happened and try to find out what causal factors were at work. For practical purposes, we discuss a man's present or past behaviour in terms of what it is or was rather than what one might imagine it to have been. We attempt to understand it in terms of known causes.

The view of human beings here outlined, that there are known causal factors for many entities, in limited situations, does not rule out the possibility of novel or creative activity. As a matter of fact, new ideas arise in the minds of some men, new developments take place in all areas of human experience. In so far as cause-effect relations are known and this knowledge can be applied, situations (conditions and causes) can be established to facilitate the origin of new entities. The psychology of invention and creativity is subject-matter concerning which some information is available. For example, great musicians do creative work if they have acquired, and are encouraged to develop, technical skills and a background from which to draw, as with Sibelius and Brahms, from the folk music of their cultures. A scientist invents a new drug because of his knowledge of chemistry and biology, careful study and much investigation of the problem before him. True, a flash of insight or an apparent accident, as with the discovery of penicillin and insulin, may open up the final step. But these factors operate on a well-stocked and inquiring mind. It is, of course, the case that one cannot set out to make Mr A a musical or medical genius and be always, even frequently, successful. Nor can Mr X invariably do it for himself, making use of available material. In summary, our present knowledge of cause-effect relations does not rule out the possibility of novelty and creativity; indeed there are known causes, in some instances, of creativity and novelty.

VI

All entities have the characteristic: 'individual'

A person relying on comprehensive experience finds that all entities[1] have the characteristic 'individual'. Hence, each entity is different from every (any) other entity. One is not the other. Each entity is a distinct ingredient in the total content of experience. None is reducible to something else. For example, a match is not a human body, nor is it a mind. Likewise green is not a shape or truth.

The individuality of these entities is obvious. However, when dealing with a number of matches, a number of human bodies, a number of minds, it is necessary to examine carefully the nature of the individuality of entities which are members of one class or group

---

[1] Either many-occurrence entities or an entity which is one occurrence of a many-occurrence entity.

of entities (particular occurrences of a many-occurrence entity). For example, in what way is each match in a box of matches different from all other matches in the box? Likewise, in what way is one human body different from all other human bodies in a large group of men and women? Further, in what way is each mind different from all other minds present in a large group of human beings?

In the context of comprehensive experience the answers are as follows. Each item in a box of wooden matches (a typical example of inanimate physical objects) made by the same (one) machine and from the same (one) slab of wood, is individual in the sense that one is not the other. Each is an individual because numerically[1] different (distinct) slivers of wood are involved, and different blobs of chemical compound composing the heads of the matches.

The question arises as to whether, for example, each match is a unique individual in the sense that each has characteristics[2] which no other match possesses. The further question arises as to whether each match is a unique individual in the sense that the different slivers of wood involved (basic entities) have cell components and structures which vary from match to match such that no complete repetition of structure or sorts of cells takes place.

For all practical purposes it may well be admitted that under the conditions noted (made by the same machine out of the same slab of wood) the matches in the box may have the same shape and size characteristics. However, it is possible that under a microscope it might be found that variations occur, so that no match has exactly the same shape and size characteristics as any others in the box. As a matter of fact this is a type of investigation which is not ordinarily undertaken. Even if it is found that there is no uniqueness in the shape and size of each numerically individual match, nevertheless each individual match does have a unique characteristic. It alone occupies a specific spatial location at a specific time. This is so, ultimately, because the basic entity of a match, wood, is such that no (numerically) other piece of wood or any other gross physical entity can share its spatial location at a specific time. Concerning the question of whether or not each match has cell composition and structure which no other match embodies, this again is a topic which is not ordinarily considered; and information may well not be available at this time. In

---

[1] As indicated by the process of counting.
[2] Other than numerical.

brief, even if after careful examination it is found that cell composition and structure of the matchsticks lack any unique individuality, each match still does have unique space occupancy at any one period, as well as numerical uniqueness.

The preceding discussion of matches applies equally well to the question as to whether each of a number of human bodies is characterised by individuality. One body is not another; each is numerically distinct from all others. The question as to whether or not a human body has unique individual characteristics such as shape and size, which are not possessed by any other human body, is a topic which has not been gone into with sufficient thoroughness. Even if it is never settled, the fact remains that, as in the case of inanimate physical objects, each human body has one unique characteristic, namely unique individuality of spatial location at a specific time. In addition to the spatial characteristic, it is important to note that each individual human body so far examined has another unique characteristic, namely uniquely individual fingerprints. The very complex question of whether or not each human body, in a large group, has uniquely individual cell components and structure is again a question which has not been thoroughly investigated. If and when this question is settled, it will not effect the unique individuality of each human body which is based on spatial and fingerprint distinctions noted.

A discussion of minds is complicated by the fact that while matches and human bodies are parts of a public world, each mind is private. Minds other than one's own mind can only be 'examined' on the basis of indirect evidence. It is obvious to a person that his mind is not the mind of any other member of a social group. Each mind is numerically distinct. The familiar question arises: is each of these individual minds uniquely individual? Does each mind have characteristics which no other mind possesses? Further, is each mind as such uniquely (not just numerically) different from every other mind?

Available evidence seems to indicate that minds as such, apart from numerical differences, do not differ in 'component stuff'. They are all mental. Thus any examination of the problem of the possible uniqueness of numerically individual minds must focus on characteristics. As noted above, while the mind is aware of its own characteristics, it can only rely on indirect evidence concerning the characteristics of other minds.

Concerning mental activity and content (characteristics) of minds present in a social group which is a vast mass-media-dominated environment, there may appear to be considerable evidence to show that each mind does not have unique individuality of characteristics. It is painfully obvious, it may be claimed, that, for example, the particular thoughts and feelings of many minds, while numerically different, do not differ in nature (sort). Even if there are some differences, where a few hardy souls swim against the tide, it may be claimed that all minds react to a loud noise with fear. However, if all minds have something in common, this does not rule out the possibility that each has some unique characteristic not possessed by any other mind.

The fact of the matter is that, at the present stage of human knowledge, it seems to be the case that the question cannot be solved. Enough is not now known about minds in a social group, let alone all minds, to find out whether or not any one has characteristics which no other mind has, that is, uniquely individual in characteristics, or is uniquely individual as such.

It may be objected that the minds of a few of the world's outstanding persons do have unique individual characteristics. For example, there is only one Shakespeare, only one Mozart, one Plato. However, in all these cases reference is made to unique overt behaviour which is interpreted as indicating the presence of unique mental activities and content. The difficulty here is that it may well be the case that several minds *might* have had the same (though possibly numerically distinct) ideas which occurred to Plato, Mozart or Shakespeare, but did not report them.[1] One cannot decide with certainty that the mind of any of these men mentioned is a unique individual because it has unique individual characteristics.

However, consider a person. A person is a combination of a body and a mind. Here some unique individuals can be found. No other person so far discovered, did or does what Plato did. A similar comment is appropriate, it is noted that each person's body has the distinctive, unique individual characteristic of a fingerprint, and spatial location at a specific time. Here again is the basis for the unique individuality of each person.

So far the discussion of the characteristic individual has been chiefly concerned with the individuality or unique individuality of particular

---

[1] At least two men had in mind the theory of evolution. The first to publish it was not Charles Darwin.

physical objects and minds. Specifically the question dealt with was this. In what sense is a match, a body, a mind, individual—particularly when it is compared with other matches, other human bodies, other minds—that is having the individuality of members of a class?

It is important to stress what was noted in passing at the beginning of this discussion of individuality, namely that what have been termed 'many-occurrence entities' are characterised by unique individuality. For example, wood (which occurs frequently) is characterised by a unique individuality. It is definitely not green (which also occurs frequently). Likewise it is not mind (which occurs frequently) or mirror image (which occurs frequently). What has here been reported concerning wood with reference to the others can equally well be said of any of them concerning the others. In general all many-occurrence entities, basic, characteristic or resultant, are characterised by unique individuality. It is not merely a case of numerical difference. Each entity as such is not reducible to any of the others. This of course does not deny the fact that they may and do have some characteristics in common.

Each concept[1] is a unique individual. For example, the concept green is not the concept wood or the concept mind or the concept match. Similarly each of the other concepts is not any of the others. This is not merely a case of numerical difference. It is a difference in nature and relational characteristic.

The question arises as to whether or not a unique concept is exclusively naturally linked with each unique individual (in both senses of the term noted above). As background, it is to be realised that a simple concept is not exclusively linked with any one entity as far as numerical individuality is concerned. For example, the concept match is linked with each of the large number of matches in a box.

In so far as a particular match has the unique individual characteristic of occupying a specific space at a specific time, this can be referred to by (is exclusively linked with) a complex concept which as such refers exclusively to that uniquely individual match. For example, one can use a complex concept: the match on the north-east corner surface of the table in my office on Friday November 15, 1968. None of the ingredient simple concepts in this complex concept is linked exclusively to a particular match, but the complex concept is.

A complex concept is exclusively naturally linked with each unique

---

[1] Each particular occurrence of the entity 'concept'.

human fingerprint. The complex concept has one ingredient, 'fingerprint', which is not exclusively linked with a specific fingerprint and it has another ingredient which is uniquely linked, namely a complex concept of the unique nature of the specific fingerprint.

A simple concept is exclusively linked with each unique individual person, such as Shakespeare, Mozart, Plato. A complex concept is also available, as in the case of Plato, 'The man who wrote the *Republic* about 385 B.C.

As noted previously, at the present stage of human knowledge, it is not known whether or not each mind is uniquely individual and whether or not any cell component and structure (in a match or a human body) is a case of unique individuality. The question as to whether or not there are simple or complex concepts naturally linked to each of these entities (cells, etc.) cannot now be settled. It will be recalled that the discussion of matches and human bodies is regarded as dealing with typical cases of inanimate and animate physical objects.

It is not proposed here to go into more complex and detailed examination of this general problem. However, in passing it may be pointed out that apparently a social group is exclusively linked with a complex concept, though in some cases there may be a simple concept, for example 'Canada'. The complex concept 'United States of America, 1876–1968' is the same sort as the one discussed in connection with a particular match.

VII

Identity

The preceding discussion of individuality has an important bearing on consideration of the continuity of an entity, or as it may be expressed, 'identity' of an entity during a temporal duration. In order to determine that an entity continues, it must be clear that one is dealing with a unique individual in distinction from all other entities, and not several different entities in temporal sequences.

Further comments are required. Despite the fact that individual physical objects such as matches, bodies occupy, a unique spatial position at a specific time, it is of course the case that on occasion their position is changed. Hence there is a danger that one may lose sight of a particular match. However, it can be given a distinctive identifying mark which serves to show its distinction from others, at least in a limited situation. For example, a number of matches may be shaken up in a box and thus their spatial position changed. But if a purple dot previously has been placed on one, that is sufficient indication enabling one to keep track of that individual match. The same procedure can be followed in dealing with other physical objects including animate ones. The fingerprint differentiation can be used in keeping an eye on individual human bodies despite changes in position and other changes. The question now to be considered is this: what is the basis of the continuity of an entity?

An inanimate physical object is the same in the sense of being continuous, that is retains its identity, if during the period of time its basic entity is not replaced by another basic entity, even though there may well be changes in many of its characteristics. For example, a white matchstick may be painted green yet remains the same (continues), but with a different colour. Indeed its length might be considerably reduced and the comment would apply. On the other hand if a woollen sock is darned and re-darned to the extent that none of the original wool content (basic entity) remains then it is not the same sock, even if the new woollen sock (new basic entity) has the same shape, size and colour characteristics (in the sense of two occurrences of a shape, a size, a colour) of the original wool component, the sock. Consider the ingenious question: how about a situation where half the original wool component remains and half the wool component is new? To this the reply is: part of the sock is the same and the rest is not. There is both continuity (retention) of some of the wool, and replacement of some of the wool.

The situation is far more complicated in the case of a complex living organism (the human body). It is commonly accepted that all cells in the human body are replaced by new ones in the course of seven years. On the other hand it is contended that some biological components are handed on from generation to generation and remain the same (unchanged). Be that as it may. If it is a matter of fact that there is replacement of many cells by others in the course of seven years, nevertheless there is still a continuity of biological development which constitutes the sameness (it is one and continuing) of the biological organism. Thus though there are vast changes in shape, size and many other characteristics of biological organisms it is still the same biological organism as long as it involves the same (one and not another) process of biological development regardless of the replacement of some cells by others or even though there is not the literal retention of some biological components, such as genes and chromosomes.

As far as comprehensive experience is concerned, there is no continuity of a mind's activities or content in the same sense of continuous occurrence. There are periods of dreamless sleep in complete unconsciousness.

Consider next the case of a mind which loses most of the characteristics which it once had. It is no longer able to think clearly, its range of emotional reaction is limited. Despite these changes it is still the same mind, the basic entity has not been replaced by another. A person's mind when he is a child, an adult, and later perhaps the victim of senility, is the same mind, but there are of course drastic changes in its characteristics. It is obvious that 'sameness' is here being used to mean not absolute denial of change, but rather continuing in spite of change.

It is to be noted that the continuity of a mind is not dependent on the process of remembering or any other characteristic. It is the basic entity, the mind, which engages in remembering.

The foregoing comments on the continuity of mind are based on what a person's awareness of mind reveals, namely that over his lifetime his mind continues. Despite lapses into unconsciousness he is aware of his own mind when he awakes.

The fact that Experiential Realism accepts only those entities which are present to awareness, and offers statements concerning them only in so far as these reports are supported by awareness, seems to lead to difficulties when it is claimed that a mind continues when it is not aware of itself. The fact that a persons' mind is not aware of itself, or of its activities and content when the person is alseep, and further that an external observer viewing the person's body can detect no indication of the presence of a mind in a sleeping body, does not force one to admit or contend that no mind is present 'in' the sleeping person's body. When a person awakes from a dreamless sleep, his mind is aware of itself as a familiar entity, specifically it is the same entity as before sleep, and not another. The situation is like that when a mind is aware of its body's right hand as a familiar particular object. The fact that one is not aware of one's hand all the time, indeed that no one is, does not lead a person to doubt that it was there when unobserved. It is contended that a physical object, such as a chair, continues in existence even though no one is looking at it, because its basic entity does so unless some destructive agency eliminates it. Hence a physical object is there when we look again. The situation is the same with reference to a person's own mind.

There is no evidence to show that basic entities drop out of the universe during a period when no one is aware of them. Once it is established, as it can be, that an entity, for example a basic physical entity, a basic mental entity or a concept cannot be generated or destroyed by the mental activity awareness,[1] in other words, they do not have an internal relation to awareness, it follows that the removal of awareness does not produce the removal of that entity physical, mental or concept.

The situation concerning minds is this. A mind concludes that there were lapses of awareness on the basis of reports from other people concerning events in the environment of which it has no memory and hence did not have any awareness. One is justified in contending that the mind is there for an extended period, even though not present to awareness all the time. This comment is set in the context of the report that some entities are found in comprehensive experience to have brief duration, for example, a cloud of smoke or a flash of inspiration. Other entities have a longer life span. They continue until destructive force overcomes them. A person's right hand is one such. His mind is another. A person can distinguish the 'endurance for a period unless destroyed' characteristic on the basis of a suitable period of continuous observation. This does not involve being aware of the entity during the entire period of its continuing existence. For example, a person can be continuously aware of his mind or his hand for twenty-four hours, because of this characteristic of 'long-span' continuity. In observing a cloud, one finds it to lack long-term continuity. In the normal course of events it is quickly removed, while this is not the case with minds and hands.

The topics discussed above with reference to physical objects and minds have been dealt with as far as concepts are concerned.[2] Hence these matters will not be considered here.

The preceding discussion has incidentally called attention to the fact

---

[1] A person is aware of the fact that a mind does generate some mental entities, (memory or imagination images). Also a mind can remove these entities by refraining from the generative process. However, there is no evidence, that is, one is not aware of an act of awareness performing this generative function for basic physical and mental entities.

[2] See Chapter 4, p. 96 and Chapter 10, pp. 252–3.

that the terms 'same' and 'identity' are used in several senses and hence there is danger of serious misunderstanding unless qualifying terms are added or careful reference is made to the context. This point must now be emphasised. The term 'same' is used to refer to (*a*) a particular entity (such as a match) which continues in existence for a period of time. At any moment it is the same entity. (*b*) The fact of class membership may be the entity meant. Two occurrences (for instance spots) of blue are termed the 'same' colour. 'Identity' is used (i) as a synonym for the first (*a*) use of 'same' above to refer to continuity of a particular entity, usually continuity despite some change. The term 'identity' is also employed (ii) as a synonym for 'individuality', that is an entity is itself and not something else. Further 'identity' is (iii) a synonym for essential characteristics, or the basic nature, of an entity, as when one asks about the identity of a person or a thing (or how one identifies an entity).

There is nothing in comprehensive awareness which provides a firm answer to the question of personal immortality. As far as this presentation is concerned, there is no reliable (non-imaginary) awareness of a mind existing during its life independent of a body or after the destruction of the body with which it has been associated. It is, of course, the case that some men have claimed to have this awareness. A person should not be dogmatic in this or any other matter. He can only report what he has and has not experienced, or what he is prepared to accept on someone else's word, after a reliability check. However, it is relevant to note that hope sometimes leads people to indulge in imagination without recognising that this is the case.

VIII

Personality differences

The dominance of various types of mental entities in the activities of human minds is a topic of great importance. Here, the fact of individual differences or, at least, differences of sort must be reiterated. Some human beings are obviously creatures of selfish desire; others—a few —proceed on the basis of ultimate concern for ideal principles. In a few men, reasoning is a dominant factor; in others, when reasoning occurs, it is the handmaiden of emotion. There is no one detailed pattern which is characteristic of all men. Nor can it be claimed, on the basis of comprehensive experience, that inevitably all men are destined to be miserable or happy, good or evil. Sufficient evidence is lacking.

IX

Deity

An entity has the characteristic deity when it is of the greatest importance and influence. In the context of primitive experience, the entity may be a stick, a stone, or imaginary beings with human characteristics. Such entities arouse fear, awe, reverence and are regarded as sources of overwhelming power. In the context of comprehensive experience the emphasis is not on power in the sense of brute force but on a concern for the highest values known to man. Here power takes the form of 'lure', not external pressure.

Deity, thus understood, does not imply unbending 'letter of the law' morality untempered by mercy. Nor is deity involved in the ability to build something very big, for example a universe.

There is deity (shown in the concern for the highest values known to man) in the lives of some of the great Hebrew prophets and it is pre-eminently present in the activities of Jesus of Nazareth, as described in some passages of the Gospels. Further, this characteristic is found in a few people today, as in some phases of the life of Albert Schweitzer and also 'nameless ones' who serve their fellow men with unselfish devotion—some parents, teachers, clergymen, doctors. It is important to realise that this characteristic (concern for the highest values known to man) is not found only in the behaviour of those who call themselves Christians.

The question arises: is this deity entity present in other than human beings, that is, other than Jesus and a few other superior men and women? Some people, for example the great mystics, claim to experience an entity other than human, characterised by deity. There is also the 'scientific' experience referred to by William James as that of the 'Divine More'. There is an inflow of energy of a sort which indicates the presence of something like 'oneself at one's best'. As has been noted, there is no support in such experiences for thinking of God in terms of Imperial potentate or ruthless moralist. The preceding discussion of causal relations indicates that there is no experience of a First Cause. Nor is there awareness of a super-mind or person (analogous to the human mind, or person) who is a lover of, and producer of order in the universe after the fashion of a human contractor, planning and building a tidy and beautiful subdivision.

X

Space and time

Concepts have no spatial or temporal characteristics. These characteristics are restricted to physical objects, physically based resultants, minds and (some of) their characteristics. The temporal characteristic is that of involvement in an irreversible sequence of change. Consider for example the growth of a plant (physical object). Cases of the spatial characteristic of physical objects are, for example, (i) location with reference to other physical entities or (ii) distance between at least two basic physical entities, or aspects of their characteristics, that is the boundaries or extent of each of several patches of colour on the surface of a physical entity. In a less rigorous sense (than in the case of physical entities) mind (and its characteristics) has spatial location. As I think, my body (with mind) is located in my chair in my office. The experienced location of some mental entities is that they are mentally spatially located where they are experienced to be. A memory image, for example, has spatial characteristics in the sense that it has a specific shape and size. Mental time may be different from physical time. Here again, mental time is what it is experienced to be.

Physical space and time can be correctly or incorrectly observed. One can, also, distinguish normal from abnormal spatial and temporal characteristics of mental entities.

Various types of measurement of spatial and temporal characteristics are available. There is an apparent relativity in space and time because of the techniques and conditions of measurement and the context in which entities are found. But this does not destroy the objectivity of these characteristics in their context. The question as to whether or not there is one all-inclusive time series or spatial organisation cannot be settled by an appeal to awareness because all entities are not available.

In understanding many entities (concepts are an exception), a reference to both spatial and temporal characteristics is required. For example, an automobile accident takes place at location X at time Y. Some entities present in awareness give rise to problems which are dealt with by the imaginative formulation of scientific theories such as multi-dimensional space, various space-time systems, in short, relativity theory. Here again is a set of problems which are the primary concern of specialists.

8

VALUE

Sorts of values and value-opposites

Value is a characteristic of entities. Several distinctions should be noted: (*a*) true, moral, beautiful, pleasure, as such are characterised by value. In this sense they may be termed 'intrinsic values'.[1] There are other modes of value, for example (*b*) entities (including those which as such are valuable) are characterised by value (on occasion, not always) when they are instrumental in the reaching of some (any) goal. When they function in this fashion, they have instrumental value (they are valuable as means). Obviously, instrumental value does not belong to entities as such. It is acquired by entities because of their relations and functions in specific situations. (*c*) In a sense every entity has value since every entity is an ingredient in some situation, and that situation would not be what it is without that entity. This sort of value may conveniently be termed 'ingredient'.[2]

It is to be noted in passing, that in the context of logic, any entity to which an abstract 'variable' symbol refers is termed a 'value' of that symbol.

This chapter will be concerned chiefly with the following intrinsic values: true, moral, beautiful. Related to each of those there is what may be termed an 'intrinsic value-opposite' namely false, immoral, ugly.[3] These latter entities are sometimes termed 'negative values' in

---

[1] The phrase 'intrinsic value' is used because it is less cumbersome than 'entity characterised by value intrinsically'. It is of course the case that true, moral, etc., which are characterised by value, are characteristics of entities, for example propositions, persons, etc.

[2] In addition (*d*) some entities are valuable because of the value of their characteristics, as with a man because of his morality. (*e*) Some entities are valuable because of the value of their consequences. (*f*) Some entities are valuable because of their possible or potential values. For the purposes of this chapter attention will be focused on modes of value *a–c*.

[3] Pain is also an intrinsic value-opposite.

contradistinction to true, moral, beautiful which are termed 'positive values'. However, this type of labelling involves difficulties since, in a sense, the phrase 'negative value' is, on the face of it, a contradiction in terms. It is, of course, roughly speaking, a convenient form of expression if its use is properly understood, as the opposite of true, moral, beautiful. It must be admitted that 'intrinsic value-opposite' is a cumbersome phrase, but it is required in order to avoid confusion.

Just as some entities on occasion (in some situations) have the characteristic 'value' because they are means to some end, so on occasion some entities have the characteristic 'value-opposite', because they interfere with or prevent the attainment of some goal. For example when rain interferes with having a picnic it is a case of value-opposite—likewise when fear prevents careful thinking.

It is obvious that a complex situation may have more than one intrinsic value characteristic or specific value-opposite. For example, a man who makes true statements may live a moral life and have a beautiful face. However, a person who is physically beautiful may be immoral and show no concern for scientific truth. Also, an ugly man may indulge in falsehood, in some cases, and yet be moral. Consider the case of a false statement about the location of the intended victim of a lynching party.

Instrumental and ingredient value, and value-opposite

Before proceeding to a detailed discussion of the main topic of this chapter, namely the intrinsic values true, moral, beautiful, and their intrinsic value-opposites, it is advisable to add a few clarificatory comments concerning entities which have an instrumental or an ingredient function and are characterised by value of these sorts.[1]

It was pointed out that true, moral, beautiful, also false, immoral, ugly, are entities which, in some instances, serve as instruments (means) which lead to some goal. In this case these entities have instrumental value. For example, because a woman is beautiful others notice her. The same is the case with ugliness. As part of a specific situation, such entities also have ingredient value.

[1] This is a simplified analysis of the so-called extrinsic mode of value. The term 'instrumental' may be used to refer to one type of means rather than as a synonym for 'means'. Further, in a sense an ingredient may be regarded as a means. The complexities of value theory will be dealt with in a subsequent volume.

Entities which are not intrinsically characterised by value on occasion serve as means which facilitate progress towards a goal. For example, reasoning, desiring (mental activities), fear, anger (mental content), concepts such as democracy or money and physical objects, such as chairs and tables may function as instruments in achieving a goal. None of them as such is characterised by intrinsic value. They take on the characteristic value as they function as means. For example, a person sits on a chair to eat his dinner at a table. He thinks about democracy and its financing and then applies that thought to the improvement of conditions in his country.[1] He desires these results and feels fear and anger while he contemplates failure. This leads to renewed effort. Such entities of course have value as ingredients in the situation.

It should be realised that entities which have instrumental value may lead to goals which are characterised by one or some of (*a*) intrinsic value, (*b*) intrinsic value-opposites, (*c*) other entities which have instrumental value, (*d*) entities which are on occasion value opposites, with reference to specific goals, (*e*) entities which have no value characteristics other than ingredient.

Technically speaking, intrinsic values are invariant, that is, all entities which have value intrinsically have it in all occurrences of that entity. For example, all occurrences of true, beautiful, moral, are cases of the presence of value intrinsically. On the other hand, reasoning, desiring, anger, fear on some occasions have instrumental value, on other occasions they do not. Likewise on some occasions true, beautiful, etc., have instrumental value, on other occasions they are value-opposite, or neither. Hence the instrumental value of entities is not invariant. In the case of ingredient value, however, the characteristic is invariant.[2]

One additional introductory comment is in order. When the characteristic value is present, it is present in varying degrees. Thus comparisons can be made in terms of amount of value. In general there is a higher degree of value in intrinsic values, that is, entities characterised by value intrinsically, such as true, moral, beautiful, than there is in entities which have instrumental value such as thinking, desiring, a chair, the concept money, or ingredient value.

[1] Obviously, he is dining alone. His charming wife and daughters are absent!
[2] Intrinsic value opposites are invariant. Value-opposites' characteristics based on interference or prevention are not invariant.

True-false

The term 'true', as here used, refers to the characteristic of some propositions, images or concepts, namely that they accurately report the situation they purport to report, that is they are supported by facts.[1] The 'accurate report' or 'supported by facts' characteristic should not be interpreted as implying that there must be even an approximation to photographic reproductions of the entity (or entities) referred to. The proposition 'The table is brown', when true, does not look like a brown table. Nor need there be a paralleling of structure. Of course, in some cases this is so when one states the proposition expressed by the sentence 'The cat is near the mat.' The nearness of concepts 'cat' and 'mat' in the proposition is similar to the relation of the entities referred to. However, the structure of the proposition 'The causes of World War One were many and varied' does not parallel in any obvious sense the very complex situation to which it refers.

It is of course the case that some (few) ideas (mental images) which are true are accurate representations of a situation which they report. For example, a memory image of the face of a mantel clock in one's boyhood home may well be a fairly accurate pictorial representation of at least some of the characteristics of that physical object.

As such, a descriptive proposition, image, or concept is either true or false with reference to a specific situation, even though no one is asserting it or aware of it, or is aware of this 'accurate report' characteristic or its absence.

It is obvious that the term 'true' is used in senses other than that of accurate report. It may be employed to express agreement, approval, encourage confidence in a proposition and so on. For example, Mr A may state the proposition 'Mr B is a trustworthy person'. Mr C says, 'True' (to express the concept true) in order to indicate agreement. However, these and other uses should not blind one to the fact that the term is most commonly used to refer to the 'accuracy of report' characteristic of a proposition or image or a concept. Indeed, in most cases, failing this 'basic function' use of the term, the other uses would not have much plausibility or relevance. For instance, unless Mr C (in the illustration above) regards the proposition about

---

[1] The terms 'entity' and 'fact' are used as synonyms.

Mr B as an accurate report (a true proposition) he will not express agreement (using the word 'true' for that purpose). In any case, regardless of the term used, the main concern in this brief discussion has been to examine what is involved when a proposition, an image, or a concept or idea is an accurate report. (See Chapter 18, pp. 400–14 for further discussion of uses of the term 'truth'.)

III

Moral-immoral; justification for using the terms 'morally good' and 'morally evil'

The term 'good' is frequently used as a synonym for 'moral'. However, unless care is taken, confusion and misunderstanding may occur. This is so because 'good' is employed ambiguously to denote a wide variety of different characteristics. It refers to (*a*) moral value, (*b*) instrumental value (means to any goal), (*c*) a goal of any type, (*d*) efficiency in any type of activity. The term 'good' is also used (*e*) as a label for a value of any sort, (*f*) to influence the behaviour of oneself or others and (*g*) indicate an attitude of approval or some other positive 'pro' attitude.

In order to clarify the various uses of the term 'good', a few illustrations are required. One may call a dog 'good' in order to express approval, or influence its behaviour, even though none of the characteristics to which the term also applies is present. The dog is not moral, there is no reference to a means leading to an end. There is no reference to a goal. One is not referring to the dog's efficiency in any activity or a value of any sort, except ingredient value. Turning from the dog, a person may refer to the efficiency of a burglar, a football player or a pot by using the word 'good'. There is no intention to designate morality or any characteristic other than efficiency and ingredient value. A child may refer to candy as good. Obviously, he is stating a goal, or in other cases referring to a means to the goal, for example pleasure. Here again, no question of morality or efficiency is raised. An act of assistance may be termed good as a means but it may be lacking in efficiency, clumsy. It may be habitual behaviour and not a goal of activity, nor does it involve an expression of approval or an attempt to influence the behaviour of others.

Since markedly different characteristics (and some which overlap) and concepts are referred to by the same inscriptions and sounds, it is essential, in order to avoid confusion, to add explanatory qualifying terms and concepts, such as 'moral' good, 'instrumental' good. The term or concept 'right' is used as a synonym for 'good' in some of its various usages.

The two terms 'wrong' and 'bad', have almost as extensive multiplicity of usage as 'right' and 'good' ('goal' being an obvious exception). The term 'evil' is usually more restricted in its scope, being employed chiefly as a synonym for 'immoral'. However, consider 'This is an evil-smelling brew!'

A difficulty also arises because of ambiguity in the use of the term 'moral'. It is used in a broad sense, referring to a 'moral situation', to make a reference to both value of a specific type, morally good, and its relevant value-opposite, immoral. It is also used in a narrow sense, as noted above, to refer to values only. Thus, both self-sacrifice and killing someone raise moral issues in the broad sense; while in the narrower sense one regards only self-sacrifice (under certain conditions) as moral and killing someone (under certain conditions) as immoral. Thus in order to avoid confusion it seems advisable to use the phrases 'morally good' and 'morally evil' in preference to 'moral' and 'immoral', when the distinction needs to be made clear.

It has been pointed out that in the main use of the term 'true' it has as a synonym 'accurate report' which serves to clarify the meaning of the term 'true'. The situation is different in the case of 'morally good' or 'beautiful'. These terms do not have meaning-clarifying synonyms. They refer to unique characteristics which cannot be further specified or appropriately referred to by some other term with well-established meaning. It is also the case that 'accurate report' ('true') refers to a unique characteristic. A unique characteristic cannot be explained in terms of some other entity. As the result of comprehensive experience, a person is aware of these characteristics (entities): true, morally good, beautiful. The same general comments (just made about true, morally good, beautiful) apply also to false, morally evil, ugly.

It is possible to indicate situations in which these characteristics occur by means of illustrations. However, they cannot be equated with these situations.

Minimum ingredients of morally good and morally evil behaviour (with examples)

Having attempted to avoid misunderstanding concerning the use of inscriptions and sounds, so that attention can be focused on specified facts, let us now turn to an examination of situations (the entities) to which the terms 'moral' and 'immoral' or (in the preferred usage) 'morally good' and 'morally evil' refer. These are characteristics of human behaviour, internal and external, and hence of the persons who behave.

The conditions under (situations in) which these characteristics are found have one, some, or all of the following factors: (*a*) dynamic mental content (feelings and emotions) and mental activities (such as believing, willing, intending. When these produce actions they are termed motives, (*b*) intention, that is specific plans (content); (*c*) action[1] (overt bodily activity), which involves persons and the rest of the environment. More exactly, specific sorts of dynamic mental content and activities, specific sorts of intentions, specific sorts of actions are crucial.

It is very important to note that no one of these or all of them can legitimately be identified with 'morally good' or 'morally evil' as such; nor should they, one or all of them, be regarded as essential or exclusively important factors in constituting behaviour[2] morally good or evil. The context in which any one of these factors occurs is of the utmost significance in determining whether or not the entities 'morally good' or 'morally evil' are present in the situation.

Contrary to the view stated above, it may appear for example, that any one of the following factors as such, without reference to anything else, is morally good or constitutes it: (*a*) loving,[3] that is

---

[1] In some cases the distinction between motive and intention is blurred since some motives, essentially dynamic causal factors, involve an infusion of the element of intention, that is the specific goal in view. For example, one desires or wills some definite goal. On the other hand, an emotion such as anger may be a blind reaction to a stimulus without any specific intended goal in view. A person merely gives vent to his anger. Nevertheless in many instances an emotion such as anger is focused as the result of an intention. The term 'action' is here restricted to overt publicly observable activity.

[2] The term 'behaviour' refers both to (*a*) internal and (*b*) external activity.

[3] As noted in Chapter 2, Section I (Mind), strictly speaking the terms 'loving' and 'hating' do not refer to distinctive mental activities. Rather it is a case of the emotion love or the emotion hate being directed towards some entity. However, in the interests of convenience in statement, and in accordance with ordinary

experiencing the emotion love, (*b*) having the intention to help a friend, (*c*) transporting a person to his place of employment. Likewise, it may appear that each of the following factors is, as such, morally evil or constitutes it: (*a*) hating, that is experiencing the emotion hate, (*b*) having the intention (plan) to make a person miserable, (*c*) knocking a person down.

In order to examine the general point of view advocated in this book, and in an attempt to meet the specific objections just noted, consider the following. If a person loves the brutal and selfish exercise of power, he is morally evil (one cannot neglect the object of his love). Likewise, if a person hates his fellow men he is morally evil. In some cases, in attempting to understand a situation, one must supplement a consideration of the emotion not only by a reference to its object, but also note whether or not an appropriate action occurs, or at least is attempted. For example if a person hates the brutal and selfish exercise of power, his behaviour is morally good only if, in addition, he at least attempts to prevent such exercise of power. Similarly, a person who loves his fellow men is morally good only if in addition he gives tangible signs of his love. Mental activities, as such, also are not the decisive factors in determining morally good or evil behaviour.[1] For example, the desiring of the suffering of others is morally evil. The desiring of the success of others is morally good, if an attempt is made to assist.

Let us now turn to examine cases where specific intentions or specific actions may appear to be identical with, or decisive in constituting a situation morally good or morally evil, but actually this is not so.

Consider the following somewhat complex situation. A merchant, motivated by love of excessive profit, has an intention of helping a friend, but with the ulterior purpose (intention)[2] of selling him inferior merchandise (a car) at a big profit, and proceeds to drive him to his place of employment. This is not a case of morally good behaviour,

---

usage, the terms 'loving' and 'hating' will be used in this chapter (as well as 'love' and 'hate'). It would be unnecessarily cumbersome, for example, to employ the locution 'directing the emotion love toward' instead of 'loving'.

[1] As in the cases of emotions such as love and hate the 'object' of the activity must be considered and, in some instances, other factors.

[2] It should be obvious that in this and other illustrations a person intends (activity) his intention (what is intended). Hence in referring to an intention it is redundant to mention that it is intended. Strictly speaking the intending activity is not usually strong enough to function as a motive, that is a sort of mental cause.

despite the intention to help (offer a drive) and/or the action of driving to the place of employment. On the other hand, a parent, motivated by love, may have an intention of making his child miserable, and then proceed to restrict his supply of candy and so produce this result. This is moral behaviour if the situation is such that the child's health requires it. If a man knocks another individual down, motivated by love for that person, with the intention of saving him from a rain of bullets, this is morally good behaviour.

To repeat, no one factor (dynamic mental state [i.e. content or activity], intention, action) can be considered in isolation, since this isolation does not actually occur, as far as comprehensive experience is concerned. The presence of moral goodness or moral evil occurs in the context of some or all of these factors, but moral goodness or moral evil are not constituted by them or identical with any or all of them.

It will have been noted that the preceding discussion of morally good and morally evil behaviour has focused attention on men in their relations to other men. A man's dealings with himself have not been considered in terms of illustrations. However, the same general line of discussion applies. There is of course morally good and morally evil human behaviour when no other persons are present. A man who derives pleasure from imagining suffering is behaving in a morally evil fashion. A man who desires to save a person (himself) from control by evil passions and proceeds to do so is behaving in a morally good fashion.

In some cases of morally good or morally evil behaviour, motive and intention may not be present in awareness—a person acts on the basis of a well-established habit. Here it must be realised that the habit of action is the result of previous motives and intentions which have faded into the background to such an extent that they are no longer present factors. However, in view of their relation to the habitual action they have a bearing in determining whether or not the person's behaviour is morally good or evil. For example, a person who habitually supports the Red Cross by writing a big cheque is behaving in a morally good fashion if the basis of the habit was love of fellow men and his intention was to help suffering humanity.

The immediately preceding line of exposition takes the form of providing illustrations and reporting the presence of the characteristics 'morally good' or 'morally evil'. It is a case of an invitation to see for oneself.

It may be objected that surely some actions are, as such, morally evil, for example, telling an untruth or causing the death of another human being.

However, here again, the action must be set in its context. If a person motivated by love has the intention of sparing a seriously disturbed friend's feelings, and tells her (the lie) that her hat is beautiful, this is morally good behaviour. Likewise, if a person motivated by love of family intends[1] to terminate the career of a dope-mad intruder with obvious murderous tendencies, and does so, that again is not morally evil behaviour. It is morally good, if no other alternative is open in defence of one's family. The once familiar, 'Thou shalt not bear false witness', 'Thou shalt not kill' refer appropriately to cases where, for example a person motivated by hatred, intends to deceive for selfish purposes and proceeds to do so, or (again) motivated by hatred, intends to destroy 'unnecessarily' another human being and does so.

It is advisable at this point to consider complications which arise. For example, if a man is motivated by love of a friend and it is his intention to help that person, and he takes reasonable care, yet the action misfires, this is morally good behaviour, even if the consequences are disastrous. For example, suppose Mr A stops his car in order to give his friend Mr B a ride. But the brakes unexpectedly screech and Mr B jumps and falls into a big mud puddle. Such action by A is inefficient and hence bad in a sense. However, it is not morally bad (evil) behaviour. Consider the case of a person who is boiling with hatred and intends harm. He performs an action. The action, contrary to his expectations, is efficient in producing desirable consequences. This action is good in the sense of being efficient in producing benefits, but it is part of morally bad behaviour. Take, for example, the case of business man, Mr C, who hates and intends to harm a competitor, Mr D. He spreads rumors that D has leprosy. He does it in such a blatant fashion that the public see through it and turn from C to give their business to D.

Additional ingredients

Implicit in the preceding discussion is the claim that, in the case of dynamic mental states, intention and action, such as those illustrated

---

[1] This is a convenient way of referring primarily not to the activity of intending but rather to what is intended.

above, a person's behaviour is characterised by either moral good or evil. This is so even though there is no choice involved at the time, or any conscious or habitual concern for moral good or evil as such, or even awareness of these characteristics, or extensive knowledge of consequences of actions. This means that a small child, a person who is mentally ill, or even an animal on occasion engages in morally good or evil behaviour.

However, Experiential Realism does not deny that behaviour is found to be morally good or evil in situations where, in addition to the above specified minimum conditions (certain sorts of dynamic mental states, intention, action), other factors are present. A person may be aware of (knows) the presence of the characteristics 'morally good' or 'morally evil' in his behaviour. He may engage in a process of choice in selecting a motive, an intention and its related action. He may habitually function in this fashion. He may have a considerable knowledge of the consequences of his action.

Indeed, these factors may facilitate his achievement of morally good or morally evil behaviour. In the interests of simplification, illustrations will be of morally good behaviour. If a person is aware of moral goodness and a number of occurrences of it, this may stimulate him to sample those sorts of occurrences of moral goodness for himself. Adequate knowledge of the facts of human behaviour will enable a person to select intentions which best express his motives (such as love of a woman) and also what actions best serve his purposes. Some knowledge may save a person, for example, from focusing love (and hate) on inappropriate entities as far as morally good behaviour is concerned. If a person habitually chooses morally good behaviour, this of course will facilitate the achievement of morally good behaviour. As in the case of any activity, sound physical and mental health and a wide range of experience and maturity are of assistance.

However, these so-called additional factors are not ones which must be present if morally good or morally bad behaviour occurs.

Consider the following situation: A child or a simple uneducated adult is motivated by love, has an intention of helping a blind person across a busy street and proceeds to do so. He is compelled by love. He does not make a choice between this behaviour and other possible ones. He does not engage in a sophisticated (or any other) consideration of the morally good (characteristic of his behaviour or standard). He has never concerned himself with such matters. He is not acting on the basis of habit. He is not aware of possible consequences in any detailed or extensive sense. He is in poor mental and physical health, nevertheless he behaves in a morally good fashion.

Consider a Nazi storm-trooper who seizes a Jew and kills him, motivated by hate, intending to kill him. The Nazi is compelled by hatred. No choice is involved. He has no knowledge of the difference between morally good and morally evil. The issue does not arise for him. He is not aware of the consequences of his behaviour, except in the most obvious sense. His behaviour is not habitual. The situation under consideration is a case of the first time he had met a Jew. Nevertheless his behaviour was morally evil.

It may seem that the terms 'morally good' and 'morally evil' are here being used in an inappropriate sense, when applying them under so-called minimum conditions. The crucial point is that reference is being made to characteristics of human behaviour which are found in the cases referred to in the illustrations. Such behaviour is usually termed 'morally good' or 'morally evil'.

The claim that behaviour cannot be morally good or morally evil unless it involves additional factors such as choice, knowledge of good and evil, knowledge of consequences and so on, is an undue concentration on supplementary factors which are involved in some instances of these sorts of behaviour (as illustrated), but need not be present in order that such behaviour may occur.

In any case, the emphasis on additional factors seems to result from a concern for another question, that of responsibility and the related problem of praise and blame, reward and punishment. These topics will be considered shortly.

It follows from the preceding discussion that from the point of view of Experiential Realism a person is morally good if he engages in morally good behaviour. Similarly a person is morally evil if he engages in morally evil behaviour.

IV

Responsibility—praise, blame, reward and punishment

It will have been obvious that the moral goodness or evil of human behaviour can occur in the context of a causal situation. Whether or not a cause in a limited situation is internal (for example a strong eruption of desire) or external (such as social conditioning), a specific item of behaviour is immoral if it has the characteristic of moral evil. Likewise a person is morally good, in a typical situation involving emotions, intentions and actions, even if he is swept off his feet by the lure of some great saint who exerts an overwhelming lure.

At this point it is relevant to be reminded of some conclusions reached in a preceding discussion[1] so that they may be applied to the present topic. In most specific limited situations, some internal and external causes and conditions can be identified. On the other hand, some phases of human behaviour cannot, at the present time, be set in a causal pattern, particularly if one goes far back in time.

Why some people succumb to the lure of moral evil, and others react to the lure of good behaviour, why some people are not swept along by any lure, but rather they calmly choose after due deliberation, cannot be ultimately answered. We do not now have a complete causal explanation for the complex behaviour of any person in the context of the total situation of his environment, present and past and his complete heredity. The facts of behaviour can merely be reported on the basis of the present stage of development of comprehensive experience.

Nevertheless, regardless of the presence or absence of causes, specific sorts of behaviour are morally good or morally evil.

The fact that we cannot at present find out whether or not every entity has a cause does not rule out the advisability of providing stimuli in an attempt to influence behaviour. Some such stimuli are known to be effective causal agencies in some situations. It seems absurd not to use available educational factors. But in dealing with a human being in a complex and changing situation, accurate prediction or absolute control of results is difficult in some cases and impossible in others.

In the context of the preceding remarks some comments on praise and blame, rewards and punishments are in order. In the first place it must be noted that there is an important, though not absolute, difference between these two pairs of entities. Praise is essentially a case of applying a value judgement. It is a statement that behaviour is characterised by, for example good—moral or some other type. Blame is (*a*) the assigning of a value-opposite judgement and also (*b*) the assigning of responsibility. These judgements are not necessarily reward or punishment. They may be merely statements of facts, that

---

[1] See Chapter 7, pp. 170–91.

behaviour is good or bad (and a person is responsible). In the context of comprehensive experience, rewards (benefits or improvements in a situation) and punishments (deterioration in a situation) in their varying forms are (ideally should be) stimuli designed to produce changes in a present situation. These are forward-looking, educative rather than backward-looking (retributive). It is of course the case that in some instances praise and blame (in the sense outlined above) may function as rewards and punishments in the sense just discussed.

Some preceding remarks require further clarification. It may appear that a person is not subject to the judgements morally good or morally evil unless he is responsible for his motives, intentions, and actions. Further, the question arises as to whether a person is responsible for his choices, his store of knowledge, or lack of it, and the state of his health. The entire discussion is complicated by the fact that the term 'responsibility' is employed in at least two different senses.

(a) The term is used in cases where immediately preceding internal initiative (not immediately external compulsion) is causally efficacious. Hence a person is responsible in the sense that 'he did it'.

If a person desires to and intends to help a friend and does so, he is responsible. If a man is a kleptomaniac and steals a watch, he is responsible in the sense that he stole the merchandise. That is in this limited situation the decisive causal impetus was internal. The same comment applies to the case where a man shot a friend, not knowing that the gun was loaded, or the case of a man who once knew the date of the founding of his university, and has forgotten it. In all cases he did it.

On the other hand if a person sneezes and blows a candle flame against the curtain, thus causing a fire, he is not responsible. He did not do it if the sneeze was caused by pollen—the decisive initiating cause in this situation is external. It is internal in the case of the kleptomaniac. (It is to be noted that all these comments refer to limited situations as specified). However, since some preceding events are known to have contributed to make a person what he is, and hence determine, at least in part, what he decides to do, and his ability to do it, he is not responsible in the sense of being independent of the past, heredity and environment. True, we cannot prove complete causal sequence, but neither can we show that a person is not controlled by past causes. Some causal influence can be noted.

The claim that a person could have done otherwise in his behaviour in a specific situation is ultimately pointless, as was noted previously.[1] What he did he did (or did not do). That is all that we can know. Of course, remorse for not doing something in the past may function as a cause for producing that result in the future.

Just because a person behaves in one way in the past, or other persons have, this does not demonstrate that he is able to do it in the future, or now. In cases where he does not, the situation has changed. A might-have-been is merely a possibility which as a matter of fact was not actualised. However, as was noted previously, a recognition of causal efficacy does not rule out the occurrence of something new in human experience.

(b) The term 'responsibility' is used in a second[2] sense. A person is responsible if he is capable of performing specific activities, including that of profiting from specific stimuli. He is not responsible, in this sense, if he is not. A child is not capable of adult behaviour. He should not be held responsible for (be expected to perform) that sort of behaviour. He is capable of profiting from instruction, on an elementary level. He is responsible in the sense that one can expect him to derive benefit from this instruction. In many cases what a person can do and cannot do is definite and can be ascertained. The situation of course can change with the passage of time.

The question of excusing a person in the sense of refraining from (a) making the judgement, evil or wrong, and (b) assigning responsibility in the first sense (that he did it)—rather than blaming him for what he does or does not do), arises traditionally in the context of discussion of behaviour which is characterised by moral evil. But it can be extended to include some other form of badness.

From the point of view of comprehensive experience, a person who is hurled by a violent gust of wind through a shop window (that is the decisive causal initiative is external) should not be blamed for breaking the window. Rather he should be excused. He did not do it. His behaviour was not morally evil; he didn't desire or intend it.

There is a second and very important sense of 'excuse'. A person who as a matter of fact is unable to perform some physical or mental activity (if he is not responsible in sense b) because of some internal or external factor or combination of them, should be excused in the sense of not being expected to perform these activities. Likewise a person who cannot refrain from morally evil behaviour should be excused.

[1] See Chapter 7, pp. 188–91.
[2] A third sense not directly relevant here is 'of high repute', 'trustworthy'.

However, if his behaviour is morally evil, or deficient in any sense, he should not be excused in the sense of withholding the relevant value judgement. The behaviour of the thoroughly indoctrinated Nazi in desiring to kill, intending and then killing a Jew, is morally evil.

In the context of comprehensive experience, one concludes that if a kleptomaniac in a specific situation steals a watch he is not able to act in an honest fashion. It is to be noted that the kleptomaniac in this case is responsible for stealing in sense (*a*) the initiating cause was internal in this limited situation. Since he is incapable of refraining from stealing despite instruction and punishment, he is not responsible in the second *b* sense. In general because of lack of capacity we excuse (do not expect) children, savages and the mentally ill from the requirements of civilised living. To this extent they are not responsible in the second sense. But we do not excuse them in the sense that their defects in behaviour are disregarded. Their behaviour is not immune from the value judgements: morally good, morally evil.

In many cases of actual behaviour, what a person is able or not able to do[1] is simply what he does or does not do. In some cases this varies from instance to instance. In other cases there are well-established patterns.

As has been noted earlier, if a person is swept along by the overwhelming desire to achieve saintly behaviour and does so, he should be praised and rewarded as long as the initiative is internal. The absence of the exercise of choice or the ability to do otherwise, and the other factors mentioned—do not have a bearing on the relevance and appropriateness of praise. Reward is appropriate if he is able to profit from it. The same requirement is involved in the use of punishment. Thus though we excuse a person in the sense of not expecting him to behave in a specific fashion (because of lack of ability), he is not thereby beyond the applicability of (excused from) criticism (his behaviour is morally wrong) and punishment (if he is capable of benefiting from it).

It is of course the case that, coupled with blame and punishment, there may be kind and friendly attitudes and deeds as part of the educative process. In many instances these are essential if improvement is to be achieved.

---

[1] The question of normal physiological or mental capacity is not raised here, for example ability to walk or run but not fly (unaided by machinery).

V

Reputed relativity of morally good and morally evil behaviour

It may appear that moral good and evil are completely relative to time, place and many other factors. It is obvious that there are different moral codes and that they offer conflicting advice. There are contradictory lists of vices and virtues. Hence, it may seem that there are no specific objective[1] morally good or evil characteristics found in human behaviour (or firm value ideal concerning human behaviour). This view leans heavily on the experience of children, savages, and uncomprehensive adults. But in the context of comprehensive experience, these comments (based on cultural and personal relativity) appear in a different light. The experience of the child, the abnormal, the uncomprehensive, should not be used to cast doubt on the experience of the adult who is 'comprehensive' in his reference. In the experience of the latter sort of person, it is correctly recognised, for example, that the action of dancing, linked with specific motives and intentions, constitutes a situation which is characterised by morally good, in the context of a private party for one's friends, in one's home, today. On the other hand, behaviour involving dancing was morally evil during the Gold Rush days in the Yukon in Roaring Gulch Saloon (the action plus the then operative motives and intentions). Thus the apparent differences of opinion concerning behaviour involving dancing does not justify the relativity view in the sense of denying firm factual ingredients in the fields of morality and immorality. Rather, it emphasises the importance of context and the related motives and intentions which are involved.

As a matter of fact, there is considerable agreement concerning the moral goodness or evil of some specific sorts of behaviour, among both comprehensive and uncomprehensive persons. For example in all social groups, helping one's colleagues in time of war, as the result of an intention to do so, plus a feeling of brotherhood, is regarded as morally good. Murder of one's colleagues, based on an intention to do so, motivated by hatred, is considered morally evil. Sexual relations among close blood relatives, linked with relevant intentions and motives, is assigned the same status.

However, it should be noted that the mere fact of agreement does

---

[1] These characteristics as such are not dependent on human generation or their relation to human beings.

not prove the correctness of a point of view. There was a time when all men agreed that the earth was flat or that foreigners were, as such, enemies. At one stage in the world's history, a few scientists accepted the theory of evolution while the majority of men rejected it. Up until recently it was assumed by the majority of Englishmen that God was on the side of 'the biggest battleships'. The view that force, accompanied by destructive intentions and the motive of hatred, is not the morally best instrument of national policy is still not subject to approval on the part of all inhabitants of this planet.

The mere fact of disagreement does not prove that there is no firm, non-relative, basis for judgement. The disagreements may be due to lack of careful examination of a very complex situation. In other words, one explanation of disagreement is that the experts are correct and the non-experts incorrect.

VI

Obligation

In discussing human behaviour in general and the characteristics morally good or evil behaviour in particular, the term 'obligation' is used. Several senses must be distinguished.

(*a*) The term is employed to refer to a mental entity, a feeling. A feeling of the obligation sort arises either because of (i) the 'pressure' of the social environment which a person is afraid to oppose because of threatened punishment, or (ii) the 'lure function' of an ideal. When a person feels within himself (is aware of) a compulsion to translate a luring moral ideal into actual moral achievement that is a moral obligation feeling. In other words, the compulsion feeling is directed toward morally good behaviour.

In any case, a feeling of moral oligation[1] does not bestow, or in itself constitute, moral goodness. As in the case of other proper motives, there must be reference to object and in some cases linkage with intention, and in most cases translation into action in such a fashion as to be characterised 'moral goodness'. When a feeling of obligation is aroused by and involves not the lure of a moral ideal but social pressure, linked with fear of threatened punishment, the situation

---

[1] This more common locution will ordinarily be used rather than the stronger-sounding but more accurate 'feeling of the moral obligation' sort.

is quite different. To take an obvious example: if a feeling of obligation is socially engendered as indicated, behaviour is not morally good even if intentions and actions are otherwise acceptable. The man who writes a fat cheque intending to help the poor, motivated by a feeling of obligation because of fear of reprisal if he doesn't, is not behaving in a morally good fashion.

(*b*) The term 'obligation' is used also to refer to a different entity (that is other than a type of feeling). Obligation in this sense involves the carrying out of the requirements of a situation. In other words a situation requires something of a person. Hence he has an obligation. Living human beings have a tendency to continue living. Each living human being finds himself in a physical environment in which there are also other living human beings. The life situation requires a person to partake of food and drink. In this sense he has an obligation to eat and drink. The question arises: are there any moral obligations in this sense of the term 'obligation'? The answer, in the context of comprehensive experience, is that there is such an obligation. Specifically, in order that any person may live (and continue to do so) in a shared physical environment with other human beings, there are a number of requirements. Among the requirements of social life (in this broad sense) are: telling the truth, refraining from killing, at least under some circumstances, and likewise repaying services or benefits— coupled with the appropriate intentions and motives, such as willingness to cooperate. In this sense there are moral obligations in the context of group life.

A person may change from one specific social group to another, but he cannot thereby escape moral obligations such as those mentioned above. These obligations exist as long as one remains in a social group even though a person is not aware of obligation (in sense *b*) or formally accepts it, or feels it (obligation in sense *a*). If a person is not aware of such obligation, this is an indication of inferiority of some sort. Thus, by being a member of a group, a person is in a general situation involving specific moral requirements and this fact imposes specific obligations. These requirements (obligations) can be and are stated as guiding principles.

A further point is to be noted concerning obligation. In the case of the second type, a person is subject to the moral obligations of the sorts mentioned even though at a specific time he is unable (because of internal or external factors—or both) to measure up to the requirements of the situation in question. For example a child, as a member of a particular society, has as obligations morally good sorts of behaviour. If he is, as a child, unable to discharge these obligations, he should be given an opportunity to develop in such a fashion so that he can meet these obligations on a future occasion.

Even though an adult, because of lack of abilities, never reaches the point where he discharges his obligations, they are still relevant to him. He has merely failed to measure up to the requirements of the situation.

The only way to avoid moral obligations based on membership in society (where there are other human beings) is by natural death or suicide or being put to death by others. It may appear that complete withdrawal into the life of a hermit is another possibility.

Yet can a hermit actually avoid moral obligation based on the requirements of the situation in which he exists? The answer is no. As a member of the human race, that is the social group which shares a very large physical environment—the situation which he cannot avoid as long as he lives—he has some moral obligations. Specifically: the continuation of life involves moral behaviour of the sorts mentioned above.

It is further to be noted that if one concentrates exclusively on our hypothetical hermit, the requirements of his own life (isolated from the rest of society) involve him in moral behaviour. For example, he must be 'honest' with himself in his dealings with his non-human environment.

It is of course the case that society may continue for a long time, human life can continue for a lengthy period, even though a considerable number of its members do not practise moral behaviour. However, a few men whose behaviour is morally evil can destroy society and, indeed, in the day of the atomic bomb, the entire human race. In brief, since human life depends ultimately on the practice of morally good behaviour on the part of all members of the human race (one person[1] can by morally evil behaviour destroy a society or the human race), as long as a person continues to be a member of society, moral requirements (obligations) are placed on him. Even if one person exists alone on the earth he has moral obligations to himself. Thus death is the only way by which a man can avoid these obligations, either his own death or the elimination (death) of the entire human race, for instance though nuclear war.

In order to round out the discussion of obligation, one other (c)

---

[1] A scientist who has become a hermit and has with him a lethal instrument world-wide in efficacy.

major use of the term should be noted. When a person wishes to achieve some goal, he must use the appropriate means. For example, when one wishes to get from London to New York as quickly as possible he is obliged to fly.

The preceding discussion of obligation in sense *b* that is, the require-ments of a situation, may be interpreted in terms of the 'means to end' analysis. In other cases the requirements for the continuance of life alone or in society are in an obvious sense means to these ends.

(*d*) A fourth use of the term 'obligation' has to do with cases where a person makes a binding promise. He is thereby under obligation to honour his promise. Whether or not honouring his obligation is morally good or morally evil depends on the context of motives and intentions. For example, having promised to pay back a hundred pounds to a friend, if the friend demands it when drunk, then imple-menting the obligation would be morally evil if one hated him and intended to harm him. Not implementing it would be morally good if one were motivated by sympathy and intended to save him from financial loss.

VII

Beautiful-ugly

A beautiful entity may have form (pattern), specific sensory char-acteristics, express emotion or convey concepts, involve some specific reaction, individual or social, satisfy some end or desire, but the entity is beautiful ultimately, not because of these facts, but because it in-volves the characteristic 'beautiful'. Some of the characteristics (as listed above) may be present and yet the entity is not beautiful.

Consider, for example,

> Roses are red,
> Violets are blue,
> Sugar is sweet
> And so are you.

OR

> Spring, Spring
> The bird is on the wing,
> Absurd, Absurd,
> The wing is on the bird.[1]

The preceding discussion of the apparent relativity of good is equally relevant to the discussion of beauty.

VIII

The comparison of values and value-opposites

Some clarification (however brief) must be provided for the introductory comment that the characteristic value is present in varying degrees (amounts), hence various entities and situations can be arranged in order or value. The situation is indeed complex. It is to be remembered that entities which are characterised by value-opposite may have value of the instrumental sort, they are involved in the achievement of ends. Any entity has ingredient value. Within groups of entities which are characterised by value-opposites, a ranking can be noted. A situation involving both value and a value-opposite can be found to be as a totality on balance, either a case of value or value opposite.

The following few brief illustrations are merely reports of what is found in comprehensive experience. Here again, as in the case of other ultimate questions, an appeal can only be to see for oneself.

Degrees of moral good present in two situations can be compared, also can degrees of moral evil. For example, there is more moral goodness in a situation where a person motivated by love of his fellow men embarks on a campaign of slum clearance, carries it through to a successful completion and derives great pleasure therefrom—than a simple case of Mr A enjoying the success of Mr B. Likewise, enjoyment of the slaughter of a million human beings is morally worse than hatred of one human being.

Degrees of beauty can also be compared as well as degrees of ugliness. Miss Universe is more beautiful than Miss Podunk Centre (unless Miss Podunk is Miss Universe). A polluted stream in the middle of a vast industrial complex is more ugly than the face of Socrates.

---

[1] An illustration of 'how not to do things with words'!

An intense pleasure which has a long duration has a higher degree of value than one which is less intense and of short duration. A pain which is very intense and of long duration is worse than a pain of slight intensity and short duration.

A morally good life takes precedence over a beautiful picture.[1] Morally evil behaviour is worse than an ugly picture. A person who is characterised by ingredient value, and very little instrumental value, or beauty, or moral goodness—is of less value than a beautiful cathedral which is instrumental in inspiring morally good behaviour. This involves the claim that the man has developed to the full extent of his potentialities. However, the building of a cathedral does not take precedence over the provision of a wide range of educational opportunities for the members of a community.

Another sort of evaluation may also occur, for example, in a situation where a person with a beautiful face behaves in an immoral fashion. The total situation is, on balance, one of value-opposite. On the other hand, when an ugly person behaves in a moral (morally good) fashion, this situation is one of value. These evaluations presuppose limited situations. Of course moral good may result (in a broader situation) from a limited situation which is morally evil. A programme of reform is aroused by the presence of suffering. But that does not change the evil of the limited situation. It is a case of an entity (suffering or pain) which is as such characterised by value opposites; nevertheless it also has an instrumental value.

[1] Strictly speaking, value is a characteristic of morally good. A life which is morally good has value by virtue of its characteristics. Thus, in this sense, value is not directly a characteristic of the life in question. However, it is a convenient locution to refer to such a life (that is, a morally good one) as valuable. The same comment refers to the value of a beautiful picture. Strictly speaking, value is not directly a characteristic of the picture. It is a characteristic of a characteristic (beauty) of the picture. The case is different concerning instrumental and ingredient values. Here value is a characteristic of entities, not of characteristics of entities. More specifically, value is a characteristic of entities when they have an instrumental function or are ingredients in a situation. It is this entity which is an instrument or an ingredient and hence valuable. It may appear that since, for example, instrumental function is a characteristic of an entity, it is the instrumental function which is characterised by value analogously to morally good and beautiful. This, however, is not the case, the analogy does not hold. It is the entity which is used to produce results or produces them itself, and here it has an instrumental function. When this happens it acquires value. The instrumental function as such does not have value. It is the way in which the entity in question is valuable. The same general comments apply to the ingredient characteristic of entities.

A pleasure which as such is characterised by value may, in a wider situation, be linked with behaviour which is evil. In this case the wider situation is, on balance, a case of value-opposite.

The question arises as to the range of a situation which a person should consider in evaluating an entity. For example to what extent should a man consider other men? Specifically, should he sacrifice himself for the welfare of others yet unborn? Likewise, should a person with creative powers and an excellent education, a high degree of morally good behaviour and a deep appreciation of beauty, attempt to obtain and retain conditions, physical, mental and social, which enable him to continue on this level of behaviour? Specifically, to what extent should he be prepared to stress his own value and the requisite condition, even at the expense of others? The best that a person can do in such complex situations is to take into consideration the widest possible range of entities and attempt to achieve the highest possible degree of value in this comprehensive situation. No simple formula will suffice. In any case where value-opposites exist, there is a moral obligation[1] to effect the greatest possible improvement.

The ability to be aware of value and value-opposite characteristics, and make complex rankings such as those just mentioned, is one of the great achievements of comprehensive experience. Much exposure to, and the careful examination of, such situations is necessary. But this evaluative skill, like other human activities, can be developed and used with confidence in fairly extensive situations, at least in a general fashion. A thoroughly comprehensive approach is an ideal to which human beings can approximate—the degree of apprehension in the future cannot be predicted. Present restricted competence in some cases gives ground for hope, in spite of many instances of woeful inadequacy.

The preceding remarks about beauty and the comparison of the values and value-opposites of various entities, and situations, are extremely general and require a great deal of clarification. However, these extensive topics do not fall within the scope of this book. Brief comments are included here merely to indicate the general position of Experiential Realism with reference to these problems. It is obvious that many other aspects of value have not been considered in this chapter.

[1] In the second sense (above).

227

9

EXPERIENTIAL REALISM

I

Outline of the most general characteristics of entities

A comprehensive examination of the world experienced by human beings leads to the conclusion that the vast complexity of this realm can be sorted out in a relatively simple general fashion, thus providing the inclusive yet adequate grasp of fundamental factors which some men seek.

As outlined in the preceding discussion, Experiental Realism reports that in the world a person finds: (*a*) entities that are basic and (*b*) entities that are characteristic of basic entities. It is to be noted (*c*) that some characteristics of basic entities also have characteristics. There are, in addition, (*d*) so-called physically based resultants which are neither basic nor characteristic, but have characteristics. Some basic entities may have as components several basic entities. There are various combinations of basic entities. No basic entity is experienced without characteristics. Entities are either simple or complex.

It is essential to realise that in discussing the characteristics of entities, reference is being made to a specific situation which may be either normal or abnormal. What constitutes a normal situation concerning many entities can be determined, for example for bean plants, human beings, sticks, minds or memory images, as far as comprehensive experience is concerned.

Usually in listing the characteristics of an entity a person focuses attention on that entity in a normal situation.

As in the preceding chapters, the summary (and additional comment here presented) will focus on many-occurrence entities. However, frequently in providing illustrations, a particular occurrence of an (a many-occurrence) entity will be examined. Such a particular occurrence (that is the particularity of occurrence) is, as noted previously, an entity in the sense that, like anything else here under discussion it is present to awareness. Thus, for example, wood is a many-occurrence entity. A particular piece of wood is an entity.

It has been pointed out that in examining the characteristics of a many-occurrence entity, for example a leaf, it is found that particular leaves differ one from the other, for instance in shape, size and in colour. Some are oval, others pear-shaped, some are large, others small, some are green, others red. However, it is still the case that all these leaves, despite their differences (variations) are characterised by some shape, size, colour. In this sense one can legitimately report that among the characteristics of the entity leaf are shape, size and colour. On the other hand, obviously one cannot claim that the many-occurrence entity leaf has the following characteristics: green, two feet by four feet, oval.

It is to be emphasised that a leaf has colour because green for instance is characterised by colour and the leaf is green. Similarly, a leaf has size because it is large, shape because it is oval. The same situation applies to some other characteristics. For example a leaf is valuable because it is beautiful, has a numerical characteristic because it is one entity and so on. Obviously, length and width, for example, are characteristics of characteristics. In this case of course particular occurrences of those entities vary considerably.

A further point must be made at the risk of introducing confusion in some minds. It is the case that there are many particular oval leaves, green leaves, large[1] leaves. In other words; oval, green, large are many-occurrence entities. Indeed oval leaf, green leaf and large leaf are many-occurrence entities.

Experiential Realism reports that comprehensive human experiencing finds three main types of basic entities: physical, mental, and concept. Basic physical entities (such as wood, metal) are characterised by length, width, thickness (hence shape, size), bounded by a surface (hence, smoothness or roughness), resistance to pressure, heat, cold, colour, weight and, in some cases, by odour or taste.[2] Basic mental entities (minds) are characterised by a number of (i) activities, such as awareness, being interested, choosing, desiring, generating images, willing, reasoning, and (ii) entities which are contents such as memory images, emotions.[3]

It is important to realise that memory images which are character-

---

[1] This, of course, is a relative term.
[2] See also discussion of potential characteristics, pp. 31–2.
[3] See Chapter 2 for a more detailed list.

istics of mind may have as characteristics: colour, shape, size, and many of the other characteristics of basic physical entities which are listed above. Mirror images (physically based resultants) also have many of these characteristics.

All basic physical and mental entities, also concepts and physically based resultants, and their characteristics, have relational, value and numerical characteristics. They are also characterised by individuality and reality. Other characteristics, though not as widespread in their occurrence, are very extensive in range and must be noted, if one is to stress the most general and fundamental features of the vast world of entities of which a 'comprehensive' human being is aware. These additional characteristics are change and endurance.[1]

In some instances they are characteristics of entities basic or characteristic. In the case of physically based resultants, for example shadows, such entities are either components (such as colour) or characteristics of components (such as length).

The fact that physical objects (that is (*a*) basic physical entities or (*b*) a basic physical entity with specific characteristics, such as a table), minds and concepts have some characteristics in common ('shared') may seem to present some difficulties. If this is the case, how can they be differentiated? However, the fact that the wood of a physical object (table) is characterised by red and so is a memory image of the table, does not present serious difficulties. The inherent characteristics of the wood and of the memory image are different. One is physical, the other is mental. One memory image, one concept, one piece of wood, are not reduced to sameness or some approximate similarity because each is characterised by one.

The preceding remarks on fundamental (most of them being invariant associates) and most general characteristics of entities will now be further illustrated as a clarification of the point of view of Experiential Realism.

Physical objects, minds, concepts, physically based resultants, and their characteristics are all real, in the sense that they are 'there',[2] entities found in experience. No entity can be reduced to (regarded as the same as) another. For example, entities such as length, colour,

---

[1] See Experiential Realism's use of the term 'neutral': Chapter 2, p. 63, Chapter 4, p. 92.

[2] The term 'reality', of course, is used in many other senses, for example, to refer to (i) a non-artificial or (ii) a non-observed state of affairs, such as a postulated 'underlying' reality.

awareness, memory image, deserving cause, value, five, shadows, wood, are all real. Each entity is characterised by individuality in the sense that it is what it is and not something else. Further, it is erroneous to claim that for example, wood is characterised by wood, or red by red. A characteristic is always some other entity than that of which it is a characteristic.

Possibility and actuality

Some entities have the complex relationship of possibility (possible) to actuality (actual).

For example when an architect first planned Talbot College, he formulated a complex concept (and no doubt a complex imagination image and numerous blue prints). This complex concept was characterised by possibility. When the building (a physical object) was constructed, it was an actuality (was characterised by actuality) in relation to the complex concept which was its plan. On the other hand, the complex concept mermaid, as created by some imaginative person, could serve as a possibility, but in this case there is no actuality corresponding to this possibility. Nevertheless a person knows what, if it were present, would constitute (be characterised by) actuality.

It is essential to realise that the actuality characteristic, in the possibility-actuality situation, is not restricted to physical objects (and their characteristics). A person using concepts may consider the possibility of being aware of an imagination image of an elephant and then generate an actual imagination image of an elephant (a mental entity).

It is to be noted that the term 'existence' is used as a synonym for 'actual' in these sorts of situations. In this sense what is termed 'actual' or 'existence' is a characteristic of such entities. For example Talbot College exists (is actual), a mermaid does not exist[1] (is not actual).

Returning to the main theme: a person using a vague concept may consider the possibility (the concept is characterised by possibility) of formulating an exact relativity formula, and then proceed to develop that formula. Here the actual (what is characterised by actuality) is a proposition formed of concepts. The term 'existence' is not customarily used to refer to such a conceptual formula, rather the term 'subsistence' is employed (and in general in referring to concepts).

Of course the possibility-actuality relationship may be in effect

[1] As a fish-lady(!) in the physical world.

even though no person is aware of it. One should not be misled by the fact that the preceding illustrations involve a person who is aware and acts.

The situation is further complicated by the fact that any physical object or mind or physically based resultant (and its characteristics) is loosely termed 'actual' (actuality) or 'existent' even though there is no obvious possibility-actuality situation in clear focus. For example, a particular building is termed 'actual' or 'existent' even though it does not involve contrast with a concept which may be regarded as (formulating) a possibility. The point being made is that in such situations one is being confronted by a building or an imagination image (for example of an elephant) or a shadow, and not merely by a concept. Here again the terms 'actual' or 'existence' refer to an entity which is characteristic of physical objects, minds, physically based resultants, and their characteristics, in other words they are not concepts, but rather entities to which concepts refer. In this sense actual (existent) is a characteristic of some entities and the terms 'actual' and 'existent' are legitimate predicates in sentences which refer to tables, imagination images and mirror images (that is entities which are physical, mental or physically based resultants).

At this point, it is well to refer briefly to the characteristic 'potential'. This is a sort of 'possible' but in a different sense from in the preceding discussion. There, a distinction was made between (a) what might be but had not yet occurred and (b) an actual occurrence. Here the term 'potential' is used to indicate that an entity, under certain conditions does occur. In many cases the term is used to indicate that the entity has occurred and will occur again (if conditions are suitable). For example gunpowder has the potentiality to explode, electricity to shock. Knowledge in storage is a case of potentiality in the sense that given proper conditions it, being content or skill, will again be present.

Change and endurance

The characteristics change and endurance are not found in all entities. Concepts endure but do not change. Whether or not they are eternal cannot be now determined. A basic physical entity, under many conditions, undergoes changes of characteristics very slowly and endures for a considerable temporal period. A basic mental entity is characterised by various activities, hence change is involved. However, some activities continue (endure) for a considerable period of time as do some relevant contents. Also characteristic patterns of changing activities endure in a general sense. Some particular contents and activities do not endure. They come and are gone. True, the coming may require a very brief duration of time. However, in any case a basic mental entity endures during extended periods of time.

Relations

There are many sorts of the characteristic 'relation'. The most fundamental, and general, in the sense that all others are cases of it, is the relation 'characteristic of'. More specific relations[1] are the spatial, temporal, causal and organic relations and various sorts of logical relations and numerical ones. Each entity, because of its individuality, has the relation of difference with reference to the rest.

Physical objects are in causal relations (are efficient causes) with some other physical objects, and, in some cases, with minds. The same is the case with minds, in other words, minds produce physical and mental effects. Spatial and temporal relations characterise basic physical entities and their characteristics. Temporal relations and specific sorts of spatial relation characterise basic mental entities and their characteristics; likewise physically based resultants. Concepts are neither temporal nor spatial. Concepts have natural and man-made relations with other entities. As a result of some of these relations mentioned above, more specific relations are found.

In so far as physical objects, minds and concepts have established (continuing or recurrent) relations with each other, the basis of order is established.

Entities which are characteristics are either inherent (for example physical, mental, physically based resultant, colour, shape, relation, value) or associate (such as length, red, morally good, cause, basic). It is to be noted that each entity has only one inherent characteristic, but may and usually does have, a number of associated characteristics.

A concept has as associated characteristic linkage with some other entity. However, the other entity as such is not a characteristic of the concept. Likewise the other entity, though actually linked with the concept, does not have the concept as one of its characteristics. In other words the relationship is characteristic (in both cases) but the relata are not.

[1] In addition to possible-actual.

Simple-complex

Some entities are simple, that is no distinctions can be found within them; for example green, pleasure, beautiful. Others are complex, meaning that distinct entities are found within the entity, in relations (and with other characteristics), for example wood, table, horse, deity, society. Some clarificatory comments are in order.

Consider first complex entities. Wood is composed of a number of specific sorts of cells. These cells are components of wood. The cells are in a specific pattern of arrangement. This arrangement (relational characteristics of the cells) is constitutive of the wood in the sense that without these relations there would not be wood. The sort of grouping of cells is compound. The wood here in question is no longer part of a living tree. It must be emphasised that wood is not just cells. It is a complex entity composed of cells in a specific pattern of arrangement, and forming a compound. Given this, the entity wood is present.

A table is a compound composed of pieces of wood, a top and four legs (to simplify discussion at this point, the fact that wood is complex is not here emphasised). As in the case of the wood, the pattern of arrangement of components is spatial. This pattern of arrangement—the relation of components in order to produce the table shape, otherwise the entity is not a table—is constitutive. Thus a table is its components in a specific constitutive arrangement. Another arrangement of these components would be another entity, such as a pedestal. Size is also a constitutive characteristic. Given the same shape—size differentiates a table from a footstool.

A biological organism, is composed of a number of cells[1] of various sorts in constitutive relationships which are not just spatial but also organic.

In the case of what has been termed 'deity' in this discussion, the components are, at least in part, moral goodness and concern, both theoretical and practical, for the entities beautiful and true. These are closely interrelated and developed to a very high degree. These relational and quantitative characteristics are constitutive. Deity consists of these components with those characteristics. Without some of those components or characteristics one is for example confronted in the case of a medium degree of moral goodness and little concern for beauty—by a decent human being.

---

[1] The legs of a horse are, of course, components. However their status relations are not exactly the same as the legs of a table.

A society is a group of human beings (components) organised in a complex pattern of relationships (constitutive characteristics). Lacking some of the relations, a group of persons degenerates into a mob. There is no longer a society.

In summary, a complex entity is its components and the characteristics of its components which are constitutive of the complex entity. In other words a complex entity is not just its components or just the constitutive characteristics of its components. There is a difference between a number of cells and a piece of wood. There is a difference between a table and a complex spatial pattern. In any case, characteristics are always characteristics of some entity. It is essential to realise that a complex entity does not downgrade its components.

In brief, a complex entity is a distinct entity. It is distinct because of its components and the characteristics of these components which together make the entity distinct—in the sense covered by the preceding illustrations.

Simple basic entities with their characteristics, although there is a togetherness of distinct entities, do not count, in the context of comprehensive experience, as instances of complex entities.

In the case of basic physical entities, many characteristics are not within them. This is also the case with concepts. Many mental characteristics are, roughly speaking, within the mind. But—and this is crucial—the relations of basic entities and their characteristics are not constitutive of basic entities and their characteristics.

Turning to simple entities such as green, pleasure, beautiful, no components can be found similar to cells in wood, the legs of tables, etc. Further, green, pleasure, beautiful are not ultimately distinguished one from the other in terms of shape, size, pattern of arrangement of components or any other characteristics. Indeed there are no patterns of arrangement of components because there are no components.

It is therefore obvious that simple entities are not open to analysis in the sense that complex ones are.

Internal-external relations; body-mind concepts

Many cause-effect and other relations between entities, technically speaking, are termed 'internal'. In other words, without these relations entities would not exist. Many relations are external, that is not constitutive of the entity or involved in the production of it.[1]

Some clarification of the preceding comments is in order since this topic was not fully covered in the discussion of causation in Chapter 7. When a body causes its related mind to feel pain, or when a mind causes its body to raise its arm, or one inanimate physical object (a cue) causes another (a ball) to move, the relations are internal, as far as the pain, the movement of the arm or the movement of the ball are concerned. In other words, the pain would not occur, the movements of the arm and ball would not take place without the causal relation specified.

On the other hand, it is to be noted that in all cases of the occurrences of a new characteristic of an already existent entity, the entity which is the cause is not dependent for its existence on being in a causal relation to some entity. For example, a billiard cue, a physical object, is not brought into existence by the fact that it is used in a game to hit against and cause a billiard ball to move. Thus, as far as causation is concerned, the relation is external, not constitutive of the entity which is the cause.

When, for example, two physical objects are side by side and do not influence each other, or two minds are members of a common culture but do not influence each other, this relational characteristic is external in both cases.

So far attention has been focused chiefly on causal relations as far as characteristics are concerned. The question now arises as to whether or not there is causal efficacy of the mind in producing an inanimate physical object, that is whether or not an inanimate physical object (such as a chair or a piece of wood) is internally related to a mind. There is the related question as to whether or not a mind is produced by its body—is internally related to it.

Comprehensive experience indicates that a mind cannot, by mental initiative alone, produce a physical object either animate or inanimate. A mind for example, cannot will into existence a human body or a match, even though it can generate entities such as an imagination image. Despite the fact that all our contacts with physical objects involve awareness, the process of awareness does not create the object of which is aware. In short, a physical object is not internally related

---

[1] For a discussion of constitutive relation other than cause-effect see Chapter 3, pp. 90–1.

to any mind even though a mind can, on occasion, produce new characteristics in its body (its body being already present).

Concerning the question as to whether or not a basic physical entity can produce a mind, hence whether or not a mind is internally related to any physical object, a number of facts must be considered.

Up until the present no mind has been found apart from an accompanying body. An external observer discovers that some bodies (dead ones) do not have associated minds. It has also been noted that on occasion a living body is present but that there is no evidence[1] of a mind, for example when the body is sound asleep. When a person awakes there is evidence of the presence of a mind. Do these factors lead to the conclusion that a mind is produced by its body? As far as comprehensive experience is concerned the answer is no. Just because one entity is present and another has periods of absence and recurs as far as an external observer is concerned, does not prove that the relationship is causal. Incidentally, when there is awareness of both body and mind (as by a person of his own mind and own body), both are present for a relatively long period. Yet no person is aware of the continuous existence of his own or any other body, during the span of a week. The decisive issue to be settled is this: is a mind aware of a mind being generated by its body? The answer is no. Of course a mind is aware of some of its characteristics, for example pain being produced by its body, but this is a case of production of characteristics, not the production of the basic entity, mind itself. Obviously a mind could not be aware of its being produced because it would not be there to be aware of its production by its body. One person cannot be aware of another person's mind at all. So he cannot observe the other person's body producing the other person's mind. Thus, in terms of appeal to awareness, the question cannot be settled as to whether or not a body produces a mind. There is no awareness of this happening. This of course does not rule out the possibility.

In observing a very young child one can note that, as his body develops, his mental activities and contents do also. This seems to indicate the causal dependence of a mind on a body. A comment on the basis of comprehensive experience is simply this: what one observes is two roughly parallel processes of development. It is of course the

---

[1] In distinction from awareness of the entity. See discussion of knowledge about other minds, Chapter 6, pp. 157–8.

case that some of the mind's characteristics cannot occur until there is bodily development. But the mind as such is not its characteristics.

A child, almost immediately after birth, gives every indication of possessing a mind with an admittedly limited range of characteristics.[1] It is known that a person's body begins its career when two cells unite at the time of conception. What produces his mind or when it begins is not open to awareness. No appeal to observation of other persons, is appropriate because what a person knows about other persons' minds is based ultimately on what he knows immediately about his own mind.

A simple concept (as a basic entity) does not have internal relations of the causal sort (either efficient or final) to physical objects, minds or other concepts. That is, it is not dependent for its subsistence on them. The concept 'bomb' is not constituted in a causal sense by its relation (linkage) to a specific bomb or a pile or bombs. Also, it is not a characteristic of the concept that there must be a linkage with even one existing bomb. However, when a bomb is made, the concept has a characteristic: linkage with that bomb. Before the existence of a bomb, linkage with bombs is a potentiality.

In the case of complex concepts the situation is different in that the togetherness of simple concepts to form a complex depends ultimately on external entities. For example, the concepts 'atomic' and 'bomb' were brought together by human imagination to form the complex concept 'atomic bomb'. In due course the togetherness of the concept had another basis. There existed a bomb made of fissionable atomic material: the concepts were then together because of their natural linkage with entities which were now together in the physical world.

In view of the above facts, it is the case that complex concepts are internally related to other entities (that is would not be present without these relations). In the case of combination in imagination, the relation is causal. When an atomic bomb had been made, the togetherness of the concepts to form a complex one is not directly based on a causal function. Rather it was an instance of conceptual togetherness on the basis of natural linkage with entities which are now together. Of course causal efficacy and indeed final causation were involved in making the atomic bomb.

---

[1] That is, desires and feelings are expressed and this serves to indicate the presence of another mind. See preceding discussion.

II

Deity

The characteristic 'deity' is found in human behaviour but there is no sound evidence of it (now) in the physical world otherwise. There is, however, awareness of the impact of something other than human beings which seems to be concerned with the characteristic of deity in human beings. But the assumption of a God with the characteristics of (*a*) a superhuman but still man-like Judge, Contractor, Imperial Potentate, or (*b*) a metaphysical First Principle, is the work of 'fantastic' imagination. However, on the basis of entities of which one is aware, one cannot legitimately deny the non-imaginary existence or subsistence of anything which is not experienced.

Among the ingredients of comprehensive experience are entities having value characteristics, such as, true, beautiful, morally good. Present as characteristics of basic and other entities are particular occurrences of these and other values.[1] In short, values are entities which are found. Value is not bestowed by human reactions. Of course, the existence of a specific value in a specific entity, such as a beautiful picture, is due to human effort. In other cases, as with a sunset, this is not so.

It is here suggested that the entities referred to in the preceding paragraphs of this Chapter are the fundamental ones found in comprehensive human experience. These basic entities, physically based resultants and their characteristics must all be taken into consideration if one is to obtain an adequate understanding of men and their environment. The concepts which refer to these entities are the fundamental concepts in terms of which an adequate world view must be formulated, or more specific problems dealt with.[2]

III

Questions answered and unanswered

As far as Experiential Realism is concerned, a number of human problems remain unsolved. There is no awareness of the origin of the

---

[1] Technically stated, true, beautiful, morally good (which are characteristics of some entities) all have the characteristic value.

[2] These, of course, must be supplemented by the addition of less general concepts which refer to the less general characteristics of entities as discussed in previous chapters.

world or its fate. There is no awareness of a future life for man. Many details of the nature and functioning of physical objects and minds are not now open to comprehensive human awareness. The question why, in the sense of an ultimate explanation, cannot now be answered. It is to be noted that 'why?' may involve a request for information about (*a*) a purpose or (*b*) any means leading to a result. In the last analysis, one can only report what he finds. In some limited situations the question why can be answered, as with, 'Why did the book fall?' Answer, 'It was pushed off the table'. And if it is asked, 'Why was it pushed?' the answer is, 'Because I wanted an uncluttered surface on which to do some writing'. But the question as to why my muscles function as they do can be answered in only a superficial and partial sense—a further 'why' quickly occurs. In brief, some causal sequences are open to awareness. Other occurrences cannot now be placed in a causal context.

In some cases, in a limited situation, men can initiate change in themselves and their environment. In other cases, they cannot. The immediately preceding remarks should not be interpreted as a sad-faced pessimistic admission of complete human failure and inadequacy. These admissions of limitation must be set in the context of a recognition of the wide range of successful dealings with specific human problems. For example it is possible in comprehensive human experience to avoid deficiencies in the activities of being aware of, and interpreting, many of the entities in the world (including oneself). Artificial abstractions, that is the neglect of present entities, or the neglect of genuine distinctions, such as between imaginary and non-imaginary, can be overcome. In comprehensive experience at its present stage of development, there is awareness of a wide range of basic physical entities, mental entities, physically based resultants and concepts, and also awareness of many of their characteristics. The extent of these achievements is here claimed to be greater than will be admitted by some philosophers and scientists.

IV

The human person

The human person is a very complex creature indeed. A person (his mind) is aware of his own mind and his own body linked in close mutual causal interaction. This creature experiences violent emotions and, on occasion, relatively profound thoughts. There is a confusing mixture of morally good and immoral behaviour, awareness of beauty, and opaqueness to it. There is desire for wisdom, and yet adherence to prejudice and ignorance. None of these ingredients is the one fundamental characteristic of all men and women. No simple formula can be applied to human beings. Men are neither exclusively almost angel nor almost lower animal. Further, there are profound individual differences. It is well to remember the fact of change as well as that of endurance. He who attempts to predict the future of mankind in detail is on shaky ground. The comprehensive man tries to make a better (future) self and environment (physical and mental).

v

The basis of Experiential Realism

Experiential Realism, as here envisaged, is concerned to observe, with equal care, the three types of basic entities (and also physically based resultants) and their characteristics. It does not assign superior status to any one of them in the sense of claiming that any can be identified with or reduced to any other. No basic entity is produced by another. Some entities, however, are more valuable than others. Vast, partial mysteries remain within the range of what is experienced. What is beyond human experience is a blank mystery, though the boundaries of the realm of mystery are being steadily reduced.

Experiential Realism is firmly based on carefully interpreted ordinary experience and the experience of specialists in various fields. Experiential Realism, as here outlined, attempts to formulate a general, unified, inclusive report of fundamental many-occurrence entities, which are found in the world of comprehensive human experience, as well as some particular occurrences of them. There are some specific comments as well, concerning a wide range of more restricted human problems.

It is not the purpose of this present general introductory sketch to deal with some important responsibilities which have been accepted by some who are termed philosophers, namely, the provision of specialist detailed information and in some cases advice in the fields of logic, ethics and aesthetics. However, the outline of Experiential Realism presented in this volume corrects some errors of specialists and non-specialists who neglect or misinterpret some aspects of comprehensive human experience in these areas.

Implicit in Experiential Realism is a specific attitude concerning the natural and social sciences. In the days before special sciences were separated out as independent disciplines, philosophy covered all these fields and, of necessity, considered them in great detail. There was no one else to do the job. Now that, for example, psychology is coming of age, it is inappropriate for philosophers to engage in minute discussion of psychological entities, for the sake of rounding up facts. In other words, as was stated at the beginning of this study, a philosopher should profit from the general conclusions reached, and basic concepts and techniques employed, in the sense of using such data (and others) in attempting to achieve a comprehensive view of man and his environment, or in attempting to deal with problems which transcend any one special field of knowledge. The same is true of the relations of philosophers with all the other sciences, natural and social. There is a tendency on the part of some philosophers to duplicate work already more effectively done by scientists. One concern of the philosopher as far as science is concerned, should also be to correct errors of omissions and interpretation on the part of some scientists. However, a philosopher should concentrate on the logic of scientific concepts and procedure only in cases where scientists omit adequate concern for these matters. These topics (logic and philosophy of science) however, fall outside the scope of this introductory volume.

It will be obvious, from the nature of this introduction, that Experiential Realism contends that philosophers should not consider (*a*) that the study of the use of words is their main concern or (*b*) alternatively that philosophical problems are linguistic, or (*c*) that words are our best source of information about facts. The areas in which philosophers have special competence—logic, ethics, aesthetics, epistemology and metaphysics—should be approached in the context of a general comprehensive, yet simplified, view of man and his environment. Excessive concentration on one subject matter, to the exclusion of other basic human problems in the fields of fact and value, will defeat the purpose of philosophy as envisaged in this discussion.

Whether the term 'philosophy' be used in the comprehensive fashion here employed, or, for example, equated with logic (in some use of this term), the question ultimately to be faced is this: is the comprehensive approach worth attempting and possible of at least a degree of attainment? These questions of value and fact, in the last analysis, must be settled in terms of the experience of the individual who is confronted by these complex problems.

It was admitted at the beginning of this study that some people who claim to have comprehensive experience state that they do not find some of the basic entities (and physically based resultants) and characteristics to which I have been referring. Specifically, for example, many philosophers and non-professionals in this field claim that they are not aware of concepts, a basic mental or physical entity or specific value characteristic as here described. Physically based resultants seem very queer indeed. They quite legitimately demand evidence.

Those who doubt some or all of the details of the report here labelled 'Experiential Realism' may charge that this so-called description or report is based on self-deception resulting from wishful thinking, previous conditioning, and other distorting factors. In the last analysis, the only evidence available for the presence of entities reported by Experiential Realism is awareness of them. One can only invite the doubting Thomases to look again.

In dealing with a complex physical situation, or even a mental one, this procedure frequently produces the desired results, if apt suggestions and techniques are used to guide the process of observation. Concerning so-called intangible entities such as concepts, as here described, and value characteristics, the matter is more difficult. But the fact that, with the passage of time, people who once found no beauty in a symphony or a sunset—or could not think abstractly, now do, is a ground for at least some hope.

An appeal to a chain of reasoning, a stringing together of concepts to make propositions and a proceeding from one proposition to another and so on to a conclusion concerning other entities, may satisfy the user. But actually no one will be convinced by this type of 'proof' unless the concepts and propositions and structure of argument, leading to the conclusion, are all supported in some fashion by the person's experience of entities to which the propositions refer.

The appeal to the authority of a man, a book, or an institution or a technique, may be effective in providing agreement among members of an 'in-group'. But a person will accept the word of an authority only on the basis of his own experience. It is, of course, the case that a person may accept an argument or an appeal to an authority on a basis other than objective factual support. It may be a case of the decisive influence of some emotional factor, aroused by the personality of an exponent, or craving for security at any price.

Central to the entire discussion is the claim that some human beings can, and do, achieve a comprehensive awareness of many entities present in experience.

The author of this study has attempted to present a report concerning men and their environment. It is offered as a stimulus for further discussion.

SECTION TWO
EVALUATION

PREFACE

Section One of this study has been concerned with the statement of one view of the nature of philosophy and an introductory sketch of a philosophy based on comprehensive human experience. It has been entitled Experiential Realism.

In Section Two other views of the nature of philosophy will be considered. The work of representative philosophers will be evaluated by reference to comprehensive experience. It will be contended that many philosophies, on occasion, suffer from some or all of the following interrelated defects:

(i) they are partial, in that they omit some of the entities present in a complex situation.

(ii) they misinterpret the entities they discuss.

(iii) they engage in unjustified flights of imagination.

(iv) there are serious inconsistencies.

Since many philosophies either directly or implicitly involve criticisms of Experiential Realism, the indication of their defects constitutes, in part, a clarification and defence of Experiential Realism.

On the other hand, a number of representative philosophies, on occasion are, like Experiential Realism, in accord with comprehensive experience. In other words Experiential Realism is in agreement with many representative philosophies concerning many fundamental questions.

In this attempt to provide a comprehensive report of the main ingredients of men and their environment, I have found the work of A. N. Whitehead very helpful. Many of his specific insights are here accepted; so is his general view of the nature of philosophy.

In this section and particularly in the concluding chapter this point will be illustrated, and in this sense Experiential Realism will be supported by quotations from Whitehead. Here, as in other instances of quotations agreeing with Experiential Realism, it is not a case of quoting authorities which are accepted without question. Rather it is a matter of showing that Experiential Realism is not alone in its views of men and their environment. Further it seems wise to take advantage of vigorous statements by men of great skill in communication.

It will be noted that some phases of Whitehead's philosophy, namely some theories, are rejected on the grounds that they are flights of speculative fancy unsupported by comprehensive experience.

In any case Experiential Realism should not be regarded as a patchwork eclecticism. It is a report of comprehensive experience. It is in agreement with some philosophers at some point and not at others.

In general, an evaluation of representative philosophers serves to place Experiential Realism in proper perspective.

It will be noted that, on occasion, in evaluating other philosophies there is reference to the criterion provided by Experiential Realism. This of course is a convenient locution. The criterion, strictly speaking, is comprehensive experience. In any case, the philosophical position here termed Experiential Realism is (a) a report of what is present in comprehensive experience and also (b) the critical evaluation of other philosophies in the context of comprehensive experience. Of course the term Experiential Realism also refers to (c) the activities, that is the techniques involved in reaching these conclusions, and the use made of them.

In referring to representative philosophers, their point of view will be stated before they are subjected to evaluation. This is necessary in order to focus attention on what is under consideration. Further, in the twentieth century even professional philosophers are sometimes not familiar with the work of some of their contemporaries. This is even more obvious concerning many philosophers of the past. Outlines of points of view being evaluated are also necessary to assist the general reader. Quotations,[1] at crucial points, are provided in order to avoid misrepresentation. It may be contended that some of the work of representative philosophers here criticised embodies views which are no longer held by them, or were abandoned in the case of those no longer living. This may well be so. Their writings are here referred to as effective presentations of specific points of view. The point of view is being evaluated. It is identified by reference to the man who formulated it.

A few very influential contemporary philosophers receive the lion's share of attention in the process of critical evaluation. This seems necessary in order to bring into the clearest possible contem-

[1] In identifying quotations, reference is frequently made to readily available recent reprints rather than to original editions. This has been done, at the risk of apparent lapse from scholarship, in order to facilitate ready reference.

porary focus the distinctive features of Experiential Realism. However an attempt is made to set the issues raised in philosophy in broad perspective. The past is not neglected.

However, in this introductory presentation, it is not claimed that all alternatives to Experiential Realism have been accorded a comprehensive consideration, in detail.

It is to be hoped that the immediately preceding paragraphs will serve to answer some criticisms which may occur to some readers of Section Two.

For example, it may appear that excessive attention is paid to linguistic philosophy. The objection is that this type of philosophy has been superseded by new trends. Further, it may be claimed that the criticisms here offered are familiar to all. Hence it would be better to pay more attention to new trends.

My reply is as follows: (a) linguistic philosophy, in various forms, is still very much alive in some circles and hence critical comment is still appropriate. The 'familiar to all' objection is open to question.

Further comment is still relevant on the grounds that it is one major approach to philosophy from which much can be learned. In any case, as noted above, linguistic philosophy provides a convenient contemporary frame of reference for the understanding and appreciation of Experiential Realism.

(b) Some of the so-called new trends are, for the most part, (i) lineal descendants of linguistic philosophy and or (ii) embody old trends—which obviously are discussed in this book. Be that as it may these comments do not apply to some other contemporary philosphies, however they have not been neglected.

It may be objected that some great names are missing from the list of those considered, or that insufficient attention is paid to some men or trends in philosophy. Thus, for example, it may seem that Plato, Aristotle, Aquinas, Kant, Hegel, Phenomenology and Existentialism do not receive their just due.

At this point I can only reiterate my previous statement. In this introductory presentation, it is not claimed that all alternatives to Experiential Realism have been accorded a detailed discussion. However, I do claim that sufficient reference, for my stated purposes, has been made to other views (if not in all cases to other philosophers by name)—to indicate the major strengths of Experiential Realism in contrast with the weaknesses of other views concerning the basic problems under discussion in this book.

10

BASIC ENTITIES

I

Errors concerning basic entities

Comprehensive experience indicates that there are three types of basic entities: mind, physical object, concept. An examination of the views of some representative philosophers concerning these entities provides illustrations of the sorts of defects in philosophising mentioned in the Preface.

Partial plus misrepresentation of the nature of an entity

(*a*) Berkeley, for example, contends that there is only one type of basic entity, namely mind. It is reputed to be an *'active, indivisible substance*, (p. 79.)[1] A mind engages in various activities such as perceiving (knowing) willing, imagining, remembering (p. 41). Colours, and shapes which are seen, odours which are smelled, resistances which are felt in the process of touching, are examples of what Berkeley calls 'ideas' and regards as mental content. They are 'supported by, or exist in minds' (p. 80). Thus, Berkeley is, in part, reporting non-imaginary entities found in a person, that is mind and its activities and content. However, he misinterprets the nature of mind (terms it substance) and the status of colours, shapes, etc.

According to Berkeley, what are ordinarily termed 'physical objects' are actually a collection of ideas which occur together. Thus an apple is a collection of the colour, smell, taste, texture, which are experienced in conjunction. As for concepts, so-called abstract general ideas, Berkeley contends that they are only particular ideas. Any generality is dependent on the wide use of a word or other 'sign' (pp. 41, 97). Here again he is guilty of serious misinterpretations.

[1] All references are to T. E. Jessop (ed.), *The Principles of Human Knowledge*, T. Nelson & Sons (London 1949).

(*b*) Another variation of an explanation of physical objects in terms of minds (misinterpretation) is found in the work of Leibniz and Whitehead. Leibniz engages in introspection and finds three main sorts of mental activity and related contents, (i) intellectual, (ii) sensory and emotional (iii) unconscious. He assigns each of these sorts of activities and contents to active agents which he terms 'monads'· The physical world, on this theory, is composed of unconscious monads.[1]

Whitehead is even more bold in the sense that, having introspected a moment of his own conscious experience, he attributes something at least similar to the components of physical objects.[2] Specifically this involves attributing (a case of misinterpretation) to a stone, moments of experience characterised by feeling, subjective aim, enjoyment, and other entities ordinarily claimed to be found only in high-grade human beings.

It is important to note that both Leibniz and Whitehead accept a realm of concepts—ideas of reason (Leibniz), eternal objects (Whitehead).[3]

(*c*) Another sort of 'one basic entity' approach involving misinterpretation of the nature of an entity is found in Hobbes, who contends that everything is matter and all that happens is motion.[4] However, in addition to these objects, on occasion he inconsistently is prepared to admit a distinct, though inferior status (another type of misinterpretation, that of status) to mental activities and content. They are termed 'fancy'. In any case concepts are dealt with in terms of words, that is words replace concepts.[5]

In the context of comprehensive experience, the reaction to any point of view, such as those just noted, which declines to accept the presence of any one (or more) type of basic entity, is simply that such entities are found. One can argue ingeniously, or expound vigorously, and these philosophers considered above have, that such is not the case. But in the last analysis these arguments or expositions

---

[1] See G. W. Leibniz, *Selections*, P. Wiener (ed.), Charles Srcibner's Sons (New York 1951), pp. 524, 537–8.

[2] See A. N. Whitehead, *Process and Reality*, Macmillan, New York, 1929, pp. 176–9; *Adventures of Ideas*, Cambridge, 1933, Chapter 11; *Modes of Thought*, Macmillan, New York, 1938, p. 228.

[3] See Leibniz, *Selections*, pp. 538–40; *Process and Reality*, p. 32.

[4] See T. Hobbes, *Leviathan* in *The English Philosophers from Bacon to Mill*, E. A. Burtt (ed.), Modern Library, New York, 1939, p. 131.

[5] These are examples of the error of misinterpretation, see fn. 1, p. 255.

collapse in the face of comprehensive experience. This general fact will be developed in detail in subsequent specific discussions of minds, physical objects and concepts.[1]

Misinterpretations of the status and nature of an entity

(a) The philosophy of Plato, in his so-called 'middle dialogues', departs from comprehensive experience in a fashion different from the 'elimination' approach ('only one type of entity' misinterpretation of the nature of entities) to some basic entities just under discussion. Plato accepts the presence of minds, physical objects and concepts. However, he assigns ultimate importance, that is reality, to only one of them: concepts (Forms, Ideas). These entities are reputed to be eternal, the basis of knowledge, and when exemplified in some particular case, the cause of that particular case. Thus Plato contends that a picture is beautiful because the Form Beauty[2] is exemplified there. Further it seems to him that knowledge implies the grasp of something permanent in contrast with the continually shifting content of mere opinion.

The realm of physical objects, characterized by change, is for that reason assigned a low status. In so far as a mind or soul has kinship with, concern for, the realm of eternal Forms, it is superior to the physical world. But some aspects of mind or soul are, like the physical world, affected by change and hence the mind or soul, as such, is not on the exalted level of importance occupied by the Forms.[3]

A person who relies on comprehensive experience reacts to the Platonic stress on concepts by pointing to the misinterpretations of the nature and status of concepts. A person does experience concepts, which endure for some time. Whether or not these are eternal cannot be determined. As far as comprehensive experience is concerned,

---

[1] It appears that Experiential Realism is in general agreement with phenomenology. For example Husserl claims that the business of philosophy is to attempt an exact description of phenomena, that is what is present to consciousness (awareness). See *Ideen*, Niemeyer Halle, 1913, pp. 10 ff. However, the contention that a person is not aware of the characteristics mental or physical—rather they are interpretations (involving presuppositions)—is contrary to comprehensive experience. Likewise a phenomenalistic reduction, which stresses a search for essences (concepts) and concentrates on them in the meaning and knowledge situations, is a case of the fallacy of the partial.

[2] Words referring to forms are capitalised.

[3] See Plato, *The Republic*, F. M. Cornford (ed.), Oxford University Press, London, 1941, pp. 181–9, 217–20, 345–6.

concepts do not exercise the (efficient) causal function attributed to them by Plato. The relation of the concept Beauty to a beautiful painting is merely the relation of natural linkage.

The qualification (in brackets) in the preceding sentence is important. While a concept, as such, is not the efficient cause of an entity to which it applies in a complex situation, a concept may function as a final cause, that is, as a luring goal. Thus a person aware of the lure of the concept beauty may decide to paint a beautiful picture and proceeds to do so. Here Plato would approve.

As far as knowing is concerned, comprehensive experience stresses the basic requirement of awareness. One can be aware of a concept, of course, but one can also be aware of a mind or a physical object. All three types of entities are cases of knowledge. Hence, again, Plato's interpretation of the status of a concept is incorrect.

In brief, if one accepts as criteria of reality or exalted status, Plato's list of characteristics: eternal, cause of other basic types of entities, the basic ingredient in knowledge—it is obvious that concepts do not measure up.

As far as comprehensive experience is concerned, minds, physical objects and concepts are equal in status in the sense that they are all inescapable ingredients in the world, in this sense real.[1] One cannot be generated from another (or others) as far as comprehensive experience can at present ascertain. Likewise, there are no present grounds for using change or lack of it as status determiners. It must be made clear that basic entities and their characteristics differ in value despite equality in status (in the sense here employed). For example, actual morally good behaviour is more valuable than the concept morally good. It is more valuable to create one work of art than to have one meal.

(b) The philosophy of Kant provides a number of illustrations of misinterpretations of the status and function (nature) of entities. The world of physical nature and the realm of concepts are downgraded—mind becomes fundamental.

In the course of the consideration of how (certain) scientific knowledge is possible in the face of Hume's criticism of causality (and Kant was convinced that it was possible), he discusses the status of the physical world. Specifically he refers to the laws of physical

[1] Everything is something, which in its own way is real. When you refer to something as unreal, you are merely conceiving a type of reality to which that "something" does not belong.' Whitehead, *Modes of Thought*, p. 95.

nature. Kant states that 'the highest legislation . . . must lie in ourselves'. We must realise that there is 'universal conformity to law' in nature because of 'the conditions of the possibility of experience which lie in our sensibility and in our understanding'. In short Kant states that 'nature is derived from the laws of the possibility of experience in general'.[1]

Kant makes it clear that these laws or principles of the possibilities of experience are provided by the mind. Specifically the mind is equipped with categories (concepts) such as substance and causality (p. 55) and forms of sensibility, space and time (p. 31).

The procedure of assigning such priority to mind over the physical world and concepts is set in the context of and admission that his view is not that of Berkeley. Kant states that there is a world beyond mind. We cannot know it as it is in itself, but only as it appears to us. How it appears to us, we determine (see pp. 36, 42, 62). In this sense our mind gives form to the world we know. Indeed Kant is prepared to admit that a person does not know his own mind as it is in itself, only as it appears to him (p. 82).

Kant's claim that the entities and characteristics of the world of nature which we experience are the result of our mental reaction to the unknown objects which exert pressure on our senses, finds no support in comprehensive experience. When I see a table, there is no awareness of my mind imposing space and time forms or organising sensory impact under the category of substance. When I push the table across the floor, it is not a case of my mind imposing a category of causality. In the context of comprehensive experience a mind finds space and time characteristics and also causality and, in one sense of the term, substance, in the world which it observes. Further, there is no adequate evidence to support the claim that concepts (categories) are mental or produced by the mind.

It is of course the case that there are in all probability entities beyond the present range of experience. However, when Kant sets up an absolute limit which cannot be extended, he is indulging in unjustified dogmatism.[2]

---

[1] I. Kant, *Prolegomena to any Future Metaphysics*, L. W. Beck (ed.), The Liberal Arts Press, New York, 1950, p. 66. See also, pp. 53 and 65. Hereafter all references will be made to this volume.

[2] See comment by Merleau-Ponty: 'The world is there before all reflection and it is completely artificial to make the world derive from our synthesis. . . . my reflection . . . ought to recognise, besides its own operations, the existence

Unjustified imagination plus partial and misinterpretation

(*a*) There is a third type of philosophy which stands in opposition to comprehensive experience. It selects one of the basic entities present in comprehensive experience and uses it to suggest a thought model. This is then employed to construct, in imagination, entities[1] to which ultimate reality (a case of misinterpretation) is assigned. For example Lucretius claims that the universe is composed only of minute physical particles (hence this is an instance of a partial view) too small to be seen, which by their combinations constitute the physical objects and minds (misinterpretation) of which one is aware in comprehensive experience.[2] These 'invisible' entities are creations of imagination, based on small physical objects which have been seen and touched.

Lucretius offers what he contends is adequate circumstantial evidence for the existence of atoms. A stone slowly erodes; we feel wind and mist. In no case do we see or touch atoms but, says Lucretius, they must be postulated to account for what we do see and feel.

It is the case that Lucretius's theories have an instrumental function in scientific investigation. But the main comment, based on comprehensive experience, is simply this: in trying to describe (report) the non-imagining world, one must avoid imagining and its results.

In brief, it is advisable to admit an unsolved problem rather than to accept an imaginary solution. Thus in trying to formulate an adequate description (report) of the world, a person does not need to take Lucretius' views seriously, except as an example of one type of mental activity, imagining. Even if one contends that his world view, though imaginary, has merit in an instrumental sense, it is still open to a serious criticism. It operates on the basis of materialistic assumptions. The partial and hence inadequate nature of an attempt to explain or describe everything in the world in terms of matter has been pointed out frequently and need not be repeated here.

(*b*) In formulating his theory of the Absolute Mind, F. H. Bradley proceeds in a general fashion roughly similar to that of Lucretius. However, there are drastic differences in the results which they produce. Further, he engages in inconsistency, he contradicts himself.

of the world. . . . Reality must be described and not constructed, nor constituted.' (See *Phenomenologie de la Perception*, Gallimard, Paris, 1945, p. iv.

[1] It is interesting to note that the entities stressed by Berkeley, Hobbes, Leibniz, Whitehead and Plato, are non-imaginary.

[2] See Lucretius, *The Nature of the Universe*, R. E. Lotham (ed.), Penguin Books, London, 1951, pp. 28, 35–7.

Bradley focuses attention on the fact that in a moment of human feeling by a mind, there is experience of a whole which includes diversities and yet is not split into absolutely separate elements. Using this as a model, he proceeds to indulge in a flight of spectacular (fantastic) imagination and claims that 'the Absolute holds all possible content in an individual experience where no contradiction[1] can remain'.[2] According to Bradley finite minds and physical objects are not real, not ultimate components of the world. Rather they are 'appearances', mere phases of one entity. They are ingredient in and dependent on its all-encompassing reality (p. 285). That this Absolute individual is mental is for Bradley beyond question. 'To be real, or even barely to exist, must be to fall within sentience. . . there is no being or fact outside of that which is commonly called psychical existence' (p. 127).

Since this type of philosophy, Absolute Idealism, is not discussed elsewhere in this study, a more detailed treatment of it will occur in this chapter than in the case of other theories so far mentioned. Since Absolute Idealism is not very familiar these days fairly extensive quotations will be employed.

Despite his claim that the Absolute is one real experience, which is superior in status to finite minds and physical objects which are mere appearances, Bradley tries to 'save' the appearances. He states: 'Nothing in the universe can be lost, nothing fails to contribute to the single Reality' (p. 453). However, a crucial qualification is introduced which indicates unmistakably that Bradley is engaging in a very rigorous programme of alteration. In short, he departs from the findings of comprehensive experience and embarks on a flight of imagination. He contends that 'every finite diversity is also supplemented and transformed' (p. 453). Having stated: 'Everything in the Absolute still is that which it is for itself', he proceeds to contradict himself and (p. 453) remarks: 'we can hardly say that the Absolute consists of finite things, when the things, as such, are there transmuted and have lost their individual natures' (p. 469. See also pp. 161–2).

Bradley's Absolute not only transmutes finite entities such as minds and physical objects. Time is banished from the one reality. The only genuine development is 'of principle' not succession in time. In a

---

[1] Which arises, says Bradley, if entities are regarded as separate and distinct in their own right.

[2] F. H. Bradley, *Appearance and Reality*, Clarendon Press, 9th edition, Oxford 1930, p. 130. All references are to this volume.

rare burst of poetic language, Bradley declaims: 'The Absolute has no seasons, but all at once bears its leaves, fruit, and blossoms' (p. 442). Personality, truth, beauty, goodness, are 'appearance distinctions' which do not apply to the Absolute, that is, do not as such find a place in the one all-inclusive experience (p. 472).

As noted previously, Bradley contends that our experience provides clues as to the nature of the Absolute; for example, the unity of a moment of feeling which retains diversity. There is also the contention that appeal to experience refutes the claim that subjects and objects are 'standing separate and on [their] . . . own bottom' (p. 128). It is, however, not surprising to find him admitting that at best our ideas of the Absolute are 'abstract' and incomplete. But he contends that (and the restriction italised is crucial) the 'main features, to *some extent*, are within our own experience' (p. 140, emphasis added).

Let us now turn to a consideration of the 'circumstantial evidence' sort of argument used by Bradley to justify his imaginative postulation of an Absolute Mind which is admittedly beyond human experience in many important respects (pp. 161–2). Thus he refers to 'the right to postulate . . . an unknown supplementation of knowledge' (p. 457). For example, Bradley contends we must assume an area of knowledge which our admitted ignorance hides, otherwise there can be no recognition of ignorance.

He also uses a similar plea in support of his claim that the universe is one reality. It consists in arguing that if one advocates a theory of many reals one is thus forced to recognise relations. If a person accepts relations, he is forced to admit a higher unity to account for the relations (p. 18).

This argument, however, involves a view of the nature of relations which must be considered carefully.

In a very subtle and complicated argument, it is contended that if a person takes relations seriously, he becomes immersed in inescapable complications. Consider a lump of sugar as a set of qualities, for example, whiteness, sweetness, hardness, in a complex pattern of relations. If we consider the relations to be part of the qualities, then they add nothing new. If the relations are considered to be different from the qualities, then there is a gap and another relation is required. Indeed one is faced by an infinite series of relations to bridge the gap—none of which is successful, since relations are being regarded as separate and distinct entities (pp. 16–28).

The reactions to Bradley's theory of the Absolute, based on comprehensive experience, take the general form which applies to any work of unjustified imagination: interesting, but not to be assigned a higher status than the non-imaginary world of comprehensive experience.

Turning to details, it must be pointed out that there is no justification in comprehensive experience for the down-grading of finite persons, or physical objects, or the denial of reality to time and value distinctions such as truth, beauty and goodness. Even when Bradley claims to be describing human experience, he is frequently inaccurate and at least partial in his appraisal. It is simply not the case that all being and existence is experienced as mental, or that when we examine human experience seeking reality, we find one whole of feeling. As for relations, Bradley simply overlooks the fact that relations relate. Part of his difficulty with the lump of sugar is that he neglects the fact that the qualities are related because they belong to one block of sugar (that is, a basic physical entity). In any case, relations are entities found in comprehensive experience—an infinite regress does not yawn before us, nor is there a need for an underlying unity to provide for relations. Such an entity is not present to awareness. Nor is it necessary to postulate an all-inclusive knower against the background of whose knowledge our ignorance becomes identifiable. In comprehensive human experience, it is possible to realise that one has more to learn, without assuming that somewhere someone (some entity) knows everything.[1]

Mixture of non-imaginary and unjustified imagination[2]

Some philosophers, in formulating a world view, rely on a mixture of entities found in the non-imaginary world of comprehensive experience and some entities which are created by imagination. Thus John Locke contends that a physical object is composed of a set of

---

[1] It will be obvious that these criticisms of Bradley's Absolute have considerable kinship with the views of a great critic of Absolute Idealism when it was in its hey-day, William James. 'The relations between things, conjunctive as well as disjunctive, are just as much matters of direct particular experience, neither more so nor less so, than the things themselves.' Also 'the directly apprehended universe needs . . . no extraneous trans-empirical connective support, but possesses in its own right a concatenated or continuous structure' (*The Meaning of Truth*, Longmans Green, London, 1909, pp. xii–xiii).

[2] Although no section heading mentions *inconsistency*, illustrations of this defect have been noted in the work of Hobbes, Bradley and Locke.

qualities, concerning which we have non-imaginary ideas and an underlying substructure which is supposed, that is, imagined, to be present. As Locke himself says, a person makes 'a supposition of he knows not what support of such qualities which are capable of producing simple ideas in us'.[1]

Locke's approach to mind is similar. In addition to experienced mental activities and content there is imagined to be an underlying 'I know not what' in which these activities and qualities inhere (see pp. 295–6).

The reaction based on comprehensive experience to this mixture of imaginary and non-imaginary approach to physical objects and minds is by now surely predictable. Imagination must be kept in its place and not given equal status with the non-imaginary when proposing to deal adequately with basic entities and their characteristics. The underlying defect in Locke's treatment is that he contends one is not aware of mind as basic entity, that is, an active agent, or of physical basic entities, in which characteristics inhere. This, to put it simply, is contrary to comprehensive experience. Therefore it is not necessary to have recourse to imagination in order to account for mental activities and content, or the togetherness of the characteristics of physical objects.

Locke inconsistently uses the term 'substance' to refer to (*a*) physical objects and minds in their entirety, that is, substratum and qualities, or (*b*) the underlying substructure alone (*re* substance in general).

Substance

At this point some comments on the theory of substance are in order. From Aristotle onwards the term 'substance' has been applied to specific entities which are basic in the sense that other entities are assigned to them but they (substances) are not attributed to other entities. In this sense the basic entities discussed by Experiential Realism might be termed 'substances'. However, this term has not been used because over the years the term substance has acquired the implication of isolation, lack of genuine relations with other entities. Thus Descartes, proceeding in a rationalistic fashion, argued that a mind substance and a body substance, since one could be thought of without thinking of the other, one (the mind) could

---

[1] John Locke, *Essay Concerning Human Understanding*, in *The English Philosophers from Bacon to Mill*, pp. 294–5. All references are to this volume.

survive the extinction of the other (the body). Hence they are, in this sense, separate.[1] Locke's discussion of knowledge reflects this same substance-oriented 'gaposis'. According to him a mind substance is directly aware only of its own activities and content (ideas). It can only assume that some of those ideas represent qualities possessed by a physical object (pp. 264–5).

Leibniz aptly states this mutual exclusiveness of substances, and the gaps in the world which are implicit in this theory: 'The monad . . . is merely a . . . substance. . . . There is . . . no way of explaining how a monad can be altered or changed in its inner being by any other creature. . . . The monads have no windows through which anything can enter or depart.'[2]

In opposition to the isolation aspect of traditional notions of substances, comprehensive experience shows that what we can or cannot conceive does not settle what is the case in the world of non-imaginary facts, specifically whether or not a mind can get along without a body. As against Locke and his epistemological gap, it is pointed out that, under suitable conditions, a mind is aware of physical objects. Leibniz's ascription of absolute windowless exclusiveness to minds is not supported by comprehensive experience. The contents of bodies influence minds and vice versa in the sense that characteristics are altered by interaction.

II

Views of philosophy opposed to Experiential Realism

This introductory chapter will be concluded by brief references to two views concerning philosophy which take issue with Experiential Realism. On examination it becomes obvious that they suffer from serious defects.

Philosophy reflects temperament or emotional conflict

Experiential Realism claims to offer an accurate report of the main features of men and their environment in so far as these entities are

[1] See R. Descartes, *Meditations*, L. J. Lafleur (ed.), The Liberal Arts Press, New York, 1951, pp. 69–70.

[2] G. W. Leibniz, *Selections*, P. P. Wiener (ed.), Charles Scribner's Sons, New York, 1951, pp. 533–4.

now open to human awareness. It is contended that in some cases at least this project is successful. An entirely different interpretation of philosophy states that one's philosophical views on any topic are to be understood as primarily an expression of temperament or emotional conflict.

William James developed this idea at the beginning of this century: '[A philosopher's] temperament really gives him a stronger bias than any of his more strictly objective premises. It loads the evidence for him one way or the other, making for a more sentimental or . . . hard-hearted view of the universe.'[1] He lists the philosophical emphasis which results from either of two opposed sorts of temperament, sentimental (tender-minded) or hardheaded (tough-minded). A tough-minded person is empiricist (governed by facts), sensationalistic, materialistic, pessimistic, irreligious, fatalistic, pluralistic, sceptical. On the other hand, tender-minded philosophers are rationalistic (going by principles), intellectualistic, idealistic, optimistic, religious, free-willist, monistic, dogmatic (pp. 11–12).

This general emphasis on the importance of psychological factors (of an emotional type) in shaping philosophical theories is, in this age of psychoanalysis, given considerable prominence. For example Lazerowitz contends that 'we can be reasonably sure that a philosopher who . . . with complete assurance maintains that change is unreal is, under the guise of making a scientific statement, covertly reassuring himself against certain feared changes and giving expression to the wish that certain things or conditions remain as they are.'[2]

The influence of temperament and deep-seated fears upon the thought and action of human beings is well known. However, it is contended by Experiential Realism that, if care is taken, the effects of these factors can be eliminated. The history of natural science shows that it is possible for a man to put his emotions behind him and view the facts without bias. Whether or not this result has been achieved in the case of Experiential Realism is for the unbiased[3] to decide.

Philosophy should be limited to logic

It has been contended by Experiential Realism that philosophy is an

---

[1] W. James, *Pragmatism*, Longmans Green, New York, 1948, p. 7.

[2] M. Lazerowitz, *The Structure of Metaphysics*, Routledge and Kegan Paul, London, 1963, p. 69.

[3] Unbiased except for a 'bias', if such it be, towards an 'accurate report'.

attempt to formulate a world view, and hence become involved in what is termed 'metaphysics' and a related epistemology, and also to deal with a number of complex questions in the fields of logic, ethics, and aesthetics. Many contemporary philosophers suggest that philosophy should be limited to what, broadly speaking, may be termed 'logic'.

For example, A. J. Ayer contends that philosophy's function is to 'clarify the propositions of science by exhibiting their *logical* relations, and by defining the symbols which occur in them'.[1] It is essential to note then, in Ayer's opinion, 'to ask for a definition of "material object", . . . is to ask how propositions about material objects are to be translated into propositions about sense contents' (pp. 64–5).

There are further jobs for a philosopher, namely to make sure that a scientist's beliefs are consistent and to focus attention on the criteria which he uses to determine whether or not propositions are true (p. 45).

A fundamental aspect of this type of philosophy is clearly stated by Ayer, thus: 'The propositions of philosophy are not factual, but linguistic in character . . . the characteristic mark of a purely logical enquiry is that it is concerned with the formal consequences of our definitions and not with questions of empirical facts' (p. 62).

The preceding quotations indicate what Ayer means when he says that philosophy is analysis.

Ayer is quite prepared to admit that his determination of the scope of philosophy is likely to be challenged. Is not metaphysics a branch of philosophy, as well as logic?

In reply, Ayer admits the need of being in 'accord to some extent with the practice of those who are commonly called philosophers' (p. 51). He admits that metaphysics has been called 'philosophy', but contends that great philosophers such as Locke, Berkeley, Hume and indeed Plato, Aristotle and Kant were chiefly concerned with the type of activity—analysis—which Ayer likes to regard as the full scope of philosophy[2] (p. 52).

[1] A. J. Ayer, *Language, Truth and Logic*, Gollancz, London, 1936, pp. 12–13 (emphasis added). See also p. 62. All references are to this volume. There is considerable quotation from Ayer in view of the claim frequently made by contemporary philosophers that they have been misrepresented. It is the case that Ayer has in some respect gone beyond this book. It is used as a classic exposition of a point of view.

[2] It is only fair to call attention to a more recent discussion by Ayer. He states: 'From the early Greeks, philosophers have been concerned with the

Referring to Locke's *Essay*, Ayer states that Locke appears 'to have seen that it was not his business as a philosopher to affirm or deny the validity of any empirical propositions, but only to analyse them' (pp. 52-3). Thus, according to Ayer, Locke 'devotes himself to the purely analytic tasks'. Ayer nevertheless admits that empirical propositions are a small segment of the book. In any case, Ayer contends these empirical considerations in the *Essay* are part of the field of psychology, not philosophy. Further, there is no metaphysics in Locke's philosophy.

In reply to all this, after a careful reading of Locke's *Essay*, one can only emphasise that Locke did not restrict the scope of philosophy as rigorously as Ayer claims he did. Some analysis, in Ayer's sense, does occur in the *Essay*. However, as Ayer admits, some of its content is concerned with matters of fact. Contrary to him, it is not just a 'small portion'. There are many empirical statements which are offered as being true—accurate reports of facts. This, to use Ayer's own stated criterion (p. 51), is the practice of Locke, who is commonly termed a philosopher. Ayer does use the phrase 'to some extent' in claiming that his view of philosophy is in accord with those who are called philosophers. This is his escape hatch. If metaphysics is to be understood in Ayer's sense of 'neither tautologies or supported by sense experience', then there is considerable metaphysics in Locke's *Essay*, specifically his discussion of substance—in particular the substratum aspect. This issues in his own assumptions concerning representative perception—substrata are postulated as supporting sense experience.

To say, as Ayer does, that Berkeley 'did not, in fact, deny the reality of material things. . . . What he denied was the adequacy of Locke's analysis of the notion of a material thing' (p. 53), is a misleading oversimplification. It is the case that Berkeley noted some of the difficulties in Locke's theory of substance and its implications for perception. However, Berkeley did deny the reality of matter, reducing what is termed 'matter' to a collection of ideas. Ayer is, of course, correct in pointing out that Hume rejected metaphysics in the sense of Locke's theory of substance (p. 53). However, the following remark is open to serious question: Hume 'has been accused of denying

question of what there really is: but in more recent times this mainly takes the form of trying to show that something, which . . . appears to be, is not.' 'Philosophy and Language', in *Clarity is not Enough*, H. D. Lewis (ed.), George Allen and Unwin, London, 1963, p. 410.

causation, whereas in fact he was concerned only with defining it' (p. 56). Actually, in discussing causation, Hume was primarily concerned with factual questions, not logical ones. He referred to the fact of constant conjunction and expectation of repetition, and denied that one could experience actual (factual) connection of cause and effect, or the exertion of force. On the basis of these factual observations, he changed the meaning, that is, referents of the concept cause. But obviously definition was not his 'only' concern. In any case, it is clear that Hume had a number of practical concerns such as escape from superstition in religion and other unsupported theories.

In general, then, the reply of Experiential Realism to Ayer's view of philosophy is summarised thus: the word 'philosophy' has been used in many senses as Ayer admits. His suggested restricted use (to logic) is a possible one. However, when he claims that those who are recognised as great philosophers were primarily concerned with what Ayer terms analysis, Ayer is simply disregarding facts.

11

LINGUISTIC PHILOSOPHY

I

The use of words (preliminary comments)

It is important to consider with care, and in some detail, the contemporary claim, noted in passing at the end of the preceding chapter, that the chief, or only, business of philosophy is to examine the use of words. While making it clear that they are not directly concerned with basic entities and their characteristics (of all types), many philosophers stress their profound interest in 'the way in which we speak about them'.[1] A great deal of time is devoted to considering how a large number of specific words, phrases and sentences are used. In the course of this analysis, attention is focused on what is not, indeed what cannot be said in statements, as well as what is being said. Likewise, concerning single words or phrases, a distinction is made between what they are used to refer to and what they are not used to refer to. Also, linguistic[2] philosophers are most emphatic in pointing out that words are used not only to refer but for many other purposes.

The term 'word' is employed by linguistic philosophers in the two senses mentioned in Section One of this study: (*a*) Inscriptions and sounds as such are termed 'words'. (*b*) The term 'word' is also used to indicate that an inscription or sound is in an established meaning-situation.

In discussing the use of words, linguistic philosophers seem to be dealing with several related topics:

(1) An inscription or sound (word in sense *a*) has a place or function in a meaning-situation, that is, it is a symbol (word in sense *b*). In this sense it has use.

(2) In establishing the meaning-situation, an inscription or sound is given a definite linkage with another entity; it is used in this process

[1] A. J. Ayer, *Language, Truth and Logic*, Gollancz, London, 1936, p. 61. Hereafter this book will be referred to as *L.T.L.*

[2] A convenient widely used but not entirely satisfactory label.

of establishment. For example it is decided to link 'table' with the physical object table.

(3) Once the linkage has been firmly established, a person can refer to or express an entity (meant) through the medium of the symbol (use it for that purpose).

(4) On the basis of this established linkage shared with others, a person can report (inform), express or influence the behaviour of himself and others by, for example, uttering sounds which bring into focus, or focus on, entities meant. In this sense one can use words in the second sense of the term to report, inform, express and influence behaviour.

(5) When words, either in the sense of (a) inscriptions or sounds as such or (b) inscriptions and sounds in a meaning situation, are put together to form sentences, this is another sense of the term 'use'.

A careful examination of the context in which linguistic philosophers employ the terms 'word' and 'use' will usually indicate the sense in which they are employed. These philosophers are not always very careful to bring into clear focus the distinctions outlined above.

It is well to note, at the beginning, that the terms 'use' and 'usage' are sometimes employed as synonyms. Several linguistic philosophers take issue with this procedure. In the course of their comments they throw considerable light on the use of 'use'. For example, Ryle somewhat waspishly remarks that those who confuse the distinction between 'use' and 'usage' are perpetrating 'a howler; for which there is little excuse'.[1] In his view, usage is a case of 'the accustomed', fashion or vogue. On the other hand, 'use' refers to a skill or technique. Specifically, when one learns to use an entity such as a word, a traveller's cheque or a paddle, one is learning how to do something. It is not a case of acquiring sociological information about what other people do. However, Ryle is prepared to admit that 'techniques are not vogues—but they may have vogues' (p. 177).

Flew's[2] comment on the latter point is highly significant, and in accordance with the view of Experiential Realism. 'No word could be said to have a use except in so far as some language group or subgroup gives it a use. . . . The *uses* of words depend subtly on the

---

[1] 'Ordinary Language', *Philosophical Review*, vol. LXII, no. 2, p. 174. Hereafter this will be referred to as O.L.

[2] Except in the case of private language. See Chapter 12, pp. 285–7.

correct *usages* of words . . . what is *correct* usage of any language group depends ultimately upon *actual usage*.'[1]

In any case the linguistic philosophers here to be considered are anxious to differentiate correct use from incorrect use of words, phrases, and sentences. The criterion of correctness is standard, ordinary use. (Ryle, O.L., pp. 180–1; Flew, *E.C.A.*, p. 14.)

Attention is focused, to a considerable extent, on the ordinary use of ordinary words. The following remark by Flew is typical and revealing: 'It has been noticed that the conceptual equipment provided by ordinary (here opposed to technical) language is amazingly rich and subtle . . .' (*E.C.A.*, p. 14). However, it is recognised that in some cases it is advisable to use technical terms (Ryle, O.L., p. 170).

II

Erroneous reports on referential use

After these preliminary remarks, let us turn to an examination of some typical discussions of the use of words, found in the work of linguistic philosophers. Key passages are quoted in the interests of accuracy in presentation and because specific critical comments are focused on these passages.

'Mind': Ryle

Ryle points out that we talk about scholars, judges, lorry drivers, etc. and the places where they operate. However, ' "Mind" is not the name of another person, working or frolicking behind an impenetrable screen; it is not the name of another place where work is done or games are played; and it is not the name of another tool with which works is done'.[2]

Ryle's negative and positive contentions concerning the use of the term 'mind' are effectively summarised in the following statement:

'To talk of a person's mind is not to talk of a repository which is

[1] *Essays in Conceptual Analysis*, A. Flew (ed.), Macmillan, 1963, pp. 7–8 (emphasis added). References to Flew are to this volume. Hereafter it will be referred to as *E.C.A.*

[2] G. Ryle, *The Concept of Mind*, Barnes and Noble, New York, 1949, p. 51. Subsequent references to Ryle are to this volume, unless otherwise noted. Pagination is the same in Hutchinson's University Library edition, London, 1949.

permitted to house objects that something called "the physical world" is forbidden to house;[1] it is to talk of the person's abilities, liabilities and inclinations to do and to undergo certain sorts of things, and of the doing and undergoing of these things in the ordinary world' (p. 199).

Referring to specific cases, Ryle contends that when we verbally distinguish absent-minded persons from those who are not, we do not refer to shadowy occult covert extra episodes, but rather to varieties of overt (public) behaviour (p. 25). In a similar fashion he discusses the difference between hearing an expected and an unexpected note in a musical presentation (p. 299).

A supplementary line of argument is offered to the effect that if mental words were used to refer to non-behavioural events (in standard ordinary use), we should have a supply of words for this purpose. But as a matter of fact we do not. As Ryle expresses it: we are able to talk about what we see and hear, but those who claim there are mental private impressions lack linguistic equipment (p. 242).

However, an appeal to comprehensive experience reveals that a very extensive vocabulary is available and is used in referring[2] to private non-behavioural mental activities and content. A glance at the writings of the existentialists is sufficient to make this point.

It is to be remembered that Ryle is claiming to report how 'mental' words are employed and not employed in ordinary standard fashion.[3]

As a matter of fact, in ordinary standard use the word 'mind' is used to refer to a 'place' where 'work is done' and 'games are played'. Intelligent men solve problems and play intelligent games without a body quiver or a tendency to quiver. In a general sense of the word, 'mind' is used to refer to a type of tool. This word 'mind' is used to refer to a kind of entity different from matter, abilities, inclination or overt behaviour. The word 'mind' is used to refer to a repository of

---

[1] 'A second theatre of special-status incidents' (p. 167).

[2] While Ryle and others use terms such as 'talk' or 'name', I have employed the more inclusive term 'refer'. When a person is 'talking of' or naming, he is engaged in the activity of meaning of the referring sort. He makes use of a sound or inscription, in the context of a meaning situation, to refer to some entity meant. He is using words in the *b* sense of the term.

[3] That Ryle and many other linguistic philosophers are, on occasion, erroneous in their reputed reports of the ordinary use of words is shown, for example, in the Glossary, Appendix to this book.

entities which are not found in the physical word, such as memory and imagination images. 'Absentmindedness' refers to a state of mind, not only to a type of behavioural expression of it. In general, the word 'mind' is not employed to refer to a special sort of bodily activities.

Some of those who differ from Ryle are not thereby committed to the absurd position Ryle attributes to them. When, in the context of comprehensive experience, the term 'mind' is used, it is not an attempt to refer to 'another person working . . . behind an impenetrable screen'. Rather it is a case of referring to an entity present in awareness. Hence, a person who does not use the term 'mind' as Ryle claims it is (or should be used) is not driven into a metaphysical mare's nest, such as unnecessary duplication involving an imaginary realm of occult entities.

'Feeling', 'know': Austin

In order to illustrate further the tendency of some linguistic philosophers to provide inaccurate reports concerning the use of words, consider the following. Austin contends that 'most feelings we do not speak of as either mental or physical, especially emotions, such as jealousy or anger itself: we do not assign them to the *mind* but to the heart'.[1]

As at matter of fact, in standard English use, we refer to feelings as mental states and to their physical manifestations. The claim that we ordinarily talk of emotion as not mental but as belonging to the heart is a strange reliance on a relatively specialised use of the word 'feeling', in poetry. This restriction neglects other more common standard uses of emotion words.

At this point it is worth while to consider Austin's very influential discussion of the use of the term 'know'. 'To suppose that "I know" is a descriptive phrase, is only one example of the *descriptive fallacy*, so common in philosophy.' He then points out that 'utterance of obvious ritual phrases, in the appropriate circumstances, is not *describing* the action we are doing, but *doing* it' (O.M., p. 174).

Thus Austin contends that the word 'know' has a performative, not a descriptive function. Specifically:

'When I say "I promise", a new plunge is taken: I have not merely

[1] J. L. Austin, 'Other Minds', *Aristotelian Society Supplementary Volume* XX (1946), pp. 179–80. Hereafter this paper will be referred to as O.M.

announced my intention, but, by using this formula, . . . I have bound myself to others, and staked my reputation, in a new way. Similarly, saying "I know" is taking a new plunge. But it is not saying "I have performed a specially striking fact of cognition, superior, in the same scale as believing and being sure, even to being merely quite sure": for there is nothing in that scale superior to being quite sure. . . . When I say "I know", I *give others my word*: I *give others my authority for saying* that "S is P".' (O.M., p. 171)

The analogy with 'promise' presents some difficulties for Austin. He states, 'When I say "I promise" I have not *merely* announced my intention'.[1] By implication, 'promise' has some descriptive function. Indeed, 'know' does involve doing something. But this performative use is based on the descriptive use of know and does not eliminate it as Austin seems to suggest. Unless it is admitted that A is familiar with and successfully recognises X—saying that he knows X is not giving anything or setting up an authority. The claim by Austin that 'know' does not refer to a 'cognition, superior in the same scale as believing and being quite sure . . . there is nothing . . . superior to being quite sure', is an unnecessary complication. In any case Experiential Realism, employing standard use, does report that to know is superior to being quite (that is fairly) sure.

Thus the standard use of 'know' has both a descriptive and a performative function. To deny this, as Austin does, is to set up a special technical restricted use of the term 'know'.[2]

Erroneous reports by Wittgenstein, Feigl, Ayer

Wittgenstein considers the case: ' "When I imagine something, or even actually see objects, I have got something which my neighbour has not." [Wittgenstein then comments]. . . . What are these words for? They serve no purpose.'[3]

---

[1] O.M., p. 171 (emphasis added).

[2] Heath aptly points out that many words have several ordinary uses. He remarks: 'To the vast majority of modern linguists, "Standard English" is no more than a trade-label annexed to a particular dialect, and has no special status or authority, apart from the (irrelevant) social approval accorded by those who happen to speak it.' P. Heath, 'The Appeal to Ordinary Language', *Clarity is Not Enough*, H. D. Lewis (ed.), George Allen and Unwin, London, 1963, p. 186. See also page 193. In some cases the fault is more serious. Some linguistic philosophers are simply guilty of a faulty report of language use; see pp. 198–9.

[3] L. Wittgenstein, *Philosophical Investigations*, Blackwell, Oxford, 1953, p. 120. Subsequent references to Wittgenstein are to this volume.

Here again is an inaccurate report of how words are used in a standard situation. When a person says he is imagining something, the words do serve a useful purpose. They refer to a mental process and content.

A faulty report of the use of individual words is found in Feigl's discussion of the mind-body problem. This version, while admitting a difference between mental and physical words, and hence the inappropriateness of translating mental in terms of physical, nevertheless contends that ultimately both sorts of words have the same referent. He then proceeds to point out that 'Utilising Frege's distinction between ... "sense" ... and ... "referent" ... we may say that neurophysiological terms and the corresponding phenomenal terms, though widely differing in sense and hence in the mode of confirmation of statements containing them, do have identical referents'.[1]

On the basis of comprehensive experience and ordinary standard use, one must reject this fine-spun line of argument. The reliance on the 'morning star'–'evening star' illustration is a case of the unjustified employment of an analogy. The star is found to be one physical object despite the fact that two different names are applied. The use of mental and physical words in the body-mind case is not an analogous situation. In the context of ordinary standard use, the mental words refer to one type of entity, and physical words to another type. It is obviously incorrect to claim that they have the same referent.

Ayer's discussion of the use of ethical terms involves him in a peculiar mixture of accuracy and error. He contends that ethical terms do not refer to anything—they merely express emotions. This is contrary to ordinary standard use where a distinction other than purely emotional is made between 'You stole the money' and 'It is wrong for you to steal money'. However, Ayer is in accord with the standard ordinary use when he points out, correctly, that ethical terms are used to express emotions, arouse feelings and influence behaviour. (*L.T.L.*, pp. 158–60)

However, it is to be noted that when Ayer argues that any statements about God are non-sensical since they do not express propositions, he is again using words in a special fashion, namely words are not significant unless they refer to sense experience, or a tautology is

[1] H. Feigl, 'Mind-Body, Not a Pseudo-Problem', *Dimensions of Mind*, S. Hook (ed.), New York Univ. Press, N.Y., 1960, p. 30.

involved (*L.T.L.*, pp. 172–5). But in ordinary and comprehensive experience words are sometimes used to refer to what is not sensory (and no tautology is involved). Indeed many people in standard use employ the term God in this fashion.

III

What one can say or not say

So far the discussion of the ordinary use of (ordinary) words has been concerned with the use of individual words. Another phase of the use of words will now be considered, namely what one can say or not say—which sentences are acceptable and which are not.

'Know I am in pain': Wittgenstein

In discussing the question of pain, Wittgenstein states: 'It can't be said of me at all (except perhaps as a joke) that I know I am in pain. What is it supposed to mean—except perhaps that I am in pain?' (p. 89).

This, in the context of comprehensive experience, is simply not the case. People regularly say that they know they are in pain. There is no attempt to joke in making such a statement. Further 'being in a certain state' is not and should not, in standard use, be equated with 'knowing that one is in that state'.

'Know how to use a sentence': Ryle

Equally incorrect is Ryle's statement about what we cannot say, that is specifically ask, in the following example: 'We cannot ask [a person] whether he knows how to use a certain sentence. When a block of words has congealed into a phrase we can ask whether he knows how to use the phrase' (O.L., p. 178).

As a matter of fact[1] a number of sentences are available as verbal units for purposes of factual reporting, expressing emotions, asking questions and ceremonial purposes. It is perfectly appropriate to ask whether or not a person knows how and when to use them.

Ryle's argument in support of his position to the effect that there are no dictionaries of sentences—only of words and phrases (O.L.,

---

[1] Ryle's argument from analogy involving the ingredients of a pie, that is the ingredients are used but not the pie, in the same sense of use—is not impressive.

p. 179) is contrary to fact. There are, in large and adequate dictionaries, examples of complete sentences in which words are appropriately used. Further, manuals designed to help a person use a foreign language for tourist purposes are set up chiefly in terms of equivalent sentences in one's native tongue and the foreign languages.

In some cases, as is correctly pointed out by Wittgenstein, some remarks are unsuitable. However, at least some of the examples he uses are such that these statements would not likely be made in the normal course of events. It hardly seems worth while to mention them as unsuitable. He refers for example, to a situation where various people on occasion are given an electrical shock. Wittgenstein points out: 'If I make the supposition that I can feel the shock even when someone else is electrified, then the expression "Now I know . . ." becomes quite unsuitable. It does not belong to this game' (p. 123).

IV

Therapeutic function of linguistic philosophy: Wittgenstein and Ryle

One feature of the work of linguistic philosophers is what they claim to be their therapeutic function. Specifically, they contend that if a philosopher uses a word, phrase or sentence in a fashion contrary to ordinary standard use, or is not familiar with ordinary standard use, he is likely to be beguiled into unjustified flights of speculative fantasy and hence generate imaginary-pseudo problems. Thus it is very important to focus attention on ordinary standard, correct use, in order to avoid, or cure such errors and remove pseudo-problems. The following remarks by Wittgenstein are typical:

'There must not be anything hypothetical in our considerations . . . description alone must take . . . place. . . . Philosophical problems . . . are solved . . . by looking into the workings of our language, . . . *in despite of* an urge to misunderstand them. The problems are solved, not by giving new information, but by arranging what we have always known. Philosophy is a battle against the bewitchment of our intelligence by means of language'[1] (p. 47).

---

[1] In this context, Wittgenstein made his famous remark: 'What is your aim in philosophy?—To shew the fly the way out of the fly-bottle' (p. 103).

More specifically, and in illuminating detail, Wittgenstein remarks: 'When philosophers use a word—"knowledge", "being", "object", "I", "proposition", "name"—and try to grasp the *essence* of the thing, one must always ask oneself: is the word ever actually used in this way?' (p. 48)

Thus, Wittgenstein claims that if a person adheres to the everyday use of words, he will not be misled into assuming, as metaphysicians do, that a word must refer to an essence which is common to all entities to which a word applies, a theory which generates innumerable problems.

In Wittgenstein's opinion, the entities imaginatively assumed by metaphysicians are a 'house of cards' which should be flattened without a qualm.

Thus, when confronted by a use of words which is contrary to ordinary standard use, a proper and acceptable alternative statement should be provided, or the offending word or phrase should be eliminated. Reputedly sound translation techniques have been developed for this purpose.

Thus Ryle recommends the elimination of the phrase 'in the mind' since 'its use habituates its employers to the view that minds are queer "places", the occupants of which are special-status phantasms' (*C.M.*, p. 40). The translation technique is also illustrated in Malcolm's claim that 'the use of the philosopher's sentence, "People are aware of their dreams", is the same as the use of the sentence, "People have dreams".'[1] In this fashion many mind-body pseudo-problems are avoided or solved, that is, removed.

A comprehensive examination of the standard use of the words involved in the preceding illustrations indicates that the word 'mind' is used by some theorists to refer to a queer, occult, shadowy, special-status phantasm. However, it is also employed to refer to an important entity which is present in comprehensive experience and hence, the phrase 'in the mind' should be retained. In any case the word 'aware' does not involve the same meaning as the word 'have'.

In general agreement with Experiential Realism's criticism of this eliminative type of translation prospect, consider Waismann's criticism of behaviourism for trying to reduce statements such as 'What a conceited fellow' to a series of statements referring to various patterns

---

[1] N. Malcolm, 'The Concept of Dreaming', *Philosophical Psychology*, D. F. Gustafson (ed.) Doubleday (Anchor), New York, 1964, p. 269.

of behaviour. 'The whole thing rests on a naivete—that there is one basic language into which everything else must be translated.'[1]

In like fashion it is legitimate to take issue with those who attempt to reduce statements about physical objects (for example, *L.T.L.*, pp. 75–6) to statements about sense data. Here again Waismann is vigorously cogent. 'We have simply to recognise that a statement about a cat is a statement about a cat: and not a truth-function of sense-datum statements, or an infinite class of perspectives, or an infinite group of sensibilia, or heaven knows what.'[2]

In brief, it should be obvious that the devotees of words, who have been considered in the preceding sections, sanction some standard use of words and reject other standard uses of these words. Also, they claim some uses of words to be standard which are not standard. The same general comments apply to discussions by linguistic philosophies of what we can say and what we cannot say in sentences.

v

Philosophy and language which is not ordinary: Ayer

So far attention has been focused on philosophers who claim to be concentrating on the ordinary standard use of words, phrases and sentences. There are those who contend that it is the business of a philosopher to employ words in fashions which are not ordinary or standard. For example, this is particularly the case in instances when a philosopher engages in a process of translating a statement which may lead to pointless metaphysical flights of speculation—into one which does not encourage such an enterprise. A sentence such as 'The author of *Waverley* was Scotch' seems, to the gullible, to imply that there is an entity to which the phrase 'the author of' refers—an entity which is not part of the familiar word of scientifically respectable entities. It is then proposed by the therapist that we translate this sentence into the following: 'One person and one person only wrote *Waverley* and that person was Scotch.' Ayer remarks that the 'One person and one person only' locution is not standard English usage, while 'the author of *Waverley*' is. However, according to Ayer, a

[1] *Logic and Language*, A. Flew (ed.), Doubleday, New York, 1965, p. 246.
[2] *Ibid.*, p. 245. See also *P.I.*, p. 180.

philosopher who is about his proper business will prefer the former to the latter in order to avoid a slide into metaphysics.[1]

Experiential Realism takes issue with those who would replace actual use by some unnecessary[2] preferred use. In apparent general agreement with the opposition to Ayer, Wittgenstein remarks: 'Philosophy may in no way interfere with the actual use of language; it can in the end only describe it' (*P.I.*, p. 49). Nevertheless, paradoxically, inconsistently, Wittgenstein on occasion does state that misunderstandings can, and should 'be removed by substituting one form of expression for another' (p. 43). Yet on the other hand he contends that 'It is clear that *every* sentence in our language "is in order as it is". ' (emphasis added).

VI

Philosophical problems only verbal or logical: Ayer, Ryle, Wittgenstein and Putnam[3]

A number of contemporary philosophers are in general agreement with the contention expressed by Ayer that a philosopher should not be 'directly concerned with the physical properties of things. He is concerned *only* with the way in which we speak about them' (*L.T.L.*, p. 61, emphasis added). This leads in some instances to the conclusion that since philosophers are concerned only with words, therefore philosophic problems are purely verbal or logical, despite their apparent concern with questions of fact.

Thus Ryle contends that philosophy has always been engaged in the discussion of concepts, that is, has 'had something to do with the use of expressions'. More specifically, when a philosopher deals with problems in the field of perception, he is not concerned with questions (factual ones) which are of interest to opticians, physiologists or psychologists. What a philosopher 'is after is accounts of how certain

---

[1] *L.T.L.*, p. 86.

[2] If it is noted that the phrase 'the author of' refers to a group of concepts, it is unnecessary to attempt to preserve meaning (referents) by substituting a reference to a physical entity. The translation technique here under consideration (Ayer's) tries to operate in terms only of physical entities.

[3] It will be obvious that this section is an expansion of the topic discussed in Chapter 10, pp. 261–7.

words work [i.e., are used] namely words like, "see", "look", "over-look", "blind", "visualise" and a host of other affiliated expressions' (O.L., p. 185, emphasis added).[1]

In like fashion, Wittgenstein asks: 'Could a machine think?—Could it be in pain? . . . But a machine surely cannot think!—Is that an empirical statement? No. We only *say* [that] of a human being (*P.I.*, p. 113, emphasis added).

Consider also Ayer's very revealing comment concerning universals (concepts): 'The assertion that relations are universals provokes the question, "What is a universal?"; and this question is not, as it has traditionally been regarded, a question about the character of certain real objects, but a request for a definition of a certain term.' Similarly 'to ask what is the nature of a material object is to ask for a definition of "material object" ' (*L.T.L.*, p. 64).

On the basis of comprehensive experience one must object strongly to the description of philosophy provided by the linguistically oriented philosophers referred to above. One must, of course, admit that if they wish to restrict the word 'philosophy' to the study of language use, they will do so. However, that is not standard ordinary use. Further, and more important, it is simply not the case that many of the traditional philosophical problems are linguistic, not factual.[2]

In the context of the preceding comments concerning the linguistically oriented type of philosophy, one can quickly reject part of the statement by Putnam, that body-mind problems are 'wholly linguistic and logical in character'. When he paradoxically proceeds to discuss facts he perpetrates another type of error. 'The various issues and puzzles that make up the traditional mind-body problem are wholly linguistic and logical in character: whatever few empirical "facts" there may be in this area support one view as much as another.'[3] Indeed, he goes further and contends that a computer can perform activities usually assigned to minds but which need not be.

That Putnam refers to empirical facts in the context of this dis-

---

[1] See also Ayer's remark: 'The problem of giving an actual rule for translating . . . sentences about sense-contents, which may be called the problem of the 'reduction' of material things to sense-contents, is the main philosophic part of the traditional problem of perception' (*L.T.L.*, pp. 75–6).

[2] See Chapter 10, pp. 261–4. See also P. Heath, 'The Appeal to Ordinary Language', *Clarity is not Enough*, H. D. Lewis (ed.), George Allen and Unwin, London, 1963, p. 254.

[3] H. Putnam, 'Minds and Machines', p. 72, *Minds and Machines*, A. R. Anderson (ed.), Prentice-Hall, New York, 1964.

cussion of philosophical problems is to his credit. However, he is quite incorrect in claiming that they 'support one view [of the mind-body problem] as much as another'. As has been pointed out earlier, the empirical facts support the view of Experiential Realism and do not sanction, for example, any version of the identity theory. It is simply naive to state, as Putnam does, that all the basic issues arise with reference to a sophisticated type of computer and hence, 'have nothing to do with subjective experience'. Just because both a mind and a machine can retain data and answer questions, that does not indicate that there are not two different types of basic entities and their characteristics present, particularly in view of their experienced difference.

VII

Lazerowitz on metaphysical theories

Another variation of the 'things are not what they seem' theme, which does not fall exactly within the scope of the topics previously discussed, is represented by the work of Lazerowitz. He examines the language used by philosophers in the light of a psychoanalytic approach, as was noted earlier (Chapter 10, pp. 260–1). Specifically, Lazerowitz contends that statements of metaphysical theories actually are not attempts to make factual statements which can be determined true or false (p. 25).[1] This being so, metaphysical theories (statements of theory) cannot be refuted, and controversy in the area cannot be settled (p. 63). It must be realised that Lazerowitz is not contending that metaphysicians have 'a mistaken idea about actual use in common speech' (p. 63). Thus, metaphysical statements cannot be corrected by referring to standard use. Rather, metaphysical statements are beyond correction because, when a metaphysician uses language, he is 'linguistically creative, not wrong'. He is engaged in a process of 'language innovation' (p. 64). The changed use of words is deliberate, if not conscious. It develops in order to deal with an emotional problem.

In view of their *modis operandi*, their language innovation in order

[1] All references are to *The Structure of Metaphysics*, Routledge and Kegan Paul, London, 1963.

to solve emotional problems, Lazerowitz contends that metaphysicians not only disregard established verbal usage but also other facts, for example change or rest (pp. 63–4). For then there is no point in referring to facts at all if one is engaged in metaphysics. The sort of 'language innovation' in which, according to Lazerowitz, metaphysicians engage, is illustrated in the following statement: 'For some people the word "change", in addition to its ordinary meaning, which they do not give up in their everyday conversation, has the private [unconscious] meaning of catastrophic change. . . . The hidden sense of the philosophical statement "Nothing really changes" is "No changes which would create anxiety in me are real" ' (p. 70).

Lazerowitz makes a further important point:

'[Some] philosophers subjectively rewrite language by casting out the word "change", . . . and they do this in a mode of speech, i.e. in the ontological idiom, which both conceals from themselves what they are doing with the word "change" and gives rise to the notion, which with unconscious duplicity they accept, that they are stating a fact about the world of physics' (p. 70).

From the point of view of comprehensive experience, one must quickly point out that, while some philosophers in general and some metaphysicians in particular, are not dealing with factual issues, others are. They would not admit, nor should they, that their statements are neither true nor false nor their disagreements beyond solution. Both Plato and Lucretius claim that their theories—Forms (Plato) and Atom (Lucretius)—have factual support which is relevant to settle disagreements. It is the case that philosophers sometimes change the meaning of familiar terms. Usually it is an extension or limitation of use. It is not a case, as Lazerowitz seems to claim with reference to the changes, of permanent disagreement, that words are completely changed in their private, that is philosophical use—for example, everything is called 'change' by Heraclitus, everything is called 'permanent' by Parmenides. Both men, as Lazerowitz admits, add a qualifying term 'real' which issues in a new phrase or term, that is, it is actually a case of 'really change' applying to everything or 'really permanent' applying to everything. Of course Lazerowitz is correct in pointing out that words take on associated meaning, that is 'change' becomes linked with 'dreaded'.

Experiential Realism does not propose to deal with the exponents of alternative views primarily in terms of what roughly may be termed psychoanalysis. However, the effects of emotions, attitudes, temperament, etc. on philosophers have been noted. (See Chapter 10, pp. 260–1, Chapter 19, pp. 419–21.)

VIII

Words (or logic) legislate: Ryle, Ayer and Flew

Some philosophers who rely on what they claim (in many cases mistakenly) to be the standard use of words—seem to slide on occasion, despite strong denials that such is the case, into the position that words, or the principles of logic, legislate what other entities must be.

Consider for example Ryle's remarks (*C.M.*, p. 205) designed to show that the reputed distinction between the physical and the mental world is spurious:

'It is true that the cobbler cannot witness the tweaks that I feel when the shoe pinches. . . . The reason . . . is not that some Iron Curtain prevents them from being witnessed by anyone save myself, but that they are not the sorts of things of which it *makes sense to say* that they are witnessed or unwitnessed at all, even by me' (*C.M.*, p. 205, emphasis added).

Likewise, Ryle, referring to the authority of logic, states: 'You cannot, in logic, hold my catches, win my races, eat my meals, frown my frowns, or dream my dreams, so you cannot have my twinges, or my after-images' (*C.M.*, p. 209).

Consider also Ayer: 'For the fruitlessness of attempting to transcend the limits of possible sense-experience will be deduced, not from a psychological hypothesis concerning the actual constitution of the human mind, but from the rule which determines the literal significance of language' (*L.T.L.*, p. 19).

This procedure is open to a number of serious objections if one relies on comprehensive experience. In general it neglects the function and status of words and the principles of logic. At best they give information about the world of facts. They do not legislate or dictate what the facts are.[1]

An interesting variation of the 'reliance on language approach' as authoritative concerning facts, is found in Flew's reference to languages other than English and most other European languages. He points out that there are many languages where the subject-predicate distinction is barely made, and in general do not operate in terms of the similarities and differences with which we are familiar. Further, there are languages which do not embody the concept 'cause'. All this, in Flew's opinion, serves 'to discredit ideas that the subject-predicate distinction must be inextricably rooted in the non-linguistic world, that the notion of cause is an indispensable category of thought, and that language must reflect the ultimate nature of reality.' (E.C.A., p. 6.)

As far as comprehensive experience is concerned the following comments are in order. If a language does not take into account entities such as causation and the subject-predicate distinction, this is an indication of the inadequacy of the language, since such entities are found in comprehensive experience. Any language, be it European or non-European, is not the final arbiter or source of information about facts. However, Experiential Realism does not claim that 'the notion of cause is an indispensable category of thought'. In some cases it is appropriate to admit that in thinking of some entities, at the present stage of human experience, the concept 'cause' does not apply because causation has not been found. Further, Experiential Realism, based on the present state of comprehensive experience, does not claim to delineate the ultimate nature of reality, but rather to report what entities are experienced. If 'reality' means 'are there in experience', then language does reflect reality. One cannot, however, claim to deal with ultimates in any absolute sense, only ultimates as far as comprehensive experience is concerned. But to repeat, the final authority is not language or logic. Words are instruments. Their usefulness for any purpose depends on their relations to facts. As sources of information, they are at best second-hand reports possessing varying degrees of adequacy. Logic either reflects facts or is an unsupported imaginative creation.

[1] See Chapter 4, pp. 101–3, Chapter 5, pp. 130–2.

Words as a source of information: Austin

This chapter began with an examination of the work of those who contend that philosophy should be concerned only (or primarily) with the use of words or concepts, and that an investigation of physical and mental facts should be left to others. It will be pointed out in subsequent chapters that these philosophers have actually paralleled this linguistic approach with a number of empirical statements about minds, physical objects and concepts. This tendency has already become apparent in some cases.

Some linguistically oriented philosophers are quite prepared to stress the point that a study of language use is an appropriate way of obtaining information about facts of all types.

The following statement by Austin merits careful attention: 'our common stock of words embodies all the distinctions men have found worth drawing, and the connections they have found worth marking, in the lifetimes of many generations.'[1]

He proceeds to suggest that this source of information is likely to be more 'sound' in at least 'ordinary and reasonably practical matters' than the results of a brief session of armchair speculation.

However, Austin has no delusions of grandeur with respect to ordinary words as a source of information. As he aptly remarks: 'Ordinary language has no claim to be the last word' ('Plea', p. 11). This is so because ordinary language embodies the results only of ordinary and practical experience. It does not reflect, adequately, the more abstract intellectual experience or the results of recent scientific developments. Nevertheless, when the worst is said of ordinary language, it is still worthy of consideration. Thus Austin states:

'Superstition and error and phantasy of all kinds do become incorporated in ordinary language and even sometimes stand up to the survival test (only, when they do, why should we not detect it?). Certainly, then, ordinary laaguage is *not* the last word: in principle it can everywhere be supplemented and improved upon and superseded. Only remember, it *is* the *first* word' ('Plea', p. 11).

Having thus contended that language, both ordinary, when properly

[1] J. L. Austin, 'A Plea for Excuses', *Proceedings of the Aritotelian Society*, LVII (1956–7), p. 8. Hereafter this paper will be referred to as 'Plea'.

purified, and technical, is a respectable source of information, Austin proceeds to put 'concentration on words' in proper perspective, at least as far as comprehensive experienced is concerned. 'When we examine what we should say when, what words we should use in what situations, we are looking ... not *merely* at words (or 'meaning', whatever they are or they may be) but also at the realities we use the words to talk about' ('Plea', p. 8).

The same general point is made even more succinctly thus:

'Words are not (except in their own little corner) facts or things: we need therefore to prise them off the world, to hold them apart from and against it, so that we can realise their inadequacies and arbitrari-nesses, and can re-look at the world without blinkers ... we are using a sharpened awareness of words to sharpen our perception of, though not as the *final arbiter of, the phenomenon*' ('Plea', p. 8, emphasis added).

Austin's stress on the necessity of a careful examination of words—the need to hold them 'apart from and against' the world in order to 'realise their inadequacies and arbitrariness' and hence the need to come to grips with the phenomena which constitute reality in the sense just noted—is completely in accordance with the view of Experiential Realism. Austin has been quoted at length to show that Experiential Realism is not alone in its discussion of the status of words.'[1]

[1] See also Ayer's support of this general point of view ('Philosophy of language', p. 412) and his contention that Wittgenstein has the same position (p. 420).

12

WORDS AND MEANING

I

Effective referential use of words: Flew, Wittgenstein, Paul and Pears

In the discussion of the use of words in Chapter 5, it was stated that after comprehensive experience it is possible to use some words[1] effectively in reporting information about physical objects, minds and concepts, as well as to influence behaviour and express emotions.

Flew takes a firm stand, in agreement with Experiential Realism, against those who are pessimistic concerning the acquisition of this competence.[2] With reference to this matter Wittgenstein makes the forthright comment: 'If it is asked: "How do sentences manage to represent?"—the answer might be: "Don't you know? You certainly see it, when you use them." For nothing is concealed.'[3]

Wittgenstein, nevertheless, raises some important objections to this general confidence concerning the use of words. Attention is focused on the problem of teaching a person how to apply a word (in the first sense of the term, an inscription or sound) correctly. He remarks that it may appear that one can define the number two by pointing towards two nuts. 'But [objects Wittgenstein] . . . The person . . . doesn't know what one wants to call "two"; he will suppose that "two" is the name given to this group of nuts!' (*P.I.*, p. 13).

The reaction of Experiential Realism (as noted in Chapter 5) is that, despite the admitted initial difficulties, care in using the pointing method finally produces satisfactory results. In comprehensive

---

[1] In the second sense of the term, that is a sound or an inscription in a meaning situation, see Chapter 5, pp. 132-7.

[2] *Essays in Conceptual Analysis*, A. Flew (ed.), Macmillan, London, 1963, p. 17. Hereafter this book will be referred to as *E.C.A.*

[3] Wittgenstein, *Philosophical Investigations*, Blackwell, Oxford, 1953, p. 128. Hereafter this book will be referred to as *P.I.*

experience the name 'two' is used properly and it is not confused with
the word 'nut' when two nuts are present.

Paul, in general agreement with Experiential Realism remarks: 'In
saying that the word "fovea" is to stand for a thing, . . . and at the
same time pointing to an instance of a fovea, . . . we say [and do]
all that any physiologist requires in order to be able to use the word
successfully.'[1]

Pears aptly points out that another common way of teaching the
use of a word, namely by mentioning a synonym, ultimately depends
on the effective use of the pointing (ostensive) techniques (*Logic and
Language*, p. 280).

II

*Language—public physical frame of reference: Wittgenstein and
Wellman*

It is contended by some of those who are devoted to the public
physical world in general, and to the importance of language in
particular, that language can only be used if there is some public
physical frame of reference which serves as a criterion to which words
can be significantly linked, and their use taught and checked. Without
this public foundation there can be no language. Thus it is argued that
there can be no language available to refer to what is completely
private, involving no public expression.

Let us examine a typical exposition of this theme provided by
Wittgenstein. He faces the question as to how a person learns the
name of a sensation, for example pain. Wittgenstein suggests an
answer. When a child hurts himself and cries, he is taught words to
use as a substitute form of expression of pain (*P.I.*, p. 689).

In support of this general line of approach, Wittgenstein asks:
'What would it be like if human beings shewed no outward signs of
pain (did not groan, grimace, etc.)? Then it would be impossible to
teach a child the use of the word "toothache" '[2] (*P.I.*, p. 92).

---

[1] G. A. Paul, 'Is there a problem about sense data?', *Aristotelian Society
Supplementary Volume* XV, 1936, p. 64. Hereafter this paper will be referred
to as *Paul*.

[2] It seems appropriate to quote at some length from Wittgenstein in order
to avoid misrepresentation. Further—critical comments are directed to those
specific passages. In any case, in dealing with Wittgenstein this is ordinary
standard usage!

In like fashion he asks, and assumes a negative answer: 'Could we . . . imagine a language in which a person could write down or give vocal expression to his inner experience—his feelings, moods, and the rest—for his private use?' there being no public criterion (*P.I.*, p. 88).

On occasion, Wittgenstein takes a much more extreme position. Having contended correctly that it is impossible to have a shared ostensive definition of private sensation, he then incorrectly claims that also there is no criterion, no public point of reference for the use of a term referring to a sensation (*P.I.*, p. 92). This position is contrary to and contradicts what he seems to be saying in a previous quotation, since he has been referring to criteria, such as crying, groaning, which operate in some cases of sensation. (See *P.I.*, p. 89).

The reaction of Experiential Realism to Wittgenstein's insistence on public criteria for the use of words can be illustrated by turning to his specific query as to how the word 'toothache' could be taught to a person who showed no outward signs, such as groaning, etc. The answer is simple. If it is found by a dentist that a person possesses a very decayed tooth and a normal reaction system; then, despite his stoic self-control, the patient can be told that his inner feelings, which he refrains from expressing, are a case of a toothache. It is to be noted that the decay of the tooth is a public fact and so serves as a criterion for an inner state. In any case, the patient can point at, or focus on, his toothache in his inner awareness. Further he can use the word again if the pain occurs again. He now has his own inner criterion.

In fairness, it must be noted that Wittgenstein, in general terms, refers to a 'do this and you will experience a sensation' situation. He then remarks: 'Can't there be a doubt here? Mustn't there be one, if it is a feeling that is meant?' (*P.I.*, p. 186). The reply to Wittgenstein is simply that in some cases there may be doubt. But if care is taken, in view of standard patterns of human reaction, there seems no justification, in comprehensive experience, for contending that there 'must be' doubt in all cases.

Further, imagining a case of a person who invents a private language to refer to his own sensations, does not present the difficulties which Wittgenstein envisages. It is quite possible for a person to invent a private language to refer to his inner states and use it consistently. Indeed, many people keep a diary in which they record, in a private language, reports of their own sensations, feelings, plans, business transactions, etc. to preserve secrecy from prying eyes.

C. W. Wellman's comment concerning Wittgenstein's contention that criteria for the use of words must be external and public is worthy of note: 'Until some reasons are produced for this view, it remains a dogmatic assumption which may be questioned.'[1]

The position of Experiential Realism is also in accord with that of Feigl, who points out that: 'Even if we *learn* the use of subjective terms in the way indicated, [by Wittgenstein] once we have them in our vocabulary we *apply* them to states or conditions to which we, as individual subjects, have a "privileged access".'[2]

III

Many uses of words: Wittgenstein, Ryle, Hobbes and Austin

In discussing language, Wittgenstein aptly stresses the point (in agreement with the discussion in Chapter 5) that words singly or in combination are used in countless ways. New uses are continually coming into existence. In this context Wittgenstein refers to language games (*P.I.*, p. 11).

This phrase 'language game' has great significance for him. Examples are illuminating:

'Giving orders and obeying them
Describing the appearance of an object. . . .
Reporting an event. . . .
Forming and testing a hypothesis. . . .
Making up a story; and reading it. . . .
Asking, thanking, cursing. . . . (*P.I.*, pp. 11–12).

It should be obvious from these examples that while the phrase 'language game' sometimes refers merely to linguistic performance,

[1] 'Wittgenstein and the Egocentric Predicament', *Mind*, April 1959, p. 225. Consider also Ayer's comment concerning Wittgenstein: 'When he denies the possibility of a private language . . . he is fashioning a mould into which the facts must be made to fit'. His position is 'not derived from an open-minded study of the way in which . . . any . . . language happens to work.' (A. J. Ayer, 'Philosophy and language' in *Clarity is not Enough*, H. D. Lewis (ed.), George Allen and Unwin, London, 1963, p. 421).

[2] H. Feigl, *Dimensions of Mind*, S. Hook (ed.), New York University Press, 1960, p. 25.

nevertheless more generally the term covers not only linguistic performance but also related bodily activities in a broad context.

As a matter of fact, it appears to many philosophers that a language is analogous to, or is, a sort of game. In other words, using language is playing a game. It is argued that rules are very important. This general point of view is stressed by Ryle: 'There are rules to keep or break. Learning to use expressions, involves learning to do certain things with them and not others.'[1]

The notion that the rules of games and hence of language are arbitrary and artificial is clearly expounded by many. 'As a matter of fact there is no natural basis for the rule in baseball that "three strikes constitutes an out". Similarly, there is no natural basis for the linkage of the English word "green" with the colour green.'[2]

The reaction of Experiential Realism is that indeed in the case of many words, there is no obvious or natural linkage with any other entity. Entities do not present themselves initially 'complete with neat, agreed, label'. To that extent, the linkage of many words and other entities is arbitrary and artificial human invention. Rules stating these linkages are in this sense arbitrary and artificial. Exceptional cases are those in which the sound of a word imitates the sound of an entity to which it is linked, as with 'hiss' and the hiss of a snake.

Wittgenstein, like Ryle, points out that acquiring a language is like learning any game (*P.I.*, p. 5). It involves instruction. As a matter of fact,[3] in most cases a person must learn from instruction by others and remember the artificial linkages of the content of a specific language, with concepts, minds, physical objects. However, there are notable exceptions which involve sounds which express emotions. The emotive use of language does not depend in all cases on a process of instruction. A groan or sigh is not a word[4] (in the second sense of the term) that is restricted to any one language which has to be specially learned, as is the case with the English word 'green' or 'ouch'. The linkage of the groan or sigh with an emotional state, in the absence of pretending, is rather obvious to a person who is aware of both. The relevant concepts may not be as quickly obvious to all

---

[1] G. Ryle, 'Ordinary Language', *Philosophical Review*, Vol. LXII, no. 2, p. 173. Hereafter this will be referred to as O.L.

[2] Similar examples are readily available.

[3] That is in the context of comprehensive experience.

[4] Groans and sighs are included in the class of words and are regarded as part of language.

men but are open to comprehensive awareness. Likewise, without instruction from others, an observant person may come to use a groan or sigh as indicating a state of fatigue, a dangerous object, or it may function as a suggestion that the object be avoided.

Rules[1] are useful reminders of how words are used in referring, reporting, expressing emotions and for practical purposes. These rules are frequently mentioned in teaching the use of words. Where one has learned to use words, rules are implied. But many words, quite apart from natural linkage as noted above, are linked with other entities without initial deliberate planning in the sense of setting up specific rules and then proceeding to implement them, as in the case of games like monopoly or basketball. Taking a cue from the procedure of children, it seems that sounds are uttered and gradually specialised in their linkage with specific entities in the interests of efficient behaviour. Thus initially a child applies the word 'dog' to any animal and 'dada' to any man. Gradually he becomes more definite in his use of these words. In like fashion, among adults, the word 'star' initially refers to any heavenly body. Later, a distinction is made between stars and planets. On the other hand, for example, the term 'communication media' has been gradually extended from application to books to include television. Once these linkages are well settled, rules may be formulated to state these linkages.

Nevertheless, some specific words are deliberately set up and linked with specified entities in accordance with rules which are in effect and decisive from the beginning. Consider the following examples of the invention of some words, and the rules of their use. When a new entity is invented or discovered, new words are invented and their use specified at once. The terms 'radio-telephone', 'communication satellite' are typical cases. However, it is essential to note that rules are here established by people to meet the requirements of a situation. In this sense also rules are not ultimate.

When the linkage of words with other entities has been established and words accurately report (describe) the situation before one, the question arises as to how the words are put together to form a sentence, specifically what determines the relative position in the sentence of nouns, verbs, adjectives, and so on. This appears to be a relatively arbitrary matter varying from language to language and usually occurs initially without deliberately setting up specific guiding rules. However, some control may be exercised by the structure of the situation

[1] See Chapter 5, pp. 130-2.

referred to. Nouns and adjectives are side by side because the adjectives refer to characteristics of entities. The latter are referred to by nouns. Efficiency in referring, also aesthetic effect, may have some bearing on the arrangement of words. In determining the sentence structure in cases of the practical uses of language, the purpose involved exerts an influence in arranging words. Also, effectiveness in producing the desired results is important. Ways of putting words together in sentences are thus established. However—and this is fundamental— the words used if one is concerned with an accurate report of facts rather than a flight of fancy, depend on the facts which are being reported. The facts determine or control what one can say or not say about an objective situation.

Thus, in brief, many rules are summaries of language use and are as such not arbitrary nor in any ultimate sense regulatory or constitutive of the language.

Hence, in most instances, the structure of a language and the use of individual words is not analogous to the application of rules of a game unless the rules of the game report an unplanned and gradual development. Some game rules are of this type.

However, most game rules initiate the use of what is involved in the game and do not report a gradual development uncontrolled by rules. This, of course, as noted, is the case with some words, namely those invented to apply to new situations and their usage are specified from the beginning. Thus, in summary, a comparison of language and games must lead to the conclusion that the rules in the two cases in many instances have different origins and functions, depending on their subject matter.

It is the case that some men, on some occasions, play with words. That is to say, they do not intend any referential reporting or practical function in any serious sense or even any function expressive for example of the emotions. They are merely amusing themselves and perhaps others. In most instances when men use language it is a serious business; language is an instrument employed in an attempt to effect an adequate adjustment to their environment. They are not merely playing a game, in the sense of a frivolous withdrawal from life's major problems. However, it is only fair to admit that some games are not mere frivolous enjoyment. Some games are serious preparation for life. Such games and much of language use thus do have kinship at this point. They are serious attempts to come to grips with the environment in which men find themselves.

The position of Experiential Realism concerning the justification for, or control of, the use of language outlined above in this Chapter and preceding ones finds support among a wide range of philosophers.

Thus Hobbes remarks: 'A man . . . had need to remember what every name he uses stands for, and to place it accordingly, or else he will find himself entangled in words, as a bird in lime twigs, the more he struggles the more belimed.'[1]

In like fashion, Austin refers to adjuster-words, 'words . . . by the use of which other words are adjusted to meet the innumerable and unforseeable demands of the world upon language.'[2]

Also worthy of note is Wittgenstein's comment that 'it is possible to do physics in feet and inches as well as in metres and centimetres; the difference is merely one of convenience. But even this is not true if, for instance, calculations in some system of measurement demand more time and trouble than is possible for us to give them' (*P.I.*, p. 151).

In another passage, while noting that language may be invented as one invents a game, nevertheless, on the other hand, use of a language may be formulated on the basis of the laws of nature as well as controlled by a purpose. 'To invent a language could mean to invent an instrument for a particular purpose on the basis of the laws of nature (or consistently with them); but it also has the other sense, analogous to that in which we speak of the invention of a game' (*P.I.*, p. 137).

The inappropriateness of assigning final authority to rules in all games, language or otherwise is also noted by Wittgenstein: 'And is there not also the case where we play—and make up the rules as we go along? And there is even one where we alter them—as we go along' (*P.I.*, p. 39).

In any case Wittgenstein, in a striking passage, is in accord with the position of Experiential Realism concerning the status of rules, specifically those of grammar, when he states: 'Grammar does not tell us how language must be constructed in order to fulfil its purpose, in order to have such-and-such an effect on human beings. It only describes and in no way explains the use of signs' (p. 138).

---

[1] T. Hobbes, *Leviathan*, in *English Philosophers from Bacon to Mill*, E. A. Burtt (ed.), Modern Library, New York, 1939, p. 142.

[2] J. L. Austin, *Sense and Sensibilia*, Oxford, 1962, p. 73. This and the immediately following statements by Wittgenstein are reproduced here because they are frequently neglected by those who worship at the shrine of Wittgenstein.

Indeed, it is to be noted that in coming to grips with an unfamiliar language, learning it, the form of reference is not rules but the 'common behaviour of mankind' (*P.I.*, p. 82).

IV

Incomplete analyses of meaning: Wittgenstein

The preceding discussion provides a useful foundation for a further examination of meaning. It will be recalled that in Chapter 5, it was noted that the term 'meaning' has four main senses. These bring into the focus of attention four main aspects of the meaning situation. For example, an inscription or sound has meaning (a characteristic) when it is a symbol pointing to (relation of meaning) an entity (entity meant). The inscription of sound then can be used in pointing to (activity of meaning) that entity (entity meant).

Many contemporary discussions of meaning are partial in that they do not take into consideration all aspects of a meaning situation. Indeed, there are those who deny that some aspects of the meaning situation are ingredients in it.

It would appear that Wittgenstein covers two aspects of meaning in the following brief statement: 'Can I not say: a cry, a laugh, are full of meaning? [have meaning] . . . much [entity meant] can be gathered from them' (*P.I.*, p. 146).[1]

On occasion Wittgenstein states several different even more restricted approaches to the meaning situation. 'In order to get clear about the meaning of the word "think" we watch ourselves while we think; what we observe will be what the word means!' (*P.I.*, p. 104) ('entity meant' emphasis). More generally: 'the *meaning* of a name is sometimes explained by pointing to its *bearer*' (*P.I.*, p. 21). This is a statement of the so-called referent[2] theory of meaning.

On the other hand Wittgenstein, in some discussions, stresses the use of words. 'For a *large* class of cases—though not for all—in

---

[1] A later remark is a good candidate for the 'circular definition' bin. ' "The meaning of a word is what is explained by the explanation of the meaning" ' (*P.I.*, p. 149).
[2] That is, entity meant.

which we employ the word "meaning" it can be defined thus: the meaning of a word is its use in the language' (*P.I.*, p. 20).

On occasion Wittgenstein engages in a vigorous rejection of the referential theory of meaning. He thus leaves himself open to the charge of inconsistency in view of his acceptance of it on at least several occasions. 'It is important to note that the word "meaning" is being used illicitly if it is used to signify the thing that "corresponds" to the word.' The following illustration is regarded as crucial: 'When Mr N. N. dies one says that the bearer of the name dies, not that the meaning dies. And it would be nonsensical to say that, for if the name ceased to have the meaning it would make no sense to say "Mr N. N. is dead" ' (*P.I.*, p. 20).

The reply on the part of Experiential Realism to this attempt at *reductio ad absurdum* concerning the referent aspect of meaning, is briefly this. As a matter of fact, one of the uses of the word 'meaning' is to focus on the thing to which the word is linked. When Mr N. N. dies, the physical referent of the name has gone out of existence—in other words this part of the meaning situation has died. The name N. N. still has meaning because one can refer to a memory image or a picture of Mr N. N. (entity meant).

Ryle offers a criticism of those who stress the referent aspect meaning exclusively, though in doing so he seems to deny that there is a referent aspect in the meaning situation. He considers it strange that there should be philosophers who take 'the meaning of an expression ... to be an entity which had that expression for its name. So studying the meaning of the phrase "the solar system" was supposed or half-supposed to be the same thing as studying the solar system.' (O.L., p. 172).

Further, he contends that the referent theory involves, at least in many cases, a realm of queer extra entities which are not part of the physical or mental world, namely essences or universals, for instance, what the words 'if', 'ought', and 'limit' refer to (O.L., pp. 172–3). Ryle's main objection to the referent theory of meaning is based on his conviction that the 'meaning is use' theory is the correct one.

Thus he remarks: 'We are accustomed to talking of the use of safety pins, bannisters, table knives, ... and gestures; and this familiar idiom neither connotes nor seems to connote any queer relations or any queer entities' (O.L., p. 172). The same is the case when using words.

In reply, on the basis of comprehensive experience, it seems appropriate to remark that words are used to refer to the solar system. It is, of course, a common assumption among philosophers that words such as 'if', 'ought', and 'limit' have no genuine and respectable referent, as distinct from other words. Nevertheless, concepts are not queer—they are among the entities found in comprehensive experience.

It should be obvious from the previous discussion that Experiential Realism is opposed to any attempt to claim that referents or, more broadly, entities meant are the only ingredients in the meaning situation, that they are the only entities to which the term 'meaning' appropriately applies. Thus the referent theory, if it claims exclusive jurisdiction, is not supported by comprehensive experience. The same comment applies to those who place exclusive emphasis on the use of words, or any phase of the meaning situation.

At this point, it must be made clear that at least one version of the 'use' theory of meaning contends that the meaning of a word is its use in accordance with rules. Thus, learning the meaning of a word is learning the rules of its use. Knowing the meaning of a word is knowing the rules of its use.[1]

The preceding discussion of the secondary status of rules, that they are either descriptions of more or less haphazard linking of symbols and entities meant, or indications of determination on the part of people to establish a rule of linkage to meet some need, is relevant here. The fundamental importance assigned to rules, by the 'use' theory of meaning, leaves it open to serious objection—that this is an emphasis on a partial, and induced, peripheral aspect of a complex situation. There is, in addition, the previously noted ambiguity of the term 'use', and hence the conclusion that in some senses 'use' is identified with meaning and in other senses it is not.[2]

v

Meaning and verification: Schlick, Flew, Ayer and Waismann

There remains to be considered a discussion of meaning which concentrates on verification. Thus Wittgenstein claims that 'Asking

---

[1] For example Ryle states: 'If I know the meaning of a word or a phrase I know something like a body of unwritten rules, or something like an unwritten code or general recipe. What I know is, in this respect, somewhat like what I know when I know how to use a knight or a pawn in chess' (O.L., p. 179).

[2] See Chapter 5, pp. 138–40.

whether and how a proposition can be verified is only a particular way of asking "How d'you mean?" ' (*P.I.*, p. 112).

Clarification of this approach to meaning is provided by M. Schlick.[1] He manifests a queer, inconsistent shift from the statement that the meaning of a sentence is that to which it refers, to the contention that the process of verifying (finding out whether a statement is true or false) defines or is the meaning. Verification in principle (p. 58) is stressed. He admits that a statement is meaningful even if verification never occurs. In brief, all that is necessary is that conditions can be indicated under which its truth or falsehood could be determined. He confuses (*a*) how we come to know the truth or falsehood of a statement with (*b*) its place in the complex meaning situation. The whole position is vitiated by the claim that all meaningful statements are either true or false. As a matter of fact works of fiction are meaningful, but the questions of truth or falsehood, and the checking on truth or falsehood, do not arise. In any case, unless a person first knows the meaning of a proposition that is what is involved in its meaning situation, he cannot check it.

Another variation of the meaning-verification theme is worthy of note. Flew contends[2] that one way (indeed he seems to imply it is the best way) to find out the meaning of a person's assertion or to determine if it has any meaning at all, is to ascertain what he would regard as counting against its truth, that is what would falsify it. In other words: 'to know the meaning of the negation of an assertion i.e. what enables one to negate ... is to ... know the meaning of that assertion.' This contention is based on the claim that 'to assert that such and such is the case is necessarily equivalent to denying that such and such is not the case.'

Flew then invites us to consider a religious person who claims that God loves men. This person, when confronted by what may appear to be negative evidence, refuses to accept it. He interprets everything that happens as supporting the assertion that 'God loves men'. Thus there is no support for the negative statement 'God does not love men'. Then, argues Flew, the negation of the assertion 'God loves men' has no meaning. It is not supported by any evidence as far as religious devotion is concerned. If this is the case, since the negation

[1] See *Logical Positivism*, ed. A. J. Ayer, Free Press, New York, 1959, pp. 86–7, 91–2.
[2] All references are to *New Essays in Philosophical Theology*, A. Flew, ed., S.C.M. Press, 1963, p. 98.

of the assertion has no meaning, therefore the positive assertion has no meaning. This follows from Flew's contention that to know the meaning of the assertion is to know the meaning of the negation.

On the basis of comprehensive experience, it is relevant to note a serious objection to Flew's ingenious arguments. As pointed out elsewhere, it is the case that truth and meaning are two distinct entities, not one and the same entity.[1] Turning to Flew's more distinctive point, namely his emphasis on the importance of meaningful negation of an assertion, it is interesting to discover the nature of meaning is interpreted in terms of presence of a referent, not strictly speaking as a process of verification. In other words, if no fact can be found to refute an assertion the negation is unsupported; it has no referent meaning. In any case there is a fundamental objection to Flew: it focuses on the unsound contention that assertion is necessarily equivalent to the denial of its negation. This is simply not the case. When an assertion is made and accepted, it follows as a consequent that its negation is denied. Just because nothing can be found or nothing is accepted as refuting an assertion, does not deny meaning to that assertion. For example, so far nothing has been found to refute the contention that the law of gravity applies to physical objects (everything is interpreted as supporting it). In this sense the negation of an assertion of the law of gravity has no support, that is no meaning (referent). This does not deny meaning either to the assertion of the law of gravity or to its negation for that matter. In brief, Flew's addiction to the reputed importance of 'nay-saying' is unjustified. In any case the statement 'God loves men' has meaning even quite apart from whether or not evidence supports it or does not support it or how available evidence is interpreted.

In fairness to Flew, it must be noted that he would contend that, even though no falsification of statement of the law of gravity has yet been achieved, it is possible to indicate what would constitute a falsification of it. However, it is only appropriate to point out also that it is possible to envisage a situation which falsifies the claim that God loves men, such as universal and eternal malicious torment for all men regardless of their behaviour.

In any case this concern with the possibility of falsification must be placed in proper perspective. When confronted by a black pen and the statement 'This pen is black', it seems silly to raise the question as to what would falsify the statement—if one operates in the context

[1] See Chapter 5, pp. 136-7.

of comprehensive experience. However, in situations such as the religious question one is relying to a degree on circumstantial evidence, and care must be taken to determine whether or not the available evidence supports or falsifies the statement about God loving men. Likewise, in dealing with complex scientific hypotheses it is important to bear in mind what would constitute support and what would constitute falsification. Thus, in brief, a concern with falsification is legitimate in some situations and irrelevant in others—if one operates in the context of comprehensive experience and the concern is with truth and falsehood rather than meaning.

In general the claim that many concepts are polar, that they are linked pairs and hence one cannot know the meaning of one without knowing the meaning of the other (for example true and false), is open to serious objection on the basis of comprehensive experience. To take an example, a person who at birth is malformed and all his life experiences nothing but excruciating pain, is well aware of the meaning of pain but has no awareness of pleasure.[1]

Incidentally, opinions as to what constitutes the verification of propositions vary. Ayer takes a restricted view, limiting the data of verification to actual or possible sensory observation (See *L.T.L.*, pp. 14–20).

As a matter of fact, one is aware, in comprehensive experience, of data other than those of sense-observation, which may be referred to in the course of verification.

Waismann's remarks on the complexity of the problem of meaning are worthy of note: 'A sentence in a novel is meaningful, if (i) it is correct English, i.e. not a broth of words, and (ii) it fits in with the other sentences. This *meaningfulness has nothing . . . to do with verifiability*. (That, by the way, is why Fiction is not false).' Waismann then notes that a rule, a definition, a request, a question are meaningful, though verifiability is not involved. He further suggests: 'There may even be a sense in which metaphysical statements have a meaning.' In brief, his position is this: 'The trouble with the Logical Positivists was that they attached too rigid an import to "meaningfulness" and lost sight of its ambiguity.'[2]

[1] See discussion of concave-convex by C. K. Grant, 'Over concepts and metaphysical arguments' in *Clarity is not Enough*, H. D. Lewis (ed.), Routledge and Kegan Paul, London, 1963, p. 265.

[2] F. Waismann, 'Language Strata', *Logic and Language*, A. Flew (ed.), Doubleday, New York, 1965, pp. 241–2 (emphases added).

13

MIND

I

Opposition to Experiential Realism's view of mind

Experiential Realism reports that a basic entity of the mental type, a mind, carries on many mental activities and possesses a number of mental contents. These activities and contents are its characteristics. Each such basic entity, each mind, is aware of itself and its characteristics.[1] This phase of Experiential Realism is exposed to various sorts of criticism which are involved in alternative views of men and their environment.

Examples: Hume, Wittgenstein and Ryle

Let us consider representative samples. David Hume contends that even the most careful and thorough investigation does not reveal the presence of a basic entity of the mental type. All that one can find are impressions and ideas. In other words, it is possible to discover perceptions but not a perceiver. Many people when confronted by perceptions assume that there is a perceiver who possesses them. According to Hume, this is an unjustified flight of speculative fancy.[2] A. J. Ayer deals in similar fashion with basic mental entities. He further accords the same treatment to a typical mental activity. Ayer

---

[1] That this is not an isolated report is obvious from the following: 'But besides all that endless variety of ideas or objects of knowledge, there is likewise something which knows or perceives them, and exercises diverse operations, as willing, imagining, remembering about them. This perceiving, active being is what I call mind, spirit, soul, or my self. By which word I do not denote any one of my ideas, but a thing entirely distinct from them, wherein they exist.' G. Berkeley, *The Principles of Human Knowledge*, T. E. Jessop (ed.), vol. 2 of *The Works of George Berkeley*, London, 1949, pp. 41–2. See also C. A. Campbell, *On Selfhood and Goodhood*, George Allen and Unwin, London, 1957, pp. 82–3 and A. Castell, *The Subject in Philosophy*, Macmillan, New York, 1965, pp. 56–9.

[2] See D. Hume, *Treatise of Human Nature*, Book I, Section VI.

accounts for what he considers to be erroneous views by referring to deception by grammar. Specifically, he suggests those who believe in 'acts of sensing' are fooled by the grammatical fact that sentences which they use to describe their sensations contain a transitive verb. Similarly, those who contend that the self is found in sensation are misled by the fact that sentences which are used to report their sensation have a grammatical subject.[1]

The 'great master' of many contemporary philosophers states that thinking is not an incorporeal process. He contends that the phrase 'incorporeal process' is used only by those who are proceeding in a 'primitive' fashion.[2]

Wittgenstein also makes use of what purports to be an empirical technique in denying the presence of the mental activity consciousness. He reports what happened when he tried to fix his attention on his 'own consciousness'. 'I stared fixedly in front of me—but *not* at any particular point or object. My eyes were wide open, the brows not contracted (as they mostly are when I am interested in a particular object). No . . . interest preceded this gazing. My glance was vacant' (p. 124).

The reply of Experiential Realism is that, as a matter of fact, there is an object, that is the activity of consciousness, in the case in question. The stare is vacant as far as physical objects are concerned, but that does not mean that one cannot be aware of mental entities. The reported absence of a wrinkled brow in the case of turning attention to one's own consciousness is in many cases inaccurate. Wittgenstein actually says brows are 'mostly' wrinkled when one is interested. When a person concentrates on observing a mental process his brows are usually wrinkled.

Wittgenstein denies the presence, not only of some typical mental activities, but also of some typical mental content. He claims that 'remembering has no experiential content. Surely this can be seen by introspection? Doesn't *it* shew precisely that there is nothing there, when I look about for a content?' (*P.I.*, p. 231).

Gilbert Ryle, in his influential book *The Concept of Mind*,[3] contends

---

[1] See A. J. Ayer, *Language, Truth and Logic*, Gollancz, 1936, p. 222. Hereafter this book will be referred to as *L.T.L.*

[2] L. Wittgenstein, *Philosophical Investigations*, Blackwell, Oxford, 1953, p. 109. Hereafter this book will be referred to as *P.I.*

[3] *The Concept of Mind*, Barnes and Noble, New York, 1949. Hereafter this book will be referred to as *C.M.* The pagination is the same in the Hutchinson's University Library edition, London, 1949.

that traditional philosophy, typified by Descartes, has set up a two-world theory concerning the human person. Mind for Descartes is a ghostly, shadowy, mysterious, hidden, occult, primitive and imaginary realm in complete contrast to the bodily (physical) machine. He takes issue on numerous occasions with those who claim that there really are basic mental entities which engage in non-physical activities and possesses non-physical contents. This theory, he claims, is a disreputable lapse into mythology (*C.M.*, pp. 54, 87, 155). He admits that devotees of the 'dogma of the ghost' claim that they are able to observe introspectively such entities. However, Ryle argues that this is actually not the case (*C.M.*, p. 83) for example with reference to feelings.

Likewise he states: 'Roughly [speaking] imagining occurs but images are not seen. . . . [A person who claims to remember his nursery] is not being a spectator of a resemblance of his nursery, but he is resembling a spectator of his nursery' (*C.M.*, pp. 247–8).

Critical comments

On the basis of comprehensive experience, Experiential Realism replies to the views just outlined, that the acceptance of mind (as a basic mental entity need not be a reflector of mere superstitition, unhealthy withdrawal from the world, merely an emotional, pre-scientific liking for ghosts. It is, of course, the case that some theories of mind are the results of superstition and wishful thinking and reflect an other-worldly fanaticism which issues in a down-grading of the body and the familiar world of everyday experience. However, the preceding discussion (in Section One) should have made it clear that mind is one type of entity found in comprehensive experience. Experiential Realism is not other-worldly, nor does it down-grade the body.

Let us consider next the charge that those who claim to find a place in the world for basic mental entities and their activities and content are the victims of deception by grammar or the careless use of concepts. The reply of Experiential Realism is that grammar, words and concepts, when properly used, bow ultimately before the authority of facts. Experiential Realism reports that there are mental facts found in the experience of human beings who rely on comprehensive experience. Hence the grammar, words, and concepts used by Experiential Realism are sound.

It is interesting to note that Ryle and Wittgenstein, who deny the existence of some mental processes and contents, but not always the same ones, nevertheless agree with Experiential Realism in accepting others.

Thus Ryle is prepared to admit on occasion, despite some passages where he seems to get rid of all of them, that there are private, non-imaginary contents which do not belong to a ghostly shadow world. 'The technical trick of conducting our thinking in auditory word-images, instead of in spoken words, does indeed secure secrecy for our thinking. . . . But this secrecy is not the secrecy ascribed to the postulated episodes of the ghostly shadow-world' (*C.M.*, p. 53). These entities, he emphasises, are not seen or heard in the same way (or sense) as we see and hear physical objects, but they are 'seen in the mind's eye' or 'heard in the head'.

In clarifying this point, Ryle reports a recollection of a boyhood experience of watching a blacksmith at work. 'I can vividly "see" the glowing red horseshoe on the anvil, fairly vividly "hear" the hammer ringing on the shoe and less vividly "smell" the singed hoof' (*C.M.*, p. 252).

One cannot but wonder how it is that when Ryle remembers his nursery he claims he is aware of no images whatever (it is just a matter of 'resembling a spectator'), but when he remembers a blacksmith's shop he is well provided with images. In accepting this type of experience Ryle is most anxious to delineate his opposition to sense-data theories commonly accepted by philosophers, because they set up an artificial epistemological gap.[1]

Also highly significant, in view of his 'denial statements', noted earlier, about thinking, that is an incorporeal mental process, is Wittgenstein's paradoxical remark: 'Why should I deny that there is a mental process [of remembering]? . . . To deny the mental process would mean to deny the remembering, to deny that anyone ever remembers anything'[2] (*P.I.*, p. 102). The acceptance by Wittgenstein of the process of 'introspection' a mental activity) has already been noted in the case of ruling out the presence of an imagination entity (content). He also uses this approach to the problem of certifying the presence of much data. Thus: ' "When you were swearing just now, did you really mean it?" This is perhaps as much as to say:

---

[1] See Chapter 16, pp. 349–55.

[2] It is to be noted that 'mental process' in this instance 'means nothing more than: "I have just remembered" '.

"Were you really angry?" And the answer may be given as a result of introspection' (*P.I.*, p. 170).

The preceding examination serves to indicate a rather impressive tendency to indulge in inconsistency on the part of Ryle and Wittgenstein at least as far as their general approach to mental activities and content is concerned. Even more obvious is the defect of a partial report as far as comprehensive experience is concerned.

Ryle considers it highly significant, and destructive of confidence in the existence of mental entities that, while observations of planets require instruments, and can be interfered with, there is nothing analogous concerning for example a twinge (*C.M.*, pp. 205–6). The obvious critical comment from the point of view of Experiential Realism is that different types of entities are observed in different fashions. While instruments are required in some cases, they are not in others. The absence of instruments in some instances does not rule out the possibility of observation (awareness) in these cases. Further, the observation of any entity can be interfered with.

Concerning introspection, Ryle correctly notes that some traditional theories of mind claim that 'minds possess powers of apprehending their own states and operations superior to those they possess of apprehending the facts of the external world' (*C.M.* p. 154). Further, introspection is free from error.

However, Ryle seems to think that, quite apart from traditional theories, introspection is as a matter of fact an unreliable source of information because it reflects the interests and theories which the observer holds (*C.M.*, p. 165).

Two remarks in reply are in order here. If this be the case, Wittgenstein's use of introspection to support his view of mind and its characteristics is open to question. In any case, Ryle's critical comment is not decisively destructive. What he says about introspection is correct in some instances, but, as has been pointed out in the earlier discussion of Experiential Realism, it is possible in introspection to avoid personal bais. Further, under proper conditions a person is able to be aware of both internal and external entities with equal efficiency.

There seems to be little point in Ryle's suggestion that what is claimed to be introspection is frequently only retrospection. He admits that in the 'same way' that he can catch himself scratching, he can catch himself daydreaming (*C.M.*, p. 166). A critic can legitimately ask how Ryle catches himself in a piece of day-dreaming unless by introspection.

It is contended by Wittgenstein that a serious problem arises when a mind attempts to observe (be aware of) itself performing its own activities, because this is a case of doing two things at once.[1] Relying on an analogy, he remarks: ' "When one thinks something, it is oneself thinking"; so one is oneself in motion. One is rushing ahead and so cannot also observe oneself rushing ahead. Indeed not' (*P.I.*, p. 132).

The reply of Experiential Realism is that if the analogy is to be taken seriously, it must be noted that one, as a matter of fact, can observe onself running. Further, thinking and running are different sorts of activities. In any case, as a matter of fact, a basic mental entity is aware of itself performing its activities. In short, a mind or person can do two things at once. In like fashion, the sting is taken out of Ryle's contention (p. 164) that even if there were the postulated ghostly mind and its states, there would still be the very serious problem of a person attending to two things at the same time. One, the state and the other, the process of observing the state. Ryle admits that this is not logically fatal and then he gives an illustration of a person doing two things at once!

In general it must be admitted that many philosophers consider there is a problem involved in being aware of one's own acts of awareness. Specifically, this seems to involve an infinite regress. It is argued that act of awareness A is required in order to be aware of act of awareness B, but an act of awareness C is required to be aware of act of awareness A and so on and on. This, however, is a pseudo-difficulty. A person is aware of his own acts of awareness. The plausibility of the 'infinite regress' argument arises from (*a*) neglecting the complex nature of awareness in this situation[2] and (*b*) applying to awareness an objection based on an unjustified process of abstraction and fragmentation which is irrelevant to this situation. A complex process of awareness is not analogous to an infinitely complex physical mosaic composed of absolutely separate and distinct pieces held together by an infinite number of drops of glue, each separate and distinct from any other, requiring another to hold them together. It is therefore wrong to try to interpret mental entities as though they were physical. Further,

[1] See previous discussion of trying to observe one's own act of awareness (consciousness), this chapter, p. 299.

[2] See Chapter 2, pp. 66-7.

just because nothing in the physical world has 'self-awareness' does not justify a denial of the fact that an agent (a basic mental entity) is aware of his own self engaged in the process of being aware (of an entity).

Ryle is opposed to the report by Experiential Realism that recognition (in many instances) involves the awareness of the linkage of an appropriate concept to an entity present in awareness. He argues that when a person recognises a tune 'He need not, for example, be . . . "subsuming" what he hears "under the concept of the tune" ' (*C.M.*, p. 227). It is argued that a person could not understand what is meant by applying an abstract concept to a tune. A person, in observing, is vigilant and things (notes) happen as he expected them to happen.

The reply of Experiential Realism is that there is, of course, the case that a person who recognises a tune may be vigilant in noting that things happen as he expected them to happen as the tune develops. But this is a by-product of the recognition which may or may not occur. A person may recognise something and then forget it—disregard it completely, almost at once. It has been noted,[1] however, that in cases of a feeling of familiarity when confronted by an entity, a concept need not be present, and that such experience is termed 'recognition'. But this is not the issue here discussed by Ryle.

An erroneous approach to recognition is found in a discussion by Wittgenstein. He admits that on coming into his office he recognises his desk, it does not seem strange to him. 'And yet it would be misleading to say that an *act of recognition* had taken place.' He suggests that error arises because people assume that recognising always involves 'comparing two impressions with one another. It is as if I carried a picture of an object with me and used it to perform an identification of an object as the one represented by the picture' (*P.I.*, p. 157, emphasis added). Wittgenstein obviously believes that no such process of comparison takes place.

Wittgenstein's difficulty here seems to be that he does not wish to use the phrase 'act of recognition'. He is, however, willing to talk in terms of 'not being surprised'. In any case a distinctive activity is taking place—the desk is treated as a familiar object. The really serious objection to Wittgenstein at this point is that he seems to be claiming that those who talk about an act of recognising are 'always' referring to a process of comparing two impressions, or as if a person carried

[1] Chapter 2, p. 66.

around a picture with him which is used for comparison with an actually experienced object. If the comparison holds up, recognition occurs. This is a parody of what frequently happens in recognition, in either sense of the term, though this comparing process may occur in a few cases. In most instances of familiar objects, that is in recognising one, a person does not carefully compare a picture (mental or physical) with the physical object desk before admitting that it is his. Nor does he claim to be doing so, as Wittgenstein contends, when an act of recognising occurs.

II

Further support for Experiential Realism's views on mental activities and content: Yolton, Humphrey, Scriven and Price

It is now appropriate to point out that the negative views concerning mental activities and content as expressed by Wittgenstein, Ryle, and Ayer are not only rejected by Experiential Realism, and at some point by some of these men themselves, but also by a number of other contemporary philosophers.[1] Quotations, rather than second-hand summaries, will be employed to make this point as clearly and vigorously as possible.

For example, John Yolton notes with approval that 'Price's account of recognition is that it is an instance of concept using. For example, "When I have an image of a dog, it is through the concept dog that I recognise it." [2] However, a concept for Yolton is not a basic entity. It is a disposition.

The legitimacy of Experiential Realism's contention that awareness extends beyond the range of sense data is supported by the investigations of the eminent psychologist George Humphrey. 'It seems probable that the psychology of the future will include among its descriptive concepts something very close to . . . non-sensory awareness' (*Thinking*, Methuen, 1951, p. 120).

The presence of consciousness (awareness) as a fact is stressed by Michael Scriven and Whitehead. 'Everyone knows what "conscious" means; everyone knows he is conscious when he is thinking or

---

[1] The same point with reference to some contemporary philosophers has been made concerning minds, (basic mental entities). See p. 298.

[2] J. Yolton, *Thinking and Perceiving*, Open Court, La Salle, 1962, p. 95. Hereafter referred to as Yolton. See also pp. 61–2.

remembering, watching or reading.'[1] 'Of course, consciousness, like everything else, is in a sense indefinable. It is just itself and must be experienced.'[2]

And as far as the nature and status of introspection is concerned, the following telling remarks by Price are worthy of note: He describes what happens in introspective awareness thus: 'When someone maintains, as I want to, that there is such a process as introspection, he is maintaining: (1) that there are private occurrences or experiences ... (2) that such private occurrences can sometimes be attended to or scrutinsed by the person who has them; (3) that such introspective scrutiny is a genuine source of information, a way of finding things out about one's own experiences; (4) that though the occurrences one finds out about are private ones, they are nonetheless publicly describable, since the information one gets by means of introspection can be imparted to others, who can *understand* one's introspective reports whether or not they believe them.'[3]

III

Entities termed mental are actually physical

So far attention has been focused on statements and refutations of the view that basic mental entities (minds) and some mental activities and some mental content cannot be found, if one exercises care in observation—hence those who believe in such entities are deceiving themselves. There is the supplementary point that the reputed methods of observation of such entities are inadequate.

A closely related series of criticisms constitutes, as it were, the positive side of this line of criticism of the position of Experiential Realism. It is argued by many philosophers that, when one observes accurately what is present when one is confronted by something termed 'mental', one does not find anything other than physical entities and their characteristics.[4]

---

[1] *Minds and Machines*, A. R. Anderson (ed.), Prentice-Hall, Englewood Cliffs, 1967, p. 34. Hereafter this volume will be referred to as Anderson.

[2] A. N. Whitehead, *Adventures of Ideas*, Cambridge, 1933, p. 347.

[3] H. H. Price, *Dimensions of Mind*, S. Hook (ed.), New York University Press, 1960, pp. 80–1.

[4] This is obviously implied, in at least a few instances in the preceding discussion.

Computer analogy

In recent times this general point of view has been supported by reference to the function of a complex type of machine, the computer.

It is stated by some devotees of computers that the reputed differences in type between machines and minds are not genuine. Machines produce activities which many men claim are the exclusive prerogative of minds. Likewise, some of the so-called distinctive characteristics of machines are found in minds. For example, it is now possible to construct a self-adjusting machine which profits from its variations in activity and hence parallels some aspects of the learning process in a human being (its mind). On the other hand, some human activities are repetitive like those of a simple machine. Consider, for example, the mechanical nature of mental habits. Typically, Turing remarks that one cannot make a distinction between minds and machines on the basis that machines do not make mistakes, because as a matter of fact they do (Anderson, p. 19). Likewise (p. 21), it is fallacious to argue that a machine cannot do anything new. It can. Machines can learn (p. 27). Also relevant is Ninian Smart's comment (Anderson, p. 107), that not only machines can produce identical parts. Nature can create identical twins. Therefore we cannot make a distinction between nature and artefacts on this basis, that is of producing or not producing identical items.

Typical also of this climate of opinion is J. J. C. Smart's point that it is possible to construct a self-producing machine. He says in general: 'I am inclined to accept the physicalist thesis that living creatures just are very complicated physio-chemical mechanisms' (Anderson, p. 105).

It is only fair to point out that such devotees of computers admit that, at the present time, it is not possible to be certain that computers in all cases can do what minds are reputed to do. But nevertheless they believe or can imagine computers duplicating some activities, and hence by implication assume, or specifically state, that this is support for the claim that what are regarded as distinctively and exclusively mental and hence non-physical activities, are actually physical. Thus Turing remarks in characteristic fashion (Anderson, p. 13) that he believes that in about fifty years 'it will be possible to program computers . . . to make them play the imitation game [that is, imitating human conversation] so well that an average interrogator will not have more than 70 per cent chance of making the right identification after five minutes of questioning.'

With disarming candour, J. J. C. Smart admits that at the moment we do not find artefacts, that is machines that have feelings. Nevertheless, it need not be always the case. Maybe in the future we shall find cases where machines do have feelings (Anderson, p. 105).

In similar vein, Scriven states his credo: 'I now believe that it is possible so to construct a supercomputer as to make it wholly unreasonable to deny that it had feelings' (Anderson, p. 42).

On the basis of comprehensive experience, the reply to this series of speculative statements is that just because a computer and a person can do, for example, a mathematical calculation, or answer questions, this does not prove that they are the same or function in the same fashion.

On the level of mind there are, of course, machine-like activities. But on this level, there are also depths of feeling, insight, courage, devotion, which, as far as one can now determine, are beyond the range of any machine. Experiential Realism is in accord with Scriven who points out that 'Consciousness is not a property which can be detected in a machine by any physical examination, because it cannot be identified with any physical characteristics of a machine' (Anderson, p. 39).

Expressions of faith, references to 'maybe', 'suppose' and what is 'conceivable' are interesting. But this is very thin ice on which to propose to skate with the degree of confidence which some devotees of computers obviously feel when they approach the question of mind.

Brain processes

A variation of the 'no difference between physical and mental' theme focuses on brain processes. Concerning the status of consciousness and brain processes Wittgenstein states: 'This idea of a difference in kind is accompanied by slight giddiness, which occurs when we are performing a piece of logical sleight-of-hand' (*P.I.*, p. 124). The preceding discussion of mind leads a person relying on comprehensive experience to the conclusion that the remark by Wittgenstein just quoted indicates that he himself may very well have been indulging in a logical sleight of hand in so far as he disregards differences. Seriously, the presence of slight giddiness is surely not to be taken as a necessary symptom of error in dealing with a philosophical problem.

In so far as logic reflects facts, the concepts of consciousness and brain processes cannot be fused. They do reflect differences in kind.

Yolton aptly remarks, in accordance with comprehensive experience: 'No matter how many correlations we may find in the physiological and neural structure with conscious awareness, no matter how close the isomorphism, the act of being aware is distinctively different from such correlates' (Yolton, p. 34). See also, S. Hook (ed.) *Dimensions of Mind*, p. 45).

More specifically, Scriven notes that intelligence cannot legitimately be attributed to a brain as such. 'The human brain is a physiological mechanism, no more intelligent than a muscle. Certainly the brain is an indispensable component of an intelligent being . . . the relative intelligence of various creatures may be deducible from their brain structure. But it is the creature that is intelligent, not the brain' (Anderson, p. 37).[1]

Behaviour of human bodies

Some of those who claim to find only physical entities, when they observe accurately activities and contents which are regarded as mental, concentrate their attention on the actually or possibly observable behaviour of human bodies. Indeed, they contend that mental activities are sorts of behavioural activities of human bodies. Wittgenstein illustrates this view with characteristic simplicity and vigour: 'What's it like for me to expect him to come'? I walk up and down the room, look at the clock now and then, and so on' (*P.I.*, pp. 130–1). In similar fashion desiring and wanting are treated behaviouristically.

Wittgenstein is quite prepared to admit that this external approach to what some people regard as internal mental activities is open to possible objection and may arouse feelings of dissatisfaction. However, in effect he interprets this as a case of an unjustified emotional, even pathological reaction. The following remarks are typical. Consider the case of being guided while copying doodles. Wittgenstein reports:

'I notice nothing special; [i.e., a distinctive in kind mental process] . . . [yet] *afterwards* no description satisfies me. It's as if I couldn't believe that I merely looked, made such-and-such a face, and drew a line. . . . And yet I feel as if there must have been something else; in particular when I say *"guidance"*, *"influence"*, and other such words to myself.

[1] Ayer aptly remarks that a devotee of physicalism 'has convinced himself on *a priori* grounds that no other way of interpreting [mental states and processes] is possible.' (A. J. Ayer, 'Philosophy and Language', in *Clarity is not Enough*, H. D. Lewis (ed.), Geroge Allen and Unwin, London, 1963, p. 422.)

. . . Only then does the idea of that ethereal, intangible influence [erroneously] arise' (*P.I.*, p. 71).

It is interesting to note that on occasion, even in the midst of this objectivistic approach to activities regarded as mental, there is an admission that there are entities which are not publicly observable behavioural activities. Thus, in discussing 'reading with feeling' (*P.I.*, p. 214), he refers to inflection, emphasis, facial expression. But also there is mention of pictures (images) which come to mind.

Further, Wittgenstein suggests that the whole controversy as to whether overt behaviour is the expression of internal states, as claimed by anti-behaviourists, is rather pointless. Thus he remarks: 'A doctor asks: "How is he feeling?" The nurse says: "He is groaning." A report on his behaviour. But need there be any question [as to whether] . . . the groaning . . . is really the expression of anything? Might they not, for example, draw the conclusion . . . "we must give him more analgesic" ' (*P.I.*, p. 179).[1]

Turning to a critical examination of Wittgenstein's examples, a series of objections occurs to a person who relies on comprehensive experience. The identification of expectation of arrival with bodily behaviour is not justified. A person only carries out these activities as the result of a general state of (inner) emotional tension. Likewise there is more to being guided than merely looking; drawing, wrinkling the forehead. These overt activities result because one intends to be guided by the doodle and by concentration on it duplicates by drawing the pattern of the doodle. The intending and concentrating are mental activities which are found, not imagined because one is misled by words. Wittgenstein is indeed correct in reporting a feeling of dissatisfaction when attempting an over-simplified peripheral, purely external description.

Wittgenstein's contention that one does not need to bother with internal states—rather, in the case of the groaning man, it is appropriate to focus on purely external matters—is simply an addiction to a partial approach. It is the case that in most instances groaning is the expression of some internal condition. The specific internal state must be identified before it is appropriate to prescribe a suitable specific treatment.

Gilbert Ryle presents a more complicated version of the 'one world'

[1] See also *P.I.*, pp. 60, 61, 75, where Wittgenstein claims that while mental processes exist, as in understanding, they are not essential. What is fundamental is overt activity.

(physical)[1] treatment of mind than that usually found in Wittgenstein. The emphasis on the overt and public is supplemented by a stress on what is not publicly observable in the sense of being capable of being seen or recorded by a camera.

Ryle invites us to consider the trippings and turnings of a clown. He claims these are the working of his mind because he did it on purpose. Ryle contends that 'tripping on purpose is both a bodily and a mental process, but it is not two processes, such as one process of purposing to trip and, as an effect, another process of tripping' (*C.M.*, p. 33).

By way of clarification Ryle contends that the bodily activity of the clown is mental because it is characterised by skill. 'To recognise that a performance is an exercise of a skill is indeed to appreciate it in the light of a factor which could not be separately recorded by a camera.' However, he contends that a skill cannot be so recorded, not because it is an 'occult or ghostly happening', but because it is not an occurrence at all. Rather it is a disposition. By way of further clarification he says: 'A disposition is a factor of the wrong logical type to be seen or unseen, recorded or unrecorded' (*C.M.*, p. 33).

In like fashion, and again apparently attributing an unjustified decisive status to logic, Ryle remarks concerning a human being: 'His life is not a double series of events taking place in two different kinds of stuff.' He proposes to account for the apparent differences between types of entities largely in terms of the applicability or inapplicability to them of logically different types of law-propositions and law-like propositions' (*C.M.*, p. 167).

As has been noted previously, Ryle is quite prepared to accept an area of privacy other than camera-escaping dispositions—indeed of mental entities, in the sense of Experiential Realism. He reports seeing in the mind's eye the blacksmith of youthful experience.

The mixture of emphasis on the public and the private is well illustrated in the following statement:

Overt intelligent performances are not clues to the workings of minds; they are those workings. Boswell described Johnson's mind when he described how he wrote, talked, ate, fidgeted and fumed. His description was, of course, *incomplete*, since there were notoriously

---

[1] It is to be noted that Ryle sometimes claims he is not offering a materialistic position; rather he is examining the use of words. However, his performance is obvious even if on occasion he will not admit it.

some thoughts which Johnson kept carefully to himself and there must have been many dreams, daydreams and silent babblings which only Johnson could have recorded' (*C.M.*, pp. 58–9, emphasis added).

The general reaction of Experiential Realism to the materialist-behaviouristic approach to mind, with its denial of the distinctively non-material, and its concentration on overt behaviour, coupled with a paradoxical admission of privacy, is that it is not necessary to interpret the mind and its characteristics in terms of the public phenomena of the physical world in order to escape the errors and excesses of some traditional views. In any case, the worship of matter is as blind as the worship of ghosts, and can be and sometimes is equally dogmatic and obnoxious. The preceding remarks apply not only to various forms of behaviouristic psychology, but also to the so-called scientific explanations of the Marxists which make the content of man's mind a mere reflection of social processes which ultimately depend on the struggle for material commodities.

The external approach, that is the emphasis on publicly observable behaviour depends for whatever plausibility it has on taking other people as illustrations. It is, of course, the case that we cannot penetrate behind the behaviour of other people and directly experience their own distinctively different mental operations.

The treatment of the internal in terms of behavioural dispositions is inadequate. It simply neglects the complexity of the non-public experience of human beings. As just noted, Ryle himself does not stop at this point. In any case, when a clown tumbles with skill his so-called purpose cannot be explained in terms of a bodily disposition. He frequently thinks, using concepts, about what he is going to do next. He formulates a purpose mentally and carries it out physically. It is not clear how Ryle can pretend to do justice in physical terms to Johnson's thoughts, dreams, and 'private babblings' which he kept to himself. Perhaps Ryle does not propose to do so! In any case, logic and the applicability of 'law-like propositions' are not the ultimate bases for distinguishing entities. Rather, because they are distinct this fact is reflected in logic and relevant propositions.

The presence of some mental processes and contents, which are not to be regarded as physical objects, is admitted by Ryle and Wittgenstein. To this extent they are in agreement with Experiential Realism.

The psychoanalytic approach to mind: Freud and Sartre

Some final comments are in order. They have to do with the view of mind based on a psychoanalytic approach. A person is aware of (*a*) dreams and of the presence of (*b*) physical entities, which seem to have no physical causes, for example hysterical symptoms, and (*c*) of mental aberrations. It is then imaginatively assumed that there are entities in the subconscious or unconscious of the sorts indicated which are never open to awareness, but must be postulated to account for what is present in awareness. In the case of Freud, the disreputable content of some dreams is said to indicate that the hidden forces are even more disreputable, being essentially sexual. Other psychoanalysts refer to less disreputable hidden forces, such as the mastery motive.

This general attempt to explain the known in terms of the imaginary unknown is interesting though somewhat fantastic speculation. However, these theories have some valuable therapeutic applications. They are indeed, in some cases, useful instruments. But they should be recognised as such and not regarded as accurate descriptions or reports of mental entities. Nor should these imaginatively assumed entities be assigned decisive causal importance in all human behaviour, because this conclusion is not based on comprehensive experience.

Sartre, one of the leading contemporary Existentialists, develops a significant view of the human mind. It is the emergent result of an act of reflection. A useful summary of this theory, which is stated in more simple terms than those provided by the author, is found in Desan's study of Sartre.[1] It is pointed out that Sartre in 'La Transcendance de l'Ego' contends:

'We do not ... need the "Ego" as the unifying link of our representations. Phenomenology is able to show that consciousness is defined by intentionality: i.e., consciousness is consciousness of something; consciousness that $2 + 2 = 4$, consciousness of being hungry. These objects, and not the Ego, are the specifying elements of my consciousness. ... The Ego, according to Sartre, is the result and creation of the reflexive act. There is usually no Ego when I read a book or drive a car. Then suddenly I become aware of what I do; I reflect. The result

[1] W. Desan, *The Tragic Finale*, Harper and Row (Torchbook), New York, 1960, pp. 27–8.

is that I am aware of my-driving-a-car or reading-a-book. Consequently, we should not in the prereflexive act say "I am conscious of a chair", but rather: "There-is-consciousness-of-a-chair." As soon as reflection arises, we apprehend and constitute the Ego.'

Experiential Realism replies that a person is aware of his own basic mental entity engaged in consciousness, even though admittedly the presence of the mind, as agent, is not always or usually in clear or central forms of attention. It is contrary to comprehensive experience to claim that the mind as agent (ego) is constituted from time to time as the result of an act of reflection. Further, objects of consciousness (content) are not the basis for specifying the consciousness as mine. This is particularly the case with two plus two equals four, which is shared by many minds.

14

PHYSICAL OBJECTS

I

James's theory of neutral entities

A discussion of the traditional theory of neutral entities, at this point, will serve as a transition from the preceding chapter to this one. This theory contends that there are entities which are, as such, neither physical nor mental but, in varying arrangements, take on the status of physical or mental entities.

William James provides a clear, vigorous and very influential exposition of this point of view, though he ordinarily uses the term 'pure experience' rather than 'neutral' entity. He makes the 'supposition that there is only one primal stuff or material [pure experience] in the world, a stuff of which everything is composed.'[1]

James, as is frequently the case in formulating his theories, finds it necessary to qualify his initial reference to 'one primal stuff'. Thus he remarks that 'there is no *general* stuff. . . . There are as many stuffs as there are "natures" in the things experienced' (*R.E.*, p. 26). These natures are sensible entities such as space, flatness, brownness, heaviness. Thus this position involves the assumption that there is only one type of stuff, but there are many sorts of this stuff, that is many different natures. 'Experience' is a collective name applied to all these sensible natures.

Proceeding to develop his theory, James contends that 'a given undivided portion of experience, taken in one context of associates, plays the part of a knower, a state of mind, . . . while in a different context the same undivided bit of experience play[s] the part of a thing known' (*R.E.*, p. 9).

James provides significant illustrations. A specific bit of pure experience such as a room, in the context of a series of 'sensations,

[1] William James, *Essays in Radical Empiricism*, Longmans, Green, New York, 1922, p. 4. See p. 26 for use of the term 'neutral'. Hereafter this book will be referred to as *R.E.*

emotions, decisions . . . expectations', is part of the 'inner' life of a person, his 'field of consciousness' a 'subjective state'. The same bit of pure experience, the room, in the context of 'physical operations, carpentering, papering', etc. is part of the physical world (*R.E.*, pp. 13–14).

James is quite prepared to admit that his theory seems open to obvious and serious objections. For example: thoughts and things are so patently different. How can one claim that 'the self-same piece of pure experience' is thought or thing, depending only on context? (*R.E.*, p. 27) Specifically, a thing such as a poker which has been in a fire is red, hot and heavy, but can one sensibly contend that a thought about it has these characteristics? The implied answer of the critic, of course, is: No.

James attempts to meet this objection by pointing out what is admittedly the case, that some characteristics are shared by thoughts and things, for example: beautiful, focal, interesting, confused, causal and even (contrary to Descartes) extension (*R.E.*, pp. 29–30). In like fashion, he is prepared to argue that the wetness of physical water and the heat of physical fire are not confined to this realm. 'When the [corresponding] mental state is a vivid image, hotness and wetness are in it just as much as they are in the physical experience' (*R.E.*, pp. 31–2).

The reaction of Experiential Realism to this general point of view is that, despite the fact of admittedly similar characteristics—for example redness, flatness, heat may be characteristics of both physical objects and of imagination images—nevertheless mental states are different from physical things, quite apart from context. A house made by a carpenter is not the same as a sensory image of a house; a fire burning on the hearth is different from a vivid imagination image. One of the important areas of difference is that by personal initiative one can immediately revive the image of the room or the fire, but this is not the case with reference to the physical room or the physical fire once they have been destroyed.

As a matter of fact James falls into an obvious inconsistency when he admits a distinction between mental and physical which is not merely a case of difference in context. He makes the distinction in terms of 'energetic' or 'non-energetic'. For example, a physical fire always burns a physical stick, a mental fire never burns a physical stick and only sometimes burns a mental stick (*R.E.*, pp. 32–3. See also *R.E.*, p. 14).

As a further general criticism, apart from the charge of inconsistency, it is to be noted that these so-called neutral entities are creations of imagination. The theory is based on a misinterpretation of types of entities, such as a mental image (of fire) and fire. Both types of entities are stated to be not what they are experienced to be in comprehensive experience, that is mental or physical as such. Rather, they are said to be of one type of entity, namely, neutral 'building blocks' in different arrangements. Thus, an imaginary realm, reputed to be more ultimate than physical and mental entities, is set up.

Turning from an examination of entities such as room and fire to space, flatness, brownness, heaviness, it is the case that these latter entities are neutral[1] in the sense that they may be characteristics of either physical or mental entities, of pokers or imagination images of pokers. However, it is not the case that either pokers as physical objects or imagination images of them are composed, without remainder, of such entities as space, brownness, flatness, heaviness. There is, in the case of a poker, a basic physical entity, namely metal. In the case of the imagination image, a mental entity has the characteristics listed.

In brief, there is no foundation in comprehensive experience for the fundamental features of James's theory. One is aware of (finds) physical objects, minds, concepts, also physically based resultants and characteristics neutral or otherwise. There is no non-imaginary experience of this reputed process of 'constructing out of mental entities'. In any case, there is no awareness of minds, physical objects or concepts as being composed of non-imaginary neutral entities of the type under discussion.

II

Berkeley

A theory of physical objects which takes issue with Experiential Realism is that proposed by George Berkeley. A few remarks are in order to supplement the preceding general discussion of his world view.[2] Berkeley contends that 'all the choir of heaven and furniture of the earth, in a word, all those bodies which compose the mighty

[1] See use of the term 'neutral' in the context of Experiential Realism: Chapter 3, p. 79; Chapter 4, p. 92, fn. 3.
[2] See Chapter 10, p. 250.

frame of the world, have not any subsistence without a mind, that their being is to be perceived or known.'[1] This theory of physical objects is set in the context of Berkeley's claim that the world is revealed to careful observation, is composed of minds, ideas, relations, and notions. Implicit in this position is the assumption that in perceiving, the only possible content is mental. An appeal to comprehensive experience indicates that many of the data of perception, if the term is used normally, are mental content (in the case of introspection, which is inner perception) for example, imagination images. Nevertheless, much of our perceiving has as its objects not mental content, but rather basic physical entities and their characteristics. These basic physical entities and their characteristics are experienced to be not mind-dependent. We can manipulate our imagination images by sheer mental effort. We cannot do this with physical objects. There is no awareness of mental generation in the case of physical objects. But, more fundamentally, the stuff and context of mental content are found in comprehensive experience to be decisively different from that of physical objects. As a matter of fact, a person relying on comprehensive experience has no difficulty in distinguishing as mental a memory image of a pen from the pen as a physical object.[2] As will be noted later, the appeal by Berkeley to 'some eternal spirit' to provide a common world involves him in serious difficulties.

III

A collection of appearances or sense data: Russell, Price and Nunn

The fact that perceiving a physical object under varying conditions involves different experienced entities has led some philosophers to formulate a theory of physical objects which differs markedly from that of Experiential Realism. It is denied that there are basic physical entities, each characterised by one shape, one size, and usually one

---

[1] G. Berkeley, *Principles of Human Knowledge*, T. E. Jessop (ed.), vol. 2 of *The Works of George Berkeley*, Nelson, 1949, p. 43. Hereafter this book will be referred to as Berkeley.

[2] In like fashion Austin comments: 'I may have the experience of dreaming that I am being presented to the Pope. Could it be seriously suggested that having this dream is "qualitatively indistinguishable" from actually being presented to the Pope? Quite obviously not.' J. L. Austin, *Sense and Sensibilia*, Oxford, 1962, p. 48.

colour (unless, for example, it is a nation's flag) and so on. The experience of differing colours, shapes, sizes under varying conditions of observation, leads to the conclusion that a physical object should be regarded as a collection ('family') of 'aspects' ('appearances', 'sense data'), of differing coloured shapes, each patch of shaped colour having a specific size. This is a simplified presentation of the theory, since it does not refer to other sorts of sense data. Some of these 'appearances' are present to sense awareness at a given time. Other aspects are capable of being present to sense awareness.

As an example of this theory, consider Russell's statement that 'when I see a penny what I perceive is one member of the system of particulars which is the monetary penny. . . . There are closely similar unperceived particulars (sensibilia) which are other members of the monetary penny.'[1] Russell suggests that the aspects in the collection which composes the penny, are related in accordance with the laws of perspective, though each entity (appearance, or sensibilia) occurs in a private space. It might seem plausible, in view of the claim that a penny has spatial location, to assume that the group of appearances which constitutes for Russell the penny, would have a focal point. However, he takes a negative position. Thus the centre of a group of appearances contains no member of the group, not even an ideal member (*Analysis of Mind*, p. 98).

Some philosophers accept the 'family of appearances' view of Russell, but add other ingredients in attempting to deal with the nature of physical objects. Price, for example, contends that among the family of sense data there is a group which constitutes a 'nucleus'. This is termed a 'three dimensional solid'. This fundamental addition to Russell's theory of a family of sense data (appearances) is based on the attempt to take seriously the causal efficacy which is open to observation when physical objects (Price uses the phrase 'material thing') are observed with care. Thus Price claims that a material thing in addition to being a family of sense data has a 'physical occupant' ingredient which exercises the causal efficacy.[2] It is further contended that this physical occupant has intrinsic qualities which make possible its causal efficacy. However, these qualities and what underlies them are not open to observation, though the exercise of causality is

[1] B. Russell, 'Physics and Perception', *Mind*, N.S. vol. XXXI, 1922, p. 483. See also *The Analysis of Mind*, G. Allen and Unwin, London, 1961, pp. 98, 134.

[2] H. H. Price, *Perception*, Methuen, London, 1964, p. 291. (Hereafter this book will be referred to as H.H.P.)

(*H.H.P.*, p. 294). Incidentally, the physical occupant ingredient not only exercises causal efficacy, it also constitutes resistance to impact by other entities.

This general Kantian practice implicitly involved in Price's claim that the intrinsic qualities of physical objects are not known, is supplemented by an even more Kantian admission. There seems to be an assumption that material thing-hood is an a priori element in experience which is provided by the mind (*H.H.P.*, pp. 102, 169).

Experiential Realism rejects Russell's theory because, when experienced under varying conditions, a penny, for example, is not experienced to be composed of a series or cluster of different-shaped sensa (namely patches of colour). In this instance one is aware of a basic physical entity, a piece of metal. Under suitable conditions a person is aware of the shape (circular) and colour (brown) characteristics of the basic physical entity.[1] In other cases, one is aware of

[1] Recent relativity theory may seem to cast doubt on the confident claim that a person can know the characteristics of physical objects and that for example, a basic physical entity has only one length. The variation argument shifts from referring to variations which are experienced, to the claim that as a matter of fact, under conditions of very rapid velocity, a basic physical entity undergoes change in length. How then can one specify what the length characteristic is? In short, in a cosmic context, what is the proper condition for accurate observation? Consider the speed of the yardstick lying on the surface of the earth and also the speed of the same yardstick whizizng through space at a vastly increased velocity. Which is the proper locale in which to investigate the length—the earth or some point in space?

In general, as noted, Experiential Realism leaves to scientists the responsibility of answering technical questions about the characteristics of basic physical entities. However, there is a comment to be raised. Is it not the case that relativity and its implications of change in length of a basic physical entity is a theory, an imaginative construction, developed in an attempt to explain or interpret data present to awareness? Is it not the case that, so far, no one has been aware of change in length depending on a vast increase in velocity? In any case it is well to remember Whitehead's comment that the mathematics and physics which he learned at Cambridge in the early 1880s had to be abandoned by the turn of the century (See Lucian Price, *Dialogues of Alfred North Whitehead*, Little, Brown & Co., Boston, 1954, in which he reports a conversation on September 11, 1945).

However, in cases where the length and weight are different, due to changes under varying conditions of heat and location, we are not, at least in all cases, in the realm of theory. It is possible in some instances to determine what the characteristics of an entity are under specific conditions. It is also possible to determine what are suitable conditions for accurate observation in a specified situation. (See discussion of this general problem in Chapter 3, pp. 77–9, 88–9).

physically based resultants, varying elliptically-shaped patches of colour. Further, the entities experienced by a person when confronted by a penny are not found to be in a series of private spaces. The basic physical entity, its characteristics and relevant physically based resultants are together in one spatial situation.

Price's attempt to correct this deficiency in Russell's theory involves him in serious difficulties. He correctly notes the 'resistance' characteristic of material things (physical objects). Causal efficacy is known to be a characteristic of some such entities but, contrary to Price's apparent position, not of all such entities. The Kantian denial of knowledge of basic entities is excessive. We are aware of metal (a basic physical entity) in the case of the penny. We are aware of, immediately know, not only causal power on occasion, but also many other characteristics. We know that the physical occupant is characterised by length, shape, size, colour and so on.

T. P. Nunn's discussion of physical objects exercised a profound influence in both Great Britain and the United States on a group of philosophers called 'New Realists'. His views will serve as an example of this position (the phases which are relevant here). Nunn contends[1] that physical objects are composed of the data of sense; further, all sense data are objective, not mind-dependent. So far, this is similar to Russell's view discussed above. However, this theory contends that the different shapes, colours, sizes, which are experienced when confronted by a physical object are equally a part of it, while Russell notes 'wild data'. Further, everything of which we are aware is part of the physical universe. The refusal of Experiential Realism to accept a doctrine which assigns an unlimited range of contradictory characteristics to physical objects is obvious. Seen shapes, sizes, colours, etc., are sorted out in terms of one set of characteristics. The rest have the status of physically based resultants, or mental content.

The New Realists' claim that all entities present in awareness are part of the physical world presents serious difficulties when one considers cases of illusion, imagination, memory, dreams. S. Alexander attempts to deal with the problem in terms of squinting or misplacing.[2]

It is indeed the case that physical squinting produces a distorted result, a seen shape is not the actual shape of an object, but on the basis

[1] See for example, his contribution to the Aristotelian Society symposium, 1909–10, on: 'Are Secondary Qualities Independent of Perception?'
[2] See S. Alexander, *Space, Time and Deity*, Macmillan, 1927, vol. II, Chapters 7 and 8.

of comprehensive experience one must deny that the entity actually is physical—it is a physically based resultant. It is the case that when I imagine a tree growing out of the roof of my house, a process of misplacing has occurred. However, in some cases the entities which are misplaced in imagination are mental not physical. Of course, it is possible to be confronted by an actual physical roof and imagine, using a mental image, a tree growing out of it.

IV

Austin

There is another ingenious theory of physical objects which is generated by the apparent problem arising from the varying experiences of the same physical object. J. L. Austin begins by raising an interesting issue: Why shouldn't we be prepared to admit that material things are extremely variable, undergoing continuous change, for example in their real shapes, colours, temperatures, sizes, and all their other characteristics? Indeed, Austin is quite prepared to 'go much further' and accept the notion that when I offer you a cigarette 'there are really *two* material things (two *cigarettes?*), one that I see and offer *and* one that you see and accept.'[1]

As far as comprehensive experience is concerned, the answer is simply that a person cannot legitimately say (accept) these things because physical objects, under conditions of ordinary social environment, are not constantly busy changing their real shapes and other characteristics from moment to moment to the degree assumed by Austin. Further, when Mr A. gives Mr B. one cigarette, it is absurd to say that two material objects, two cigarettes, are involved in the transaction. The experience of the two men may be different. One may see a real round tip, the other an elliptical shape, that is a physically based resultant. But to repeat, the two experiences are concerned with one basic physical entity.

V

Physically based resultants and Ryle

The entities which in the content of Experiential Realism are termed 'physically based resultants' are dealt with in Ryle's discussion of our

[1] J. L. Austin, *Sense and Sensibilia*, Oxford, 1962, p. 58.

experience of round objects as elliptical. Incidentally, Ryle prefers to talk about plates rather than pennies. He characteristicaly uses 'what we say' as a primary source of information in the course of his treatment of this topic.

The important question is whether there is an elliptical shape present in experience. Ryle's answer is that 'a person without [previous commitment to] a theory feels no qualms in saying that the round plate might look elliptical . . . [or] looks as if it were elliptical. But he would feel qualms in following the recommendation to say that he is seeing an elliptical look of a round plate [i.e., an elliptical sense datum].[1] In other words there is not an extra something, a 'look', or to speak technically a sense datum, which has an elliptical characteristic (a patch of colour). Thus Ryle is simply denying the presence of one type of entity found in comprehensive experience, namely, physically based resultant. It is to be noted that the 'looks' or 'looks as if' locution is a superficial approach to the problem. The crucial point has to do with what a person is aware of in this situation. In this case admittedly he is not aware of the characteristics of a physical object.

VI

Secondary qualities: Descartes, Locke, Ayer and Whitehead

It will have been realised that Experiential Realism rejects a very venerable tradition to the effect that the so-called 'secondary qualities', for example, colour, odour, taste, heat and cold, do not actually belong to (are characteristics of) physical objects.

Descartes provides an influential argument in support of this traditional view. He proposes to rely on ideas which are clear and distinct in human understanding (reason). This involves a rejection of reports derived from sensory experience. He offers a twofold justification. As the result of his education he became convinced that the method of mathematics was the only reliable source of information open to human initiative. He gave at least lip-service to divine revelation, accepted on faith. But to repeat, human knowledge can be obtained only by the careful use of reason, that is by accepting only ideas which are so clear and distinct they cannot be doubted and

---

[1] G. Ryle, *The Concept of Mind*, Barnes and Noble, New York, 1949, p. 216 Hereafter this book will be referred to as *C.M.*

proceeding as one does in geometrical reasoning.[1] The only possible alternative is reliance on sense experience, but obviously it, and imaginative manipulation of the data of sense, is unreliable. In his famous 'piece of wax' illustration, he notes that everything reported by sense experience concerning a piece of wax is denied by what is found after the wax is melted. Yet it is the same piece of wax. Obviously its real characteristics are not changed, but what sense experience reports is riddled with change. Ergo sense experience is unreliable.[2]

What then does reason (awareness of concepts) discover about physical objects, what ideas are clear and distinct? Our ideas, for example, of heat and cold are hopelessly confused. We cannot decide whether heat is the absence of cold or vice versa. Ideas of colour, sound, odour, taste are equally confused. But we do have clear ideas of shape, size, length, width, depth, position, movement, duration, number (the so-called 'primary' qualities). These then are the real qualities of material substance. (Incidentally, Descartes claims he has a clear idea of substance (*Meditations*, pp. 38–9).

Locke, in opposition to Descartes, contends that knowledge is based on sensation. He states[3] that primary qualities, that is real ones, are those which are 'utterly inseparatable from the body, in what estate soever it be . . . in all the alterations and changes.'[4] He points out that if we take a grain of wheat and proceed to divide it and then divide the parts and continue the process, as long as we can still see it . . . we find material particles which have as qualities: solidity, extension (length, width, depth), shape, motion or rest and a numerical characteristic.

However, according to Locke the situation is entirely different with reference to colours, odours, tastes, heat and cold, pleasure and pain. It is readily admitted, for example, that pain is not really a quality of a physical object. Rather, it is a mental reaction to a physical stimulus. Why then regard heat as a quality (characteristic) of a physical object, in view of the fact that one and the same fire at one distance arouses an experience of (idea of) heat and when one approaches nearer an experience of pain? Concerning colour, consider

---

[1] R. Descartes, *Discourse on Method*, Part II.

[2] R. Descartes, *Meditations*, Liberal Arts Press, New York, 1951, p. 27.

[3] *Essay Concerning Human Understanding*, Book II, Chapter VIII.

[4] In *The English Philosophers from Bacon to Mill*, E. A. Burtt (ed.), The Modern Library, New York, 1939, p. 265. Hereafter references will be to this book.

the fact that an object, when light is present, is experienced as coloured, but the colour disappears when light is removed. On the basis of his claim that real qualities remain regardless of change in a situation, colour is denied the status of a real (primary) quality, likewise, heat, as well as of course pain (p. 267).

Locke proceeds to offer other 'evidence' which, unfortunately for him, is not as plausible as some of his other submissions, even in the the context of his own basic principle, namely that real qualities remain despite change in the object or the situation. In the argument now under consideration he points out that if a person takes an almond and starts pounding it, the colour changes from white to 'dirty' grey, the sweet taste is replaced by an oily one. Hence, there are not real qualities. Likewise, it is noted that the same dish of water feels cold to one hand and hot to another. He remarks that there is no corresponding change in shape, from square to globe (pp. 268-9). However, the crucial point he overlooks is that, as a matter of fact, there is a change in shape in the case of pounding the almond. Consider also the more striking case of Descartes's piece of wax. Before heat is applied, it is a solid cube; after melting it is a circular puddle of fluid. Turning back to Locke's earlier argument which states that there are always shape qualities when one divides a grain of wheat, it is also the case that there are always colour characteristics, though individual shapes and colours are replaced by other individual shapes and colours. Thus his argument works against so-called primary qualities as well as against secondary ones.

It is important to realise further that Locke goes beyond sense awareness of small physical particles and postulates the presence of invisible particles reputed to possess the so-called primary qualities only. He bases his argument on an appeal to what must happen in the seeing of objects. Invisible particles must travel from the object to the observer's eye. Further, even though we do not see the material components of air and water, they must have them.

Be that as it may, Locke contends further that among the real qualities of physical objects are powers to produce changes in (a) the primary qualities of objects and (b) to produce ideas in minds. Concerning the former, obviously fire produces changes in a piece of wax, namely, shape and size. Further, the experienced colour, odour, taste, heat, pain which many people assign to physical objects are, in Locke's view, only ideas in human minds. These ideas are generated as results of the impact of minute physical particles on the eye which then affect the nervous system of the person. These ideas exist only as long as a mind is aware of them. The particles in question here, Locke claims, possess only primary qualities.

In refutation of Locke's position, several further remarks are in order in the context of comprehensive experience.

It was pointed out earlier that, in the case of a specific physical object, if conditions are suitable, and light is one of them, one is aware of the actual colour characteristics of that physical object. Likewise a person can find that a specific, particular, object, such as a cup of tea, has specific taste and odour characteristics. These are, in the experience of an expert tea taster (if conditions are suitable for awareness), entities which are just as 'mind-independent' as the depth of the fluid in the cup. A volume of fluid has specific temperature characteristics on which experts agree, as they agree concerning its shape and size. Other taste, odour, and temperature entities as experienced by the non-expert, or under abnormal conditions of observation, merely indicate the varieties of human experience and the differences (physically based resultants) which result when conditions for awareness are not satisfactory for the awareness of characteristics of basic physical entities. Further and crucially, pleasures and pains are experienced as mental while the other characteristics are not. They are found to be either characteristics of physical entities or physically based resultants. It is to be noted that sounds are not characteristics, rather they are physically based resultants. If physical facts are changed, as in crushing an almond, it is not surprising that the actual colour changes.

Specifically, in dealing with a cup of tea, or a vibrating bell, the experienced odours, tastes, sounds and thermal entities are not subject to organisation or removal by an act of mental effort as such. This is only possible when one is dealing with pleasures, pains and the content of imagination and, to a lesser extent, memory.

It seems plausible to suggest that this technical, 'professional' philosophical distinction between so-called 'primary' and 'secondary' qualities merely reflects an addiction to geometry (mathematics) in the interest of scientific efficiency or philosophic presupposition. Specifically, geometry is not interested in colours, odours, tastes, etc. In the case of Descartes there is further a devotion to abstract reasoning, regardless of sense experience. This general geometrical orientation, as such, does not guarantee the accuracy of the theory of primary and secondary quantities, despite its admitted instrumental value. It involves, in some cases, such as Locke, a theory of insensible particles or other minute entities which are imaginary (that is not seen or touched and recognised as physical).

Thus, in brief, all the characteristics both so-called 'primary' and 'secondary' under consideration are equally entities found to be characteristics of physical objects, with the exception of sound, pain and pleasure.[1]

A difference (apart from being distinct entities, for example colour and shape) can be noted between qualities (characteristics) of physical objects on the basis of the way one becomes directly aware of them, and their relation to the objects they characterise. For example: (a) length, width, thickness, depth, shape, size, resistance to pressure, and some relations are seen and touched; (b) colour is seen but not touched, weight is felt by touch but not seen; (c) length, width, thickness, shape, size, resistance to pressure, weight and colour are experienced as located in or on the physical object (basic physical entity); (d) taste characteristics also are experienced as located at or in the physical object; (e) similarly, odour, heat and cold characteristics but they, in addition, are experienced as extending out from it with diminishing intensity.

Experiential Realism obviously takes issue with Ayer, who suggests that the use of the term 'real' with reference to the characteristics of material objects involves the matter of convenience in measurement, or more specifically the situation in which the discrimination, say in the case of colour, is most conveniently made.[2]

As far as comprehensive experience is concerned 'convenience' does not settle the issue as to whether or not a physical object has or has not a specified characteristic, if an entity is a characteristic. The question is settled by accurate observation. Of course, having found what the characteristics of a physical object really are, this knowledge is very useful—convenient—in dealing with the object.

The general point of view of Experiential Realism concerning the

---

[1] Relevant here is Whitehead's forthright statement: 'The objectivist holds that the things experienced and the cognisant subject enter into the common world on equal terms. . . . I am giving the outline of what I consider to be the essentials of an objectivist philosophy adapted to the requirement of science and to the concrete experience of mankind. . . . It appears from this interrogation that we are *within* a world of colours, sounds, and other sense-objects, related in space and time to enduring objects such as stones, trees, and human bodies.' A. N. Whitehead, *Science and the Modern World*, Cambridge ed., 1946, p. 110.

[2] See A. J. Ayer, *Language, Truth and Logic*, Gollancz, 1936, pp. 81, 82.

so-called distinction between primary and secondary qualities finds support in the work of a number of philosophers. Whitehead remarks with, characteristic irony that if so-called secondary qualities are seriously considered to be ideas in a person's mind, we must change our approach to nature and ourselves. Nature no longer should be adored by poets: 'the rose for its scent', 'the sun for its brilliance'. 'The poets . . . should address their lyrics to themselves, and should turn them into odes of self-congratulation on the excellence of the human mind.'[1]

Ryle, relying on a verbal orientation, points out (*C.M.*, p. 220) that 'Secondary quality adjectives are used and are used only for the reporting of publicly ascertainable facts about common objects.' More specifically, he suggests (*C.M.*, p. 221) that arguments for the subjectivity of secondary qualities are apt to hinge, in fact, upon an interesting verbal trick. Adjectives like green, sweet and cold are assimilated to adjectives of discomfort, and their concepts, like paralysed, scalding, chilly.

VII

James

A superficial reading of some of James's remarks about physical objects and their characteristics, when he is not expounding the neutral entity theory, seems to cast doubt on their status as basic physical entities with characteristics. Consider the following: 'What shall we call a thing anyhow? It seems quite arbitrary, for we carve out everything, just as we carve out constellations, to suit our human purposes.'[2]

But this is very misleading unless it is put in its proper context.

'We carve out groups of stars in the heavens and call them constellations.'

'In all these cases we humanly make an *addition* to some sensible reality, and that reality tolerates the addition. All the additions "agree" with the reality; they fit it, while they build it out.'[3]

---

[1] Whitehead, *Science and the Modern World*, p. 169.
[2] W. James, *Pragmatism*, Longmans Green, New York, 1948, p. 253.
[3] *Ibid.*, pp. 252–3.

In other words, the process is not actually arbitrary. Rather, it is a case of making additions to entities already there. 'Reality means that we submit to them, take account of them, whether we like it or not.'[1]

In short, we human beings named the Big Dipper, we count its stars. But the stars are there to be named and counted.

[1] W. James, *The Meaning of Truth*, Longmans Green & Co., London, 1909, p. 68.

15

CONCEPTS

I

No concepts: Halloway, Merleau-Ponty, Wittgenstein, Ayer and Pears
Experiential Realism reports that concepts are among the basic entities
found in the context of comprehensive experience. These concepts
are neither mental nor physical nor physically based resultants nor
characteristics of such entities.

Halloway states a typical criticism: 'There is no escaping the
conclusion that the presence of a "concept" . . . cannot be confirmed
by observation.'[1]

If 'observation' is used in a restricted fashion, to refer only to
sense experience, of course concepts cannot be observed. But as found
in comprehensive experience, concepts are data of non-sensory
awareness.

There are a number of philosophers who claim that the function
assigned, by Experiential Realism, to concepts in recognising entities
actually is performed by other entities. Indeed there are no such
entities as those termed 'concept' by Experiential Realism. Thus an
eminent phenomenologist, Merleau-Ponty, contends that the recognition of objects consists in naming. For example, when a person says:
'This is a table', there is no concept 'table' in his mind under which
he subsumes or classes the object. The word (sound or inscription)
carries the meaning and in applying it to the object 'table' he
recognises it.[2]

In opposition to the general contentions that words are quite
sufficient to perform the functions assigned to concepts, Experiential
Realism reiterates the fact that some persons are aware, in complex
mental processes, of entities which are not words, and cannot be

[1] J. Halloway, *Language and Intelligence*, Macmillan, London, 1951, pp. 42–3.
[2] See M. Merleau-Ponty, *Phenomenologie de la Perception*, Gallimard, Paris,
1945, p. 206.

reported by words. Specifically a person can identify or recognise a complex situation and yet it can't be reduced to any type of behavioural process, or mental entity.

Since this is an important topic, another illustration will be considered. In introducing a description of concepts in Chapter 4, of this study, it was pointed out that concepts are involved in, indeed make possible, the understanding of language, in many instances. Wittgenstein takes issue with this interpretation of what happens when, for example, a person reads and understands a newspaper. He contends that concepts are not mentioned in an adequate description of the event. Further, and to him of the utmost importance, in checking whether or not understanding has occurred, there is no reference to the presence or absence of concepts, rather to a person's verbal performance. Specifically, 'We should . . . say that he had read a sentence if he . . . was afterwards able to repeat the sentence word for word or nearly so'.[1]

There is the related criticism that those who regard concepts as basic entities are the victims of self-deception concerning the general nature of the meaning situation. Coupled with this is the contention that there is a thoroughly effective way of escaping from this erroneous view.

Ayer's version is that we are misled concerning descriptive words and phrases. Specifically, the unwary mistakenly assume that every phrase must refer to either an existing entity or a subsisting one, in other words to a concept (or universal). Such phrases as 'round square' and 'The present King of France' obviously do not refer to existing entities. It is assumed they must refer to subsisting ones, to concepts. Ayer contends that such words and phrases, when subjected to proper translation techniques, lose their 'power to mislead'. For example, it should be pointed out that one is referring to particular entities, not general ones. The statement 'Round squares do not exist' can be translated into 'There is no one thing which has both round shape and square shape'.[2] Each of the fundamental words obviously refers to a particular entity open to sense experience.

Pears offers the following diagnosis and recommended cure: 'general words were tacitly assimilated to proper names,' that is, it

---

[1] L. Wittgenstein, *Philosophical Investigations*, Blackwell, Oxford, 1953, p. 61. Hereafter referred to as *P.I.*

[2] See A. J. Ayer, *Language, Truth and Logic*, Gollancz, 1936, pp. 68–9. Hereafter this book will be referred to as *L.T.L.*

was falsely assumed that because proper names refer to an entity, therefore, general words refer to a general entity, a concept. However, this is a faulty analogy. When this is recognised one wisely refrains from postulating concepts.[1]

As a variation of this theme, Pears contends that devotees of concepts (as discussed in the context of Experiential Realism) falsely assume that if one word is to be used to refer to a number of different entities, there must be something in common involved, and that common element must be a concept (universal, essence). Pears objects that this is an illegitimate demand for a generality which is really 'specious'.

To those who insist that there must be at least one universal (similarity), in order to justify the use of one word in referring to several entities, Pears replies: Why not merely say people just recognise similarly, in other words, a concrete characteristic (*L.L.*, p. 279).

In the course of dispensing with universals (concepts), when trying to account for the use of one word in referring to several entities, Wittgenstein gets rid of even a common concrete characteristic (as well as a common concept). Consider, for example language games. He states: 'I am saying that these phenomena have no one thing in common which makes us use the same word for all, . . . they are related to one another in many different ways. And it is because of this . . . that we call them all "language".' There are in short, only 'family resemblances' (*P.I.*, pp. 31–2).

The reaction of Experiential Realism to these related criticisms of its treatment of concepts takes various forms. To begin with, it is interesting to find that on occasion Wittgenstein inconsistently is prepared to admit the presence of something common in a group of sentences. Thus he states: 'The thought in a sentence is something common to different sentences' (*P.I.*, p. 144).

It is important to note that as far as comprehensive experience is concerned, concepts are not posited to account for the use of a word to refer to a number of objects or to account for a concrete common quality (Pears) or family resemblances (Wittgenstein). When there are a number of games, this is simply a case of many occurrences of the entity: game. The concept game is naturally linked to the entity. Further, it is reported that concepts are entities which are found in

[1] D. Pears, *Logic and Language*, A. Flew (ed.), Doubleday, Anchor Book, New York, 1965, p. 267 (referred to hereafter as *L.L.*).

comprehensive experience. Many concepts (all simple ones) are not imaginary human creations resulting from self-deception based on mistaken theories. It is, of course, obvious that some complex concepts are creations of human imagination, such as 'The present king of France', 'round square', but such complex concepts are composed of single concepts which are not, as such, creations of human imagination. There is no awareness of any such generation.[1]

A concept, as a matter of fact, is linked with a word when a word is used to refer to a number of objects. This is so because the concept is linked with the object. Further, as noted, concepts are involved when one recognises similarity or family resemblances among objects.

Wittgenstein's attempt to deal effectively with 'reading and understanding' without referring to concepts, and their linkage in propositions, is an illustration of a typical peripheral (partial) approach. It is correct as far as it goes, but it leaves out an important ingredient, namely the awareness of propositions, since it concentrates on words (apparently inscriptions as such) alone. As a matter of fact, a person can repeat words which he has seen before and this does not demonstrate he has read them—if reading (with understanding) is to be distinguished from seeing. Thus Wittgenstein's descripion of reading (seeing and understanding) does not turn out to be adequate.

II

Generalisations

One ingenious theory contends that while there are concepts, they are not correctly described by Experiential Realism. Specifically, it is claimed that a concept is a generalisation which results from human experience of particular mental or physical entities or both. This generalisation is formed by leaving out differences and retaining a common element, that is, a sort of composite photograph formed by superimposing a number of individual ones. Another theory contends that some particular entity, mental or physical, is taken as a focal point in attention and then used with a generality of reference. For

[1] S. Alexander, *Space, Time and Deity*, vol. I, Macmillan, 1927, p. 232, claims that universals (concepts) are found (p. 208). They are neither human generalisations nor abstractions. Incidentally, Alexander reports that there are concepts for individuals, for example Napoleon (p. 316).

example, Locke refers to a process whereby 'ideas taken from particular beings become general representatives of all of the same kind'.[1]

From the point of view of Experiential Realism, these theories are a misinterpretation and inaccurate report of a number of important aspects of comprehensive experience. There is no non-imaginary experience of the so-called building up by a process of generalising from concrete particulars to a 'composite picture' (mental) image formed by fusing a number of particular views of a class of entities, for example, of humanity. Such a composite picture can be imagined but, when a person thinks (for example) 'in general' of humanity, such a mental entity need not be present.

Also, in thinking of humanity, one does not necessarily, as a matter of fact one does not, always have in awareness a memory or an imagination image or a particular man which serves as a symbol, in general reference, for all other men. Such entities, if present, are peripheral, incidental accompaniments.

It is of course the case that the term 'concept' is used in different ways. For example, words (inscriptions and sounds) are sometimes termed 'concepts' (*P.I.*, pp. 32–3). The crucial question is this: Are there entities as described by Experiential Realism, or are there only other entities which are termed 'concepts'?

Propositions: Ayer

Referring not to individual concepts but to propositions, Ayer declines to accept the ' "metaphysical doctrine" that they are real entities'. He states: 'we may define a proposition as a class of sentences which have the same intensional significance for anyone who understands them. Thus, the sentences, "I am ill", "Ich bin krank", "Je suis malade", are all elements of the proposition "I am ill" ' (*L.T.L.*, p. 121).

In reply to Ayer's attempt to interpret propositions in terms of sentences, Experiential Realism points out that it is, of course, the case that we 'may define a proposition as a class of sentences which have the same intentional significance'. However, as a matter of fact, there is more to them that that. In comprehensive experience one is aware of propositions which are reported by corresponding sentences

---

[1] J. Locke, *Essay Concerning Human Understanding*, in *The English Philosophers from Bacon to Mill*, E. A. Burtt (ed.), Modern Library, New York, 1949, p. 281.

in different languages. To term this a 'metaphysical doctrine' is regarded by Ayer as putting a curse on it, since it goes beyond sense and tautology. But, as previously noted, comprehensive experiencing reports entities, in this case propositions, which do not involve tautologies (that is, some do not) and are not apprehended by sense.

III

Acceptance of concepts: Plato and Yolton

Many philosophers have taken concepts seriously in the sense that they have stressed the presence of this type of basic entity. The following statement by Plato is typical. He is referring to the requirement for guardians. They must be aware of 'the essential Forms [concepts] of temperance, courage, liberality, high-mindedness, and all other kindred qualities, and also their opposites, . . . [They] must be able to discern the presence of these Forms themselves and also of their images in anything that contains them'.[1]

The same point is made by a contrasting reference to people below the guardian (superior) class. 'Your lovers of sights and sounds delight in beautiful tones and colours and shapes and in all the works of art into which these [Forms] enter; but they have not the power of thought to behold and to take delight in the nature of Beauty itself' (*op. cit.*, p. 183).

Drawing support from the investigations by the Wursburg schools of psychologists, Yolton states: 'We understand or intend without the aid of images, even without the aid of words. Thinking in these instances is, I would suggest, operating with concepts freed from any base in words or images.' He also, in agreement with Experiential Realism, remarks that 'the difference between the man who merely utters certain words (i.e. sounds) and the man who understands what he says is that the latter is using concepts. . . . Concepts are the intelligible components of the world, the translation of physical sounds into meaningful units'.[2]

Price has formulated the theory that concepts are really dispositions

---

[1] Plato, *The Republic* [Cornford edition], Oxford, 1955, p. 91.
[2] J. Yolton, *Thinking and Perceiving*, Open Court Publishing Co., La Salle, 1962, p. 110. Hereafter this book will be referred to as Yolton.

or capacities. However, as Yolton aptly remarks: 'But if concepts are *only* capacities, what Price says about my recognition of the image of [a] dog is that I recognise it as a dog because I have a capacity for recognising dogs and dog-images. The term "concept" seems redundant or at last only a short-hand for "recognitional capacity" ' (Yolton, p. 95).

He then concludes: 'Concepts are so obviously present in cognition, not as dispositions nor as forces but as entities . . .' (p. 110).

However, on closer examination, it becomes evident that, on occasion, Yolton's view of the nature of concepts differs drastically from that of Experiential Realism. Consider the following statement: 'we must not only speak of mental processes; we have also to accept mental entities. Some of these mental entities (images) are inspectable and similar to properties of physical objects. Other mental entities (concepts) are not inspectable and differ radically, even categorically, from images and physical object properties' (p. 112).

A basic question from the point of view of comprehensive experience is this. What is Yolton referring to when he talks about mental entities which are as such not open to inspection?[1] To put it bluntly, why place so much emphasis, as Yolton apparently does, on what does not fall within the scope of awareness? His theory is further complicated by the Kantian-sounding statement (p. 113) that 'Concepts are the units of significance in terms of which we think about and are aware of our world. They are also the units of reality, since it is by means of concepts that a world becomes cognitively specified. The world becomes a complex fragmentation of the units of significance'.

Here Yolton gives every indication of claiming that concepts are open to awareness. In any case, the contention that mental entities are the only ingredients in thought is contrary to comprehensive experience.

IV

Problem of range of application: Wittgenstein and Waismann

Wittgenstein raises a very fundamental point concerning concepts— that of 'limit', exact range of application. Equating concept and word

[1] It seems improbable, in view of previous remarks, that he restricts 'inspectable' to what is open to sense awareness.

(inscription or sound),[1] he claims: 'I can give the concept "number" rigid limits . . . that is, use the word "number" for a rigidly limited concept.' However, the situation is different in the case of a word (concept) such as 'game': 'how is the concept of a game bounded? . . . Can you give the boundary? No' (*P.I.*, pp. 32–3).

Waismann shares this general point of view. He is convinced that most of our empirical concepts are not delimited in all possible directions.[2] Thus he states that 'Open texture is a very fundamental characteristic of most, though not of all, empirical concepts' ('Ver.', p. 123). In developing this theme he discusses the case of a person using the concept 'cat'. It is employed in referring to the familiar creature who lolls by the fireside. But, says Waismann, suppose this animal greatly increases in size, suppose it dies and returns to life again. Does the concept cat apply to this creature? He claims that there is genuine uncertainty on this point. He also uses the illustrations of a creature which looked like a man except it is only one span tall, and of metal that appeared to be gold and yet had the characteristic of radiation. If you say these cases do not occur, Waismann blithely replies: 'But it might happen.'

As far as comprehensive experience is concerned, if a material which appears to be gold radiates, then it is not gold. If a creature looks like a man and is only one span high, he is not a man. All these flights of speculative imagination merely introduce different creatures and objects, and hence new related concepts. They do not cast doubt on the known limits of concepts which apply to familiar relatively simple entities.

Wittgenstein's game illustration seems to present some difficulties. We are not familiar with all types of games. They are essentially make-believe, and the limits to human imagination are not now known. However, while the exact limits of the concept 'game', in this sense, cannot now be drawn, it is none the less now possible to distinguish the present application of the concept game and the present application of the concept 'non-game' in many instances, such as playing bridge (a game) and performing an operation to remove cancerous tissue (not a game).

---

[1] The fallacious nature of this identity claim has already been noted.

[2] F. Waismann, 'Verifiability', *Aristotelian Society Supplementary Volume* XIX (1945), p. 122. Hereafter this article will be referred to as 'Ver.'

The linkage of concepts with other concepts: Wittgenstein

Wittgenstein takes an interesting stand concerning the question as to whether or not the linkage of concepts with other concepts is, in at least some cases, controlled by factual entities to which they refer. His answer is that we should rely ultimately on rules of grammar or what a person believes about concepts, or is interested in. The full impact of his position can only be appreciated by examining his own specific statement:

'If the formation of [complex] concepts [i.e., linking of concepts] can be explained by facts of nature, should we not be interested, not in grammar, but rather in that in nature which is the basis of grammar?— Our interest certainly includes the correspondence between concepts and very general facts of nature. (Such facts as mostly do not strike us because of their generality.) But our interest does not fall back upon these possible causes of the formation of concepts; we are not doing natural science; nor yet natural history—since we can also invent fictional natural history for our purposes.

I am not saying: if such-and-such facts of nature were different people would have different concepts (in the sense of a hypothesis). But: if anyone believes that certain concepts are absolutely the correct ones, and that having different ones would mean not realising something that we realise—then let him imagine certain very general facts of nature to be different from what we are used to, and the formation of concepts different from the usual ones will become intelligible to him.

Compare a concept with a style of painting' (*P.I.*, p. 230).

It is important to note that he is not fundamentally interested in natural science and is prepared to invent fictitious 'natural science' for his purposes. Therefore there is no point in making an ultimate appeal to the actual facts of *nature* in any situation. Thus Wittgenstein seems intent on destroying the distinction found in comprehensive experience between the linkage of concepts in imagination (because of some belief or interest, regardless of actual facts) and the linkage based on facts.

It was noted in the earlier discussion of concepts (Chapter 4) that the linkage of many concepts, for example, to form complex concepts and propositions is ultimately controlled by physical or mental entities, or both. In other words, the non-imaginary linkage of concepts is given a respected place in the scheme of things. This view is shared by Hall, who remarks: 'Categorical systems are not, in the main, oriented to themselves or their rivals but to the world.'[1]

VI

A basis for some objections to concepts

It is important to realise that much of the objection to concepts, as a distinct type of entity, neither mental nor physical nor physically based resultant (nor characteristic of any of these entities) is quite understandable. Some people deny the presence of such entities, or try to replace them by mental or physical ones, in order to account for thinking, recognising, generality of reference, because of unfortunate implications which concepts have acquired in some instances. It is the opinion of such critics that, if one accepts concepts as distinctive basic entities, one is committed to a static, dogmatic approach to the physical objects, mind (and their characteristics) to which the concepts refer.[2] Further, it is claimed that those who accept concepts (as discussed by Experiential Realism) are committing themselves to an other-worldly view that assigns subordinate or no reality to the familiar world of men and things.

It is the case that these consequences have followed from the acceptance of concepts by some philosophers. This, however, need not happen. Concepts can be used as effective instruments in dealing with physical objects, minds, physically based resultants, and other concepts. In so far as concepts are found as ingredients in this world their assertion is not dogmatic. In so far as there are entities found in this world with characteristics which are sufficiently definite to be identified, the admission of concepts which refer to these entities does not condemn one to an unjustified static view. Concepts apply to changing entities as well as to enduring ones.

[1] E. W. Hall, *Philosophical Systems*, University of Chicago Press, Chicago, 1960, p. 22.
[2] H. Bergson, *Creative Evolution*, Macmillan, New York, 1928, pp. ix–xi.

16

KNOWLEDGE

I

Recapitualation: knowing and knowledge

The discussion of knowledge in Chapter 6 serves as the basis for a series of comments on the work of a number of philosophers. Recapitulating briefly, it was noted that this is a difficult topic because the knowledge situation is diverse and complex. This is reflected in the varying uses of the term knowledge. Unfortunately the diversity and complexity of the knowledge situation are frequently neglected and the term knowledge is used in a confused fashion.

On the basis of comprehensive experience, it is found that in the knowledge situation there are two main distinguishable ingredients, (*a*) the activity of knowing and (*b*) what is known. It is recommended that in the interests of clarity the term knowing be used to refer to the activity and the term knowledge to what is known, and also qualifying terms as indicated below. A careful examination of the knowledge situation shows that what is known (knowledge) takes different forms; so does the activity of knowing. Consider the following sorts: (1) when one is being aware of an entity, this is a case of immediate knowing; the entity (entities) of which one is aware, is what is known, that is 'immediate knowledge.'[1] (2) Through the medium of true propositions (and one is aware of their truth) a person has an occurrence of knowledge about[2] entities which, as such, are not present in awareness. What is present in awareness is the proposition, its truth, and the referential function. Awareness in this case is an instance of 'knowing about'. (3) When a person is performing some skill (intellectual or physical), this is a case of knowing how and also manifesting

---

[1] When recognition occurs there is immediate identifying knowing and immediate identified knowledge, otherwise it is minimum.

[2] Entities other than propositions may be involved. See full discussion in Section One.

an occurrence of 'knowledge how"[1] (4) When a person has a skill, or has available for recall a proposition which constitutes knowledge about (but in both cases there is no presence in experience, of knowledge), this is a case of 'knowledge in storage'. Such knowledge, though not present to awareness, yet is possessed in the sense indicated.

It is of course the case that, when a person is engaged in any type of knowing, the relevant type of knowledge is present, and vice versa—except in the case of knowledge in storage. Thus in the interests of simplified expression it is sometimes sufficient to mention only either knowing or knowledge.

II

Neglect of some types of knowing and knowledge: Sartre, Ryle and Wittgenstein

In discussing general or specific situations, some relevant types of knowing or knowledge are neglected by some philosophers. Thus, for example, Sartre firmly believes that all knowledge (entities known) is intuitive (involves immediate awareness).[2] This view neglects the fact that, in the case of knowing about, the entities known are not present in awareness. Similarly in the case of knowledge in storage. In the case of knowledge how, immediate knowing may or may not be involved—one can be performing some skills without being aware of what one is doing.

The works of philosophers who in varying degrees attempt to reduce mental entities to physical ones are guilty of neglect of some types of knowing and knowledge. At the risk of repeating points already made in Chapter 13 on mind, brief reference will be made to representative examples.

In discussing what Experiential Realism terms 'knowing how' or 'knowledge how' (the performance of skills), Ryle pokes fun at what he terms 'the intellectual legend'. By this he means the view that when a person actually is knowing how, he must also at the same time, or immediately preceding it, be engaged in what Experiential Realism

---

[1] See Chapter 6, pp. 149–50.
[2] J. P. Sartre, *L'Être et le Néant*, Paris, 1943, p. 220.

terms knowing about (Ryle sometimes uses the term 'knowing that'). For example, 'The chef must recite his recipes [knowledge about] to himself before he can cook according to them.'[1] Likewise a person cannot swim the best stroke without reciting to himself a set of instructions. (*C.M.*, p. 49).

More specifically Ryle states: 'Knowing how ... is a disposition. ... Its exercises are observances of rules or canons or the applications of criteria, but they are not tandem operations of theoretically avowing maxims and then putting them into practice.' (*C.M.*, p. 46).[2]

A person relying on comprehensive experience would not contend that when he is performing a skill (a case of knowing and knowledge how), he always has present also in awareness a rule or formula which he recites and follows. In attacking this so-called 'intellectual legend', Ryle manoeuvres himself into an extreme position (contrary to what he sometimes admits), which at least seems to argue that no awareness of a rule is present in knowing how. As a matter of fact, skills sometimes function without intellectual guidance—sometimes they don't.

Wittgenstein is a foremost exponent of the theory that knowledge is basically of one type only, what Experiential Realism terms knowing how or knowledge how. Thus he states, for example: 'To understand a language means to be master of a technique.[3] However, he vacillates on the question as to whether or not a formula is present in awareness when a skill is being performed.

In terms of a verbal approach, he remarks: 'The grammar of the word "knows" is evidently closely related to that of "can", "is able to". But also closely related to that of "understands" ' (*P.I.*, p. 59).

According to Wittgenstein, when a person claims to know what the next number in a series which increases by two is, given the number 1000, this does not 'simply' involve a mental process—thinking of the step from 1000 to 1002, or the apprehension of a formula. It is perfectly possible for a person to be aware of a formula and yet not understand it. The fundamental factor in the situation is the ability to write the next number if requested to do so (*P.I.*, pp. 60, 75). In

---

[1] G. Ryle, *The Concept of Mind*, Barnes and Noble, New York, 1949, p. 29. Hereafter this book will be referred to as *C.M.*

[2] Strangely enough Ryle admits correctly (p. 29) that sometimes this so-called tandem process does occur.

[3] L. Wittgenstein, *Philosophical Investigations*, Blackwell, Oxford, 1953, p. 81. Hereafter this book will be referred to as *P.I.*

brief, Wittgenstein's advice is: 'Try not to think of understanding as a "mental process" at all' (*P.I., p.* 61).

Here Wittgenstein is manifesting his dislike of relying on mental process, in the sense of processes which are hidden from public observation (*P.I.,* p. 60). He is prepared to admit that they occur, or may occur. But his point is that if they do, they are not basic in the process of understanding, which, in his view, is the ability to go on to carry out a particularly observable process such as writing or saying the next number in a series (*P.I.,* p. 61).

The reply of Experiential Realism to the Wittgenstein position is twofold. In the first place, he limits the use of the words 'know' and 'understand' to a special restricted sense, thus neglecting the other standard uses. Secondly, on the level of facts, he refuses to assign importance to inner 'hidden from public view' processes even when he admits they occur (acts of awareness). This reflects his addition to the public approach. As far as comprehensive experience is concerned there are many cases of proceeding to the next number in a series where awareness of a formula is essential. True, in some cases the production of the next number in a series may be sheer verbal habits, with no thought of the formula being present. It has already been pointed out that 'ability to do' may be in some cases potential, in other words cases of knowledge in storage. Here, of course, nothing is being done either externally or internally. Finally, it must be emphasised that Wittgenstein overlooks the fact that one can be aware of, (know immediately) physical objects, minds, concepts, and proceed to do nothing overt. One can, for example, be aware of a formula and not apply it.[1]

III

Criteria: Waismann

Experiential Realism points out that immediate knowing and knowledge, in its simplest form, is awareness of an entity. As noted in the discussion of awareness in Chapter 2, factors internal and external

---

[1] It is of course the case that one may be aware of a proposition and not understand it in the sense of not being aware of the entities to which it refers.

must be present if awareness is to occur,[1] likewise various factors can interfere with the process of awareness of entities. However, in many cases these can be discovered and corrected. This general point of view finds support from Austin. He notes that on occasion we may have initial doubts concerning the status of what as a matter of fact are dreams or mirages due to the effects of drugs, unusual lighting and so on. However, Austin remarks: 'There are recognised ways of distinguishing between dreaming and waking (how otherwise should we know how to use and to contrast the words?), and of deciding whether a thing is stuffed or live, and so forth.'[2]

In the process of becoming aware of some entities, frequently a reference to criteria is involved. In this fashion a person is aided in identifying one entity, and in particular distinguishing it from other entities. What constitutes criteria (or a criterion) for a specific entity is determined by experts in the field in which the entity in question falls. There are, of course, difficulties when dealing with complex entities. The fact remains that in many instances criteria are noted and used efficiently. The details of this achievement are, in general, the subject matter of psychology and, as noted, the concern of experts in specific fields. Additional detailed discussion is not relevant here.

However, several general comments are in order. If by criterion one means a statement of (*a*) the essential ingredients (distinguishable components or constituent relations of a complex entity) and (*b*) its distinctive characteristics—then it follows that, in this sense, there are no criteria for simple entities. For example (*a*) there are criteria in terms of bodily components and structure for the entity horse which enable one to identify it and distinguish it from the entity giraffe and (*b*) one can distinguish a horse from a giraffe in terms of what it can do. However in these senses there are no criteria for entities such as green, pleasant, causality, value. A person does become aware of each of these entities under suitable conditions. They are distinguishable one from the other—but not in terms of components or constitutive char-

---

[1] Whitehead aptly points out: 'There is a sort of sliding scale of normality in the conditioning events necessary for the perception of a given sense-object in a situation with a definite relation to the percipient event. For example, in the case of the redness of . . . [a] poker, there are the conditions for direct vision, the conditions for vision by reflection in a mirror, the conditions for alcoholic delusion' (A. N. Whitehead, 'Time, Space and Material', *Aristotelian Society Supplementary Volume* II (1919), p. 53).

[2] J. L. Austin, 'Other Minds', *Aristotelian Society Supplementary Volume* XX (1946), p. 159. Hereafter this paper will be referred to as O.M.

acteristics (because they do not have any) or, distinctive characteristics. One can, of course, refer to the characteristics of simple entities
(of the sorts mentioned), but these characteristics are not unique to
any one of them. For example, the numerical characteristic one is not a
criterion for green, pleasure and so on.

If one wishes to use the term criterion to refer to the conditions
under which one is aware of simple entities, it is the case that such
conditions can be specified as an aid in locating an entity. For example,
if a normal person is hungry and he is given food he feels pleasure.
This is a special use of the term criterion. In any case, pleasure as such
is not identified in terms of anything else or some essential ingredient
(or equated with it). Likewise value does not have as a criterion (in
the usual sense of the term) something else, another entity. It is very
significant to note that when there are criteria for an entity, the factthat
those criteria apply is something 'directly grasped'. There are no
criteria for the fact that the application of criteria has occurred, in
other words, no criteria that identify the fact that criteria apply to an
entity. This fact, when it occurs must be 'seen immediately'.[1]

Nevertheless, another problem arises, that of being aware of all
relevant characteristics of an entity under consideration and, in the
case of recognition, the relevant concepts. The matter is greatly
complicated when one considers relations between entities and evidence on which claims to know are based. There is another serious
problem, that of determining when an empirical statement has received
sufficient verification. This, however, will be dealt with more appropriately in the context of a discussion of problems involved in
determining the truth of statements (see Chapter 18, pp. 463–5).

Some extreme positions, from the point of view of comprehensive
experience, are taken by a number of contemporary philosophers with
reference to the problem of a complete description.

For example, Waismann claims that a person can never formulate
a complete description of an empirical entity. He states that he can
never exhaust the description of a material object or of a situation,
since he may always add something to it. (*L.L.*, p. 128).

However, he contradicts himself when he admits that there is
complete description, if not in the case of a chair, at least in that of a
game of chess. (*L.L.*, p. 243). The same is true of a dream. It is a
finite entity. Its relations are finite. Hence it is possible to get a complete
finite description.

[1] For a further discussion of criteria see p. 347.

Knowledge and uncertainty

The highly sophisticated argument has been offered that the word knowledge applies only in cases where a person initially is uncertain (in both senses)[1] in dealing with public facts in a process of investigation.[2] Since, it is argued, one has no uncertainty about mental entities, therefore the term knowledge does not apply; one cannot properly be said to have knowledge of private mental entities.

Two points must be made in refutation: (1) All claims to have knowledge do not involve an earlier admission of uncertainty. In some cases of experience of physical objects there is no uncertainty; (2) in some cases of mental experience there is uncertainty. For example, I am aware that I am holding a pen in my hand, recognise it as such and have no uncertainty concerning this situation. Complicated processes of scientific investigation are not necessary as far as a normal adult who relies on comprehensive experience is concerned. Likewise I am sure of a feeling of pain, recognise it as such and am certain that this is the case. On the other hand (2) there are cases where I am not certain as to whether the emotion I am feeling is injured pride or righteous indignation, or whether X is a cure for cancer.

The argument that knowledge involves uncertainty in either sense of the term is open to the objection that this is not its ordinary dictionary usage.

V

Knowledge and private experience

As noted previously, the term knowledge in its various senses is legitimately applicable, in terms of ordinary usage, to what is experienced and recognised. This includes one's own mind and relevant concepts. If a philosopher does not wish to apply the term knowledge to private experience, that is his privilege. However, his preference does not blot out the fact that a person is, on occasion, aware of his

[1] The term certainty is misleading. It has two meanings (entities meant) since it refers to (i) a mental state or attitude, or is (ii) a synonym for knowledge (what is known), for example that a proposition has adequate factual support.
[2] P. Heath, 'The Appeal to Ordinary Language', in *Clarity is not Enough*, H. D. Lewis (ed.), George Allen and Unwin, London, 1963, p. 199.

own mind and its characteristics and is aware also of appropriate concepts.

In view of the preceding discussion, one can find no justification for Wittgenstein's influential remark: ' "How do you know that you have raised your arm?"—"I feel it." So what you recognise is a feeling? And are you certain that you recognise it right?' (*P.I.*, p. 161).

This remark is contradicted when, moving in the context of comprehensive experience, he states: 'My kinaesthetic sensations advise me of the movement and position of my limbs' (*P.I.*, p. 185).

The first of these two statements from Wittgenstein reflects his famous dictum: 'An "inner process" stands in need of outward criteria'[1] (*P.I.*, p. 153).

This refusal to accept private criteria, or bases, in the knowing process is shared by Malcolm who remarks: 'How could one know that the inner state one calls "dreaming" is the same in oneself each time?'[2]

The fact remains that, contrary to Wittgenstein, there are inner bases for the identification, for the awareness and recognition of inner private states. Contrary to Malcolm, in comprehensive experience, a person does know that he has had the same dream twice (in the sense of twice dreaming he is falling down stairs) and he knows this without talking to other people or being observed by other people or by observing his own overt behaviour or checking against public facts.

VI[3]

Problem of awareness of external physical objects
Problems because of intervening physical entities: Whitehead

It has occurred to some philosophers,[4] and others, that the sense

---

[1] The point at issue here is the claim that the only way to know that an inner state occurs (and what it is) is by referring to an external publically observable occurrence. The latter is regarded as a criterion for the former. For example, in using words to refer to entities, these entities must be public. Otherwise there is no way of checking on the use of the words.

[2] *Philosophical Psychology*, D. E. Gustafson (ed.), Doubleday, New York, 1964, p. 265. Hereafter this book will be referred to as *P.P.*

[3] This section is an expansion of the discussion in Chapter 6, pp. 152–3. Some repetition is involved.

[4] See brief statement of this view by C. D. Broad in *Perceiving; Sensing and Knowing*, R. J. Swartz (ed.), Doubleday, New York, 1965, p. 38.

organs and the nervous system stand in the way of, indeed, make impossible, an awareness of an external physical object. Specifically, a stimulus must come from the physical object, pass through the appropriate sense organ, along the nervous system to the cortex and then finally issue in awareness of an entity. Thus it appears that, for example, in a case of so-called seeing a table, the process is very complex, involving many intervening entities. How then can one legitimately claim to be aware of the table (in any sense of immediate direct presence)?

There is a further apparent difficulty. On occasion sense organs and the nervous systems introduce distortions or deceptions. A colour-blind person, of a certain sort, lives in a grey world. A person who has lost a toe in an accident 'feels pressure on it' because there is pressure on some remaining part of his nervous system. Further, diseases of or damage to the nervous system and the brain seriously interfere with or render impossible awareness of concepts (which are involved in recognition) as well as physical objects. For example, the development of a brain tumour may render a person incapable of understanding English. Likewise, malfunction of brain or nervous system may lead to undetected flights of imagination involving all the basic types of entities. Such facts concerning sense organs, the nervous system and the brain lead some critics to suggest that it is difficult, if not impossible, to be sure that these instruments are functioning properly at any time in view of their tendency to malfunction, and the fact that this is frequently overlooked. How, then, can one claim to have awareness of and recognition, immediate knowing of any entity and in particular physical objects in view of a person's dependence in experience on the physically intervening brain, nervous system and sense organs (in the case of physical objects)?

It is important to note, in opposition to such criticisms, that the critics, with intolerable inconsistency, presuppose an awareness and recognition of the nervous system, brain and sense organs, and, also an awareness of the distorting effects of these conditioning factors. As a matter of fact, brains, etc. have the same status, as part of the public physical world, as the other physical objects which are claimed to be beyond the range of accurate awareness because of these intervening and distorting factors. If it is claimed that part of the physical world, such as the nervous system, can be immediately known, one cannot legitimately deny immediate knowledge concerning tables and chairs.

Whitehead aptly remarks: 'Some people express themselves as though [human] bodies, brains and nerves were the only real things in an entirely imaginary world. In other words, they treat bodies on objectivist principles, and the rest of the [physical] world on subjectivist principles. This will not do.'[1]

In short, it is here contended that when our instruments of observation (brains, nervous systems, sense organs) are functioning properly, they do not interfere, in other words 'cook' the data, add data, or come between us and entities of which we are aware. They facilitate the awareness of entities rather than generate, in whole or part, what we are aware of. Any one who claims to deal effectively with an entity implicitly accepts this general state of affairs.

It is the case that, on occasion, the sense organs, nervous system and brain (as in illness and accident) play tricks and hence interfere with the awareness of entities. However, in comprehensive experience, this can be noted and distinguished from normal experience where these difficulties do not occur. The mechanism involved may, indeed, be complex, and beyond fully detailed understanding. Nevertheless, in comprehensive experience, the distinction is made between its normal and its abnormal function in many cases.

The time-lag factor, the fact that time is required for a stimulus to come from an external object, pass across space and along the nervous system to a brain, must be faced. But there is continued experience over a period, which indicates a period of endurance without significant change in the case of many basic physical entities and their characteristics, as with the desk which a person uses for thirty years. Thus, in the case of near objects, the time-lag factor is not crucial. True, conditions may change, but the origins of change in at least some instances can be spotted. A brief time-lag in this type of perception is part of a normal situation and does not constitute a special problem. In the case of a distant star, the matter is more complicated. This problem is the business of astronomers who seem to conclude that, in many instances, the star is still there.

Epistemological gap because of substance

Doubts are cast on the possibility of knowledge of external physical objects on the basis of an assumption that there is a serious gap between

---

[1] A. N. Whitehead, *Science and the Modern World*, Cambridge, 1946, p. 113.

the object and the perceiver. This prevents awareness of the physical object as such. For example, some versions of the theory of substances give rise to a problem (artificial) in the field of knowledge. It is claimed that a mind, being a substance and hence independent of other substances, is aware only of its own ideas, which are assumed to represent in some cases, the characteristics of physical objects (another type of substance). However, there is no way of confirming this in awareness because physical objects are not open to mind.[1]

Epistemological gap because of variations in sense data: Ayer, Austin and Ryle

Another variation of this general type is very common. Variations in experience of physical objects have led some philosophers to conclude that there is no awareness of physical objects as such. Rather, in perception, a person is aware of some intervening entity which is frequently termed a 'sense datum', 'impression' or 'sensible manifestation'. Usually many such entities are involved in perception. For example, chairs and tables, as well as atoms and electrons, are known only by their sensible manifestations and are definable in terms of them.[2]

In his *Sense and Sensibilia*, Austin discusses Ayer's presentation of the function of 'sensible manifestations' in the process of perception. The general tenor of his criticisms of this approach are obviously in agreement with the point of view of Experiential Realism as developed in Chapter 3.

Specifically, Ayer refers at length to the deceptive, indeed, the illusory experiences which occur. We experience different shapes and colours when looking at physical objects, sticks partly in water are seen as bent. Mirror images and dreams are a source of deception. Hence, he contends that in sense experience we are not in the presence of basic physical entities and their characteristics.[3]

To all this Austin replies, with vigour and aptness, that the recognition of deception is only possible if one has non-deceptive experience as a criterion. He goes on to report that, in any case, people are not

---

[1] See Locke, *Essay Concerning Human Understanding*, Book II, Chapter VIII.

[2] A. J. Ayer, *Language, Truth and Logic*, Gollancz, 1936, p. 46. Hereafter this book will be referred to as *L.T.L.*

[3] A. J. Ayer, *The Foundations of Empirical Knowledge*, Macmillan, 1940, pp. 1–11.

ordinarily deceived about the status of mirror images or the characteristics of apparently bent sticks immersed in water.[1]

Further, and fundamentally, Austin contends that 'it is not only false but simply absurd to say that such objects as pens or cigarettes are never perceived directly' (*S.S.*, p. 19).

Austin's remarks about the bent stick partly immersed in water are in general agreement with Experiential Realism, concerning awareness of basic physical entities and their characteristics. The bent shape which we see is not a real quality or part of the material thing. Nevertheless a person sees the wood (of the stick) regardless of whether it is in the water or out of it (See *S.S.*, p. 30).

It is important to note that Austin on occasion seems prepared to rule out sense data entirely. Thus, in a verbal orientation, he contends that in the case of mirages, dreams, and mirror images 'We don't actually have to say . . . here that . . . he is "experiencing sense data"; for though, as Ayer says . . . "it is convenient to give a name" to what he is experiencing, the fact is that it already has a name—a *mirage* [mirror image, dream]' (*S.S.*, pl 32).

From the point of view of Experiential Realism, this approach is a case of dodging a crucial issue, namely, a positive approach to the status of the entities under discussion. Mirages, after-images, dream content, and mirror images are entities which are present in awareness. They are not physical objects; rather they are physically based resultants or mental entities. Further, most of the experienced shapes and colours of mountains and pennies and the bentness of the stick immersed in water are physically based resultants.[2] Thus, there is a place[3] in Experiential Realism for what are termed 'sense data' by some philosophers. To this extent Experiential Realism disagrees with Austin's statement noted above. However, there is agreement with him on the fundamental point that there is (direct) awareness of physical objects, that is their basic physical entities and characteristics. Sense data do not come between the perceiver and the perceived physical object, in the fashion of an opaque screen, or a series of representations.

Ryle's influential discussion of the problem of perception has

---

[1] J. L. Austin, *Sense and Sensibilia*, Oxford, 1962, p. 20. Hereafter this book will be referred to as *S.S.*

[2] See Chapter 3, pp. 79–83.

[3] This does not imply an acceptance of any variety of sense-data theory in its entirety.

kinship with Austin's at many crucial points. However, it is open to serious criticism on the basis of comprehensive experience.[1]

As in the case of Austin, Experiential Realism is in agreement with Ryle in his emphasis on the artificiality of some phases of sense data (impression, sensation) theory.

Since Ryle adds important dimensions to the discussion of perception, his views will be examined in some detail.

Ryle claims that entities which are called by some philosophers 'sense data', or as he terms them, 'sensations', cannot be observed, that is are not open to awareness (*C.M.*, p. 207). Therefore it is absurd to claim that they 'carry the freight' in the process of perceptual knowing. It amounts to this. In Ryle's judgement the term 'sensation' has a correct use, to refer to a process. It is incorrectly employed by the sense datum devotees to refer to what is claimed to be a content or entity on which the process of sensation (sensing) focuses.[2]

A typical statement by Ryle is the following:

'It is not a specialist's theory, but a piece of common knowledge, that we find out by sensation [process] that things are warm, sticky, vibrating and tough. It was, accordingly, made to seem just a more general piece of common knowledge that we have sensations [content] when we see, hear, and smell [that is, are sensing]' (*C.M.*, p. 243).

Ryle noted that we frequently use phrases such as 'feels as if', 'looks as if'. But the reference here is to a way of sensing; not to some mysterious entity; but rather to objective entities in the physical world. In brief, Ryle is objecting to the practice by sense data theorists of turning the word 'sensation' into a noun. It is essentially a verb. It is not just a question, of course, of using the word 'sensation' as a noun or a verb, or both, but a fundamental one as to whether or

---

[1] However, in commenting on Ryle's views, it is only fair to bear in mind his own dissatisfaction with what he has to say about sense experience (*C.M.*, p. 240):

'As I said in the Foreword, there is something seriously amiss with the discussions occupying this chapter. I have talked as if we know how to use the concept or concepts of sensation; I have spoken with almost perfunctory regret of our lack of "neat" sensation words; and I have glibly spoken of auditory and visual sensations. But I am sure that none of this will do.'

[2] Ryle himself is prepared on occasion to use the term 'sensation' to refer to feeling, content and emotions also some sensory content.

not in perception special mental entities are found in distinction from sensing activities (*C.M.*, pp. 216–17, 224, 242–3).

In clarifying his general position, Ryle pokes fun at those who set up glimpses and whiffs, for example, glimpses of robins, whiffs of cheese, . . . as entities which can be observed in the same way as the cheese and the robin (*C.M.*, p. 207). He claims that we do not talk about glimpses[1] and whiffs or tickles in the same way that we talk, say, about a horse race or a football match. These comments of course are in accordance with Ryle's general objection to what he terms 'the supposed peculiar objects of my privileged observation, namely my sensations [content] . . . sensations are not objects of observations at all' (*C.M.*, pp. 207, 224).

The result of this argument in Ryle's opinion is that there is no epistemological gap. 'As has been shown, listening and looking are not merely having sensations [content]; nor, however, are they joint processes of observing sensations and inferring to common objects' (*C.M.*, p. 232). The so-called problem of inference from sensations to external objects is a pseudo-problem. In observing a robin one is glimpsing, that is, having a sensation of (sensing) a robin (*C.M.*, p. 224).

As was pointed out in Chapter 11, it is claimed by some philosophers that, for philosophers, problems in the field of perception are basically linguistic. Some of Ryle's remarks are typical of this point of view and will be referred to briefly, at the risk of undue repetition, in the interests of a more comprehensive treatment of the problem.

Ryle states for example that problems of perception are 'not questions of the para-mechanical form "How do we see robins?", but questions of the form, "How do we use such descriptions as 'he saw a robin'?" ' (*C.M.*, p. 225).

Concentrating on words and phrases, Ryle claims that no legitimate use can be found for the following: 'object of sense', 'sensible object', 'sensum', 'sense datum', 'sense-content', 'sense field' and 'sensibilia'. 'To sense' and . . . 'direct awareness' and 'acquaintance' are likewise useless (*C.M.*, p. 221).

On the basis of comprehensive experience Experiential Realism is in agreement with Ryle in opposing the theory of an epistemological gap between an observer and a physical object. However, in attempting to avoid this pseudo-gulf Ryle goes too far and disregards some facts of comprehensive experience.

[1] See discussion in Chapter 14, pp. 321–2 of physically based resultants.

As a matter of fact, people do ask questions, and talk about, and observe whiffs of cheese and tickles; and in so doing they are not dealing with ghostly entities. In other words, one can and does distinguish, in talk and observation, between a piece of cheese or a muscle on the one hand, and the odour of the cheese which may linger after the cheese is eaten, and the tickle or itch which arises when the muscle is in a certain disturbed condition. It is the case, in agreement with Ryle, that glimpses are not distinct entities which can be observed. This is a case of imagining an entity to be present when actually only a process is occurring.

In his claim that when one talks about something appearing 'as if', or 'as' (for example a round penny appearing as if it were elliptical in shape), one is only referring to the physical object, Ryle is in error. When we talk about the penny 'appearing' elliptical, actually, as is obvious in comprehensive experience, this is a case of seeing a penny, seeing an elliptical shape and knowing, on the basis of past experience, that the penny is not characterised by an elliptical shape.

Ryle mistakenly thinks he has covered the problem by referring to a sort of perceiving, while, as a matter of fact, he neglects a type of entity which is perceived, and correctly interpreted, by a person, as not belonging to a penny.

Experiential Realism agrees with Ryle that many of the sense data stressed by the epistemological gap devotees (those which are said to make direct perception impossible) are fabrications of the imagination. But some data, such as twinges and tickles are private mental sense data. Thus, contrary to Ryle, we still need, in our vocabulary, such terms as 'sense data', 'impressions', 'direct awareness', etc.

Finally, as emphasised so often, Experiential Realism does not assign the exalted status to words which Ryle accords them. For example, the problem of perception in not basically a problem of how we use specified words. (See also *P.I.*, p. 180; *L.T.L.*, pp. 19, 75–6).

In passing, a further point is worth noting, concerning those who mistakenly contend that there is a screen of entities between the observer and the observed physical object—hence, there is no awareness of the physical object. Some claim that these intervening sense data (impressions, etc.) are mental (for instance, Locke, *Essay Concerning Human Understanding*, Book II, Chapter VIII). Others contend they are essences, concepts. (See Santayana, *Skepticism and Animal Faith*, Scribner, New York, 1923, Chapter VII) Russell, at one stage, is typical of those who state that they are physical. (B. Russell, *Mysticism and Logic*, George Allen and Unwin, London, 1935, pp. 150–2).

In all these cases there is little point, as far as Experiential Realism is concerned, in engaging in much further discussion. As already stressed, comprehensive experience shows that when one is aware of a physical object such as a penny, under varying conditions, one is aware of a basic physical entity and, if the conditions are satisfactory, its characteristics (its actual shape, size, colour, etc.). Otherwise, one is aware of physically based resultants in close conjunction with the basic physical entity. It must be remembered that shapes, sizes, colours, etc. as such, are neither physical nor mental nor concepts. Of course concepts apply to the characteristics of physical objects and physically based resultants. However, concepts do not constitute such entities, nor are those entities mental. In any case, when one perceives a physical object one is not cut off from it by a screen of intervening entities.

It is important to realise that those who reject Experiential Realism, and adhere to the theory that in supposedly seeing a physical object one is aware only of entities other than the physical objects, are faced with the problem of how to 'get from' the mental image (or another type of intervening entity) to the physical thing. They are forced to assume that a person's dealings with a physical object are a case of an 'animal faith', a 'working hypothesis' a 'hope' that what one is aware of in some sense represents what is assumed to be 'out there'. This artificial solution to an artificial problem, of course, is contrary to the experience of an enlightened person. A young man at a dance, under normal conditions, does not find himself confronted by a group of mental images and mutter: 'There must be a young lady here' (to account for the sense data).

What is perceived is the product of interaction, Chisholm

Another variation of the theory that a person is cut from awareness of physical objects contends that what is experienced is the product of interaction between physical objects and minds.

An interesting illustration of this approach to perception is found in Chisholm's discussion in terms of a theory of 'appearing'. His discussion is set in the context of a linguistic orientation.

Chisholm begins by raising the question as to whether by changing language a person can get away from some problems. He suggests that we do not need to say such things as ' "From the corner of the room, the table presents a diamond-shaped sense-datum." . . . We could say instead, "From the corner of the room, the table *appears* to be . . . diamond-shaped." ' This, as a matter of fact, is the way we ordinarily do speak.[1]

In language reminiscent of Ryle, Chisholm points out that when we operate in sense data language we needlessly multiply entities (which may be termed 'appearances') and get involved in all kinds of 'epistemological gap' complications and errors.[2] 'But when we speak in terms of appearing [an activity] we have only the original external objects' (*P.S.K.*, p. 174).

Chisholm candidly admits a difficulty in the recommended point of view. 'On the present version of the theory of appearing [as outlined above] it is an *objective* property of the external thing to be able to appear as it does to observers like us; but the property is *subjectively* dependent in that the object cannot appear in *any* way unless observers are present' (*P.S.K.*, p. 177).

In short, our knowledge of physical objects is based on how they appear to us. There is an essential and decisive interaction between perceiver and the external physical object. In short, in the literal sense, the 'appearing' theory does not involve the direct perception of external objects (*P.S.K.*, p. 178).

Chisholm suggests, as a solution to the problem, that, for example, in talking about a thing appearing white, instead of using the word to refer to something supposed to belong to a physical object as such, the word 'white' might be used adverbially (*T.K.*, p. 95). Specifically, we might say, then, that the word 'white', 'in what we have called its sensible use, tells us something about that state of affairs which is an object's appearing; it tells us something about the way in which the object appears, just as "slowly" may tell us something about the way in which an object moves' (*T.K.*, p. 96).

It should be obvious from previous discussion that, on the basis of comprehensive experience, a person must take serious exception to Chisholm's adverbial theory of appearing.

[1] R. Chisholm, 'The Theory of Appearing.' *Perceiving, Sensing and Knowing*, R. G. Schwartz, (ed.), Doubleday, New York, 1969, p. 171. Hereafter this book will be referred to as *P.S.K.*

[2] See R. Chisholm, *Theory of Knowledge*, Prentice-Hall, Englewood Cliffs, 1966, p. 94. Hereafter this book will be referred to as *T.K.*

Of course, one 'might say', one might use the word 'white' in an adverbial function. But, as a matter of fact, in standard English usage, it is not so employed in discussing perception.

Further, all colours are not characteristics of or results of the interaction between perceiving organisms and objects perceived. Colour is not a way in which physical objects appear, analogous to 'slowly' as a characteristic of the movement of an object. This is simply contrary to the facts of comprehensive experience.

In brief, it is contended that Chisholm is so anxious to escape from the epistemological gap problems which are involved in positing a screen of sense data, or appearances (content) between the observer and the physical object, that he has recourse to an activity, 'appearing'. He does not provide an adequate description of what is actually involved in the situation because he is the victim of an accepted analysis, and has not taken seriously the more accurate report based on comprehensive experience. In any case the fact that an object appears to a subject who is aware of it, does not rule out the possibility of being aware of the object as such.

VII

Concepts as a source of difficulty

It is claimed by many philosophers that the use of concepts involves one in very serious difficulties in attempting to acquire knowledge of various types of entities.

This is a case of (*a*) concepts guiding or determining what we 'see' and what we don't 'see', for example, in the case of a physical object which is present in the environment. Concepts, it is claimed (*b*) are particularly dangerous also as sources of misinterpretation of a complex situation, leading one to attribute, imaginatively, entities which actually are not 'there'.[1]

It is true that a person looking at a flower may (*a*) literally not see the stamens and pistil, if he is not aware of relevant concepts and hence has no guidance. Or if he does know (about) that the concept

---

[1] See A. J. Ayer, 'Philosophy and Language' in *Clarity is not Enough*, H. D. Lewis (ed.), George Allen and Unwin, London, 1963, p. 417.

357

of a species of flower is linked with a concept of a specific colour, he will notice that specific colour. In the matter (*b*) of misinterpretation, of what is present in awareness, it is notorious that a person who thinks of a member of an opposing political party in terms of the concept evil will apply the worst possible interpretation to behaviour which, as a matter of fact, is thoroughly morally good. He will, for example, imagine ulterior motives in apparently benevolent behaviour.

Thus, it appears to some people that all of us, all the time, inevitably are victims of the set of concepts which we have available, as we are aware of any entity. It is a fact that no entity is present in awareness without some accompanying concepts, apart from early childhood experience. However, it is possible, in many instances, to have only accurately relevant concepts, and a relatively adequate set, and hence avoid omissions and distortions from this source. Incidentally, this claim is made or implied by the devotees of any point of view which is used to criticise another, that is, they claim to be able to identify accurately, distorting or impeding entities, in the experiences of others. Obviously some people are not free of interference by concepts, but the possibility of escape is recognised as a goal which lies within human reach in some situations.

Specifically, it is possible to force oneself to check preconceived notions about observed facts and, thus, to find, for example, good behaviour, at least on occasion, even in the enemy camp (when it exists there). In the matter of obtaining knowledge of flowers, one's range of conceptual competence can be extended.

In general, there are many instances where entities and relevant concepts are present in our awareness, despite our previously accepted conceptual prejudices or general orientation, from which we have escaped. In any case, when a stone falls on a person's foot, he is aware of it, not because of his conceptual orientation, his interest in stones and the law of gravity. Of course, once the entity enters awareness, available concepts are put to work in the process of interpretation. Further, the impact of the object brings, if conditions are satisfactory, the relevant concept into focus, including new concepts.

The conclusion of this discussion of the so-called enslavement by concepts is that an enlightened (comprehensive) person is aware of concepts linked with other entities. Further, if the appropriate concepts are noted, and they can be in many instances, these concepts are aids to awareness and ingredients of knowledge, not barriers of effective awareness, that is knowing or knowledge.

In the context of the preceding discussion, some comments on the following diagram are relevant:

The familiar so-called 'duck-rabbit' diagram may seem to lend credence to the claim that what we see, either the head of a rabbit or the head of a duck, is controlled by our interest, or by suggestions, and hence in most cases by concepts. In other words, what we see is what we want to or are told to see. This as a matter of fact is what occurs. However, this situation is not a matter of enslavement to concepts or interests—preventing us from adequate observation of things as they are. As a matter of fact, the one diagram serves as a picture of both the head of a rabbit and the head of a duck. What we see when looking at the diagram depends on and is determined by interest or suggested interpretation. But it is not an analogous situation to not seeing stamens because we are ignorant of the concept or are not interested in them, nor is it a case of misinterpretation. The diagram as such is a picture (physical entity) of a duck's head and of a rabbit's head. The seen rabbit's head and the seen duck's head are not analogous to the seen corridor and the seen stand in the case of the diagram below.

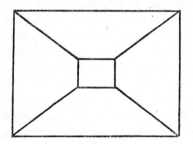

The seen stand and corridor are physically based resultants in alternating presence, regardless of attempts at conceptual control. The first diagram, to repeat, as such, is a physical picture of both a duck's head and a rabbit's head. The seen heads do not alternate in the same fashion as in the case of the stand and the corridor.

Knowledge of other minds: Hook, Ryle, Yolton, Austin and Scriven

One of the thorny and recurrent problems in the discussion of knowledge is that of the knowledge of other minds.

As noted in Chapter 6, comprehensive experience reports that it is possible, under favourable conditions, to have knowing about and knowledge about other minds but not immediate knowing or knowledge concerning them. In the approach of Experiential Realism to the problem of knowledge about other minds, reliance was placed (*a*) on an observed similarity. Specifically, one person observes bodily behaviour in another person which is similar to his own when his own body is influenced by his own mental states. On this basis he claims to have circumstantial evidence that the other body is likewise similarly influenced by a mind. This is frequently termed 'the argument from analogy'. Strictly speaking, this is not a case of an analogy. An analogy involves two situations where there are both similarities and differences. For example, death, that is the departing of life, is said to be analogous to the ebbing of the tide (of an ocean). Life and water are entities which are of very different types, but have in common a characteristic which is similar only in a very general sense. On the other hand, the two human bodies are occurrences of the same entity. The two minds are likewise occurrences of the same entity. Further, the causal relation between them in each case is a matter of two occurrences of the same entity. In brief, the factor of difference is not present in the same sense as in the instances of life and water. Hence, in the context of this discussion, the so-called 'argument from analogy' concerning the knowledge of other minds will be termed the 'similarity' argument. There is also (*b*) the acceptance of the reports offered by other people whose reliability has been accepted.

Sidney Hook rejects the 'similarity' approach for the following reason: 'Long before we are ever in a position to make such comparisons, we are already convinced that . . . humans feel because on the basis of our own feelings toward them we get an answering response which is appropriate.'[1] Here Hook is merely objecting to excessive reliance on a clear formulation of the assumed similarity. There is no reason why a clear formulation of this approach should be rejected. It is just a little more sophisticated than the more primitive

[1] S. Hook, 'A Pragmatic Note', in *Dimensions of Mind*, New York University Press, New York, 1960, p. 203.

type of experience Hook mentions in which, as a matter of fact, by implication the similarity assumption is involved. More specifically, the 'argument' is a rational analysis, while the more primitive approach is a matter of recognised appropriate reaction to a feeling, in oneself and in others.

Ryle's attack on the similarity approach is more drastic. He remarks that even if a person has privileged access to his own inner states (which Ryle for the most part rejects) there is a crucial defect in this argument. His claim is that the behaviour of people differs very markedly and therefore the 'analogy' falls flat (*C.M.*, p. 53).

The reply of Experiential Realism is that while, of course, there are individual differences in human behaviour, there are nevertheless fairly common patterns in overt behaviour. Where these occur the similarity approach is appropriate.

Another objection to the argument from similarity in overt bodily behaviour claims that a person's view of his own inner life is developed as the result of his interaction with other persons. Thus one does not start with a clear view of one's inner life (mind) and its relation to one's own body and then argue from other bodies to other minds.

The response of Experiential Realism is as follows. Granted that many of the ideas we have about the characteristics of our own minds are suggested to us by our fellow-men. They tell us we are scoundrels or expect us to be honest—and we are what they say, in some instances, as a result of their suggestions. However, all this operates in a context of a person's awareness of his own mind and some of its characteristics. They are there regardless of how others talk or act with reference to him. Further, the 'imposed by others' characteristics imply a present mind with some characteristics.

A number of contemporary philosophers are in general agreement with Experiential Realism's confidence that there can be knowledge about other minds, and in particular its use of the similarity approach.

In general terms Yolton notes with approval the fact that 'For Wisdom, "how a man looks and what he does, though it does not constitute his state of mind, provides good evidence from which we may infer his state of mind".'[1]

Of particular importance (as far as Experiential Realism is concerned) is Austin's recognition that there is natural linkage between an emotion (an inner state) and its display, in overt behaviour. 'They constitute

[1] J. Yolton, *Thinking and Perceiving*, Open Court, La Salle, 1962, pp. 66–7.

part of a comprehensive pattern.'[1] Thus Austin remarks that 'it is our confidence in the general pattern that makes us apt to say we "know" another man is angry when we have only observed parts of the pattern' (O.M., p. 181).

The 'similarity' approach to knowledge about other minds must be used with care. There are well-known instances of deliberate deception where a person pretends to have a specific emotion and behaves overtly accordingly. There is also the ever-present possibility of misinterpretation. A man may act as most men usually do when they are angry, but the exceptional person in question may merely be manifesting a desire to emphasise what he is saying. However, these problems are not insuperable, as Wittgenstein aptly remarks: 'It is certainly possible to be convinced by evidence that someone is in such-and-such a state of mind, that, for instance, he is not pretending.' (*P.I.*, p. 228).

Austin is very confident about this situation. Thus he states: 'There are . . . established procedures for dealing with suspected cases of deception or of misunderstanding or of inadvertence . . . special cases where doubts arise and require resolving, are contrasted with the normal cases which hold the field' (O.M., p. 184).

A second (*b*) source of knowledge about other minds, namely reports provided by the persons possessing the other minds, must now be briefly considered.

Though Ryle holds a view of mind less rich in content than some philosophies, including Experiential Realism, he contends there is knowledge about other minds which is obtained 'more directly' than by a similarity argument. The medium is, broadly speaking, language (including gestures). 'I find out your inclinations and your moods more directly than this [that is by so-called 'analogy']. I hear and understand your conversational avowals, your interjections and your tones of voice; I see and understand your gestures and facial expressions' (*C.M.*, p. 115).

In like fashion Austin reports: 'In the complex of occurrences which induces us to say we know another man is angry . . . a peculiar place is occupied by the man's own statement as to what his feelings are. In the usual case, we accept the statement without question' (O.M., p. 185).

The question of the reliability of another person's reports concerning his mind (whatever in one's view the mind is) obviously

[1] See O.M., p. 180–1.

raises difficulties. Here again the problem of deception and mis-interpretation are not insuperable. Thus Scriven, agreeing with Experiential Realism, remarks in general terms that 'one can have overwhelming inductive support for the veracity of an agent from areas not involving his introspective reports and extrapolate it to support a report of consciousness of [for example] pain, provided great care is taken in teaching the language of feelings.'[1]

At this point it is well to note Austin's apt remark that 'believing in other persons, in authority and testominy, is an essential part of the act of communicating, an act which we all constantly perform. It is as much an irreducible part of our experience as, say, giving promises, or playing competitive games, or even sensing coloured patches' (*O.M.*, p. 186).

In the context of the preceding discussion, the following remarks by Ryle concerning the knowing of other minds can be evaluated expeditiously. 'To find that most people have minds . . . is simply to find that they are able and prone to do certain sorts of things, and this we do by witnessing the sorts of things they do.'

Ryle then changes his approach and states:

'Certainly there are some things which I can find out about you only, or best, through being told of them by you. . . . If you do not divulge the contents of your silent soliloquies and other imaginings, I have no other sure way of finding out what you have been saying or picturing to yourself.'

He then makes a highly significant comment.

'But the sequence of your sensations and imaginings is not the sole field in which your wits and character are shown; perhaps only for lunatics is it more than a small corner of that field. I find out most of what I want to know about your capacities, interests, likes, dislikes, methods and convictions by observing how you conduct your overt doings' (*C.M.*, p. 61).

Here the problem of knowing other minds seems a simple one. We are witnessing what other people do. The mental activities which are not open to public gaze are conveniently reported to us and,

[1] M. Scriven, *Minds and Machines*, A. R. Anderson (ed.), Prentice-Hall, Englewood Cliffs, 1964, p. 42.

anyway, they are relatively unimportant. In both cases Ryle, by implication, has no worry about a supposedly insuperable problem posed by possible deception or misinterpretation. Life is gloriously simple for Ryle at this point in his deliberations.

It is, of course, the case that Ryle is primarily concerned with the overt rather than the covert. His remark that 'perhaps only for lunatics' are covert experiences more than a small corner of the field of mind—to put it mildly, reflects a prejudice in favour of the public and a practical 'disregard' of the fundamental importance of the complex inner life of great men, both of thought and action. In refutation of Ryle, consider Einstein, having an 'inner soliloquy' sitting quietly for days, indeed, for most of many months, formulating thoughts (linkages of concepts) which in due course issued in a vast range of conclusions. Among these, according to the mythology (or fact) of science, were intellectual sanctions for the Manhattan Project. These led to the production of the first atomic bomb.

IX

Sources of knowledge

Traditional discussions of knowledge are concerned with the question of the source of knowledge, ways of knowing. There have been devotees of sense and devotees of reason (the awareness of and manipulation of concepts). Some have placed strong emphasis on the methods of science or logic. What one accepts as the preferred method is reflected in what is regarded as the content of knowledge. Let us turn to a brief discussion of these interrelated matters.

Sense or reason: Hobbes and Descartes

The tracing of all knowledge to its reputed origin in sense experience is typified by Hobbes's succinct remark: 'The original . . . is that which we call *sense*, for there is no conception in a man's mind which hath not at first, totally or by parts, been begotten upon the organs of sense. The rest are derived from that original.'[1]

The opposing view, namely that sense experience is not a sound or adequate basis for knowledge, is resolutely expounded by Des-

[1] T. Hobbes, *Leviathan*, in *English Philosophers from Bacon to Mill*, E. A. Burtt (ed.), Modern Library, 1939, p. 131.

cartes. He refers to a piece of wax, and notes that the qualities we apprehend through the senses, before it is brought close to a fire, are different from those thus experienced afterwards. In answer to the question: What are the real qualities of the wax? Descartes replies: 'Certainly it cannot be anything that I observed by means of the senses, since everything in the field of taste, smell, sight, touch, and hearing are changed, and . . . the same wax nevertheless remains.'[1] Descartes contends that on the other hand, we have, for example, clear ideas of length, width, thickness, but confused ones of temperature and colour. He concludes that clear ideas are alone reliable. These are obtained by the proper use of the intellect (reason).

Descartes thus is convinced that only reason (understanding, intellect) is the agency whereby we grasp what is clear and distinct and unchanging, that is the only means by which knowledge can be obtained (*M.*, p. 31).

In a classic passage Descartes illustrates how by the 'light of nature' (reason), without any prior appeal to sense experience, one can know a number of basic principles (propositions):

'Now it is obvious . . . that there must be at least as much reality in the total efficient cause as in its effect, for whence can the effect derive its reality, if not from its cause . . . from this it follows, not only that something cannot be derived from nothing, but also that the more perfect . . . cannot be a consequence of the less perfect' (*M.*, p. 36).

The position of Experiential Realism with reference to the question of the source of knowledge in brief, is this. Knowledge (what is known), is of many sorts. Physical objects, minds, concepts, physically based resultants and their characteristics constitute immediate knowledge, if present to awareness. In some cases these entities are apprehended by sense experience, such as seeing, hearing, etc. This is the case with physical objects and some of their characteristics, also some of the characteristics of mind, namely mental content such as many imagination and memory images. Likewise one may be said to 'sense' pleasure, pain, itches, etc. However, the awareness of concepts, mind, value, and some relations is not sensory, at least in the traditional use of the term.

[1] Descartes, *Meditation*, Liberal Arts, New York, ed., 1951, p. 27. Hereafter this book will be referred to as *M*.

When one has knowledge about entities which are not present to awareness at the moment, what are present to awareness are propositions, and in some instances, words and images. It is of course the case that concepts, and combinations of them (propositions) are used in the process of reasoning, but there is no faculty of reason which grasps concepts (and propositions). A mind is aware of non-sensory entities, namely concepts (and propositions). Thus reason is not a source of knowledge in any ultimate sense. Concepts and propositions record what one is aware of. In any case it is essential to realise that the non-imaginary linkage of concepts to form a proposition requires prior sensing experience, or some other awareness, of particular entities. Thus, for example the causal principle stated by Descartes is not derived from reason. Likewise the clarity and distinctness of ideas (groups of concepts) concerning physical objects is determined ultimately by reference to the objects. A process of reasoning may bring into focus what is not known in a clearly organised fashion. A process of reasoning may provide explanatory hypotheses and so contribute to the finding of knowledge, but in the last analysis immediate knowledge (and 'knowledge about' based on it) is derived from awareness sensory and non-sensory.[1]

In the case of 'knowledge how', the possession and use of skills, awareness of the environment is present while exercising the skill. In some instances propositions are used as guiding principles.

Knowledge in storage is the result of the acquiring of knowledge of the other kinds—and its retention.

In brief, in view of the complexity of knowledge, it is simply naive to claim that all knowledge is acquired by sense experience. In some cases this is so, in others it is not. Reason is not an autonomous source of knowledge in any ultimate sense. Reasoning has an instrumental function—facilitating awareness in some cases.

In the context of these remarks, reference to those who claim that the methods and results of natural science are the key to the problem of knowledge is relevant.

[1] 'First-hand knowledge is the ultimate basis of intellectual life. To a large extent book-learning conveys second-hand information, and as such can never rise to the importance of immediate practice. . . . What the learned world tends to offer is one second-hand scrap of information illustrating ideas derived from another second-hand scrap of information. The second-handedness of the learned world is the secret of its mediocrity. It is tame because it has never been scared by facts' (A. N. Whitehead, *The Aims of Education*, Macmillan, New York, 1929, p. 79).

Methods and results of natural science: Ayer and Whitehead

Consider, for example, the confident pronouncement by Ayer: 'There is no field of experience which cannot, in principle, be brought under some form of scientific law, and no type of speculative knowledge about the world which it is, in principle, beyond the power of science to give' (*L.T.L.*, p. 44).

An appeal to comprehensive experience leads Experiential Realism to agree wholeheartedly with the following pointed and pungent remarks by Whitehead. 'The man with a method good for purposes of his dominant interests, is a *pathological case* in respect to . . . the coordination of this method with a more complete experience. Priests and scientists, statesmen and men of business, philosophers and mathematicians, are all alike in this respect.'[1]

For example, Whitehead is quite prepared to admit that measurement is a valuable source of knowledge, but it is not the whole story. One does not fully understand a man by taking his blood pressure. 'Matter-of-fact [the reputed concern of scientists] is an abstraction.' The impact of aesthetic, religious and moral entities is inescapable. They are the disrupting and the energising forces of civilisation. 'The concentration of attention upon matter-of-fact is the supremacy of the desert. Any approach to such triumph bestows on learning "a fugitive, and a cloistered virtue".'[2]

x

Deduction, induction, contradiction: Whitehead and Ayer

A few supplementary remarks on deduction, induction and contradiction are relevant at this point.

Whitehead aptly notes the dangers implicit in excessive reliance on deduction.

'The primary method of mathematics is deduction; the primary method of philosophy [a comprehensive approach to entities experienced] is descriptive generalisation. Under the influence of mathematics, deduction has been foisted onto philosophy as its

---

[1] A. N. Whitehead, *The Function of Reason*, Princeton, 1929, p. 8, emphasis added.
[2] Idem, *Modes of Thought*, Macmillan, New York, 1938, pp. 25–7.

standard method, instead of taking its true place as an essential auxiliary mode of verification whereby to test the scope of generalities.'[1]

Ayer's remarks concerning induction raise a crucial issue. 'It appears that there is no possible way of solving the problem of induction, as it is ordinarily conceived.'[2] He interprets the situation thus: 'This means that it is a fictitious problem, since all genuine problems are at least theoretically capable of being solved.' In any case he contends that 'the credit of natural science is not impaired by the fact that some philosophers continue to be puzzled by it' (*L.T.L.*, p. 47).

This refusal to be dismayed when some philosophers claim to be puzzled is in accordance with the approach of Experiential Realism. However, on the other hand, induction is a method used by natural science, and in other sorts of thinking, and should be employed even if one cannot provide guarantees that it will be effective. Thus it seems strange indeed to state, as Ayer does: 'All genuine problems are at least theoretically capable of being solved.' To set up a distinction between genuine and fictitious problems on the basis of whether or not they are capable of being solved seems unjustified. A problem is a problem regardless of whether or not it is theoretically capable of being solved. The 'capability of solution' question is in itself a problem. Further, a problem which today seems incapable of solution, even in theory, may be viewed in a more hopeful light tomorrow. It is simply a departure from standard use of language, or a reflection of some philosophers' quest for certainty or exuberant over-optimism, to claim that all genuine problems are capable of being solved.

In the realm of logic, both in its theoretical system-building and its practical applications in attempting to obtain knowledge, great emphasis is placed on the principle of contradiction as a criterion of acceptability. Whitehead issues a useful warning which serves to correct over-emphasis on the avoidance of contradiction. His remarks are not to be interpreted as a recommendation that it be shelved in all or even most cases. There are many, many situations where its use is, of course, appropriate. He states: 'In formal logic, a con-

---

[1] A. N. Whitehead, *Process and Reality*, Macmillan, New York, 1929, pp. 15–16.
[2] In so far as it involves a general statement and *all* facts have not been observed.

tradiction is the signal of a defeat: but in the evolution of real know-ledge it marks the first step in progress towards a victory.'[1]

More specifically he explains: 'A mere logical contradiction cannot in itself point to more than the necessity of some readjustments, possibly of a very minor character' (*S.M.W.*, p. 229). In effect, he is agreeing that a person should not engage in a contradiction such as 'Black is not black'. However, when one scientist reports that the atomic weight of nitrogen is X and another claims that it is $X + 1$, this is a sign that further investigation is necessary. Further, in a complex situation it may well be appropriate to report both sameness and difference. For example, a person during his career is the same person, but is different in the sense that he undergoes a process of development. The apparent contradiction of same and different is not a cause for concern.

[1] A. N. Whitehead, *Science and the Modern World*, Cambridge ed., 1946, p. 231. Hereafter this book will be referred to as *S.M.W.*

17

MAN AND HIS ENVIRONMENT

I

Causation (general discussion): Hume and Whitehead

The discussion of causation outlined in Chapter 7 regards as a cause any entity, physical or mental or concept, which produces effects, either physical or mental. This position is contrary to the views of many philosophers and scientists.

Consider the influential and widely accepted view formulated by David Hume. He states: 'When we look about us towards external objects, and consider the operation of causes, we are never able, in a *single instance*, to discover any power or *necessary connection*; any quality, which binds the effect to the cause, and renders the one an *infallible* consequence of the other.'[1] Thus he contends that all events (entities) are found to be 'entirely loose and separate' (p. 76).

Cause is defined to be 'an object, followed by another, and where all the objects similar to the first are followed by objects similar to the second.' Thus, there is present to awareness a 'constant conjunction' of discreet entities. In due course 'the appearance of a cause always conveys the mind, by a customary transition, to the idea of the effect' (*H.*, p. 79).

On the basis of comprehensive experience it is found that, as a matter of fact, the relation of cause and effect, in any situation, is not that of absolutely separate and distinct entities. True, the cause is not the effect and to that extent they are different, but in the cause-effect relation there is an experienced continuity.[2] In some instances there is an experience of force (power), as when a man is aware that

---

[1] D. Hume, *An Enquiry Concerning Human Understanding*, Open Court, La Salle, 1946, p. 64. Hereafter this book will be referred to as *H*.

[2] See for example, C. J. Ducasse, *Philosophy and Phenomenological Research*, vol. 26, no. 2, 1965, p. 177 and also items listed in the next footnote.

he forces himself to pay attention to a theory.[1] In other cases, though one is aware of a cause producing an effect (as when the impact of the cue on the ball causes the ball to move)—there is, however, no awareness[2] of the exertion of force as in the first illustration.

If 'necessary connection' means a natural linkage, such a connection is found in some cases, as in the examples given in footnote 1, below. However, there can be no claim of an 'infallible consequence', that is no exceptions can possibly occur. This is so because one cannot make claims which are certain (in the sense of established fact) about what has not been (or is) present to awareness. Thus, there can be no legitimate claim of certainty about causal relations in the future no matter how often they have held in the past.

By proposing to define causation in terms of 'constant conjunction' and 'expectation'[3] of conjunction, Hume neglects the essential nature of causation and refers to peripheral factors. In other words, his treatment of causation is partial.

Even if a cause produces an effect only once, that is, there is no constant conjunction (as when Leonardo painted the Last Supper), it is still a cause if it produces its effect.[4] The same is true with reference to the first occurrence of a cause-effect relation, which is repeated, for instance, an atomic bomb explosion and its resultant cloud of dust. Even though the cause-effect sequence was repeated in the case of the bomb, the fundamental factor is not the repetition, but the producing of the effect by the cause. It is of course the case that, having observed a sequence of cause and effect on many occasions, one comes to expect it to continue, and predict it, but this is not an

---

[1] See for example S. Alexander, *Space, Time and Deity*, Macmillan, New York, 1927, vol. I, p. 8. Likewise I. A. Melden refers to 'cases in which force of mind, great effort, or great struggles are involved as habit is resisted or temptations conquered' (*Essays in Philosophical Psychology*, D. F. Gustafson (ed.), Doubleday, New York, 1964, p. 61). Whitehead reports that when a bright light causes him to blink he has a 'feeling of causality', that is of force and continuity from the light to the blink (A. N. Whitehead, *Adventures of Ideas*, Macmillan, New York, 1929, pp. 265–6).

[2] As noted on several occasions, the 'awareness' locution is employed to report the presence of an entity. The only evidence that an entity is present is that one is aware of it.

[3] The habit of expecting it to recur.

[4] See C. J. Ducasse, 'Determinism, Freedom and Impossibility', *Determinism and Freedom* (S. Hook, ed.), Collier Books, New York, 1961, p. 164. See also B. Blanchard, 'The Case for Determinism', same volume, p. 27.

essential character of the causal situation.[1] In any case there are constant conjunctions 'which are not causal situations', as where spring follows winter and we expect it. 'Constant conjunction' and expectation are not enough.

Awareness of a sort of sequence of events no doubt assists one in identifying a new cause and a new effect of this sort, on first occurrence. For example, the first time an atomic bomb was exploded its cloud of dust was identified as an effect because of previous experience of bombs producing clouds of dust. It might be argued that the first explosion of an atomic bomb, since it was a bomb, is simply a case of a well-known constant conjunction, that is, an explosion—cloud of dust. But to repeat, the essential nature of a cause is that it produces effects. Even when confronted by an object, which cannot be assigned to a specific sort or set in the context of a familiar constant conjunction, one can be aware of its causal function, on occasion. That is, when its causal impact is unmistakable its effects obviously follow from it. For example, if a person pours an unknown (to him) fluid over his hand and it produces a severe burn, he has no legitimate doubt of its causal efficacy, even it he does not know it is an acid.[2]

However, in general agreement with Hume, Experiential Realism admits that the first time a person, such as a Laplander, experiences an object of an unfamiliar class, for instance a 'lifesaver' candy, he cannot know, merely by looking at or thinking about the lifesaver as such, that it produces nourishment and a pleasant taste. Knowledge of its causal efficacy requires experience of its ability to produce effects (results). They, the effects, cannot be rationally deduced independently of such experience.

Further discussion of causation can appropriately occur in the context of an examination of the problem of the relation of body and mind.

II

Body-mind: Leibniz and Spinoza

There are philosophers who argue that mind cannot causally affect body, and vice versa, because they are different types of entity. One

---

[1] See Ducasse, above article, pp. 163–4; Blanchard, above article, pp. 26–7.

[2] See A. N. Whitehead, *Process and Reality*, The Macmillan Co., New York, 1929, pp. 290–1.

variation of this theme is found in the *Monadology* of Leibniz. He regards substances as mutually exclusive. A mind is composed of substances (monads). So is a body. Hence there is no possibility of interaction because each monad is self-contained—or as he puts it: monads do not have windows.[1]

This, however, is a case of a thought model imaginatively created out of one sort of human experience—grossly misinterpreted. There is, of course, a rich inner life of the mind but it is not cut off from external influences, or denied the exercise of influence on external entities. To regard everything in the world as composed of these exclusively inward-looking centres of mental energy is to engage in a flight of unjustified speculative fancy. In any case, such a procedure is simply contrary to the experienced interaction of body and mind.[2]

An important variation of the 'no interaction' theme is found in the philosophy of Spinoza. It is based on the theory that there is one substance, not many. He regards body and mind as attributes of substance but they are essentially different.[3] Thus while there are causal interactions between physical entities and between mental entities, 'the body cannot determine the mind to think, nor the mind the body to remain in motion, or at rest, or in any other state'. (*E.*, III. 2) His point of view is expressed in the technical terms thus: 'mind and body are one and the same thing, which, now under the attribute of thought, now under the attribute of extension, is conceived' (*E.*, III, 2 note). Because mind and body are attributes of one substance 'the order or concatenation of things [entities] is the same under whatever attribute Nature is conceived'. The resultant actual paralleling of mental and physical sequences is the source of the mistaken notion that there is interaction between them.

[1] See Leibniz, *Selections*, P. Wiener (ed.), Scribner, New York, 1951, pp. 533–4.

[2] It is interesting to find A. J. Ayer taking, at one point, roughly the same approach to the so-called body-mind problems as Experiential Realism. He states: 'The problems with which philosophers have vexed themselves in the past, concerning the possibility of bridging the "gulf" between mind and matter in knowledge or in action, are all fictitious problems arising out of the senseless metaphysical conception of mind and matter, or minds and material things, as "substances".' He then proceeds to state that there 'can be no *a priori* objections to the existence either of causal or epistemological connections between minds and material things' (A. J. Ayer, *Language, Truth and Logic*, Gollancz, 1936, p. 192). Hereafter this book will be referred to as *L.T.L.*

[3] B. Spinoza, *Ethics*, Everyman Edition, J. M. Dent, London, 1928, Book I, Proposition 10. Hereafter this book will be referred to as *E*.

His rationalistic orientation is reflected in the term 'conceived'. The point being made is that, since mind and body are conceived to be mutually exclusive attributes of one substance, that is what they are. The apparent interaction of mind and body can be explained in terms of an analogy (this is not Spinoza's)—that of the two sides of a sheet of paper. A sequence of changes in surface shape of one side of the paper, as it is bent, is paralleled by a sequence of changes on the other side. It is the case that there is no interaction of one side acting as cause on the other, it being the effect.

Spinoza does not restrict himself to an appeal as to how we (ought to) conceive mind and body. He attempts to support his 'double aspect' theory by a reference to our experience of minds and bodies. Thus he remarks for example: 'experience more than sufficiently teaches that men govern nothing with more difficulty than their tongues.' He then proceeds to refer to extreme cases and states that 'a madman, a talkative woman, a child . . . think they speak by the free decision of the mind, when, in truth, they cannot put a stop to the desire to talk.' (*E.*, III, 2 note).

As far as comprehensive experience is concerned, such an argument is not conclusive. The fact that some men talk when it would be better for them to be quiet does not prove that mind cannot, or does not, causally control body. Rather it demonstrates that one sort of mental entity (such as anger) has caused the tongue to function as it does (to wag). If another sort of mental entity, say, a resolve to be silent, had been decisive in the situation, it would cause the tongue to be dormant. The expression of one's appetites can similarly be interpreted. Some men by mental effort can prevent the expression of the desire for one more drink. In the case of other men the desire for another drink issues in the expression of that desire. The drink is taken. In both cases a mental cause produces a physical effect.

The fact that a person thinks or feels that he is free to do what he actually does not do (contrary to Spinoza) does not constitute a denial of the fact that mind can and does influence the body on occasion. It may be merely a false assessment of the type of mental cause which is operative or an ignorance of what mental causes are operative.

In some cases, of course, mental causes are not operative—only physical ones are present. The operation of the cancer virus is a case in point.

The preceding discussion of the facts of human experience serves to refute the metaphysical theory which Spinoza offers concerning the non-interaction of body and mind. It is to be noted that in the experience referred to by Spinoza, mental causation was considered. Cases of physical causes producing mental effects will be examined subsequently.[1]

Voluntary action, mental causes: Wittgenstein and Ryle

A great deal of contemporary discussion of the place of causes in human behaviour has sprung from a series of remarks by Wittgenstein concerning a situation where a person raises his arm. Some of the relevant Wittgenstein foundation comments are as follows: 'We say significantly that a thing doesn't simply happen to us, but that we do it.'[2]

He then attempts further clarification: 'When "I raise my arm", my arm goes up. . . what is left over if I subtract the fact that my arm goes up from the fact that I raise my arm?' It is important to note that Wittgenstein rules out one possible factor. He states: 'When I raise my arm I do not usually *try* to raise it' (*P.I.*, p. 161).

In general, he is proposing to reject any attempt to account for an action in terms of an act of will. He is opposed to those who think of willing as an immediate non-causal bringing about. 'When I raise my arm "voluntarily" I do *not* use any instrument to bring the movement about. My wish is not such an instrument either. "Willing, if it is not to be a sort of wishing, must be the action itself. . . ."' When I raise my arm, I have *not* wished it might go up' (*P.I.*, p. 160).

Two other remarks about willing are part of Wittgenstein's discussion: (*a*) 'I bring about the act [for example] of willing to swim by jumping into the water. . . . (*b*) it makes no sense to speak of willing willing. "Willing" is not . . . the name of any voluntary action' (*P.I.*, p. 159).

From the point of view of Experiential Realism, Wittgenstein is correct in saying that when I raise my arm it is not merely a case of the arm going up. As a matter of fact I do it. Roughly speaking he

[1] See the valuable discussion by P. F. Strawson; *Individuals*, Doubleday, New York, 1963, Chapters 3 and 4.
[1] L. Wittgenstein, *Philosophical Investigations*, Blackwell, Oxford, 1953, p. 159. Hereafter this book will be referred to as *P.I.*

seems to be referring to causal initiative on the part of the person concerned.

However, in the context of comprehensive experience, it is relevant to point out that, as a matter of fact (contrary to Wittgenstein) usually when I raise my arm I wish to raise it, and frequently I exercise an act of will, to carry out the wish, if difficulties are involved in raising it. In this sense, I try to raise my arm. In the context of the ordinary use of language it is not correct to state as Wittgenstein does that 'willing is the action itself'. Thus, willing is sometimes central in the act of raising one's arm, not, at best, a mere incidental factor, or a non-entity. It is, of course, the case that one does not appropriately say that one 'wills willing'. As a matter of fact, a person under certain conditions engages in an act of will. The act of willing functions as a cause for action, or is an ingredient in action (in one sense of action), in many instances. The causes for the act of willing are many and varied. If a person jumps into the water, he as a result has a will to swim, if he is a certain type of person. On the other hand, a person sitting on a deck may have a will to swim because of the example of his friends, or a desire for exercise.

In claiming that willing is not an 'immediate non-causal bringing about', Wittgenstein is not open to objection. However, he is obviously contrary to comprehensive experience when he contends that 'I do not use any instrument' when I raise my arm voluntarily. Will is an instrument (at least on occasion), while the nervous and muscular system are always such.

It strikes one that Wittgenstein is so anxious to remove what he considers to be mistaken explanations, or rather descriptions of what is involved in raising one's arm—apart from the arm going up—that he has neglected to give a positive answer to his question.

In any case, Ryle, stressing a verbal approach to the place of will in action, is simply incorrect when he contends that no-one ordinarily, apart from technical nonsense, ever refers to an act of will, strong or weak, being exercised in order to produce physical results.[1] In refutation, consider, for example, the then gallant soldier, Petain, who in World War I expressed a will which was influential in the battle of Verdun—'They shall not pass'.

[1] G. Ryle, *The Concept of Mind*, Barnes & Noble, New York, 1946, p. 64. Hereafter this book will be referred to as *C.M.*

Ryle continues his attempt to eliminate commonly accepted mental causal entities. Motives, for example, he claims are primarily dispositional. They are not causes which produce effects. Rather, the so-called cause-effect relation is merely a case of the motive and its manifestations. Specifically, it is wrong to claim that vanity is a feeling which as an occult cause produces an effect (*C.M.*, pp. 86, 110).

He provides the following illuminating clarification. Motives, being dispositions, do not determine a person to action in a particular situation any more than the brittleness of glass is the cause of glass shattering. The glass is caused to break (for example) by the impact of a stone. Human action is caused by some preceding factor. The disposition and the brittleness are present but they do not exercise causal efficacy. Consider another example. A polite man passes the salt when it is requested. But the cause of passing is the request, not the disposition to be polite. In any case a disposition is general in nature and hence cannot legitimately be regarded as the specific cause for a specific effect (*C.M.*, p. 113).

A number of criticisms of Ryle's view arise in the context of comprehensive experience. As a matter of fact, a feeling of vanity does on occasion cause a particular action. It is true that the situation in which the person is operating has a bearing on the origin of the feeling and the way in which it is expressed. The fact that a specific feeling may arise as a result of a propensity in a person, and when aroused expresses itself in a characteristic behaviour pattern, does not rule out its function as a cause. Such a feeling functioning as a cause has nothing occult about it. It is an entity found in the world of experience and is not the product of superstitious imagination or addiction to ghostly presences.

The references to a stone and the brittleness of glass exemplify Ryle's contention that in explaining an occurrence, a causal factor is not the only legitimate one. Specifically, he contrasts an approach to explanation based on the analogy of (*a*) 'The glass broke because a stone hit it', with the alternative (*b*) 'The glass broke because it (the glass) was brittle.'

Ryle provides a very illuminating comment concerning the second, *b* type of explanation. 'When we say that the glass broke when struck because it was brittle, the "because" clause does not report a happening or a cause . . . People commonly say of explanations of this . . . kind that they give the "reason" for the glass breaking when struck'

(*C.M.*, p. 89). Ryle claims that in dealing with human motives the second approach should be used, not the first.[1]

In the context of comprehensive experience it is appropriate to remark that the glass analogy does not hold. Motives are experienced, on occasion, to be causes, not as in the case of the brittleness of the glass, a mere condition which enables a cause to produce an effect. If the analogy is to hold, one would note that a strong feeling or emotion has an impact on a person, if he is susceptible, leading to (causing) action in a fashion similar to the impact of a stone on glass—if it is brittle—causing it to break.

Ryle argues in favour of his view that the alternative one *a* has difficulties in dealing with other people. He says: 'Even if the agent reported, what people never do report, that he had experienced a vanity itch just before he boasted, this would be very weak evidence that the itch caused the action, since for all we know, the cause was any one of a thousand other synchronous happenings' (*C.M.*, p. 90).

In reply several comments are relevant. In the first place, contrary to Ryle, people do report the presence of a 'vanity itch' before proceeding to boast. Secondly, it seems strange, in view of his preceding remarks, to find Ryle even considering a vanity itch as possibly a cause. Furthermore, to merely say 'for all we know' the cause might have been something else is not decisive. The reply of Experiential Realism is this. In some cases where due care is taken, a vanity itch is found to be, in a limited situation, the cause of boasting.

The dichotomy which Ryle sets up between causes in the physical

---

[1] Ryle's disinclination to regard motives and other mental entities as causes, preferring rather to term them 'reasons', is given an ingenious treatment by Waismann. 'An action may be viewed as a series of movements caused by some physiological stimuli in the "Only rats, no men" sense; or as something that has a purpose or a meaning. . . . An action in the first sense is determined by *causes*, an action in the second sense by *motives* or *reasons*' (F. Waismann, 'Language Strata', in *Logic and Language*, A. Flew (ed.), Doubleday, New York, 1965, p. 247).

Obviously a need for clarification arises. In the answer to the question: 'Well, now, do you believe that if you are writing a letter you are engaged in two different activities?' Waismann replies in a Spinozistic fashion. 'No; I mean that there are two different ways of looking at the thing; just as there are two different ways of looking at a sentence: a series of noises produced by a human agent; or as a vehicle of thought.' (*Ibid.*, p. 247).

This, however, is only an ingenious subterfuge. An action as discussed has a cause. It is not merely a matter of choice in interpretation.

realm and reasons in the mental is artificial.[1] It seems to be ultimately a question of the use of words. In that context, it is to be noted that the word 'reason' is frequently, in standard use, applied to causes (what produces results), as in 'What was the reason for the collapse of the building?' Answer: 'It was destroyed by a bomb blast', a physical cause. Further, the term 'cause' is (in standard use) applied to motives resulting in mental effects or bodily actions. Consider, for example: 'Worry is the cause of his pain', or 'What cause have you to denounce him?' Answer: 'I hate the fellow.'

IV

Mental causation in doubt because of lack of knowledge of machinery and extent: Hume, Spinoza, Vesey, Anscombe and Abelson

One recurring line of argument against the view of Experiential Realism, concerning the causal influence of mind on body, takes the form of a claim that serious, if not complete, doubt is cast on this theory because we do not now have adequate knowledge of the machinery of interaction, or the extent of interaction.

Specifically, Hume remarks: 'The motion of our body follows upon the command of our will. . . . But the means, by which this is effected . . . for ever escapes our most diligent enquiry' (*H.*, p. 66). Technically speaking, the supposed influence of a spiritual substance over a material one is a vast mystery. Further, he argues that if we claim to be conscious of a power of will to effect bodily changes 'we must know its connection with the effect; we must know the secret union of soul and body, and the nature of both these substances' (*H.*, p. 67). There is a further problem: 'Why has the will an influence over the

---

[1] 'For, contrary to what is sometimes alleged, causation of a physical by a psychical event, or of a psychical event by stimulation of a physical sense organ, is not in the least paradoxical. The causality relation, whether defined in terms of regularity of succession or [preferably] in terms of single antecedent difference does not presuppose at all that its cause-term and its effect-term both belong to the same ontological category but only that both of them be *events*' (C. Ducasse, in *Dimensions of Mind*, S. Hood (ed.), New York University Press, New York, 1960, p. 88). For the contention that there are mental causes, see for example, S. Alexander, *Space, Time and Deity*, Macmillan, 1927, vol. I, p. 8; B. Blanchard, in *Determinism or Freedom*, S. Hook (ed.), Collier Books, New York, 1961, pp. 26-7.

tongue and fingers, not over the heart and liver?' (*H.*, p. 67). We know of no reason for this situation (*H.*, p. 70).[1]

An interesting supplement to this argument is provided by Spinoza, who claims that since we do not fully know what a body by itself can do, we are in no position to identify reputed cases of bodily action which are caused or controlled by mental causes. Indeed we would do well to consider more carefully what a body can do by itself. He notes that animals do many things, without thought, which far surpass human ingenuity. Also sleep-walkers perform stunts which they would not dare to do when consciously controlling their activities (see *E.*, III, 2 note).

From the point of view of comprehensive experience the preceding contentions are open to serious objection. It is, of course, the case that we do not have complete knowledge of what a body or mind can do, or how they do what they do. Nevertheless, as in the case of other complex activities, one is not obliged to deny that causes produce effects on the grounds that one does not now know in detail all about the phenomena under consideration, how or why they occur. Specifically, even if one does not know exactly how or why the nervous system and muscles are used to transform a desire to raise one's arm into the action of raising it, this does not deny the fact that one is aware of the occurrence of this complex causal performance. Further, in dealing with mind-body interaction one is not obliged to accept the substance theory and all the problems entailed by it.

At this point it is relevant to consider Vesey's paper on volition.[2] He refers to Wittgenstein's remark: 'When I raise my arm "voluntarily" I do not use any instrument to bring the movement about' (*V.*, p. 43).

Vesey then contends that if a person claims that he is using his nervous system as an instrument in this case, 'he would be making what Professor Ryle might call a "category mistake joke" ' (*V.*, p. 44).

Vesey proceeds to clarify his position by claiming that when a person is said to move his arm, the actual movement is caused by certain muscles contracting or expanding. These are caused by impulses in the efferent nerves. The impulses are caused by changes in the brain. Having identified these causes, Vesey contends that the agent really does not raise his arm. Indeed he does not really cause the initial

---

[1] See also Spinoza, *Ethics*, III, 2 note and Ryle, *C.M.*, pp. 64–6.

[2] *Philosophical Psychology*, D. F. Gustafson (ed.), Doubleday, New York, 1964, 'Volition'. Hereafter this paper will be referred to as V.

changes in his brain, 'since he is not even conscious of the nature of these changes. Therefore what he *really* does cannot be anything physical at all, but must be something of an altogether different kind, namely mental' (V., pp. 45–6).

The reply of Experiential Realism to such an appeal to ignorance has just been noted. Comprehensive experience reveals the fact that a mental act is capable of producing bodily changes even if all the details of the 'machinery' (how it is done) are not fully known. However, as Vesey himself points out, quite a bit is known about the physiological process involved.

Further, it seems most peculiar for Vesey to claim that all that a man can do (cause) in the arm-raising situation is something mental, not something physical. The point is that Vesey does, contrary to the view just noted, state that a man does raise his arm. In other words he contradicts himself: 'So one does not, in this sense of "will", will one's arm to move; one simply moves it' (V., p. 44).

He also refers to 'the mental state which results in, say, a movement of one's arm' (V., p. 47).

Equally intriguing is his claim that there is confirmation of the fact that the 'mental state of willing consists in having an idea of the movement desired, which somehow triggers off the causal chain ending in the movement' (V., p. 47).

The contention of Experiential Realism that there are mental causes for physical entities, and for mental entities as well, is supported by Anscombe. However, she refuses to regard as causes some mental entities which are so considered by Experiential Realism. Thus she says: 'Mental causes are possible, not only for actions ("The martial music excites me, that is why I walk up and down") but also for feelings and even thoughts. However, she claims: 'In considering actions, it is important to distinguish between mental causes and motives.'[1]

In developing this point of view Anscombe makes two very significant points: (*a*) When a person refers to a motive 'he is not giving a "mental cause" in the sense that I have given to that phrase.' The second (*b*) pronouncement is this: 'It appears to me that the mental causes are seldom more than a very trivial item among the things that it would be reasonable to consider' (I., pp. 326, 327).

Further clarification of the first point is provided by Anscombe

---

[1] G. E. M. Anscombe, 'Intentions', *Proceedings of the Aristotelian Society* LVII (1956–7), pp. 322, 323. Hereafter this paper will be referred to as 'I'.

when she suggests that motives serve to explain actions. Using the familiar 'confusion by language' theme she states: 'We do say: "His love of truth caused him to . . ." no doubt such expressions help us to think that a motive must be what produces or brings about a choice. But this means rather "He did this in that he loved the truth"; it interprets his action' (I., p. 326).

As is usual in a word-oriented approach to a problem, Anscombe makes much of what she claims to be 'proper' use or 'the sense . . . which I [!] have given the phrase'. In this context she claims that though we do talk about motives as causes (as in 'Love of truth caused him to'), nevertheless this is not to be taken seriously or used without an approved translation.

This decision to employ the word 'cause' in a special sense is interesting as an example of neglect of standard ordinary use. But it does not help in coming to grips with the factual problem as to whether motives function to produce results. On the level of at least an apparent factual approach, Anscombe's claim that motives do not cause, rather they explain, is a peculiar point of view. The situation is, as far as comprehensive experience is concerned, that since motives cause (in the ordinary sense of the term) action, they are referred to, and thus can be used in explaining or interpreting an action. In any case, as a matter of fact, it is not the case, as Anscombe contends, that when mental causes are involved they 'are seldom more than a very trivial item among the things that it would be reasonable to consider'. To use Anscombe's own illustration—it seems peculiar to claim that excitement (resulting from martial music) which causes a person to walk up and down is a very trivial item. In brief, Anscombe is obviously neglecting facts and, in addition, contradicting herself.

Abelson is in agreement with Experiential Realism at many points when he notes that a doctor tells his patient that 'the main cause of his illness is mental [i.e., caused by mental factors] rather than physical, or when he tells another patient that a blow on his head has affected his mind'. Here are cases of psycho-physical interaction. It is pointed out that we 'often say that motives (which are mental) cause bodily motions, which are physical, and I see no reason to prohibit this mode of speech so long as we avoid the temptation to picture motives as invisible engines inside our heads'.[1]

---

[1] R. Abelson, *Dimensions of Mind*, S. Hook (ed.), New York University Press, New York, 1960, p. 270.

V

Not mental causation—actually physical

One very fundamental objection to the report by Experiential Realism that a mind exerts a causal influence on the body, takes the form of contending that what appears to be a case of mental causation actually is physical causation. This is based on the claim that anything mental is effect, not cause. Specifically, physical entities produce not only other physical entities as effects but also mental effects. For example, when a person puts a large amount of alcohol in his stomach, or has a brain tumour, he wobbles (physical behaviour). Also there is vivid imagery (mental entities). Here there is no mental entity exercising causal efficacy in the case of the wobble or the imagery. When, for example, it apears that an act of will (mental entity) causes a physical action (entity), such as raising one's arm, it is actually a case of a preceding brain state, or some other physical entity, causing the arm to be raised and also causing, as an incidental accompaniment, the mental 'act of will' to occur. In short, the mental act of will is not a cause of subsequent physical change.

As far as comprehensive experience is concerned, there are some instances in which one finds that physical causes are decisive in producing mental changes, for example vivid mental images in the case of the alcoholic. However, strictly speaking it is a case of physical stimulus (C) arousing a mind (E). The mind (C) then generates the imagery (E). On the other hand, in some instances mental causes produce mental effects. For example, in the absence of alcohol, or a brain tumour, a person by mental initiative is able to initiate a wobble or vivid mental imagery by an act of will. Brain changes no doubt occur but they are not decisive causally. One is just as clearly aware of this mental causation as he is of physical causation.

In general, it is to be noted that in its normal state the body, including the brain, functions as a neutral channel of communication for the transmission of physical stimuli on the one hand, and the effects of mental stimuli on the other. In both cases either physical or mental effects may be produced, or both. Further, the mere fact of the prior presence of one entity does not prove that it is the cause of a subsequent entity. The determination of cause-effect relations involves a reference to causal efficacy.

It must also be remembered that the function of the brain is not sufficiently understood to justify the claim that its physical entities are the only causes which influence mental entities. In discussing causation or anything else, on the basis of comprehensive experience, one must restrict oneself to what is present in awareness and scrupulously refrain from according superior status to what may be or what is conceivable. Thus comprehensive experience does not justify the attribution of exclusive causal efficacy to either physical entities or to mental entities.

VI

Physical changes stop mental events

Another line of criticism directed against Experiential Realism takes the form of pointing out that decisive physical changes can, and do, stop mental activities, and remove mental contents. For example, the diminution of a person's supply of oxygen, or a blow on the head, will produce these results. This seems to imply a superior state to the physical in the matter of causal efficacy. However, it is to be noted that, in some instances, mental initiative can stop physical activities. One can decide to hold one's breath and so stop breathing. In mental illness one may suffer psycho-somatic paralysis.

If these activities, physical or mental, are of a sufficient intensity and duration, mental process and content (in the case of loss of oxygen and the violent blow) are permanently terminated. Likewise physical processes (the life of the body) in the case of holding one's breath are terminated (and also one's mental life).

Some further examples are relevant. If part of the brain is removed, related mental processes disappear. If a person loses the will to live, he does not recover from a physical illness. If he has the will to live under the same bodily conditions, he will survive. In any case, just because an entity can remove another entity, that does not prove that the first is the cause of the second. A person can shatter a beautiful vase, or destroy a smooth running community of scholars, without being able to produce either. This comment brings into the focus of attention a problem which requires serious consideration.

VII

Equal status, body and mind

Experiential Realism regards basic mental entities as independent, as far as existence is concerned, of basic physical entities, and as being at least equal in status. There are those who contend that any mental entity,[1] either basic or characteristic is merely an incidental accompaniment of physical entities. These entities (it is claimed) owe their existence to the generating power (causation) of physical entities. So far discussion has focused on the characteristics of mind. We must now face the claim that basic mental entities are the effects of physical causes.

For a person relying on comprehensive experience, the situation is as follows. As far as can be determined by circumstantial evidence, a child at birth has, in addition to its body, some mental activities and content. For instance, it is aware of pain. This implies the presence of a basic mental entity (mind). What the pre-birth situation is, one finds it difficult to determine. The body is there undergoing growth— beyond that one indulges in speculation. Does the body at birth generate the mind (basic mental entity)? In the context of comprehensive experience both a basic physical entity and a basic mental entity are present. All available evidence shows that a basic mental entity cannot, by itself, generate a basic physical entity. Further, there is no awareness of a basic physical entity generating a mind. This is so because a person is only able to be aware of his own mind. If it did not exist, and was then generated by its body (which did exist), that mind could not be aware of its own generation.

It is conceivable that basic physical entities may generate basic mental entities. The opposite is conceivable also. But if a person restricts himself to non-imaginary comprehensive experience, there is no justification for claiming either that basic physical entities generate basic mental entities or that the reverse is the case. There is no awareness of a mind as such, for example, by fiat eliminating a basic physical entity. Likewise there is no awareness of a body eliminating a mind. However there is circumstantial evidence that, given sufficient bodily change, there is no longer a mind present in that body. Specifically Mr A has no awareness of an act of will whereby, by it alone, he destroys his own body. If Mr A's body destroys his mind, his mind would not then be aware of this occurrence. On the other hand Mr A may observe Mr B and have circumstantial evidence that Mr B's body first is in an abnormal condition and then his mind is no longer present in his body, that is his body no longer is seen to act like one in which mind is expressing control. The immediately preceding comments about the 'conceivable' are relevant here.

[1] See p. 383.

VIII

Relativity in identifying causation

A final word on causation in general is in order here. It is claimed by some philosophers that the assigning of causes in any objective fashion is impossible, because it is relative to the interests of an interpreter. This view does not find adequate support in comprehensive experience. In explaining the assassination of a president a physician may attribute death to the cessation of the flowing blood, a sheriff to the firing of a bullet, a psychologist to the passion of anger in the assassin, a sociologist to bad environmental conditions. Each is correct if it is an accurate report. The apparent differences are due to the fact that each is concentrating on a specific limited situation[1] and each situation differs in its limits or range. Some are more inclusive and hence contain others. In other words, the situation a man concentrates on may indeed reflect his interests, but within the situation the decisive cause can be accurately determined regardless of his whims or interests. In the case discussed, the situations are capable of being included one within the other. Hence each interpretation of the cause of death concentrates on one segment of a cause-effect series in a very extensive situation, that is men in their environment.[2]

The preceding discussion of causality obviously has concentrated on efficient causality. Of course, final causality cannot be overlooked, as was argued in Chapter 7, pp. 183–4. Here also Experiential Realism has kinship with Whitehead, who remarks:

'The conduct of human affairs is entirely dominated by . . . purpose . . . issuing in conduct. Almost every sentence we utter and every judgment we form, presupposes our unfailing experience of this element in life. . . . For example, we speak of the policy of a statesman or of a business corporation. Cut out the notion of final causation, and the word "policy" has lost its meaning.'[3]

[1] M. Black, 'Making Something Happen', *Determinism and Freedom*, S. Hook (ed.), Collier Books, New York, 1961, p. 42.
[2] See Chapter 7, pp. 181–3.
[3] A. N. Whitehead, *The Function of Reason*, Princeton, 1929, pp. 9–10.

Freedom: Spinoza, Hume, James and Austin

The discussion of causation raises the issue of freedom. One view is that of Spinoza, who contends that men who claim to be free, meaning free of causation, are simply manifesting their ignorance of relevant causal factors (see *E.*, III, 2 note).

Hume, on the other hand, while agreeing with Spinoza that causality (necessity) is a fact, contends that this does not rule out freedom (liberty). He states: 'All mankind have ever [always] agreed in the doctrine of necessity.'[1] By necessity, or cause, Hume makes it clear that he means 'constant conjunction' and the expectation of its continuing. And as for liberty: 'By liberty, then, we can only mean *a power of acting or not acting, according to the determinations of the will*; that is, if we choose to remain at rest, we may; if we choose to move, we also may' (*H.*, p. 99).

This confidence, on Spinoza's part, that all entities have a cause, and Hume's acceptance of necessity at least in human affairs, is not shared by Experiential Realism. As noted earlier, all that comprehensive experience justifies to date is the report that some entities in limited situations have causes. Whether all entities have causes is not yet settled.[2]

It is also relevant to note that there are those who argue that a person is free only if causal factors do not apply in some instances. Thus, James in his famous discussion of 'The Dilemma of Determinism' contends that men are free to choose, at least within limits, because there is 'a certain amount of loose play'.[3] As just noted, this confidence concerning the presence or absence of causes is not yet settled. What may at one time appear to be loose play, the absence of causes, may indeed be a case of ignorance, as Spinoza would contend.

Austin offers an ingenious verbally oriented approach to the problem of freedom which seems to equate freedom with a situation where one can say 'X did it'. Or as Austin puts it in negative form:

' "Freedom" is not a name for a characteristic of actions, but the name of a dimension in which actions are assessed. In examining all

---

[1] D. Hume, *Enquiry Concerning Human Understanding*, Open Court, La Salle, 1946, p. 85. Hereafter this book will be referred to as *H*.

[2] See Chapter 7, pp. 186–91.

[3] W. James, *The Will to Believe*, Longmans Green, New York, 1927, p. 150.

the ways in which each action may not be "free", *i.e.* the cases in which it will not do to say simply "X did A", we may hope to dispose of the problem of Freedom.'[1]

From the point of view of comprehensive experience, this is a much too easy 'solution'. Granted, in a limited situation, the causal initiative is provided by X. A further question arises—is it not the case that, in some instances, one can identify causes which result, in the limited situation, in X performing an action? He hit Y because he was angry. In other words, would it not be wise to put the discussion of freedom in as wide a context as possible? If one wishes to undertake a verbal approach, the fact remains that the term 'freedom' is used not only in the fashion noted by Austin, but in many others as noted. Indeed, there is not one problem of freedom. Several different issues are referred to by the one term 'freedom'.

X

Existentialism—the human person: Sartre

One very influential theory of the human person, set in the context of a discussion of causation and other major issues, is provided by contemporary Existentialism. Some of the chief characteristics of this point of view are covered in an admittedly brief yet very effective fashion by J.-P. Sartre in his deceptively simple little essay entitled 'Extentialism is a Humanism'. The following statement is typical: 'If man, as the existentialist conceives him, is indefinable, it is because at first he is *nothing*. Only afterward will he be something, and he himself will have made what he will be. Thus, there is no human nature, since there is no God to conceive it.'[2]

Sartre provides further clarification thus: 'Man is at the start a plan which is aware of itself . . . nothing exists prior to this plan; there is nothing in heaven; man will be what he will have planned

---

[1] J. L. Austin, 'A Plea for Excuses', *Proceedings of the Aristotelian Society*, LVII (1956–7), p. 6.

[2] J.-P. Sartre, *Existentialism*, Philosophical Library, New York, 1947, pp. 18–19. Hereafter this will be referred to as *Ex*. It is, of course, not contended that this book is a full or final statement of Sartre's philosophy in particular or of Existentialism in general.

to be ... But if existence really does precede essence, man is responsible for what he is' (*Ex.*, p. 19).

On the basis of comprehensive experience, a number of remarks are relevant. The exact meaning of the claim that at first man is nothing, and only becomes something after he has made himself, is difficult to determine. An individual human being at birth, or even at conception, is not nothing (if this means the complete absence of anything). When the transition was made, in the distant past, from pure animal to human animal, again there was not nothing at the start of the species man. If Sartre, meaning by 'nothing', something other than the present state of a man's life or the species man, it would be in the interests of clarity to say so, in the context of the statements quoted.

In any case Sartre states in this passage that at the start man is 'a plan which is aware of itself'. The process of self-creation by willing and acting then takes place. This seems to involve Sartre in the admission that there is, after all, a human nature, indeed, a human essence prior to existence, in the sense that all this is what characterises the members of the species man. Incidentally, it is difficult to make much sense of the phrase 'a plan aware of itself'. Further, the reputed self-creativity of man seems to disregard external conditioning factors.

To say that there is no human nature, concept or essence, because 'there is no God to conceive it' (*Ex.*, p. 18) is hardly decisive as far as comprehensive experience is concerned. Even if there were no God or heaven, an essence (concept) is found to be present. If one wishes not to refer to concepts or to Platonic Forms, for example, it is still the case that human beings have common characteristics.

In this connection it is interesting to find Sartre stating (*Ex.*, p. 45) that, though it is impossible to find in every man some universal essence which would be human nature, yet there does exist a universal human condition. Thus, he refers to 'the *a priori* limits which outline man's fundamental situation in the universe. . . . What does not vary is the necessity for him to exist in the world' (*Ex.*, p. 45). In short, all human beings do have definite characteristics.

Strangely enough, in view of Sartre's claim that man makes himself, he states, in apparent contradiction, that the 'force of circumstances is such that he cannot abstain from choosing one [alternatively]. We define man only in relationship to involvement. It is therefore, absurd to charge us with arbitrariness of choice' (*Ex.*, p. 51). In view of all these admissions, how can Sartre legitimately refer to a man's 'complete freedom'? (*Ex.*, p. 55).

In any case, Sartre's theory of man's freedom and self-creative activity leads him to a number of conclusions concerning the life of human beings.

In the first place he claims that values are man-dependent, and each man has responsibilities to his fellows. From this situation it follows that human life is bound to be characterised by extreme emotional disturbance. For example, Sartre states: 'To choose to be this or that is to affirm at the same time the value of what we choose. . . . nothing can be good for us without being good for all. . . . I am responsible for myself and for everyone else' (*Ex.*, pp. 20–1). This 'condition' gives rise to a feeling of anguish.

As noted previously, Sartre states that there is no God. This further 'darkens' the emotional life of man. Anguish is accompanied by a feeling of forlornness—of being absolutely on one's own. In particular 'all possibility of finding values in a heaven of ideas disappears along with Him [God]' (*Ex.*, pp. 25–6).

The reaction of Experiential Realism to this point of view can be simply stated. Sartre himself, as noted earlier, has a 'humanistic' theory of value. He does qualify this first remark by mentioning *a priori* value. As far as comprehensive experience is concerned, value characteristics and value concepts are found in experience, but their status as such does not depend on experience. They do not depend for their place in the universe on God. It is the case that the occurrence of some values is due to human initative, that is, justice as such is not a human creation but a just society is.

The desire for something to cling to, which is thwarted by the absence of God as source of values, is dealt with in the context of Experiential Realism by noting that while God[1] and values are found in comprehensive experience, they are not refuges but entities with which man can deal in an effective fashion. A man who accepts his responsibility for developing his own personality and helping others, need not feel anguish. Indeed, many such men do not have this feeling. Further, even if (and this is not the position of Experiential Realism) a man denies the existence of God and an objective status for values, it does not necessarily follow that such a person is weighted down with a feeling of forlorness. This is simply not the case. In brief, comprehensive experience gives no basis for anguish and forlornness. Rather, its approach to man and his environment is such that despite

[1] See pp. 391–3.

present terrible difficulties, confidence and hope should be the dominant notes. This is not to deny the relevance of deep sympathy and profound regret in view of human misery.

XI

Immortality; nature and existence of God: Plato, Descartes and Whitehead

We turn now to the question of whether or not a human being is immortal, and a brief examination of a traditionally closely related topic, the existence and nature of God.

Arguments for the immortality of the soul based not on awareness but on circumstantial evidence are, of course, open to suspicion. For example, the claim that morality is meaningless unless there is a next life for rewards and punishments[1] does not stand critical examination. There have been and are some men who are thoroughly moral and yet do not accept the theory of personal immortality. Likewise, the argument that if a mind concentrates on what is eternal it will become eternal, is not open to verification (to awareness). The argument that the mind or soul is by nature indestructible[2] simply begs the question.

A person who wishes to have faith in personal immortality should admit that it is a case of faith, not evidence provided in experience.

The nature of a divine being[3] has been described in terms of omniscience and omnipotence. These are entities beyond the range of human experience, except in imagination unsupported by fact. Those who argue from the existence of the world, as we know it, or from the so-called order of the world, to the reality of a being with these characteristics (existence, a concern for order) or who is responsible for them, are relying on indirect (circumstantial) evidence, and not on awareness of non-imaginary entities.

The same general comments apply to arguments for the existence of a God envisaged in the traditional fashion, based on a reference to miracles of the past (or present) (that is, setting aside the 'laws of

[1] I. Kant, *Critique of Practical Reason*, Bk. II, Chapter. II, Sec. V.

[2] Plato, *Republic*, X (608c–612a).

[3] It is not proposed in this book to deal extensively with the philosophy of religion, hence a few brief comments will suffice to round out this introduction to Experiential Realism.

nature'). What in the past were termed miracles of healing, for example where the blind see, the paralysed walk, are now produced, in some instances, by psychoanalytic therapy. Events which are not now so explicable cannot legitimately be referred to as evidence of the causal efficacy of an assumed divine being (whose existence and activities are not open to awareness), since they presupposed a setting aside of causality. In any case, even if some source could legitimately be assumed, on the basis of physical and mental miracles, most miracles do not imply the presence of a divine being who possesses deity in its highest sense. Moral and spiritual excellence is not demonstrated for example, by turning water into wine, or building something big, such as a universe.

The moral argument assumes on the basis of no sound evidence (there is no awareness of the entities mentioned), that the validity of morality requires a divine 'bookkeeper' and 'distributor' of rewards and punishments. As a matter of fact, in the normal course of events, in this world, good behaviour is rewarded and evil behaviour punished.[1] Some men are moral who do not accept the postulate of a divinely based foundation for morality in the traditional sense.

The argument, on so-called logical grounds, that an analysis of the meaning of the concept 'God', a perfect being, or one than whom no greater can be conceived, implies that nothing is lacking, since this would be a denial of perfection—hence God exists—is open to an obvious objection. What is found in the realm of concepts does not determine, or necessarily reflect, what is found in the non-conceptual world. Indeed, any validity in argument on the conceptual level concerning mental or physical entities is based, ultimately, on reference to the non-conceptual world.

It is only fair to note that one of the devotees of this type of logical approach, the so-called ontological argument, is not unaware of the impact of this critical reaction. Consider Descartes. He faces the objection that

'even though in fact I cannot conceive of a God without existence, any more than of a mountain without a valley, nevertheless, just as from the mere fact that I conceive a mountain with a valley it does not follow that any mountain exists in the world, so likewise, though I conceive of God as existing, it does not seem to follow for this

---

[1] It must be admitted that this is not obvious to many persons who take a short-range view of things.

reason that God exists. For my thought does not impose any necessity upon things.'[1]

However, Descartes continues:

'From the fact *alone* that I cannot conceive God except as existing, it follows that existence is inseparable from him, and consequently that he does, in truth, exist. Not that my thought can bring about this result or that it imposes any necessity upon things; on the contrary [and this is the point to note], *the necessity which is in the thing itself—* that is, the necessity of the existence of God—determines me to have this thought' (*M.*, pp. 59-60, emphasis added).

The latter part of this quotation seems to be a return to the causal argument, not defence of the ontological as it is claimed.

In any case, from the point of view of comprehensive experience, these defences of the existence of God have a fatal flaw. There is no awareness of a perfect being, and hence we are not led to think of 'Him' in the traditional terms.

The so-called divine being and characteristics referred to in the traditional view may indeed exist. But, if this is accepted, it will be on the basis of faith, not as the result of awareness of a non-imaginary entity (*H.*, p. 175).

It was reported in Chapter 7, on the basis of comprehensive experience, that there is awareness of a divine being—God, that is, an entity other than man which possesses the characteristic deity.[2] In general agreement with Experiential Realism's stress on the importance of first-hand experience of God, rather than circumstantial evidence, Whitehead remarks: 'Religious experience . . . consists of a certain widespread, direct apprehension of a character exemplified in the actual universe.'[3] Also: 'What . . . can be known about God must be sought in the region of particular experiences, and therefore rests on an empirical basis.'[4]

---

[1] R. Descartes, *Meditations*, Library of Liberal Arts, New York, 1951, p. 59. Hereafter this book will be referred to as *M.*

[2] A few men also have this characteristic, but to a lesser degree.

[3] A. N. Whitehead, *Religion in the Making*, Macmillan, New York, 1926, p. 86.

[4] A. N. Whitehead, *Science and the Modern World*, Cambridge, 1946, ed. p. 222.

Existence as an attribute: Ayer and Moore

It has been noted previously[1] that physical objects and minds exist, are actual (but not conceptual or other expressions of a possibility).

Thus Experiential Realism takes issue with a venerable tradition in philosophy to the effect that existence is not an attribute, that is, a characteristic. Consider for example Ayer's statement: 'But, as Kant pointed out, existence is not an attribute. For, when we ascribe an attribute to a thing, we covertly assert that it exists: so that if existence were itself an attribute, it would follow that all positive existential propositions were tautologies.'[2]

The fallacious nature of Ayer's position becomes obvious when one examines a specific case. Consider a particular brown table. In ascribing the attribute 'brown' to the table, a person of course asserts covertly (implies) that the table exists, but he is not merely indulging in a tautology. It is one thing to assert that a table is brown, and something else to state that this physical object (the table) exists. The physical object table has here two attributes (characteristics) which are (*a*) brown, (*b*) existence.

This issue can be further clarified by examination of some remarks by G. E. Moore. He argues that if you point at a tame tiger and then say 'This exists', you are not saying anything additional. In other words, you are not expressing a proposition. It is absolutely meaningless. On the other hand, when you say 'This is a tame tiger and it growls' you are saying something additional and it is meaningful.[3] ' "This is a tame tiger, and exists" would be not tautologous, but meaningless' (Moore, p. 185). Thus, while agreeing with Ayer in general, in this claim that existence is not an attribute, he disagrees as to the nature of the resultant defect. However, Moore is prepared to admit that we have to consider the possibility that something did not exist that might have existed. If something might have existed, then "does not exist" is a significant statement and true; for example, 'A tame tiger does not exist'. It follows that ' "This does exist" must be significant too' (Moore, p. 186).

[1] See Chapter 9, pp. 231–32.
[2] A. J. Ayer, *Language, Truth and Logic*, Gollancz, 1936, p. 34.
[3] See G. E. Moore, 'Is Existence a Predicate?', *Aristotelian Society Supplementary Volume* XV (1936), p. 185. Hereafter this paper will be referred to as Moore.

From the point of view of comprehensive experience, in dealing with physical facts, to say that they exist is to report that there are specific facts (actual, not mere possibilities). Hence 'exist' functions as a synonym for 'is'. It is not redundant to say that a physical object exists (that existence is an attribute, a characteristic). There is a genuine distinction between possibility and actuality. 'There is a table and that table exists' is redundant because both synonyms are used. Those who criticise the use of the term 'existence' really indicate a preference for the other term, namely 'is'.

If one starts with possibilities (a house as a possibility) and then proceeds to state that the possibilities have been actualised (the house has been built), this is to report that it now exists. This is a highly meaningful report.

As has been previously noted, the term 'is' suffers from ambiguity. When one asserts that a table 'is' brown, the term 'is' functions to indicate possession of a characteristic, namely brown. This of course is different from 'is' meaning existence.

XIII

Space and time: Whitehead

The brief discussion of space and time in Chapter 7, wherein it was reported that space and time are not basic entities, rather they are characteristics of entities, has obvious kinship with some of Whitehead's views.[1] Specifically concerning time he states: 'We are not aware of two facts, namely, a period of time and also of things existing within that period. We are aware of . . . the passage of nature. Thus the present contains within it antecedents and subsequents, and the antecedents and the subsequents are themselves endurances with temporal extensions.'[2]

Whitehead also refers to the 'passing of nature, its development,

---

[1] *Alfred North Whitehead*, 'Time, Space and Material', *Aristotelian Society Supplementary Volume II* (1919), p. 56. Hereafter this paper will be referred to as T.S.M.

[2] T.S.M. p. 46.

its creative advance'.[1] This is the basis of the so-called universality of time. Turning to space, note Whitehead's reference to the theory that 'space . . . is the outcome of certain relations between objects commonly said to be in space' (T.S.M., p. 46).[2]

[1] A. N. Whitehead, *The Concept of Nature*, Cambridge, 1916, p. 34.
[2] For a more detailed discussion of space and time and space-time, see relevant sections in A. N. Whitehead, *The Interpretation of Science*, Bobbs-Merrill, Indianapolis, 1961.

18

VALUES

False identification of moral goodness with other entities

Moral goodness has been identified with (essentially related to) a wide range of activities and other characteristics of human beings. A few examples of typical statements will bring this matter into clear focus.

Hobbes contends that 'whatsoever is the object of any man's appetite or desire, that is it which he for his part calleth *good*; and the object of his hate and aversion, *evil*.'[1]

In the general context of an evolutionary approach to morality, Spencer places stress on the ultimate importance of the adjustment of an organism to its environment. He then proceeds to state: 'Conduct is right [good] or wrong [evil] according as [it] . . . does or does not further the general end of self-preservation.'[2]

The Stoic manual prepared by Epictetus, in the midst of a discussion of specific problems, emphasises the underlying general principle of Stoic ethics: 'I will now go [to face my problem], and keep my own will in harmony with nature.'[3]

Mill's statement of the utilitarian position is typical of those who stress pleasure or happiness. 'Actions are right [morally good] in proportion as they tend to promote happiness; wrong [evil] as they tend to produce the reverse of happiness. By happiness is intended pleasure, and the absence of pain.'[4]

Another approach to good and evil is found in Hume's *Enquiry Concerning Human Understanding*. He states: 'The mind of man is so formed by nature that, upon the appearance of certain characters,

[1] T. Hobbes, *Leviathan*, in *The English Philosophers from Bacon to Mill*, E. A. Burtt (ed.), Modern Library, New York, 1939, p. 149.
[2] H. Spencer, *The Data of Ethics*, A. L. Burtt, New York, 1879, p. 26.
[3] Epictetus, *Enchiridion*, Liberal Arts Press, New York, 1948, p. 19.
[4] J. S. Mill, *Utilitarianism*, Liberal Arts Press, New York, 1948, p. 7.

dispositions, and actions, it immediately feels the sentiment of appro-
bation or blame.'[1]

A classic remark by Kant must not be neglected. 'Nothing in the
world—indeed nothing even beyond the world—can possibly be
conceived which could be called good without qualification except a
good will.'[2]

According to Aristotle the good man is he who develops his
characteristic human functions to the fullest possible extent. This
doctrine of self-development, in its technical exposition, is in summary
as follows: 'human good turns out to be activity of soul in accordance
with virtue . . . in accordance with the best and the most complete
[virtue].'[3]

The 'divine decree' foundation for moral goodness is typical in
the following: 'Thou shalt love the Lord thy God with all thy heart,
and with all thy soul, and with all thy mind. . . . Thou shalt love
thy neighbour as thyself.'[4]

On the basis of comprehensive experience, it is appropriate to note
that a person who is in his behaviour morally good may in addition
meet some or all of the following criteria: develop himself, experience
pleasure and contribute to the pleasure of others, adapt to the environment and thus preserve himself, be approved in some specific fashion,
act in accordance with so-called self-evident principles or laws of
nature, satisfy or be an object of desire or interests, follow what
are reported to be the dictates of a Divine Being, be motivated by a
sense of obligation (good will) and so on and on. However, a person
may do (or be) one or all of these things and still be morally evil.

Consider the case of Adolf Hitler. He developed himself, experienced
personal pleasure and contributed to the pleasure of millions of
others. At one stage in his career, he achieved a very effective adjustment to his environment. He was highly approved by millions of
people. He believed in what, for many men, was a self-evident
principal (natural law): the Nordic race should subdue lesser breeds.
He satisfied desires and interests of millions of men and women.

---

[1] D. Hume, *Enquiry Concerning Human Understanding*, Open Court, La Salle,
1946, p. 106.

[2] I. Kant, *Foundations of the Metaphysics of Morals*, Liberal Arts Press, New
York, 1959, p. 9.

[3] Aristotle, *Ethics*, W. D. Ross (ed.), Oxford, 1942, Book I, Section 7, 1098a.
Here Aristotle deals not only with moral but also intellectual virtues.

[4] *Matthew*, 22: 37, 39 (A.V.).

Hitler believed he was following the dictates of the gods of Germany. He felt a strong sense of obligation to fulfil a mission to purge the world of those whom he considered inferior creatures.

It is, of course, the case that none of the ethical theorists mentioned above would term the behaviour of Hitler morally good. This is because they add essential qualifications to their general statements of what constitutes moral goodness—self-development, pleasure, self-preservation and so on. Thus, for example, Mill refers to a high quality of pleasure, Spencer to the preservation of a superior sort of self and Aristotle to a particular sort of self-development. But the same general type of objection, as in the case of the Hitler illustration, can be raised with reference to the suggested qualifications. They require further qualification, and in the end, a justification for their assigned status concerning moral goodness. The question remains—why make that claim?

It is here contended that, from the point of view of comprehensive experience, the moral good or evil of a person and his behaviour is ultimately not determined (caused) by the presence or absence of the entities mentioned above, nor is it identical with them. Rather, the moral good or evil of entities depends on whether or not they manifest the characteristic moral good or the characteristic moral evil.

Further, the Hitler illustration demonstrates that, as such, the entities mentioned above are not the supreme or only goals for morally good persons. Self-development, pleasure, and the rest are goods, in some sense. But at best are only in some cases ingredients in a complex situation in which morally good behaviour occurs. In other words, these entities are peripheral. However, in so far as such entities are objects of desire or interest, they have instrumental value since they are what satisfies the desire or interest.

It is obvious that Experiential Realism is in general agreement with G. E. Moore's report that good 'is a simple quality' (but rejects its reputed non-natural status). Specifically, he remarks: 'It may be true that all things which are good are *also* something else. . . . But far too many philosophers have thought . . . that these properties, in fact, were simply not "other", but absolutely and entirely the same with goodness.'[1]

[1] G. E. Moore, *Principia Ethica*, Cambridge University Press, 1929, p. 10.

'True'—opposing views of the term; recapitulation of Experiential Realism's view

It was reported in Chapter 8 that true propositions or ideas are those which constitute an accurate report concerning that to which they refer. (The term 'true' has this standard use). This point of view is not accepted by a number of philosophers. It is claimed, for instance, that truth is a matter of coherence or usefulness, or verification. The word 'true (or the truth)' is by them used in this specialised technical non-standard sense. Interestingly enough, at least many of the same propositions are considered to be true by those theories as by those who support the 'accurate report' view of truth.

Coherence theory

It is the case that in geometry and in the affairs of ordinary life, a person frequently checks, in a roundabout fashion, on the truth of a proposition by noting its coherence with other propositions whose truth is already established and accepted. For example, one grants the truth of 'You should not steal a car' on the basis of its relation to 'Thou shalt not steal (antything)'. The coherence theory[1] of truth is that true propositions are part of a coherent system.

An obvious objection is that it is quite possible to have propositions which are part of a coherent fairy tale. These propositions are not supported by facts, that is, they are not true in the ordinary use of the term. It is, however, appropriate to realise that some devotees of the coherence theory imply that this is not a sound criterion. They are not concerned with some particular abstract group of entities. For them a proposition is true if it is part of one system in which everything actual or possible is coherently included.

However, even in this version the coherence theory of truth is not free of criticism. There is no awareness of one coherent system of entities. Further there is a difference between the fact 'accurate report' and the fact 'part of a coherent system'. If one wants to regard truth and coherence as synonymous terms and so stipulate this, so be it. However, in order to avoid confusion, it is wiser to restrict oneself to the ordinary use of 'true' and employ the word 'coherence' to refer to coherence.

[1] *Meaning and Knowledge*, E. Nagel and R. R. Brant (eds), Harcourt, Brace and Co., New York, 1965, pp. 125–6; 144–52.

Pragmatic: James

In view of the fact that William James raises a number of fundamental issues concerning truth, his work will now be examined. Because of the vigour and clarity of his presentation, considerable use will be made of quotations. Incidentally, these will serve to demonstrate that some supposedly very new contemporary views have a longer history than some of their devotees realise.

James remarks that 'the possession of true thoughts means everywhere the possession of invaluable instruments of action'.[1] There is also the striking comment: 'You can say of it then either that "it [a proposition] is useful because it is true" or that "it is true because it is useful" ' (*Prag.*, p. 204).

Indeed, James goes farther and asserts: ' "The true", to put it very briefly, is only the expedient in the way of our thinking, ... Expedient in almost any fashion; and expedient in the long run and on the whole of course' (*Prag.*, p. 222).

The reaction to this point of view, based on comprehensive experience, is: the fact that true propositions (and concepts) are useful does not constitute the essential feature of truth, namely accuracy of report. The proposition stated in English: 'If you are not good, a bogey man will get you' may be useful in making a child behave, but it is not true (in the ordinary sense). In any case, the usefulness of a proposition frequently depends on its truth. The truth of the proposition 'Bread is nourishing' is the basis of its usefulness.

In all fairness, it must be noted that the Jamesian stress on utility is, in some discussions, placed in a broad context, and the term is apparently given its ordinary use. He remaks: 'Truth, as any dictionary will tell you, is a property of certain of our ideas. It means their "agreement", as falsity means their disagreement, with "reality".' He then points out that 'pragmatists and intellectualists both accept this definition as a matter of course. They begin to quarrel only after the question is raised as to what may precisely be meant by the term "agreement", and what by the term "reality" ' (*Prag.*, p. 198).

In this context, James appropriately points out that while some ideas are copies of the objects to which they refer, others are not. A memory image of a clock may be a fairly accurate copy of the clock's face. Our idea of its time-keeping function is not (*Prag.*, p. 199).

---

[1] W. James, *Pragmatism*, Longmans, Green, New York, 1948, p. 202. Hereafter this book will be referred to as *Prag.*

However, it becomes obvious that even here he is using the term 'agree' in a rather special sense.

'To "agree" . . . with a reality *can only mean to be guided either straight up to it or into its surroundings, or be put into such working touch with it as to handle either it or something connected with it better than if we disagreed.* Better either intellectually or practically . . . To copy a reality is, indeed, one very important way of agreeing with it, but it is far from being essential. The essential thing is the process of being guided' (*Prag.*, pp. 212–13).

The general utility emphasis is supplemented by a reference to satisfaction, and in a sense, coherence. 'Any idea that will carry us prosperously from any one part of our experience to any other part, linking things satisfactorily, . . . simplifying, saving labour; is true . . . *instrumentally*' (*Prag.*, p. 58).

The remarks by James, quoted above, leave him open to the criticism, on the basis of comprehensive experience, that his views of truth are peripheral, (partial) or distorted. It is the case that true ideas (ideas accepted as true by James and almost everyone else) can be used to guide future actions. On the other hand true ideas also report present and past events. This latter point James seems either to neglect or down-grade. The 'guide up to' interpretation of 'agree with' simply does not have the status he assigns to it. The reference to satisfaction is a case of either the peripheral fallacy,[1] or a false interpretation. Further, those who hold the 'accurate report' approach to truth do not equate this with having a copy of the entity to which the true idea or statement refers.

Nevertheless, it is proper to point out that in other writings James had second, or other thoughts. These views turn out to be generally in accordance with comprehensive experience. In effect, he contradicts many of the statements just quoted. There is, for example, the candid admission that 'when we said that the truth of a belief consists in its "working" value, etc., our language evidently was too careless,' James admits that his remarks involved an erroneous stress on activity and on satisfaction, rather than objects and statements about them.[2]

[1] The entity referred to may be involved in a situation, but it is not fundamental. Many true propositions are not satisfactory, though some are. Further, truth is one entity, satisfaction is another.

[2] W. James, *The Meaning of Truth*, Longmans, Green, New York, 1909, pp. 206–7.

Note also the forthright statement: 'That these ideas should be true in advance of and apart from their utility . . . is the very condition of their having that kind of utility—the objects they connect us with are so important that the ideas which serve as the objects' substitutes grow important also' (*The Meaning of Truth*, pp. 190–1, 207–8).

Verification: James, Ayer, Waismann and Austin

The scientific emphasis on the importance of verification of hypotheses is a source of misunderstanding concerning truth (in the sense of accurate report).

Consider, for example, James's contention that 'The truth of an idea is not a stagnant property inherent in it. Truth *happens* to an idea. It *becomes* true, is *made* true by events. Its verity *is* in fact an event, a process: the process namely of its verifying itself, its *verification*. Its validity is the process of its valid-*ation*' (*Prag.*, p. 201).

James is well aware that this general point of view, that truth is made by human reaction, is such as to arouse objections. He himself states one of them effectively: ' "Truth is not made" . . . it absolutely obtains, being a unique relation that does not wait upon any process. . . . Our belief that yon thing on the wall is a clock is true already, altho no one in the whole history of the world should verify it' (*Prag.*, pp. 218–19).

James's reply to his critic is as follows: 'One verification serves for others of its kind. . . . Truth *anti rem* means only verifiability, then; or else it is a case of the stock rationalist trick of treating the name of a concrete phenomenal reality as an independent prior entity. . . .' (*Prag.*, pp. 219–20).

In comprehensive experience it is not the case that a process of checking a proposition against the entities referred to tends to make a proposition or belief true. A proposition is true or false when it occurs, depending on the factual situation to which it refers. One should not overlook the distinction between 'being true' and 'finding out' whether or not a proposition is an accurate report. In any case, as pointed out previously, James in some passages is in agreement with Experiential Realism.

Some philosophers and scientists suffer from over-addiction to the reputed need for a continuous process of verification. This leads to the claim that there can never be conclusive verification of an empirical statement. Ayer is typical of this approach. 'One cannot say . . . [a]

proposition has been proved absolutely valid [true], because it is still possible that a future observation will discredit it.' Likewise Ayer contends that 'even if it is rejected in consequence of an unfavourable observation, one cannot say that it has been invalidated absolutely. For it is still possible that future observations will lead us to reinstate it.'[1]

In similar vein, Waismann remarks that even though he may be familiar with a required testing procedure for an empirical statement, he may not have time to perform all the tests. Further, he voices a very grave doubt. He cannot be sure he knows all the tests which are required.[2] For example, he has serious, indeed, final doubts, about the possibility of verifying the statement: 'There is a cat next door' ('*Ver*'., p. 121). Seeing the animal, touching it and hearing it purr, are, in his opinion, not enough. Something may be overlooked, or new experiences may occur which give rise to doubts about the adequacy of the process of verification. Therefore, we should not be satisfied that we have reached conclusive verification.

Comprehensive experience reveals that it is not the case, in all instances of human experience, that conclusive verification of empirical statements is never reached, hence the process of verification should not be terminated. However, tentativeness is appropriate concerning some complex scientific problems, for example the behaviour of an individual ultimate physical particle in the realm of microphysics or a reputed cure for cancer. On the other hand, when a man who relies on comprehensive experience is aware, in one complex act, of a cat, and recognises it as such, it is absurd to worry, wonder and be tentative in accepting propositions reporting this fact. One careful examination is enough to settle the question. Thus, a person who generalises from the scientific realisation that a continued process of verification is necessary in some cases, is guilty of an obsession. What is advisable in complex scientific observation is not appropriate in more simple everyday situations (see Chapter 16).

A critical comment by James is relevant here: 'Science has organised this nervousness [concerning careful checking] into a regular *technique*, her so-called method of verification; and she has fallen so deeply in

---

[1] A. J. Ayer, *Language, Truth and Logic,* Gollancz, London, 1936, p. 143. Hereafter this book will be referred to as *L.T.L.*

[2] F. Waismann, 'Verifiability', *Aristotelian Society Supplementary Volume* XIX (1945), p. 127. Hereafter this will be referred to as '*Ver.*'

love with the method that one may even say she has ceased to care for truth by itself at all.'[1]

Austin's criticism of Ayer's claim that empirical statements are not conclusively verifiable is in essential agreement with the view of Experiential Realism.

Ayer contends that in order to achieve conclusive verification of an empirical statement (proposition) one must attempt the impossible self-contradictory task of completing an infinite series of verifications. Austin comments, with forthright vigour, that there are any number of 'sense statements' about which he can be, and is, completely sure.[2] Turning to a specific case, he remarks: 'If, for instance, you tell me there's a telephone in the next room . . . how could it be thought *impossible* for me to . . . [verify] this conclusively?' (*S.S.*, pp. 118–19). However, for Ayer's benefit, he proceeds with laborious irony to indicate, in detail, the obvious procedures which are used in conclusive verification.

It is, of course, possible to use the word 'truth' ('true') in many different ways. However, the type of usage must be identified, and the question faced as to whether one characteristic and one concept are involved in the different usages of words. This is necessary in order to avoid confusion. It is obvious that the usual meaning of 'truth'—accurate report of facts—is disregarded in the discussions based on the peripheral factors which have been under examination. However, these peripheral factors referred to above are significant, namely coherence, usefulness, verification. It must be emphasised again that, despite differences in theory, there is general agreement as to which factual propositions are true and which are false.

True, because of meaning or structure: Quine and Ayer

Some logicians claim that some propositions are true because of (*a*) the meaning, or (*b*) the structure of the proposition. By way of background, it is to be noted that exponents of this view point out that some statements (propositions), those termed 'empirical', are true or false depending on whether or not they are accurate reports. They are found to be true or false as the result of observation (some claim sensory observation only). Merely knowing the meaning of such

---

[1] W. James, *The Will to Believe*, Longmans, Green, New York, 1937, p. 21.

[2] J. L. Austin, *Sense and Sensibilia*, Oxford, 1962, pp. 117–18. Hereafter this book will be referred to as *S.S.* See also *L.L.*, p. 359.

statements (that is relational and entity meant or activity aspects) is not enough to determine truth or falsehood, as with 'Volcanoes erupt', 'Pigs fly'. What is found to be false might conceivably have been true in some other world and vice versa. In other words, facts establish the truth or falsehood of these statements. On the other hand, it is argued by some philosophers that there are some statements (propositions) of which, if their meaning is known, one can determine their necessary truth or falsehood, without engaging in observation. They are true or false, *a priori*. These necessary true and false statements could not have been conceived to have been otherwise in this world or any other. They are true or false in any possible world. This is so because of the meaning of their component terms and their structure. Specifically, necessarily true statements are analytic propositions. Their denial involves contradiction. Consider for example: 'All dogs are animals'. 'Snow is white or non-white.'[1]

It has been argued previously that propositions of the sort just referred to are not *a priori*, neither are they analytic.[2] Hence the view under discussion is undercut. It is only fair to point out that some devotees of necessary truth correctly admit we must rely on experience to establish the meaning of words (or concepts), that is what they refer to (*B.*, p. 27).

As has been argued earlier, there are no analytic propositions apart from these in which the predicate simply repeats the subject (for example 'Black is black'). Here truth does depend on structure, quite apart from meaning of subject and predicate[3] 'X is X'. Cases such as 'All dogs are animals' or 'Snow is white or non-white' are *a posteriori*, namely reports of experience of dogs and their characteristics. Similarly, as the result of experience of snow, we state something about the colour characteristics of snow. The same statement could not be made about a rainbow because it is experienced to be different with respect to colours. Further, for example, the concept 'dog' and the concept 'animal' are simple not complex. One does not include the other. Thus, merely by contemplating some meaningful words and concepts we do not have an escape from our experience and find truth in the cases under consideration. Their meaning and structural relation is

---

[1] See S. Barker, *The Elements of Logic*, McGraw-Hill, New York, 1965, pp. 25–7. Use is made of this elementary text in the interests of simplified presentation. Hereafter this book will be referred to as *B*.

[2] See Chapter 4, pp. 101–03.

[3] As noted, the meaning of 'is' which is concerned here, is based on experience.

established as a result of experience. They are legitimately linked, not because of their own nature but because of the natural linkages of the entities to which they refer, which in turn have natural linkages, for instance snow and colour. Thus there is no necessary linkage among words or concepts as such, nor do we obtain necessary truth or become aware of it by reasoning on the level of concepts or words. Even the proposition 'Black is black' is a report of the experienced fact that the colour black retains its identity.

Therefore if the term 'necessary truth' refers to a characteristic of words and/or concepts, independent of facts, in the cases mentioned, then there are no propositions of these sorts which are cases of necessary truth.

The claim of inconceivability of being otherwise in any possible world is no guarantee of necessary truth. As a matter of fact, any proposition, no matter how bizarre, is conceivable. If the criterion: It is necessary because its denial involves contradiction is introduced, the reply is: What is contradictory and what is not is determined by reference to the facts of experience, in the cases under consideration. It is not implicit in words or concepts as such. However, once one has observed, and thus established the meanings of words and remembered all this accurately, then it is possible to think about the words and recall whether or not they present, as a matter of fact, a true statement, as previously determined.

The only necessity a statement (proposition) of the sorts considered has is the result of the fact that no exceptions to it have been found as the result of careful observation. For example, all dogs examined have the characteristic 'animal'.

A complicated illustration of a statement which is reputed to be a necessary truth because of its logical form (structure) is the following. If no gentlemen are tactless and if all baboons are tactless, then no baboons are gentlemen. Barker (p. 28) contends that, regardless of its subject matter, any statement of this logical form is bound to be true. He does add the qualification 'provided we make sense'. He further assumes that on the basis of experience we know the meaning (that is, relation in referring to a referent) of the words we use. But to repeat, he contends that some propositions are true because of their structure (the structure of the argument which leads to them), and we can be aware of their necessary truth without recourse to experience.

Here, of course, the term true is not used in the sense of accurate report, rather it is a case of referring to a set of premises from which a conclusion validly follows. This is frequently termed logical truth. But here again, as has been pointed out,[1] the valid structure of agreement here employed is usually based on our experience of entities found in the world of experience. This, however, is not always the case. Specifically a structure of argument may be set up, which either (*a*) reflects the structure of facts, or (*b*) may merely be the result of some purpose to establish an arbitrary structure. Once this valid structure is discovered, or formulated to suit some purpose, if one wants to disregard truth (as accurate report) one can play an intellectural game and use within the structure any statements, regardless of their truth or falsehood (in the sense of accurate report). To term the result a 'necessary truth' is simply a special use of the term 'truth'. It is a report that, given the structure, the conclusion follows.

An interesting version of 'logical' truth theory—namely that a complex proposition is true by virtue of its form alone—is provided by Quine. Specifically, this involves the claim that a statement is true because of the so-called logical expressions (such as 'no', or 'if', 'then', 'all', 'some', 'it is false that') which occur, essentially, in it. For example, the statement: '*If no* Greeks are Romans *then it is false that some* Romans are Greeks.' (The logical expressions are italicised) is true regardless of what non-logical expressions are used.[2]

However, as noted before, the approved structures of logical expressions here used by Quine, which are claimed to be relevant independent of any concern for specific non-logical expressions (which presumably refer to specific entities), are as a matter of fact a mere summary of relations which are found to exist among the non-logical elements of statements which are accurate reports of facts. Specifically it is because, as a matter of fact, Greeks (or any other class of entities) are not Romans (a different class of entities) that, as a matter of fact, some Romans (or any other class of entities) are not Greeks (a different class of entities). The structure of a statement merely reflects the factual state of affairs—of which the illustration is typical of a large class of such entities.

On the basis of the preceding comments, it is clear that Experiential Realism takes issue with the point of view expressed by Ayer in the following remarks: 'When we say that logical and mathematical

[1] See Chapter 4, pp. 103–6.
[2] See Quine, *From a Logical Point of View*, Harvard University Press, Cambridge, 1953, pp. 22–3, and R. Chisholm, *Theory of Knowledge*, Prentice-Hall, Englewood Cliffs, 1966, pp. 85–6.

truths are known independently of experience. . . . We maintain that they are independent of experience in the sense that they do not owe their validity to empirical verification' (*L.T.L.*, p. 95).

Ayer then makes the damaging suggestion that 'The best way to substantiate our assertion that the truths of formal logic and pure mathematics are necessarily true is to examine cases in which they might seem to be confuted.' (*L.T.L.*, p. 96). He points to what seem to be cases where, for example $2 \times 5 = 10$, or the law of excluded middle, are refuted by an appeal to experience. It turns out that actually one has been careless in counting, or has not taken a proper case for the law of excluded middle (*L.T.L.*, pp. 96–7).

It should be noted that here in Ayer's argument there is confusion. It does not rule out the report of Experiential Realism that such truths are based on experience, in at least the sense that an appeal to experience is relevant.

In any case, Ayer's follow-up comments are worthy of note. 'The principles of logic and mathematics are true universally simply because we never allow them to be anything else.' In slightly less flamboyant fashion he remarks: 'And the reason for this is that we cannot abandon them without contradicting ourselves, without sinning against the rules which govern our use of language, and so making our utterances self-stultifying' (*L.T.L.*, pp. 99–100).

An obvious criticism is that it smacks of unbridled egoism to claim that the principles of logic and mathematics are universal, necessary truths, because we do not allow them to be otherwise, or because otherwise we would be involved in language difficulties. Further, as Waismann remarks in his discussion of language structure, this approach to logic takes one into the realm of myth (See *L.L.*, p. 245).

Specifically, the fact that the denial of some statements involves contradiction (and this fact is used as a criterion of necessary truth) does not sanctify these statements as some philosophers claim. It merely indicates that 'In the nature of things there are no ultimate exclusions, expressive in logical terms. . . . Thus inconsistency is relative to the abstraction involved. An easy intellectual consistency can be attained, provided that we rest content with high abstraction. Pure mathematics is the chief example of success by adherence to such rigid abstraction.'[1]

As noted in an earlier discussion of contradiction, some contra-

---

[1] A. N. Whitehead, *Modes of Thought*, Macmillan Co., 1938, p. 76.

dictory statements in science (for example regarding the atomic weight of nitrogen) were indications of the need for further examination. It is of course the case that some contradictions indicate falsehood, as in 'Black is not black'.

True-assert: Ayer

The deficiencies of Ayer's remarks on truth stated below are obvious. 'Thus, to say that a proposition is true is just to assert it, and to say that it is false is just to assert its contradictory. And this indicates that the terms "true" and "false" connote nothing, but function in the sentence simply as marks of assertion and denial' (*L.T.L.*, p. 122).

On the basis of comprehensive experience, it is to be noted that when one says that a proposition is true, he is not merely asserting it. Men assert many propositions which they do not say are true in any of the usual senses of truth, that is accurate report or logical truth. When one says a statement is false, he is not asserting its contradictory, or at least as far as standard ordinary or technical use is concerned. It is possible to utter contradictory statements, both of which are false. For example, 'Colours smell'. Colours do not smell. In any case, the terms 'true' and 'false' do connote and denote something. They usually indicate that a report is accurate or it is not. There is also the case of 'A conclusion follows logically'. Of course, on occasion, the terms 'true' and 'false' can be used for assertion or denial, also to indicate agreement or approval or their opposites. But any of these is only one of several uses, and not the chief or usual one.

In view of the several uses of the term 'truth', it is obvious that any one who proposes to restrict it to one is guilty of a peripheral partial approach, particularly if he neglects the most usual use, 'accurate report' which, as noted previously, underlies most of the other uses.

Various uses of 'true'; Waismann

At this point it is relevant to note Waismann's comments. He argues that, depending on the sort of statements involved, the meaning of the term 'truth' varies. To say that a mathematical proposition is true 'simply means that it can be deduced from such-and-such axioms. . . . Truth, when applied to a physical law, means roughly speaking that it is well established by experimental evidence . . . that it brings widely different things into a close connection.' To say that the light is on in my room is to do none of these things, 'it is just true because it says so-and-so is as you say it is' (*L.L.*, pp. 238–9). In other words it *reports the facts*.

III

'*Truth-function*'

The 'truth-function' approach claims that the truth or falsity of a specific sort of compound statement or proposition depends solely on the truth or falsity of its components and the components can be any statements.[1] Examine 'and' compounds. In the case of 'It is snowing and it is cold', the components are true, and hence the compound is true. Here the term 'truth', in all instances, is used in the sense of 'accurate report'. Taking the illustration: 'This chair is green and the floor is solid,' the same comments apply. However, the illustration: 'I am sitting in my chair and children like candy', while in this context true, is rather silly. The question of truth of the compound does not normally arise in such a case.

Consider disjunctive compound statements. Here the situation is similar to conjunction ('and'). The components may (some do) have a natural linkage in forming the compound. However, any two statements (that is some pairs) are not normally linked in the disjunctive relation. For example, consider 'It is raining or it is snowing'. Here the truth of one determines the truth of the compound (in the sense of factual accurate report). However, in the illustration 'I am sitting in my chair or Zulus love giraffes', the truth of one does not determine the truth of the compound, in the sense of 'accurate report'. The compound is not an accurate report of a factual situation. The alternative stated is not a genuine normal, factual alternative as is the raining or snowing case. Hence, in calling this compound (chair-giraffe) true, in the context of truth-function set-up, the term 'true' is being employed in a special sense. It is used to indicate that in this context, when any two statements are linked by the word 'or', if one is true in the factual sense, then the compound is acceptable in the truth-functional set-up, and in this sense is termed 'true', that is in a logical sense. In other words, when one is free of reference to the factual world (as in imagination), any two statements may be linked by 'or'.

A third main sort of compound proposition is the conditional,

---

[1] The following discussion takes seriously the claim of the devotees that truth-function analysis has useful, practical applications.

where the component propositions have the 'if-then' relation. It is very important to note that in some instances when the phrase 'if-then' is used, this does not indicate a truth-function situation. The truth or falsity of the compound is not determined by the truth or falsity of the components. This is the case with reference to a causal proposition (one which states a causal relation). The truth or falsity of the proposition: 'If the sun is shining, then the snow is melting', is not determined by the truth or falsity of 'The snow is melting' and 'the sun is shining'. This is so in view of the fact that there is another ingredient in the situation, expressed by the causal word 'because'.

More specifically, the truth-function situation occurs when a compound is false if the antecedent is true and the consequent is false. The compound is true in all other cases. For example (to use Barker's illustration), the proposition: 'If the Cavaliers win today, then I am a monkey's uncle', is false, if the Cavaliers win and I am not a monkey's uncle. On the other hand, the proposition: 'If I have lectured once then I have lectured a thousand times' is true if both components are true. Consider also the following examples: 'If Caesar crossed the Rubicon, then two Johnsons will have lunch together.' Though this is legitimate in truth-functional analysis, and the two statements (each of which is an accurate report) are termed a compound and a true one, this is hardly an accurate report of a complex factual situation with related components giving rise to a compound proposition. Further, the truth-functional use of 'true' sanctions the claim (for example) that 'If Bobby Kennedy is the President of the US, then China is the smallest nation in the world' is a true compound. This again is using statements linked by 'if-then' in an unusual sense independently of factual reference. (In this case both components are false in the ordinary 'accurate report' sense of the term) Also this is a case of assigning truth to the so-called compound in a sense justified only in the artificial content of truth-functional analysis, that is, truth (logical) is an appropriate, in this context, likewise 'compound'. There is nothing true about this compound in the sense of 'accurate report'.

Thus, in brief, the reaction of Experiential Realism to this discussion of the truth-functional treatment of the 'if-then' relation, in the first place notes that some of the compounds which seem quite suitable to the truth-function doctrine appear very strange to a person relying on comprehensive experience. Consider, for example, the compound composed of 'If the Cavaliers win today' and 'I am a monkey's uncle'.

This seems a very implausible candidate for the label 'compound'. In short, there is nothing in non-imaginary experience to give rise to this linkage of propositions. The question of the truth or falsehood of such compounds arises only in an artificial fashion, in logic textbooks! In other words, in the context of truth-functional analysis, the term 'compound' is used in a special sense, namely the result of a situation where the truth function rules for conditions apply. Further, the terms 'truth' or 'falsehood' as applied to components of compounds have the sense of accurate or inaccurate report. When applied to a compound they have a different, that is logical sense, either acceptable or unacceptable.

As noted at the beginning of the truth-function discussion, the preceding comments take seriously the assumption, or the claim, by some of its devotees that truth-function analysis is a useful instrument for solving practical problems which arise in human discourse. There seems less justification for that claim than some devotees would like to believe.

It is sometimes claimed that truth-function analysis as such is concerned only with formal relations, and hence that there are no commitments involved in using the terms 'true' and 'false'—no essential tie with particular factual references. It is merely a case of, for example, that if two propositions in the conditional relation are both false or both true, then the compound is true, regardless of the proposition as such, that is, what they state. If this is all that is involved, the protest outlined above, concerning the peculiarity of some compounds and the dual use of the terms true and false, is not in order.

The reply of Experiential Realism is simply this. It is of course the case that purely formal relations between abstract entities can be set up. Further, such achievements may, and on occasion do, have practical use in solving problems. But in the last analysis, if the truth-function analysis is to be of practical use it must involve itself in some commitment when the terms 'true' and 'false' are used. They must have some meaning including a referent, otherwise why apply them to propositions? Further when truth-function analysis applies some formal abstractions such as

p	q	$p \supset q$
T	T	T
F	F	T

413

to some specific propositions, and it is claimed that this structure aids in determining the truth or falsity of complex statements in human discourse, it cannot very well avoid the type of criticism noted above.

As long as truth-function analysis remains within the confines of

p	q	p ⊃ q
T	T	T
F	T	T
T	F	F
F	F	T

and permits no commitments otherwise, it is 'home free'. But it is useless except within the limits of its own world.

19

EPILOGUE

The preceding discussion in Section Two has been concerned chiefly with views alternative to those of Experiential Realism and which in effect implicitly or explicitly express destructive criticism of Experiential Realism.[1] General and specific replies by Experiential Realism to these criticisms have been noted. These replies are an attempt to provide a report of what is found in the context of comprehensive experience and, on this basis, show the deficiencies of the positions of the critics, as well as provide further clarification of and support for Experiential Realism.

I

Agreement among philosophers

Before summarising the objections raised to alternative views, it is well to remind ourselves that there is a wide area of agreement, either stated or implicit, shared by the other parties and Experiential Realism. As far as one can determine, many other philosophers accept (i) a common world of physical objects (ii) experience of one's own mental entities (iii) the presence of other persons (iv) concepts (v) value distinctions; and they agree that (vi) words or symbols are used for communication of specific and general propositions and as instruments for social interactions or to express emotions. How these entities are interpreted, of course, varies. Some philosophers, even when they explicitly refuse to accept some of these entities, imply, by their behaviour, that they are nevertheless taking them into consideration, as either imaginary or non-imaginary.

[1] *Support,* at specific points, from many sources has been mentioned.

415

Defects of philosophies which differ from Experiential Realism

When we examine entities which are discussed by philsophers who oppose Experiential Realism, it is found that these persons have no awareness of entities which are of fundamentally different types from those experienced by other men, though frequently their theories and techniques seem to suggest that this is the case. Because they take a different approach from that of Experiential Realism to these 'shared' entities, these philosophers do not agree with at least some aspects of the view of the world around us and the characteristics of human beings, as reported by other men in general, or comprehensive experience in particular.

What happens seems to be specifically one or more of the following interrelated procedures:[1]

(1) Many philosophers misinterpret the nature or status, or both, of at least some of the entities they discuss. They also misinterpret or misunderstand the statements of other men.

(2) The approach of many philosophers is partial. They omit some of the entities, basic or characteristic, of comprehensive experience. Specifically, as a result of misinterpretation of the nature and status of entities, some entities are stressed, given superior status, and the rest are (i) neglected by being disregarded, or (ii) rejected by being denied or (iii) identified with the stressed entity. Further, (iv) some philosophers, in proposing to examine or discuss an entity, do not deal with the entity as such. Rather, they concentrate on some peripheral factor in a complex situation which involves the entity in question.

(3) Unjustified flights of imaginative fancy occur. Specifically (*a*) some part of the non-imaginary content of comprehensive experience is either (i) taken as experienced or (ii) reinterpreted in some fashion and then, in either case, used as a 'thought model' to imagine a world which is considered to be the ultimate reality. (*b*) In some cases imaginary entities are employed in this fashion. The distinction between imaginary and non-imaginary is disregarded. Some or all of what is present in comprehensive experience is then given an inferior

---

[1] On the basis of the considerable discussion in Section Two it is possible to provide a more detailed and somewhat expanded version of 'defects' listed in the Preface of Section Two.

status or omitted. One result is that these thought models are then used as the basis for the assumption of artificial 'gaps' in the universe which are contrary to comprehensive experience.

Having reduced at least part of the world of comprehensive experience to inferior status, or in some cases denied its existence, or given it the other types of 'ill-treatment' mentioned in 2, nevertheless, strangely enough, such philosophers on occasion refer to the world of comprehensive experience for purposes of illustration or to justify their own theories. Further, they try to do justice to some of the features of this world within the context of their artificial and distorted theories. In any case, such philosophies attempt explanations when none is possible or justified, in the context of comprehensive experience.

(4) Some philosophers indulge in statements which are contradictory, or in general proceed in an inconsistent fashion in situations where opposing views are not justified.

Recognition of these defects by other philosophers: Wittgenstein, Whitehead and Bacon

Many of these defects, as has been noted in preceding chapters, have been identified by many philosophers in dealing with views opposed by Experiential Realism. Specific examples have been provided from time to time. A few representative general illustrations will serve as a useful reminder of this fact.

For example concerning 2, Wittgenstein aptly remarks: 'A main cause of philosophical disease—[is] a one-sided diet: one nourishes one's thinking with only one kind of example.'[1] A brief statement by Whitehead is in the same vein: 'The chief danger to philosophy is narrowness in the selection of evidence.'[2] Whitehead provides apt and pointed illustrations of those comments by referring to the deficiencies of medieval thought and contemporary science.[3]

The dangers of reliance on too restricted, too partial a method, are noted by Wittgenstein in commenting on symbolic logic. Characteristically his orientation is linguistic. Wittgenstein aptly remarks:

---

[1] Wittgenstein, *Philosophical Investigations*, Blackwell, Oxford, 1953, p. 155. Hereafter this will be referred to as *P.I.*

[2] A. N. Whitehead, *Process and Reality*, Macmillan Co., 1929, p. 512. Hereafter this book will be referred to as *P.R.*

[3] *P.R.*, p. 8; *The Function of Reason*, Princeton, 1929, pp. 40–1, 68. Hereafter this book will be referred to as *F.R.*; *Adventures of Ideas*, The Macmillan Co., New York, 1929, pp. 111, 289, 313. Hereafter this book will be referred to as *A.I.*

'The more narrowly we examine actual language, the sharper becomes the conflict between it and . . . the crystalline purity of logic. . . . The conflict becomes intolerable; the requirement [of the crystalline purity of logic] is now in danger of becoming empty. We have got on to slippery ice where there is no friction and so in a certain sense the conditions are ideal, but also, just because of that, we are unable to walk. We want to walk: so we need *friction*. Back to the rough ground!' (*P.I.*, p. 46).[1]

In dealing with 1, the misinterpretation of language, Wittgenstein points out: 'When we do philosophy [in the wrong fashion] we are like savages, primitive people, who hear the expressions of civilised men, put a false interpretation on them, and then draw the queerest conclusions from it' (*P.I.*, p. 79).

Concerning misinterpretation of the nature and function of language, one is reminded of Bacon's delineation of the so-called idols (fallacies) of the market place.

'Words, being commonly framed and applied according to the capacity of the vulgar, follow those lines of division which are most obvious to the vulgar understanding. And whenever an understanding of greater acuteness or a more diligent observation would alter those lines to suit the true divisions of nature, words stand in the way and resist the change.'[2]

The tendency of philosophers to indulge in flights of imagination, as mentioned in 3, is covered impressively in Bacon's discussion of idols of the theatre. He refers to systems of philosophy as 'representing worlds of [the author's] own creation after an unreal and scenic fashion' (*N.O.*, xliv). He points out further that such systems like 'stories invented for the stage are more compact and elegant, and more as one would wish them to be, than true stories out of history' (*N.O.*, lvii).

Whitehead also provides a vigorous warning against flights of

---

[1] See also: 'The logic of everyday statements and even . . . of scientists, lawyers, historians, and bridge-players cannot, in principle be adequately represented by the formula of formal logic.' (*Essays in Conceptual Analysis*, A. Flew, ed., Macmillan Co., 1963, p. 18.)

[2] F. Bacon, *Novum Organum* (lix) in *The English Philosophers from Bacon to Mill*, Modern Library, 1939. Hereafter this work will be referred to as *N.O.*

speculative fancy into an imaginary world which is claimed to be necessary in the philosophic enterprise. 'Do away with this elaborate machinery of a conceptual nature which consists of assertions about things which don't exist in order to convey truths about things which do exist.'[1]

In an apt statement, Wittgenstein stressed the need for philosophy to consider everything and to avoid uncritical reliance on the results of imagination for reputed purposes of explanation. As he puts it, philosophy should describe what one finds. 'Philosophy simply puts everything before us, and neither explains nor deduces anything. Since everything lies open to view there is nothing to explain. For what is hidden, for example, is of no interest to us.' (*P.I.*, p. 50. See also p. 46).

Most philosophers stress the importance of avoiding 4, inconsistency. Thus, for example, in delineating the characteristics of a philosophy which will do justice to 'every element of our experience' Whitehead states that it must be logical. 'The term "logical" has its ordinary meaning, including "logical" consistency, or lack of contradiction' (*P.R.*, p. 5).

III

Basis of philosophical errors: Bacon and Whitehead

The question arises: why is it that so many philosophers are guilty of the errors, the defects discussed above. The answer in part is as follows.

In formulating their theories, philosophers frequently are the victims of the past. They turn away from entities as they are because they are influenced by their ancestral theories. Once a philosopher has accepted a set of leading ideas, in many instances he works out a vast set of coherent consequences regardless of some of the facts. The basis of acceptance is often some emotion, for example, admiration of a personality past or present based on 'animal magnetism'. Sometimes a philosophic view reflects merely a spirit of rebellion or a feeling of inferiority.

Explanations such as these were offered long ago by Bacon in his discussion of the so-called idols of the tribe, namely errors in thinking

---

[1] A. N. Whitehead, *The Concept of Nature*, Cambridge, 1926, p. 45. Hereafter this book will be referred to as *C.N.*

common to all human beings, and of the cave, that is errors perpetrated by some individuals (*N.O.*, xli–lii). Consider for example (idols of the tribe): 'Human understanding when it has once adopted an opinion draws all things else to support and agree with it' (*N.O.*, xlvi). This happens because human understanding is no 'dry light, but receives an infusion from the will and affections' (*N.O.*, xlix). More specifically (idols of the cave): 'Men become attached to certain particular sciences and speculations, either because they fancy themselves the authors and inventors thereof, or because they have bestowed the greatest pains upon them and become most habituated to them.' (liv). He makes the further very fundamental point that

"There are found some minds given to an extreme admiration of antiquity, others to an extreme love and appetite for novelty; but few so duly tempered that they can hold the mean, neither carping at what has been well laid down by the ancients, nor despising what is well introduced by the moderns' (*N.O.*, lvi).

In like fashion Whitehead argues against the arbitrary bias which results from reliance on the temperament of individuals, the provinciality of groups and the limitation of streams of thought (see *P.R.*, p. 502).

However, it is not here proposed to stress the psychological or social origin of opposing theories, even if they are relatively or clearly obvious in some cases. All through this study an attempt has been made to refute opponents on the basis of their theories, not by reference to their feelings or cultural background. The basic problem is to determine whether or not their points of view are supported by comprehensive experience. Implicit in this approach, as noted in the first chapter of Section One, is the contention that comprehensive experience does occur. That is to say a person can and does, at least on occasion, avoid the distorting effects of internal and external entities both physical, mental and indeed, conceptual. A person who will not admit that, is in no position to make any sound factual statements concerning anything.

It is contended by Wittgenstein that philosophy functions when a person is in difficulties. Thus he states: 'The philosopher's treatment of a question is like the treatment of an illness' (*P.I.*, p. 91). A 'philosophical problem has the form: "I don't know my way about" ' (p. 49).

This indeed is the situation in some cases. However, the philosophical enterprise is not always so emotionally charged or so harassing. It is not correct to claim, as James apparently does, that a person's philosophy necessarily reflects his temperament, or as Lazerowtiz, claims that the philosophical enterprise always is a symptom of personal malaise. (See Chapter 10, pp. 260–1.) To repeat: it is certainly possible for a philosopher (as envisaged by Experiental Realism) to deal calmly and rationally with a situation before him, noting its main features, recording the results of investigation. In many instances there is no pressing personal problem of a disturbing nature, temperamental or social pressure, causing distortion. In many cases a person is interested in continuing the process of understanding himself and his world to the best of his ability. But it is not a crisis situation as when one is afflicted by a disease or is lost! This of course is not to deny that there are many unanswered questions.

IV

The status of ordinary experience: Whitehead, and Ayer

It is customary to claim that most philosophers live in another world as far as ordinary every-day experience is concerned. It is further contended that ordinary experience is not a respectable basis for adequate philosophising. There are, however, notable exceptions. With penetrating irony Whitehead points out: 'It is almost indecent to draw the attention of philosophers to the minor transactions of daily life, away from the classic sources of philosophic knowledge; but, after all, it is the empiricists who began this appeal to Caesar' (*P.R.*, p. 264).

In like fashion Ayer remarks: 'It follows that the philosopher has no right to despise the beliefs of common sense. If he does so, he merely displays his ignorance of the true purpose of his enquiries.'[1]

It is therefore advisable to mention at least briefly the position of Experiential Realism concerning this issue. It is in essential agreement with Whitehead who states: '[Some] *metaphysical notions* rest ... upon the ordinary, average experience of mankind, *properly interpreted.*

[1] A. J. Ayer, *Language, Truth and Logic*, London, 1936, p. 49. Hereafter this book will be referred to as *L.T.L.*

[There are others] for which ... occasions and modes of experience ... in some degree are exceptional.' (*A.I.*, p. 379, emphasis added). Whitehead wisely notes that present human experience was at one time exceptional. The same points are made in the apt reference to 'the Common Sense[1] of civilised mankind' (*A.I.*, p. 240).

Experiential Realism agrees with ordinary experience of mankind, properly interpreted, in many respects. It finds many phases of ordinary experience suitable bases for philosophy, not because these phases of ordinary experience are ordinary but because they are not open to objection on the basis of comprehensive experience. Specifically

(*a*) extensive awareness of physical objects and one's own mind can be achieved without distortion. It is not the case that a third party inevitably stands between in such a fashion that a person is aware only of the third party and can, at best, only assume the presence of the physical object or his own basic mental entity. (The third party might be a mental entity or a neutral or so-called physical sense-datum).

(*b*) The entities found in physical objects and one's own mind, under conditions of accurate observation, actually are the characteristics of these entities. For example, causality is a genuine relation which exists on occasion between a basic mental entity and its characteristics, between physical objects and between minds and physical objects, in both directions.

(*c*) Concerning what are termed 'concepts', and value characteristics including diety, one is dealing with what may seem to be outside the range of the ordinary experience of mankind. However, as noted in the foregoing discussion, some of the concepts and value entities mentioned come into focus when ordinary experience is properly interpreted. For example, if one understands what is involved in communication by language, that is by sounds and inscriptions in a meaning situation, and the process of recognising, one finds concepts. Some concepts, such as those involving lofty value ideals, may indeed be present only in cases of exceptional experience. The same comment should be made concerning some value qualities and the specific characteristic deity. In any case ordinary experience must be supplemented by exceptional. This fact, however, should not lead to a denial of the significance of ordinary experience.

[1] In this context it is well to note that Whitehead once defined common sense as 'Genius in homespun!'

In order to demonstrate the reliance placed on ordinary experience by Experiential Realism and its agreement with and support by Whitehead in this matter, consider the following extensive quotations from Whitehead. These are not to be regarded as a case of mere piety. They are introduced because of their vigour and cogency:

'Consider, for example, the homely illustration . . . of the angry man who knocks his neighbour down . . . amid all this ambiguity of sensa, the stubborn flux of events is asserted, that the fist of the angry man completely upset the stable functioning of his victim's body. It is not a flux of sensa which is asserted, but a bodily collapse as a result of the expressiveness of the angry man. Also the anger of the man undoubtedly affected the functioning of his own body.'[1]

Whitehead also takes a common-sense approach to the status of our value experience. This problem is placed in proper perspective as far as comprehensive experience is concerned by the remark for example, that 'The discordance over moral codes witnesses to the fact of moral experience. You cannot quarrel about unknown elements. The basis of every discord is some common experience, discordantly realised' (*F.R.*, p. 69).

With vigorous candour, he notes that 'If value [and motivation] were suddenly removed from human life, not much of this life would be left, . . . nobody would read a book, no man would be interested in any woman (or vice versa), in fact nobody would move from one room to the next and so forth' (*F.R.*, p. 14).

The report by Experiential Realism that any entity has value in the sense that it makes a difference has obvious kinships with Whitehead's views. He states:

'The base of our existence is the sense of "worth". Now "worth" essentially presupposes that which is "worthy". Here the notion of worth [value] is not to be considered in a purely eulogistic sense. It is a sense of existence for its own sake, of existence which is its own justification, of existence with its own character' (*M.T.*, p. 149).

Experiential Realism's discussion of mirror images, mirages, and other so-called (in this book) 'physically based entities', which in ordinary experience are not found in close association with physical

[1] A. N. Whitehead, *Modes of Thought*, Macmillan, New York, 1938, p. 47. Hereafter this book will be referred to as *M.T.*

objects (after the fashion of characteristics), receives general support from Whitehead. He refers to 'the wealth of sense-objects which enter into our experience as situated in events without any connection with physical objects. For example, stray smells, sounds, colours and more subtle nameless sense objects' (*C.N.*, p. 156). Significant also is Austin's remark that a mirror image is not a private mental sense datum: 'it can be photographed.'[1]

Like Experiential Realism, Whitehead objects to the setting up of artificial gaps between body and mind. To use a pungent phrase, there is mutual 'pollution'! 'Physical energy sublimates itself into zeal; conversely, zeal stimulates the body. The biological ends pass into ideals of standards, and formulation of standards affects the biological facts.'[2]

However, the world found in comprehensive experience is complex. Whitehead correctly protests against some artificially postulated gaps, but he aptly notes genuine distinctions. 'In our cosmological construction we are, therefore left with the final opposites, joy and sorrow, good and evil, disjunction and conjunction—that is to say, the many in one—flux and permanence, greatness and triviality, freedom and necessity, God and the world' (*P.R.*, p. 518).

v

Support for Experiential Realism: Whitehead and Austin

At this point it is appropriate to stress the fact that the view of the nature and scope of philosophy held by Experiential Realism is similar in many respects to that of Whitehead. He states:

'Philosophy destroys its usefulness when it indulges in brilliant feats of explaining away. It is then trespassing with the wrong equipment upon the field of particular sciences. Its ultimate appeal is to the general consciousness of what in practice we experience. . . . It is a disease of philosophy when it is neither bold nor humble, but merely a reflection of the temperamental presuppositions of exceptional personalities' (*P.R.*, pp. 25–6).

[1] J. Austin, *Sense and Sensibilia*, Oxford, 1962, p. 31.
[2] A. N. Whitehead, *Religion in the Making*, Macmillan, 1926, p. 87. Hereafter this book will be referred to as *R.M.*

The wide range of what is present in experience is carefully noted by Whitehead. He stresses the importance of considering not only the data of physics, mathematics and biology but also those of psychology, aesthetics, morality and religion (see *P.R.*, vi, and *Science in the Modern World*, Cambridge edition, 1946, pp. 165, 207, 219. Hereafter this book will be referred to as *S.M.W.* See also *M.T.*, pp. 66–7).

Worthy of note is his contention that 'the elucidation of immediate experience is the sole justification for any thought; and the starting point for thought is the analytic observation of components of this experience' (*P.R.*, p. 6). He also refers to 'the direct inspection of the nature of things as disclosed in our immediate present experience' (*S.M.W.*, p. 27. See also p. 24).

The claim that philosophers should be essentially descriptive, that they should report, is supported by Whitehead thus: 'Metaphysics is nothing but the description of the generalities which apply to all the details of practice [i.e., experience]' (*P.R.*, p. 19).

The critical function of philosophy is of great concern to Whitehead: 'One aim of philosophy is to challenge the half truths constituting . . . scientific first principles' (*P.R.*, p. 15). More specifically, scientific principles must be broadened so that a systematic organisation of knowledge may be achieved. However, a philosopher should assist scientists in the process of clarifying meanings and suggest topics for consideration. Further, a philosopher should neither attempt (*a*) to dictate to science what its duties are or (*b*) to replace the scientist in any fashion (see *M.T.*, pp. 30–1).[1]

VI

Respectability of ordinary language: Wittgenstein, Flew, Ryle and Whitehead

Experiential Realism is in agreement with those who stress the respectability of ordinary language in the context of the philosophic enterprise. For example, the complicated 'being-for-itself', 'being-in-itself' (instead of 'mind' and 'physical object') language of Sartre seems hardly necessary.

[1] It is not appropriate in this book to refer at length to Whitehead's stress that philosophy is both thought and action. For a brief treatment see A. H. Johnson, 'Some Aspects of Whitehead's Social Philosophy', *Philosophy and Phenomenological Research*, vol. XXIV, pp. 68–71; also, *Whitehead's Philosophy of Civilization*, Dover, New York, 1962.

There is the eminently sane contention by Wittgenstein that if men wish to carry on effective communication about any entity they must rely on the established use of language of every day. 'Is this language somehow too coarse and material for what we want to day? *Then how is another one to be constructed?* And how strange that we should be able to do anything at all with the one we have!' (*P.I.*, pp. 48–9).

Admitting all this, however, Experiential Realism, as previously noted, stresses the point that ordinary language is woefully inadequate in dealing with some entities. New technical terms must be developed to supplement ordinary ones. (See also A. Flew, ed., *Essays in Conceptual Analysis*, Macmillan, London, 1963, p. 18).

Experiential Realism notes with approval Ryle's remark:

'Enslavement to jargon, whether inherited or invented, is certainly a bad quality in any writer, whether he be a philosopher or not. It curtails the number of people who can understand and criticise his writings; so it tends to make his own thinking run in a private groove. The use of *avoidable* jargon is bad literary manners and bad pedagogic policy as well as being detrimental to the thinker's own wits.[1]

Nevertheless, words, ordinary or technical, must be 'kept in their place'. Their status as instruments must be properly appreciated.

In the course of a discussion of the function of language in the philosophic enterprise, one who proposes to rely on comprehensive experience will do well to remind himself of the sage comments of Whitehead:

'There is an insistent presupposition continually sterilising philosophic thought. It is the belief, . . . that mankind has consciously entertained all the fundamental ideas which are applicable to its experience. Further it is held that human language, in single words or in phrases, explicitly expresses these ideas. I will term this presupposition, "The Fallacy of the Perfect Dictionary" ' (*M.T.*, p. 235).

The nature and limitations of language, even at its best, as outlined in preceding discussions (see Chapter 1) are clearly recognised and

---

[1] G. Ryle, 'Ordinary Language', *Philosophical Review*, vol. LXII, no. 2, April 1953, p. 181. (Emphasis added).

vigorously stated by Whitehead. He does agree in general with the linguistic philosophers that 'most of the muddles of philosophy are, . . . due to using a language which is developed from one point of view to express a doctrine based upon entirely alien concepts.'[1]

He would, however, distinguish between genuine muddles and artificial ones generated by linguistic philosophers.

More specifically he notes that language is an attempt to express prior insights[2] and that attempts are frequently inadequate.[3] There is also the much needed warning: 'The abstraction, inherent in the development of language, has its dangers. It leads away from the realities of the immediate world. Apart from a balanced emphasis, it ends in the triviality of quick-witted people' (*M.T.*, p. 55).

VII

Direct insight and argument: Whitehead and Waismann

Whitehead reports that there are two major divisions within contemporary philosophy. 'The critical school confines itself to verbal analysis within the limits of the dictionary. The speculative school appeals to direct insight, and endeavours to indicate its meanings by a further appeal to situations which promote such specific insights. It then enlarges the dictionary' (*M.T.*, p. 236).

Whitehead's reference to 'direct insight' (awareness) is very significant as far as Experiential Realism is concerned. The type of philosophy here envisaged—a report and description of the fundamental entities present in human experience—does not rely ultimately on argument, on long chains of reasoning. As a matter of fact, each step of a valid argument depends ultimately on direct insight.[4]

[1] A. N. Whitehead, *The Interpretation of Science*, Bobbs Merrill, Indianapolis, 1962, p. 218.

[2] 'Language halts behind intuition' (*M.T.*, p. 68).

[3] 'It is not the case . . . that our apprehension of a general truth is dependent upon its accurate verbal expression . . . this consciousness of failure to express our accurate meaning must have haunted most of us. . . . We know more of the characters of those who are dear to us than we can express accurately in words' (*R.M.*, pp. 126–7).

[4] Whitehead deals with the topic thus. 'The justification . . . must mainly rest upon . . . direct elucidation of first-hand experience. They [philosophic views] are not, and should not be, the result of an argument' (A. N. Whitehead, *Adventures of Ideas*, Cambridge, 1933, p. 379).

The immediately preceding remarks should not be regarded as in any sense casting aspersions on a very important phase of philosophy, namely the careful study of the structure of arguments. It is essential to note the logical nature of valid argument. Nevertheless the point being made here is that in presenting arguments about facts, the final appeal is to the facts. The premises of an argument are not to be accepted as the ultimate authority for the conclusions reached.[1]

It follows that the much vaunted concentration, in some contemporary circles, on numbered premises used in the course of an argument, the solemn stating that one premise follows from another and so justifies a conclusion, the use of translation techniques, ultimate reliance on truth-function patterns (tables)—all this is either an ingenious game or a report of factual situations and approaches to them.

In brief, one statement concerning the non-imaginary world follows from another only if the linkage of facts of a complex situation justifies it. Such a sequence of argument is only a case of statements which together cover a complex situation. An argument sequence may remind a person and record for him how, from an examination of additional facts, an additional statement arises and thus follows, in this sense, the first one, that is an earlier statement of one phase of a complex factual situation. In short, what one can say in premises or conclusions concerning facts depends ultimately on facts, not on a preceding network of premises.

In general agreement with the preceding point of view, Waismann states: 'Philosophy is the breaking through to a *deeper insight*. . . . Insight cannot . . . be demonstrated.'[2]

---

[1] 'The basis of all authority is the supremacy of fact over thought' (*F.R.*, p. 64). More specifically Whitehead remarks: 'It should be noticed that logical proof starts from premises, and that premises are based upon evidence. Thus evidence is presupposed by logic; at least, it is presupposed by the assumption that logic has any importance' (*M.T.*, p. 67).

It is worth noting that Experiential Realism's report that the so-called laws of thought are reports of how a person thinks in dealing effectively with entities, is supported by S. Alexander, *Space, Time and Deity*, Macmillan, London, 1927, vol. I, pp. 204–6. See also p. 316 for a discussion of the empirical nature of arithmetic.

[2] F. Waismann, 'How I see Philosophy', *Logical Positivism*, A. J. Ayer ed., The Free Press, New York, 1959, p. 364. See also pp. 365–80.

Concluding comments

At the end of this discussion of Experiential Realism and other philosophers one point must be made clear. Obviously the references to other philosophers who support Experiential Realism, and to those who oppose, are not complete. Of necessity, in this introductory presentation, attention has been focused on a few specific cases. It is obvious that major attention has not been paid to existentialism and phenomenology as such. However, some of the main emphases of these philosophical positions have been considered. A detailed examination of these very complex and complicated philosophies does not fall within the scope of this volume.

It is appropriate to point out that detailed opposition to views supported by Experiential Realism is based on various fundamental general claims concerning method or fundamental principles. If, as Descartes long ago suggested, the foundations of a philosophic position can be shown to be defective, its efficacy in dealing with specific details is seriously undermined. Further doubt is cast if its inadequacy in a few representative specific cases is shown. It is contended that as a matter of fact Experiential Realism, by offering criticisms of the foundations of, for example linguistic philosophy, or of materialism, or Absolute Idealism, and also critical comments on some specific typical doctrine, is spared a detailed refutation of all phases of these positions. In like fashion, if support for Experiential Realism is forthcoming from various general philosophic positions, and at crucial specific points, as a result, it is not necessary to mention a great many representative names or refer to more than a sample of supporting reports of a specific nature.

There has been a great deal of quotation from the writings of those who support Experiential Realism and from those who reject it, for several reasons. An attempt has been made to present opposing points of view as accurately as possible, hence, in many cases paraphrases have been avoided in the interests of adequate presentation. On the other hand, there has been extensive quotation from those who are in agreement with Experiential Realism, at least at some points, to show that the position here termed Experiential Realism is in accordance with the views of a wide range of philosophers. Further, in some cases their words are the best available presentation of a specific report of the facts of comprehensive experience.

Concerning these philosophers, in some cases, their statements which support Experiential Realism are frequently overlooked because in other phases of their work they are in opposition to it. In other instances, the work of some philosophers is not read by those who deliberately restrict themselves to a very closely prescribed intellectual environment. Hence it is advisable to remind them of wider perspectives.

Be that as it may, I am reminded of an apt remark by Wittgenstein: 'I should not like my writing to spare other people the trouble of thinking. But, if possible, to stimulate someone to thoughts of *his own*'[1] (*P.I.*, p. x).

[1] Emphasis added!

20

Appendix

NB—'O' is a symbol for: *Oxford Concise* or *Oxford Shorter Dictionary*
'W' is a symbol for: *Webster Collegiate Dictionary*

Action: a thing done, a deed (O)

Blame: find fault with for offence (O)

                 fix responsibility (O)

Cause: what produces an effect (O)

Characteristic: pertaining to, or serving to constitute, the character of (W)

Comprehensive: inclusive (O)

Concept: idea of a class of objects (O)

                 an idea as distinct from a percept (W)

Divine: (deity) supremely good or admirable (W)

Dream: train of thoughts, images of fancies passing through the mind during sleep—or indulged in when awake (O)

Emotion: any one of the states designated: fear, anger, disgust, joy, grief, etc. (O)

Entity: a thing which has reality and distinctness of being (W)

Excuse: lessen blame, obtain exculpation from duty (O)

Experience: observation of facts or events (O)

                 what has been experienced (W)

                 the state of having been occupied in any study or practice, in the affairs of life (W)

Fact: data of experience (O)

                 things certainly known to have occurred or to be true (O)

Feeling: the general sensitivity of the body as opposed to the special senses (O)

                 what one feels in regard to something (O)

                 pleasurable or painful consciousness (O)

Image: mental representation of anything not actually present to the senses (W)

Imagination: the act or power of imagining; the formation of mental images of objects not present to the senses, especially of those not present in their entirety, hence mental synthesis of new ideas from elements experienced separately; a concept or notion created by the mind (W)

Know: have personal experience of (O)

                 to be aware of, to be versed or skilled in (O)

Knowledge:	acquaintance with fact (O)
	range of information (O)
	skill (W)
	certain understanding (O)
Language:	vocabulary and way of using it (O)
	method of expression (O)
	any means, vocal or otherwise, of expressing or communicating feeling or thought (W)
Mean:	have in mind, intend to convey, indicate object (O)
Meaning:	what is meant (O)
Mind:	the incorporeal subject of the psychical faculties (O)
	subject of consciousness, that which feels, perceives, thinks, etc. (W)
	seat of consciousness, thought, volition, feeling (O)
Motive:	a moving or exciting cause (O)
	what induces a person to act (O)
Obligation:	binding agreement, duty, indebtedness for service or benefit (O)
	any duty imposed by law, promise or contract, by social relations, etc. (W)
Philosophy:	love of knowledge, especially that which has to do with reality or the most general causes and principles of things (O)
	study of principles of human actions or conduct (O)
	system for the conduct of life (O)
	calmness of temper, serenity (W)
Praise:	commend merits of person or thing (O)
Proposition:	statement, assertion, proposal (O)
Punishment:	cause offender to suffer for offence (O)
	inflict punishment on an offender (O)
Real:	actually existent or present as a state or quality of things (O)
	actual as opposed to artificial or apparent (O)
Reason:	to use induction or deduction, or a combination of these in an effort to decide something (O)
Refer:	have relation, be directed to (O)
	make allusion to, direct attention to (O)
Responsible:	answerable as the primary cause (W)
	capable of rational conduct (O)
	respectable (O)
	reliable, trustworthy (O)
Reward:	recompense for merit (O)
Sign:	thing serving as presumptive evidence or indication of a thing (O)
Signify:	be a sign or indication of, mean (O)

Symbol:	thing regarded by general consent as representing something by association in fact or thought (O)
Think:	to form in the mind, conceive, imagine (O)
True:	in accordance with fact or reality (O)
	accuracy, correctness (O)
	genuine not merely apparent (O)
Value:	worth, utility (O)
Will:	faculty by which person decides and initiates action (O)
	power of effecting one's intentions (O)

N.B. This index is not intended to be all inclusive. It is designed to provide ready access to crucial discussions of specific topics.

GEORGE ALLEN & UNWIN LTD

Head Office:
40 Museum Street, London WC1
Telephone: 01-405 8577

Sales, Distribution and Accounts Departments:
Park Lane, Hemel Hempstead, Hertfordshire
Telephone: 0442 3244

Argentina: Rodriguez Pena 1653-11B, Buenos Aires
Australia: Cnr. Bridge Road and Jersey Street, Hornsby, N.S.W. 2077
Canada: 2330 Midland Avenue, Agincourt, Ontario
Greece: 7 Stadiou Street, Athens 125
India: 103/5 Fort Street, Bombay 1
285J Bepin Behari Ganguli Street, Calcutta 12
2/18 Mount Road, Madras 2
4/21-22B Asaf Ali Road, New Delhi 1
Japan: 29/13 Hongo 5 Chome, Bunkyo, Tokyo 113
Kenya: P.O. Box 30583, Nairobi
Lebanon: Deeb Building, Jeane d'Arc Street, Beirut
Mexico: Serapio Rendon 125, Mexico 4, D.F.
New Zealand: 46 Lake Road, Northcote, Auckland 9
Nigeria: P.O. Box 62, Ibadan
Pakistan: Karachi Chambers, McLeod Road, Karachi 2
22 Falettis' Hotel, Egerton Road, Lahore
Philippines: 3 Malaming Street, U.P. Village, Quezon City, D-505
Singapore: 248c/1 Orchard Road, Singapore 9
South Africa: P.O. Box 23134, Joubert Park, Johannesburg
West Indies: Rockley New Road, St. Lawrence 4, Barbados